The
Diary
of
Anaïs Nin

Works by Anaïs Nin

The
Diary
of
Anaïs Nin

—◄◆►—

1966-1974

Edited and with a Preface by Gunther Stuhlmann

Harcourt Brace Jovanovich
New York and London

Requests for permission to make copies of any part
of the work should be mailed to
Permissions, Harcourt Brace Jovanovich, Inc.
757 Third Avenue, New York, N.Y. 10017

The editor and publisher wish to thank the C. G. Jung
Foundation for permission to quote from
Woman's Mysteries, by M. E. Harding, copyright 1971
by the C. G. Jung Foundation for Analytical Psychology;
and William Morrow & Company, Inc. for permission
to quote from *Venture to the Interior,*
by Laurens van der Post, copyright © 1951, 1979
by Laurens van der Post. The "Magic Circle Weekend"
material (pp. 212–17) was first published by
Magic Circle Press in *Celebration with Anaïs Nin,*
edited by Valerie Harms,
copyright © 1973 by Valerie Harms.

Library of Congress Cataloging in Publication Data
Nin, Anaïs, 1903–1977.
The diary of Anaïs Nin.
Vol. 3 has imprint:
New York, Harcourt, Brace &
World; v. 4–7: New York, Harcourt Brace Jovanovich.
CONTENTS: v. 1. 1931–1934.—v. 2. 1934–1939.—
v. 3. 1939–1944.—[etc.]—v. 7. 1966–1974.
1. Nin, Anaïs, 1903–77—Diaries. 2. Authors,
American—20th century—Biography. I. Stuhlmann,
Gunther, ed. II. Title.
PS3527.I865Z5   818'.5203 [B]   66-12917
ISBN 0-15-125596-2

Printed in the United States of America
Set in Intertype Baskerville

First Edition
B C D E

Preface

Anaïs Nin died in California on January 14, 1977, just a few weeks before her seventy-fourth birthday. The final decade of her life, which to some extent is reflected in these pages, brought many things to the woman who at the age of eleven had embarked upon that long and tireless voyage into the labyrinth of her diary. Today, we have a complete French edition of those early "letters" to a lost father from her first exile in America, spanning the years 1914 to 1920. With this, the seventh and final volume in the present series, we add another segment to the already published portions drawn from the original diaries, reaching from Anaïs Nin's little-noticed début as a published writer and early champion of D. H. Lawrence in Paris at the start of the 1930s, to the agonizing yet obviously inevitable decision—described in Volume VI—to open her diary to the world, some thirty-five years later. On a universal scale, this decade produced an intense emotional response to Anaïs Nin's lifework, which led her to exclaim in 1972: "How could I have felt so weak and so passive at twenty and feel so strong now? It is so wonderful."

Indeed, the last ten years of Anaïs Nin's life were rich in recognition, acceptance, in realized ambition and, for a time at least, in increased mobility. They were also overshadowed, privately, by the growing intrusion of a cancer that eventually wrestled down her body though it never succeeded in breaking her spirit. With the same stubborn strength she had displayed throughout her life in defense of her own creation, she fought to the very last against the rapacious cells in her body. Confined for most of the last two years to the house in Los Angeles, unable to travel easily, to lecture, she tended with iron devotion to the work that still lay ahead. She oversaw the translation into English of her "childhood" diaries. She proofed, with waning strength, a selection of the erotic stories she had produced in the early 1940s as a quick way to earn a few dollars from an unpoetic "collector" but also as an artistic challenge, which only a few months after her death propelled her name for the first time onto the best-seller lists of Europe and of the United States—an irony she would surely have appreciated. She also kept a "book of pain" and a "book of music" by her bedside—the ingrained "diary habit," as she so often had called it, asserting itself to the last. But the original decision to publish portions of her diary did not extend to these final private notes. What Anaïs Nin wanted to leave with us, and leave us with, at the end of Volume VII, was not a record of pain and suffering but her impressions of a last joyful journey, the realization of an old dream: a glimpse of that magical island, Bali, where for a brief moment the enchanting fairy tales of childhood, of the mysteries of the East, of a fantastic land of golden spires, graceful people and natural abundance, could be rekindled before the onrushing bitter reality. After all, her motto had always been: "Proceed from the dream outward."

The publication, in the spring of 1966, of the first volume culled from the mountain of notebooks which had been accumulating in that famous Brooklyn bank vault, as we now know, marked a major turning point in Anaïs Nin's life. The frightening explosion she had envisioned in a dream while struggling with the decision to break the seals of her secret enterprise did indeed take place. But, like the unpredictable flow of the diary itself, the explosion that followed took forms that had been impossible to anticipate.

After the trying years of neglect as an artist, Anaïs Nin, at the age of sixty-three, suddenly found a vast and receptive readership throughout the world. At a time when the quest for self-realization, for the liberation from outmoded societal impositions, from traditional roles, had gained an almost epidemic momentum, especially among the young, her *Diary* struck a highly responsive chord. From a solitary "underground" writer who had shared her work with a small audience, who had occasionally discussed her art with a handful of interested students, she suddenly found herself transported onto the spotlighted stages of giant lecture halls. It was a difficult, if gratifying, transition. Discovered by the media, by political action groups, by militant feminists and by lonely individuals who strongly identified with her own struggles toward liberation, Anaïs Nin found herself caught up in an ever increasing groundswell of being interviewed, recorded, taped, cheered, crowded by fans, warmed by their intensely personal responses and sometimes badgered and exploited by her newfound admirers.

The private person who had confided to the diary her hunger for recognition, for a response to her lifework so long carried on in secret, almost overnight confronted the pressures of public exposure. Like her old friends—Henry Miller, Lawrence Durrell—before her, Anaïs Nin found the satisfaction of a belated triumph overlaid with the consuming demands levied upon a "celebrity," especially in the United States. The intimacy with the self, which had given such exemplary strength to the diary and which she had pursued so diligently behind her many veils, was challenged by what was asked of her most often now, that most contradictory, most difficult of all demands: to establish intimacy with the world at large.

While her name appeared emblazoned on T-shirts and (much to her amusement) cropped up in literate crossword puzzles, the work on which this very recognition was founded, the intimate diary, was gradually being transformed into something else. "The journalists ask me if I am still writing in the Diary," Anaïs Nin notes in the spring of 1972. "I answered 'yes' automatically, but one day I realized it was not true. The Diary has become a correspondence with the world. Was this what I really wanted?"

As Anaïs Nin expanded into the world at large, the world also invaded her diary. The secret notebook, the "hashish and vice" of her early days, began to bulge with clippings, interviews, travel articles, prefaces, reviews—a scrapbook of her external achievements. As mountains of letters cried out for a personal response, the laboratory of the soul was opened to the public. "I keep the Diary spasmodically, less consistently," she admits early in 1973. "I will write a lot when I am traveling or on vacation." The voice of Anaïs Nin the diarist is still there, unmistakably, but with a decreasing need for secrecy, it is addressed, increasingly, to the world "out there." With future readers looking over her shoulder, with friends asking jokingly whether they will be "in the diary," the refuge, the clandestine workshop, becomes transformed into an "open letter."

At the outset, the artistic function of the diary as a conscious creation is still unchanged. "I am preoccupied with tracking down incomplete figures to round out a story, pursue a denouement," she writes in January 1967. "I'm only excited when I find a clue, which leads me to a new facet of someone's character, or a new version of an old story, or bringing my portraits up to date. I live for the Diary." And she admits, once again: "Tonight I could not communicate with people.

There are times when the world I created and its personages seem more vivid than the ones before me."

In a letter to Robert Duncan in December 1968, she once more explains and defends her method: "We *are* strangers to each other. I did not want anything in the portrait to sadden you. The Diary, you do not seem to understand, records ambivalences, changes . . . But where is there objectivity? In none of us. Each one has his particular vision of others. We are lucky if, by love, they come near matching. . . . my concern was with understanding and seeing. The facts I jumbled in an effort to have some continuity in your life . . ."

Amidst recording, preserving outside events, the diary still serves as a mirror of self-examination, the battleground of conflicting demands, of angers repressed and ultimately understood, of the continuing search for resolutions: "Where is Anaïs? . . . I cannot keep the same feeling after a thousand exchanges. So Anaïs is now an actress. . . . I am uneasy about this new phase," she writes in October 1972. "Can one multiply, share, expand without loss of substance?" And she answered her own question: "Yes, if you can extend feeling into all you do, say, write . . ."

A month later she notes: "This year I had to reconcile the public and the personal, make them one as sincere as the other, not in conflict. Every year we have to make a new synthesis . . ." But by April 1973, she confesses: "That moment to which I respond with love and an amazing sense of communion, became finally drowned by the pressures of the crowd." In the fall of the same year, she writes: "I have returned at last to the intimacy of the Diary. . . . Last year . . . I had the feeling of living outside of myself, or of myself coming entirely out of myself to meet the world . . . but at times the constant appearance before the public created a mirror image, like an echo, which was not good for me." And she adds: "I think I am withdrawing from public life because it focuses entirely upon an idealized Anaïs . . ."

Subsequent to the initial publication of the *Diary*, the public person, Anaïs Nin the writer, had submitted to the flattering but exhausting claims of her overseas publishers. She had traveled to Japan, to London, to Paris, to a triumphant reception in Germany. The private person, during those years, had slipped away from the prosaic fetters of publishing, from inquisitive journalists, from public performance, to explore some of the places that by their very names still assumed an aura of exotic enchantment: Morocco, Tahiti, Bangkok, Singapore, Bali. With the diary displaced as her central refuge ("Life only became real when I wrote about it. Today that sounds like nonsense," we read in February 1974. "The present is real. That is why I wrote less in the Diary"), Anaïs Nin resorted to the other magic she had practiced throughout her life: movement. As she had once been transported from the "old" to the "new" world, as she had once moved from the "cold" intellectual atmosphere of an Edmund Wilson to the "warm" promise of the "children of the albatross," in her final decade Anaïs Nin shifted her focus from New York to California. Her monastic apartment on the edge of Greenwich Village became largely preempted by the wide-windowed house in Los Angeles, by its verdant garden, its glistening pool. The harsh climate of Manhattan was subsumed by the more languid air of the Pacific shore. Her travels in the Far East—that "homeland" of our childhood enchantments—were not only escape from the pressures of public life. They were but another step in Anaïs Nin's perennial search for the colorful, the non-prosaic, the potential, the unfinished. They were another expression of her undiminished capacity for wonder. Under the grinding drone of the radium-bombardment machine in a New York hospital, Anaïs Nin was able to conjure up the images of enchantment, of the exotic places she had searched out so diligently in a world where, unless you look for it, magic has become a rare commodity.

But movement, flight, exploration, the uncovering of potential, in the end also required a record that would preserve all that had been discovered, experienced. In her last notebook, Anaïs Nin jotted down some thoughts on the writer she had admired above all others; a writer who had served, perhaps subconsciously at times, as the major guidepost of her own endeavor; a writer who by the sheer magic of his craft was able to overcome the handicaps of his own life, the personal obstacles and impediments that had to be transposed into literature.

Because he penetrated the unconscious of his characters, they did not age and die in our imagination; the unconscious is a stream of revelation which is never touched by time, fashions, history. . . . He transcended time. He never fixed a date upon anything. Very few novelists escaped the stamp of time, which allows the experience to take place only once. . . .

No other writer has achieved this continuum. Is it because he explored every aspect, every mood in a state of perpetual movement, that the change is achieved each time as if each word had a thousand meanings? . . .

It is the quality of infinite depth which makes each reading a new experience. . . .

Is it that the mobility of thought and feeling was finally cornered or captured at the moment of its evolution so that the evolution never ceases? He has never described stasis, fixity, metamorphosis into stone, petrified heart and body. The life current was never interrupted, and so whenever you catch it, you are drawn into its vortex and life offers you a new vision.

The writer, of course, was Marcel Proust.

In the contest of being in and of the world and, at the same time, to retain the very qualities which separated her from the world—of being a guest at the feast, as it were, and simultaneously looking in from the outside, with her nose pressed against the glass—Anaïs Nin was severely tested in her loyalty to the course she had set upon when she first embarked upon her diary. In the end, she sided with the creation of a livable world through art, as she so eloquently expressed it before the students of the Philadelphia College of Art, when she received her first honorary doctorate: "Even beginning a diary, you see, was already conceding that life would be bearable if you looked at it as an adventure and a tale. I was telling myself the story of a life, and this transmutes into an adventure the things that can shatter you. It becomes then the mythical voyage which we all have to undertake, the inner voyage, the voyage in classical literature through the labyrinth."

GUNTHER STUHLMANN

November 1979

List of Illustrations

The
Diary
of
Anaïs Nin

[Summer, 1966]

At a lecture I am asked to pronounce my name three times. I try to be slow and emphatic, "Anaïs—Anaïs—Anaïs. You just say 'Anna' and then add 'ees,' with the accent on the 'ees.' "

A month of good reviews, love letters, appearances on television. Has the sniping really stopped? I feel like a soldier on the front, amazed by the silence of the guns, wondering if the war is over.

A month which made up for all the disappointments, the poison pen reviews, for all the past obstacles, insults. The sound of opening doors is deafening!

Suddenly love, praise, flowers, invitations to lecture. "Girl Talk" (TV show) with Elsa Lanchester. She and I sat on the couch and let the other aggressive women ramble on. It seems we both had the same expression. How shallow, noisy they are! We did not talk, just looked at each other with the same understanding.

Television interview with Arlene Francis very deep. She knew my work. She is enormously intelligent and wise.

My scrapbook is gaining weight.

The same publishers who turned down my work beg for my comments on new books they are publishing.

Rehearsal for "Camera Three." Stephen Chodoroff wrote the script. They wanted me to read the birth story but I did not have the courage. They blew up photos of Louveciennes for background. I read for half an hour. I read well but had the impression they expected fireworks and I was restrained and quiet in my reading. Partly shyness.

The Diary is selling well. Hiram Haydn thought its sale would be limited. My publisher printed only 5,000 copies. They were sold in a week! Then they printed only 2,500 more.

Book-signing party at the Gotham Book Mart. Overflow of people out into the street.

Hilda Lindley is my publicity director at Harcourt, Brace. She is a charming and clever woman, but we do not agree on the way she spends my publicity budget. She advertises in the *New Yorker,* which has done everything in its power to annihilate me, reviewing each book destructively and maliciously. Same with *Partisan Review,* or the *New York Review of Books,* which ignores me. I ask her if she does not think readers of such reviews will believe the book reviewer rather than the advertisement. It makes no sense to me. She will not advertise in the *Village Voice,* or in the Los Angeles *Free Press,* which supports me loyally. She answers that she is trying to move me away from the underground into a more general readership.

"But I was created by the underground, I belong to the underground. I want to remain in contact with them. They are my genuine readers. They supported me. The others tried to destroy my work. *Life, Time, Saturday Review,* etc."

She cannot see my point of view.

My Japanese publisher invited me to Japan to celebrate the publication of *A Spy in the House of Love.*

The beauty of Japan began on the Japan Airlines plane. In the pocket in front of me there was a fan, paper slippers, napkins and exquisitely designed writing paper. On the dinner tray the food was shaped like flowers, an orchid rested on the center of the plate. The plastic bottle containing the soy sauce was shaped like a graceful Greek vase.

The book I carried with me was *Meeting with Japan* by Fosco Maraini, an Italian writer who lived in Japan many years and loved it so deeply that he forgave the Japanese for forcing him to spend the war years in a concentration camp (he was a "foreigner" even though his country was on the side of Japan).

It was dark when we landed in Tokyo. From the taxi I saw the silhouette of the Imperial Hotel built by Frank Lloyd Wright. It seemed like that of an Aztec or Mayan temple. I could see why the Japanese chose Wright to build their most palatial hotel. The sense of aristocracy, the nobility of forms, the sense of many-layered beauty in stone, tiles, wood. It was a romantic floating palace, built on piles riding in mud, which enabled it to survive the great earthquake. As I arrived, the first thing I saw was the pool covered with lotus flowers. The Japanese baron who built the hotel had said there was no money for the pool. But Wright insisted it was essential to protect the buildings from the great fire that would surely follow an earthquake. And this

4

beautiful pool did save the hotel from the earthquake-produced fire, when the city water supply failed and the hotel employees formed a bucket brigade from the pool to the buildings.

The Imperial Hotel became the temple for international celebrities. Everyone stayed there when they came to Japan, and the many beautiful intimate corners became meeting places for the Japanese. The heaviness of the furniture was not in harmony with Japanese austerity, but whatever Wright designed had its own integrity.

Immediately adjacent was the new Imperial Hotel; in violent contrast to the garden-surrounded, romantic Wright buildings, it was a typical international high-rise, sterile, plain, monotonous. From a distance it hung like a sword of death over the last refuge of beauty in downtown Tokyo. Wright's design gave the sensation of living through many centuries; it evoked every palace or temple ever portrayed, from Egyptian to Inca. He restored to man the sense of pride and deep accumulation of experience entirely lost in modern architecture, which reduces man to an anonymous, meaningless being in an anonymous, meaningless abode, like an ant cell. Here the man who moved about in Wright's setting was a being containing memories of all the past, and strong enough to have a vision of the future, and of his metaphysical place in it. The man staying in the modern wing had no face, no identity, no existence. The restaurant was like a cafeteria. Did modern architecture know it would reduce man to a colorless, insubstantial shadow, without memory or power to evoke his own history?

It was not only the invitation of my publisher which led me to visit Japan. I was steeped in Japanese novels, in Lady Murasaki's work, in Japanese films; and one of my most important childhood readings was a volume on Japan from a collection, *Voyage Autour du Monde*. I dreamed over the illustrations. A need of beauty and meaning led me to Japan, a need of renewal, of an external world I could love. Everything suited me. The muted sounds, the gentleness of manners, the charm and graciousness of the stewardesses on the plane, the taxi driver's immaculate white gloves.

My first day in Tokyo was a Sunday, so I was free to walk about. I visited the Imperial Palace.

We believe that films give us a true image of the countries we cannot see for ourselves, but when faced with reality, I was shocked to see how much I had not been given by films. The texture, smell and tonalities were missing. The Gate of Hell was of a dark, ashy black wood with heavy iron hinges. The palace, placed high on the tip of a hill, was all white and black wood. The walls around it were of huge hand-cut stones. Black swans with yellow beaks glided in the moat water. There were gardeners everywhere in dark blue cotton embroidered with white and in white head kerchiefs. All so neat, working with precision and order, stylized. The strollers carried colorful umbrellas. It was a misty day. The air smelled of damp vines and crushed flowers and freshly cut grass. Another missing element in the films.

It was my first sight of the curved roof, curving upward, ending in a peak adorned with a carved bird seeming about to fly off. This curve, this undulating fine design pointing to the sky, is what the Japanese call "frozen music" [kureku-ongader]. And so it was, though of solid matter, its design vibrating like a stringed instrument.

In the afternoon I visited a shrine, all gold and red. The offerings to the gods were rice on lacquered trays and bottles of sake.

On Monday I met my young publisher, Mr. Tomohisa Kawade, who had just inherited the Kawade Shobo publishing house from his father. He was twenty-eight; he had the smooth, pearly complexion so often seen in the Japanese. The gold skin is tinged with the faintest flush, the eyes brilliant. My translator came too, Mr. Nakada. They took me to a tempura restaurant. A small wooden house with private rooms overlooking miniature gardens. Uncluttered room. A rush mat, a lacquered table, pillows and one ornamental scroll and flower arrangement. The women, elaborately dressed, as in familiar prints; such subtle harmonies of color. They move about on woolly socks, noiselessly. Having tea and contemplating the garden, with its sound of dripping water, creates a mood of serenity and harmony in the heart of Tokyo.

After tea we moved to the tempura bar. A circle of white pinewood, immaculate. In the center is the chef, ruling with precision and skill over big cauldrons of boiling oil. Using three-foot chopsticks like a rapier, he takes up shrimp, or string beans, or eggplant, dips it in a light batter, immerses it quickly in the boiling oil and serves it crisp and airy. Conversation was labored because everything had to be translated.

I visited the publishing house, a small, intimate building. I met the editors.

In the evening we had dinner in a geisha restaurant. A long, low table, and behind each one of us a geisha, solicitous of one's every need. They kept filling the small sake cups, making conversation. Softly, a geisha helped me to handle a small fish with chopsticks. She patted the fish for a few seconds and suddenly pulled out the entire skeleton clean and free. All this in an exquisite dress with floating sleeves, like the wings of butterflies, which would paralyze a Western woman. There was a small stage on which dancers performed after dinner. They exuded an incredible charm, young or old, pretty or not. Faces so smooth, smiles like an offering of flowers. The kimonos had a freshness, an airiness, as if just ironed, starched, never wilted. Every gesture, every modulation of voice was made with intent to please, delight, as if the dancers were born like the genii out of your own dreams to shower you with thoughtfulness. They banish all harshness of voice or color, move like the wind, surround you with the essence of care, solicitude. It is not only directed at men. I felt the benefic effects of it.

One geisha, quite young, gave me her scarf to sign. Near my signature was Ernest Hemingway's. She said, "He signed my scarf when I was fifteen."

It is no wonder men dream of this quintessence of femininity, which never seems more than a reflection of a dream.

The women of Japan are at once the most present and the most invisible and elusive inhabitants of any country I have seen. They were everywhere, in restaurants, streets, shops, museums, subways, trains, fields, hotels and inns, and yet achieved a self-effacement which, to foreign women, is striking. In the hotels and inns they were solicitous, thoughtful. It was as if one's dream of an ever-attentive, ever-protective mother were fulfilled on a collective scale, only the mother is forever young and daintily dressed. They were laborious and yet quiet, efficient, ever present and yet not intrusive or cumbersome.

They stood before you not a moment longer than necessary, not one of them seemed to be saying: Look at me. I am here. The way they carried trays and served food seemed like a miraculous triumph over clumsiness, weight. They had conquered gravitation.

I saw them at work in factories. They wore blue denim kimonos, shabby from use but clean. They kneeled, sitting back on their heels, working with the same precision of gesture as their more glamorous counterparts. Their hair was not lacquered or formed into high chignons, but neatly braided.

In the fields, the peasant women presented the same harmonious dress of coarse, dark blue denim, always soigné, even when worn. Their straw hats, their baskets were uniform, and they worked with such alignment that they seemed like a beautifully designed group dance. I watched them pick weeds, in a row, on their knees, with baskets beside them, and they picked in rhythm, without deviation or fumbling. While the women weeded, the men took care of the trees or cleaned the ponds of surplus water lilies.

The softness, the all-enveloping attentiveness of the women . . . I thought of the Japanese films, in which this delicacy could turn into fierceness if challenged, in which women startled you with a dagger or even a sword at times. What kind of modern woman would emerge from the deep, masked, long-hidden Japanese woman of old? The whole mystery of Japanese women lay behind their smooth faces, which rarely showed age except perhaps on peasant women battered by nature. The smoothness remained from childhood far into maturity.

The thoughtfulness could not be a mask; it seemed so natural, a genuine sensitiveness to others.

I collected a large number of Japanese novels, thinking I would then become more intimate with the feelings and thoughts of Japanese women. It was a woman, Lady Murasaki, who wrote the first novel around the year A.D. 1000 [*Tale of Genji*], and although it is a Proustian work of elaborate and subtle detail, although the feelings and thoughts of the personages at court are described, the author herself remains elusive. But few modern works by Japanese women are translated, and the novels as a whole failed to bring me any closer to them. The same element of feminine selflessness is present. There is a strong tendency to live according to the code, the mores, the religious or cultural rules, to live for a collective ideal. The one who breaks away is described as a monster of evil.

In one of the touring buses there was a young woman guide in a light blue uniform, a small white cap and white gloves. She was in reality homely, but her expression radiated such responsiveness and participation, such warmth and friendliness, that she kept the mood of the travels high through an arduous day. At each village the bus stopped, she sang the folk song of the region. Her voice was clear and sweet like a child's, and yet it had a haunting quality like that of a wistful flute played in solitude. Through heat, through fatigue, through harassing travelers, she remained fresh, buoyant, carrying her modern burden of work as lightly as if it had been a fan.

The children presented a different mystery: the mystery of discipline and love in such balance that they appeared to be the most spontaneous children I had ever seen, and at the same time the best behaved. They were lively, cheerful, charming, outgoing, expressive and free, but their freedom never ended in sullenness or anarchy. I witnessed a group of Japanese schoolchildren being guided through a museum who came upon an American child of their own age. They surrounded him gaily, twittering and speaking the few words of English they knew. The American child looked suspicious and withdrawn.

I thought of the gardens of Japan, the order, the stylization, the control of nature, which presented only an aesthetically perfect image. Had the Japanese also achieved this miracle of aesthetic and ethical perfection in their own nature? No weeds, no dead leaves, no withered flowers, no disorder, no tangles, no mud-splattered paths?

My publisher filled up Monday and Tuesday with interviews. After a few days of homage paid me as a writer, too long to describe, I had a lunch with my translator, Nakada; a young critic, Jun Eto; and a young novelist, Kenzaburō Oē. A lunch of many hours with interpreters, talking to other writers. The talk was recorded and published. Conversation through interpreters is frustrating. It is laborious and heavy, prevents quick interplay and direct contact.

Oē, the most modern of the Japanese writers and a left-winger, was not the writer I wanted to meet. I was far more interested in Kawabata, in Mishima and in the older tradition of Japanese novels. The first thing Oē did when we were introduced was to extend his right hand and say: "This hand shook the hand of Mao Tse-tung." Which made no impression on me at all.

He had written about Norman Mailer, the most uninteresting of American writers. I could see I was in a Japan influenced by the worst of America.

The conversation veered unexpectedly to the American Dream. I said Mailer represented the American nightmare. Oē thought there were two trends in America, one the hero who expresses the American dream, and one who expresses America's illusions. Oē quoted Al Capone: "I am the ghost of a bad dream in America." The real American dream, said Oē, was Lindbergh and J. F. Kennedy. Kennedy, he felt was a dangerous American, because he showed only an ideal face. He died before he could reveal his other face.

The conversation bored me, and I turned away from it.

Nakada is a brilliant translator and essayist, a critic and theater director. He presented me with a summer kimono and obi. I love the seriousness of the Japanese, their caring, and basic timidity. They are imprisoned in their traditional formalities but it makes intercourse harmonious and suave.

Great repressions create dualities. I feel that the selflessness demanded by their culture creates a seething unconscious.

I was only allowed into a geisha restaurant with one of my editors, Hideo Aoki, because I was a writer; otherwise women are not invited. I expected a different behavior from the new generation.

There was a big demonstration against the war in Vietnam. I had Senator Fulbright's speech, "The Arrogance of Power," translated, and it was read in public. It was a tremendous event with a vast number of people attending. The speeches were not translated into English, but one American stood up and suggested boycotting all American goods until war ceased. Another American told how many generals were on committees for manufacturing goods for the army. One company was making millions manufacturing a new bomb which makes fire cling to the body until it is consumed.

A Buddhist spoke, a noble old man, ascetic-looking. Hideo Aoki translated what he said: "Scientists are men without religion and philosophy." It was a painful confrontation of horrors.

The same day, Aoki took me to a Noh play, a profound experience in abstraction. The voices, as if disguised; the gestures, slow. The floor is so highly polished it looks like water. It is like a series of tableaux, or prints. Everything is suggested. The audience is serious, as if they were attending a mass. They follow the classical text the way musicians read scores. The young no longer attend. They prefer the vivid, dynamic Kabuki theater, which is more like a ballet or opera. The crowd talks and eats during the performance. They are gay. They know the text by heart and reserve their concentration for their favorite actor or passage. It is colorful, full of magic and violence.

In Japan I had a weeping fit. The sweetness, kindness, consideration touched me. For once in my life I felt I was treated as I always treated people.

I would fall asleep hearing the delicate music of the samisen.

I was asked American-style questions: Did I really take moonbaths? What did I play with as a child? I answered playfully: "Japanese dolls," although in reality it was in San Francisco that I discovered the exquisite dolls and began a small collection. I told them about my father, who did not believe in childish books and who gave me *The Book of Knowledge* and *Voyage Autour du Monde*. My favorite volume was *Le Japon*. What I did not say was that during my rebellious years (rebellious against my father's discipline and France's formalities) I thought I would not like Japan, but that after living in chaotic, uncouth America I found Japan elating. The American anarchy had created a destructive generation, people who threw beer cans all over the landscape and broke Coca-Cola bottles on the beach, wounding children and animals; who kept water closets in such condition that one could not use them; who threw so much popcorn and gum on the floor of movie houses that you waded in the sticky stuff, in masses of paper cups; who defaced subways, covered walls with obscenities.

I return again and again to the concept of "frozen music" in architecture, which gives the same vibration as the sound of a harp or other stringed instruments. The way the roofs of temples and palaces sweep upward like that of bird's wings in flight—a roof which flies inspired by the upward curve of the black pine branches. Often at the tip of the roof there is a carved bird or flying fish.

Lovely words like *fusuma* to describe the paper doors.

The light summer kimono is called *yukata*.

A bath is ritualistic. You soap and rinse yourself first before entering the boiling hot water, and then relax. It is a purification rite. It gives the Japanese the special tender flush of well-watered flower petals.

In one of the castle halls I saw replicas of the costumes of various periods, life-size, re-creating court scenes. The young shogun looked as beautiful as a woman.

Long trousers, twice as long as the man himself, were intended to impede the flight of a courtier if he should assassinate the shogun. Such a clever way of trapping him in his own clothes.

Many ginkgo trees were planted around the castles and temples because they did not burn easily.

The marvelous roofs were made of many layers of cypress bark, one upon the other until it reached a thickness of eight to twelve inches.

The round tips of the roof tiles were sculptured with sixteen-petaled chrysanthemums, the symbol of the emperor. In front of the coronation hall on the left was planted a cherry tree as a symbol of loyalty, and on the right an orange tree as a symbol of eternity.

Meditating on all this I realized how the lack of symbolism has made our Western world dismal and empty.

A few of us practice symbolism in our private lives.

The bus driver, the taxi driver, the policeman all wear immaculate white cotton gloves. In one department store when I went up the escalator, a young girl stood wiping the railing after each person touched it.

Men and women carry packages wrapped in large handkerchiefs of beautiful colors. Sometimes the handkerchief, the kimono and the obi are matched in color.

But not one hand-painted, lacquered Japanese umbrella in sight.

The Coca-Cola salesmen, the neon light salesmen, the black nylon umbrella salesmen have invaded Japan, doing more harm than the colonizers of old. Next to the temples, in sordid little shacks, are piles of Coca-Cola cartons, and the hideous red advertisement is hung everywhere. This outrage in a place which has beautiful fruit.

Some of the ashcans in the street are in the shape of a pelican.

When I took LSD years before and was asked if there was anything I wanted, I asked for a pagoda. Now I find that the two favorite symbols of Japan are the pagoda and the *torii*. The pagoda is a reliquary, a diagram of the universe. The *torii* is a gate of honor.

Kyoto.

A tour of the castles reemphasizes my feeling that fairy tales originated in the Orient. The grace of the architecture, the refinement of textures, the shape of the roofs, the arrangement of gardens are almost incredible. Just as the Japanese control nature to make every garden of legendary perfection, awakening the same sense of art one has before a painting, a print, a poem, they also create rules of harmony in buildings, rooms before which one gasps. The symbolic, lyrical beauty of the various teahouses, set in different positions from which to view the moon in various seasons, the simplicity which clarifies the thoughts, the aesthetic harmonies which evoke serenity, a superior level of consciousness. I was prepared for the beauty of Japan. I was not prepared for the depth of meaning, the highly evolved symbolism.

I visited the Golden Pavilion, so well described by Mishima—so beautiful that the ugly clubfooted monk grew to hate it. Its beauty was a constant offense to his ugliness, and a threat to his virility. He burned it down. It was rebuilt—all of gold leaf and flesh-colored floors like silk. It seems made of light, a reflection of the sun. Not content with its ethereal radiance, its builders made it to be reflected in a pond, so in the end it all appears like an illusion, a manifestation of spirit.

That very evening I visited a striptease show in the prostitute quarter. It was in a shabby theater, small but with a big stage. There was one old man in the audience who looked like the old man in the novel *Odd Obsession*. On the left an orchestra played jazz badly. On the right there was a room filled with mirrors and gauzy curtains. In the center the stage extended into a ramp. The women were dressed in caricatures of Ziegfeld Follies costumes, feathers and spangles; others in pseudo-Spanish, one in the traditional Japanese kimono. They danced badly, stripped badly, but then they came forward on the ramp and displayed their intimate treasures openly to the young Japanese (apart from me, no women in the audience). They played with themselves under the eyes of the eager young men with a sort of comic vulgarity. The young Japanese behaved with extraordinary decorum as no Westerners would under the same circumstances. They watched intently but they were quiet, respectful almost, certainly neither bawdy nor crude in their response.

One woman looked like a beautiful female Buddha. She exposed herself nonchalantly, with an impassive, masklike face. If the young men came too close she ruffled their hair playfully.

At that moment I understood Mishima's *Golden Pavilion,* and the ugly monk's feeling that beauty interfered with sensuality.

The women, touching their sexual parts, shaking the honey off their hands on the heads of the young men, teasing, beckoning, inviting, letting a man unwind the obis until the kimonos fell open, offering their breasts, were suddenly covered by the iridescence of the Golden Pavilion. I was so filled with gold, with light, that my body ceased to exist as a body. It had become spirit as from the effects of a dissolving luminosity.

The Imperial Palace was all grace and simplicity. The Shogun's Palace garish like all expressions of military power. The floorboards of the palace are linked by steel wires so that they sing with an eerie wail when you walk over them. They are called the "nightingale floors." They were intended to warn the shogun of the presence of an enemy. A musical warning. Has any other culture ever invented an alarm that would be pleasingly musical? Walking over this floor in socks was a whimsical experience. A symbol of Japan's obsession with beauty.

The shogun ruled by force and was hated. It was the emperor who was peace-loving, a lover of art. All the art of Japan was created and defined during early court life. In ancient times no one could travel about, the land was infested with bandits. The entire aesthetic culture of Japan—music, poetry, the tea ceremony, pottery making, flower arranging—was born in this period when they all had to turn to inner resources. The rituals, customs are recorded in the novels of Lady Murasaki. Women did a great deal of the writing in notebooks they concealed in their pillows, from which the *Pillow Book* derived its name.

One room in the Seiryo-den Hall was entirely covered by screens. The use of gold leaf and an aquamarine blue is entrancing.

I watched the craftsmen stenciling, painting silk, weaving. I watched a woodblock printer at work in his own home.

The gardens are works of art in design, planting and miniaturization. The Japanese favor green gardens, not flowers which die, but evergreens, carpets of moss. Always, the accompaniment of water from a stream directed to fall drop by drop from a bamboo pipe. Each time it stops to allow the water to accumulate, it makes a sound like one dry slap on a drum.

The Japanese admire intuition more than intellect. They have a subjective language, describing states of mind, moods.

The night before the Gion Festival (begun in A.D. 700 as a prayer against the plague) you can visit the floats being prepared in the park. The shrines and temples are open and lit by thousands of lanterns. The old priests are dressed in white robes, with high tiaras like those of the Catholic popes. They are incredibly lean, trim, erect, as if carved in wood; the most beautiful old men in the world. They present the Buddha with food on trays, a fresh watermelon carved like a flower, tea in silver cups. Acolytes, also dressed in white, pray behind grilled doors. The interplay of sliding doors, muslin curtains, incense, ringing bells is a creation of mystery and gaiety, the essence of the Japanese character, both religious and pagan. Aesthetics to please the senses, religion for contentment and resignation, to abolish fears and anxieties.

The people are gay and exuberant. Cedar wood is burning in large iron cauldrons, filling the air with perfume. Every time someone throws a coin into the copper dish for the temple, he is allowed to pull the cord of the big temple bell and to bang on the giant drum. The noise of drums, bells, laughter fill the soft, warm air.

The next day we sit on the edge of a wide street to watch the floats. They are very high, constructed in several tiers, the top one used for life-size representations of legends or stories from Noh plays, the bottom for bands of musicians. They are covered with precious tapestries, bells, carved fasciae, gold tassels, red and gold predominating.

They roll on gigantic wooden wheels pulled with huge ropes by young men dressed in their regional costumes. In front of each float walk Kyoto's men of distinction. Each float is a work of art. I noticed one Aubusson tapestry. There are Oriental rugs, frescoes, Chinese embroideries.

The crowd sits for hours in the humid steam-bath temperature wearing cardboard hats of traditional shape.

One float is shaped like a ship. Another is topped by an orange umbrella.

I love the title of one: The Float of the Chrysanthemum Water! Chinese legend says you live long if you drink the water of a river near chrysanthemum growth.

One float depicts the legend of Moso Yama. To realize the wish of his sick mother for a bamboo sprout in mid-winter, he desperately searched in the snow. God took pity on him and enabled him to find one.

Another float described Hakuya Yama as the greatest harp player in the Tsin dynasty of China. When Shoshiki, his bosom friend, died, he realized that nobody would appreciate his harp playing any longer and he destroyed his harp.

Katsura Rikyu, my favorite of the Detached Palaces. It is as if everything were built by poets, musicians, painters, to achieve supreme grace, sensuous texture, a simplicity which influences the thoughts, conveys serenity. The richness lies in the gold screens, in the silky surface of the woods, in the muted sliding doors, in the tatamis which smell like fresh-mown grass, in the hidden closets, in the lanterns. A teahouse for each season placed to watch the reflections of the moon on the pond. One teahouse for "smiling mood." Another designed to give an illusion of being at the top of a mountain, actually only eighteen feet above the ground. The illusion is created by gradations of planting. Star-shaped moss, star-shaped leaves over the lake.

A rack for lances at the palace entrance. Bamboo reeds on the windows. All these places were peopled for me by the characters of *Tale of Genji*.

Japan has no beggars, no sick people sleeping in the streets, no cripples, no ash-covered fanatics as in India or Morocco. Everybody is working, busy, disciplined. Cleanliness, being a religion, is practiced continuously. The workmen clean their faces now and then with wet towels.

The painted screens, the scrolls, the panel paintings are of such beauty that they are impossible to describe. The flowers, birds, water, animals, are all done as if from a quintessence. There is a perfect reality to them, but the selection, composition and isolation of details, give them a dreamlike quality. The background is often gold; one branch, one wing, one wave is more beautiful than a thousand branches, wings and waves. We live in an overcrowded world of overcrowded paintings, but the Japanese emphasis on space, distance and few details gives oxygen and a far greater sense of reality than our Western painting.

At the Tenryu Temple, a teahouse set on a small bridge spanning the lake portrays the ethereal quality sought by the Japanese, a quality of lightness, of transparency, of reflections in water, which make life itself seem like a volatile poem.

The pity is that Americans are always allowed to teach in Japan, and the worst American movies and the worst paperbacks are widely distributed, but very few Japanese are invited to teach in America, so Japanese culture, which would be so valuable to America, does not influence it.

In Kyoto I saw a tea ceremony in a garden, heard koto music and saw a puppet show. The puppets were almost life-size, manipulated by men wearing masks and black suits. Long, complicated stories.

The koto players, two young women dressed in purple, sat under a big red umbrella on a carpet of red felt. A monk who wore a white gown covered by a black transparent kimono carried a lighted lantern to guide people to their seats.

The garden was a continuation of the mountain and forests, a miniature replica. Pure nature is a symbol of the spirit. The Japanese are worried that hotels are being built on mountains, which are a sacred place for temples.

The geisha quarter was mysterious and fascinating. Just one street lined with simple, beautiful wooden houses with shuttered windows. Simple lanterns. Now and then a geisha in full formal attire would come out and look for a taxi to go to a dancing assignment. They are exquisitely dressed, exquisitely made up. Their glossy hair piled up with elegance, with ornaments of silver or gold leaf and flowers.

Everywhere polished floors, clean tatamis, shining lacquer trays, flower arrangements, windows open on the quintessence of a garden. Small and large trees, small and large stones. Green tea. White kimonos under black transparent muslins. The monks in black, or in orange cotton, or in white for festivals. Half the women in kimonos, half in Western dress. In Western dress they lose some of their charm.

Arrived on the day of the Feast of Tanabata. Two lovers loved each other too well and forgot their duties. He forgot his work in the fields and she forgot her weaving. The gods punished them by placing them in the sky (the Heavenly River) as Vega and Altair, who would meet only once a year. On the day of this meeting people hang wisteria branches on their door, adorned with colorful ornaments and with folded white papers containing prayers of young lovers that they might accomplish their duties and not be separated.

The hair ornaments on women's heads are works of art. Flowers, gold leaf, combs, tinsel cut in thin pieces which tinkle at each motion.

Nijo Castle, built in 1603 for Tokugawa Ieyasu, first shogun of Tokugawa family, to serve as his residence during his visits to Tokyo. The castle grounds of seventy acres are surrounded by substantial stone walls with turrets at the corner.

In most of the gardens there are no flowers, because "flowers wither and cause disturbance." The ever greenness of the gardens was intended to represent the eternal.

At the tip of the roof there is a flying fish, its tail pointing upward like a wild bird's wing.

It was here in Nijo Castle that I saw the screens painted by Japanese painters who had never seen a lion or a tiger. They painted them by reconstructing skins brought back by hunters. They assumed the lion was the male and the tiger and leopard were females.

The Japanese practice Buddhism and Shinto simultaneously because one takes care of the present and the other, the future life.

The rock garden of Ryoan-ji Temple was particularly conducive to meditation and dreaming. This state of mind is expressed here in an expanse of sand, raked in the form of waves. A few rocks stand for the islands of Japan. There are fifteen stones set in the pure white sand. These stones are arranged in five groups of five, two, three, two, three from east to west. They stand for the five sacred temples of Buddhism, while the white sand represents the sea. There is a pool, too. People sit for hours entranced, hypnotized, dreaming.

Asia discovered two remedies for the cruelty of man, art and religion. America discarded both and is drowning in hate and aggressivity. America also discarded courtesy, which comes from thoughtfulness, consideration of others. The Japanese respect each other's dignity and pride and therefore mitigate resentments and humiliation, from which crime is born. The Japanese discovered that beauty was a source of ecstasy and tranquillity. But they did not lose their sensuous concept of life. They have a highly evolved erotic art.

The dolls used in puppet shows are almost life-size and very intricate. It takes several men to manipulate them. But though they portray evil and violent characters (evil and angry monsters guard the temple gates), I have not seen one evil or angry face. It is said that it was America who introduced the idea of evil in sex during the occupation, the idea of nudity being erotic. So the Japanese adopted the striptease but do it unerotically.

At the station, with a cup of coffee you are handed a wash-and-dry instead of the customary warm and perfumed towel. But on the train everyone had his wet towel to keep face and hands clean.

At busy intersections people can pick up a yellow flag from a box and carry it across the street to warn drivers. They carefully replace it in a box at the other end. In America people steal the wheelchairs supplied by airlines for cripples, and baggage carts and market carts.

Prayers are written on strips of paper and tied to the bushes or fences around the temples. Or people burn incense sticks.

Satori is intuition, illumination, oneness with nature or human beings.

Shumi is Taste.
Kokoro is Heart.
Kimoshi is the subjective state of mind.

The visit to Nara was like a dream. It has some of the oldest temples. Moss and flowers grow on the roofs of cypress bark. It is full of old stone lanterns. Behind the temples and pagodas are restaurants so quiet, so peaceful, that the meal induces a meditative reverie.

The beauty of each item of food plunged me into ecstasy. The soup looked like a painting by Paul Klee, the little flowers and sculptured herbs floating in it so lovely that I wept! I could not bring myself to eat it.

They serve low-voiced, wearing cotton socks. One listens to the water dropping, watches the red and gold fish in the pond, dreams over the garden, which by its miniature-sized plants gives you a vast landscape in a small area.

I am eating a variety of vegetables I do not know. I recognize small green pepper, eggplant, watercress and cucumber—and a variation of the sweet potato, parsnip, dandelion, cucumber flower. I eat fried chrysanthemums.

Only the Japanese would think of serving red watermelon in a green plate. Or wrap rice in green leaves.

The legend is that in the fifth century a saint arrived in Nara mounted on a deer, and from then on deer were considered sacred. They are tame and Nara is filled with them. The traffic stops for them. Everybody feeds them. They are very bold about searching your pockets and pocketbooks, stealing whatever is chewable—chewing gum or nuts. They eat the paper around rice cakes, chew buttons off. At night a bugle call alerts them, they gather in the park. The car lights illuminate them asleep in groups of four or five. Occasionally one of them will be awake, the beautiful golden eyes unblinking.

One temple was near a thin waterfall which dropped from the mountain over rocks and was then allowed to run like a moat around the temple. People stopped to wash their feet in it. At the fountain they washed their hands.

The woods are full of small shrines.

In one of the temples a huge red wooden column had an aperture just big enough for a child to crawl through. Parents incited their children to do so. Some children were afraid, others treated it like a game. I do not know the meaning of this ritual. It seemed like a passage through the womb, a rebirth.

The Pagoda of the Horyuji Temple was particularly graceful. The roof was edged with what seemed like gold wooden beads.

The black Pagoda of Kofukufi Temple evoked the wavelike tiers of the black pine.

The hectic quality of Western life disappears. The quietness, muted sounds, are soothing like silk. The lack of clutter conducive to dreaming.

On the way to Nagasaki by bus.

Beautiful farmlands and farmhouses. The people wear traditional farming clothes, blue cotton, big hats, colored scarves under the hats. It gives the landscape a sense of unity. There is not one unkempt spot, no billboards, no discarded beer cans on the road. The rice paddies are like geometric designs.

I saw people cutting and binding the tall grass they weave into tatamis and baskets.

The general cheerfulness and gentleness of the people is soothing. On the train they buy picnic lunches in little bamboo baskets covered with colored paper. In it the various foods lie atop a bamboo leaf. The food is displayed like a flower arrangement. When the Japanese are finished eating they cover the basket with the paper again, very neatly, and slip it under their seat. Perfumed wet hot towels are passed around.

The bus ride from Nagasaki to Kumamoto one of the most beautiful of my life. It is a fertile land, every inch of it planted. The texture of the wooden farmhouses, the thatch roofs, all melt into the trees and bushes.

Part of the journey was on a ferry. On the boat they sold lunches in the usual bamboo box covered by orange paper and of course with the food arranged, a design with two shrimps, black olives and rice wrapped in bamboo leaves. The seashore was filled with boats and fishermen, sailboats.

The abstract beauty of Japanese art issues from the abstract beauty of their lives. They do not like clutter. They like to look at one flower at a time, one painting, one pot. They have a storage house for the objects of art which are not being displayed.

The ship sailing on the Inland Sea was called *Lady Murasaki.*

It was foggy so we only saw the many islands as they appear in Japanese screens, enveloped in mist, floating.

I had read about Ibusuki, hot springs, with pools under palm trees, each pool the shape of a fruit. I expected a paradise of beautiful naked Japanese. So by air, bus, train and ship I finally arrived there. The hotel was as big as Grand Central Station and devoid of charm. The pools were enclosed in a vast glass hangar similar to those sheltering airplanes or plants. The naked bathers were mostly young men, and there was one old lady with her husband and two young girls who never left the soaping stand in front of a mirror and chatted together.

Men and women wear small towels the size of a wash rag, to cover strategic parts.

At the end of the pools there was a waterfall where the men gathered. Men look natural in the midst of green foliage; women, shy and self-effacing. But I liked the Acapulco temperature, and my Japanese room. Arriving tired and dusty, and being served tea immediately was so soothing. I was given a light cotton kimono and led to the mineral baths.

I swam in the warm sea where the boiling mineral waters empty into it.

Families lounged around the hotel in fresh cotton kimonos, relaxed, showing a sensuous enjoyment of bathing.

My mattress was taken out of the closet and laid out in the middle of the room. It was four inches thick, more like a quilt. It was my first night Japanese style. I slept well.

No dining rooms. Dinner was served in the room with an attentive maid watching over one's needs, keeping the small sake cups filled. This warm wine is so subtly effective. The small cups make you unaware of how much you are drinking, and before you know it you are gently drunk.

When I left the inn this morning they gave me a small towel, a recording of a folk song and a toothbrush for the next inn.

The result of so much discipline is that you can hardly distinguish between educated and uneducated people, unless they wear a peasant costume. Manners are uniformly good. The second-class train filled with quiet and polite people. No garbage on the floor, no defacement, no obscene scribblings as in New York's subways.

Fosco Maraini's *Meeting with Japan* is a beautiful travel companion, historical, religious and human. He describes Japanese writing as based on intuition. Intuition is the quality they praise. Perhaps my love for Japan will one day be requited.

I also read Donald Keene's *History of Japanese Literature.*

Care. Everywhere signs of care. The road is watered against dust. Everyone is weeding, sweeping. No matter how poor the bamboo huts, they are immaculate. I hear a flute song. I hear the wooden clogs tapping on the cobblestones. So much wood, grass, must give off energy as a garden does. A group passed, playing on what sounded like two pieces of wood struck against each other. They carried banners I could not read.

Hong Kong.

A big city as ugly as Wall Street side by side with the most abject poverty. High-rise hotels next to Chinese living on the street, selling fruit or fish.

At the Hong Kong station I was met by "Yonie" (Johnnie). Yonie was well dressed and acted like a representative from the hotel, attending to the baggage, calling a taxi, paying for the taxi. At the hotel he introduced himself. He was a tailor, and did I want suits and dresses made? He called every day. He intercepted me as I walked out of the hotel. Yonie was a supersalesman. Finally, against my will, I bought a chongsum of raw silk.

The street was bedlam, the shops crowded. The poverty of the Chinese, the swollen stomachs of the children, were unbearable.

To walk into a good restaurant I had to leap over an open sewer and scatter begging children.

The bay and the mountains would have been a spectacle to delight the eyes, but they have been ruined by high-rise buildings. No sampans in the bay, to make room for bigger ships or because they are not proud of them.

To see the sampans we drove to Aberdeen, where 230,000 people live on boats.

In the middle of the bay is moored the Floating Restaurant. From far away it looked like a picture from Chinese fairy tales—gold, red, lanterns, reflections on the water. But from near, it was gaudy, too much red and gold, too many bright colors, ornamentations.

A woman rowed us out in a sampan to a colony of sampans and junks. Some very beautiful, with their colored butterfly-wing sails and polished teakwood. On the shore some of them were rotting away, yet people managed to live on them.

Whole families live on the sampans, three generations sometimes. They are born, live and die on them. One family was having dinner, a bowl of rice and small pieces of fish. People on other sampans were selling fish, vegetables and fruit to the ships passing by.

It was barbaric to be served a many-course dinner on the Floating Restaurant while watching such extremes of poverty. I could not eat. I wondered at the heartlessness of the tourists indulging in shopping sprees while undernourished children begged. Aberdeen was sordid, with broken baskets, rotten fruit, rags and empty cans lying about. Boats close together, a labyrinth.

Sometimes people fish for the food thrown out of big luxury ships and cook it.

How did Hong Kong ever get its reputation for glamour?

The young women are beautiful, with lovely delicate figures, flawless skins, glossy hair, graceful in their tight-fitting chongsums.

The sails of the sampans and junks look as if made of parchment, a beautiful wavy texture, shaped like butterfly wings. The women carry their babies tied in a shawl on their backs. The dogs are skeletal, starving, sick. Nowhere in the world have I seen such poverty and such callousness in the tourists or the government.

Every Western building planted among mountains, bays, coral skies, looks funereal. Every Western object is not only ugly but grim. Every native building and object in Asia has color, illumination, symbolism, transcendence. A group of sampans looks like a cluster of giant butterflies deployed for flight.

The women wear fantastic straw hats with holes in the middle for their chignons, and black cotton flounces to shade them from the sun.

Phnom Penh, Cambodia.

This is where the plane lands for the visit to Angkor Wat. The airport smelled of crushed fruit.

A quiet, spacious French colonial city. Pale yellow stucco houses, wide avenues lined with beautiful trees, the river very red from the red earth.

Pedicabs are pulled by young men on bicycles. I could not bear the Chinese rickshaws pulled by thin, undernourished old men in Hong Kong. But here the strong young men pedaling merrily were wonderfully quiet. No cars at all; how wonderful!

Temples and palaces ornamental, colorful; white stucco, red doors and shutters. Roofs of gold tiles, minarets, the tip of each roof undulating upward like the tail of a serpent.

The throne in the palace like an LSD dream of pure gold. Gold for the throne, court dress, shoes, crowns, a dream of gold.

In front of the palace, on the river, the queen's barge awaits the water festival in November. The stairway to her palace is of purple tiles. Everything in pure, clear colors, flower colors, gold, yellows, greens and sky blue. Pillars are supported by bat women.

Every now and then through the foliage of old trees there appears a gold minaret of delicate design. So many towers, minarets all pointing to the sky, have a strange elevating effect on the spirit. The builders of cathedrals knew this, but the Asian people added the bejeweled light, transparencies, illumination of color.

The more temples, palaces, minarets I saw, the more convinced I became that it was the first men to visit the Orient who inspired our fairy tales. I cannot believe that the colorless, opaque Western culture could create such images. It must have been the stories of Marco Polo which illustrated our childhood. It was a shock to every Western child to discover that jeweled palaces with gold minarets did not exist, that nowhere in France, Germany or Spain would they find a Chinese barge shaped like a swan.

It was not only the sense of beauty, of stylization, of decorative fantasy, but the theme of light and ascension, of transparency and reflecting textures which gave the metaphysical quality so highly developed in the Orient.

The nearest Europe came to it was in the use of gold leaf in religious paintings, but the colors of Venice came from the Orient.

I saw the floating houses of the fishermen at the end of wooden piers on stilts, covered with fishing nets and gently swaying on the tide.

Beauty can give ecstasy—the sight of the palace with the gold shining in the sun, its lacquered aquamarine tiles dazzling, its peaked roof in tiers looking about to fly off, topped by a serpent. In one of the open pavilions children were being trained for the royal ballet. The laughter and charm of little voices were a joyous music in itself.

I remember André Malraux's *Voie royale,* but I probably won't see the wild jungle; it must have been cut away. Nor will I meet an army of red ants, nor will I discover buried statues.

The palace shining in the sun was festive. On my second visit I noticed more details. The roof of gold tiles, edged with emerald green and turquoise blue. Against the white walls, the bright red shutters and doors were vivid.

In the royal museum, in one glass case a most incongruous, outlandish black silk umbrella and black top hat presented by the king of England. Napoleon sent a complete French country house in the worst possible taste, which they reconstructed in the garden of the fairy-tale palace. I suddenly understood [Jean] Varda's hatred of black. In Asia it is not even used for funerals.

One of the stairways was carved in the form of a serpent-dragon, painted blood-red. Dragons and elephants appear often as motifs. The statues of dancers are as exquisitely shaped as the women one sees in the street. No fatness but soft curves, a lazy, sensuous walk, placing weight on the heels, as pregnant women do.

Angkor Wat.

The hotel was a low building hidden among the trees. It faced the temple. I awakened early. I saw the monks in their bright orange robes, which they wore like a toga, with one shoulder uncovered. As their heads are closely shaven, they carry an umbrella, yellow or white or black, against the hot rays of the sun. They crossed the courtyard on their way to worship.

Sitting at breakfast on the terrace of the hotel, I watched with unbelieving eyes two elephants entering the courtyard. They were lavishly covered with embroidered rugs with gold tassels, carrying traditional-looking armchairs adorned like thrones. I tried to ride on one but it was like being tossed in a storm at sea, so I did not stay very long on my wildly undulating chair.

One visits the temples in the pedicabs. It adds to the quietness, avoids invading the temple grounds on smelly, noisy buses.

The temples lie in the middle of the jungle, where one hears the monkey chatter and bird songs. They extend over a vast area which would take weeks to visit. Some have been restored by the French, some have been left as they were found, invaded by the jungle, columns and walls and entrances strangled by the roots of the banyan tree. The roots are like giant white pythons; they can lift huge stones over a doorway like an extension of the sculpture itself.

All the walls are sculptured, representing various stages of religion, different moments of history, the life of the monks, rituals, festivities. The entire history of the temple is recorded.

One courtyard is dedicated to mural sculptures of elephants. Big celebrations were held there. The dancers lived in the temple.

There are many pools. The smell of stagnant water mingles with smells from the jungle. The dampness causes every leaf, every twig, to exude its odors. There is green moss on the steps, white moss on the statues of the Leprous Prince. It may be the white moss which gave rise to the idea that the prince suffered from leprosy.

At one moment I became separated from the group of visitors and found myself alone in a square patio on the edge of the jungle. From the deep dark green foliage a black man appeared, tall, handsome, wearing a sarong, with a necklace on his bare chest. He held out a naked sword.

Primitive fear overwhelmed me. D. H. Lawrence's "Woman Who Rode Away," legends, myths of sacrifice, supplanted reality. I thought the hour of my death had come, the white woman sacrificed to an unknown god. The man walked nobly and proudly toward me and extending the sword, said in English: "One dollar!"

One evening the dancers came to perform in front of the temple. Small, exquisite women elaborately dressed in gold and orange silks. Stylized gestures, exact replicas of the murals. They threw flower petals over us out of small baskets. The music and the dances were hauntingly beautiful.

The rain began and we all took refuge in the buses. The dancers laughed and chattered gaily. They gave their fresh-flower hair ornaments to the women in the bus.

Sweetness is their outstanding feature, like the sweetness of the climate.

Trees so varied and beautiful: banyan, jacaranda, raintree, snake tree, tamarind, yellow cassia, acacia, rubber tree, West Indian cherry, kapok, frangipani, teak, mahogany, wild cinnamon, bohdi.

Women sweep the streets with brooms made of twigs. They wear either straw hats or heavy turbans made to cushion the weight of the round, flat baskets they carry on their heads, filled with bananas, pineapples or sugar cane.

The museum built to shelter statues removed from the temples is all in orange stucco and dark wood, a perfect setting for the statues of Shiva, Vishnu, and other Hindu deities. There were many variations upon the statues of Buddha, skeletons of Cambodian barges, ancient nine-tier umbrellas, carved wood and carved stone.

They all give the feeling that the people who struggled to build such temples were of noble race, and even poverty could not diminish their dignity and pride.

The more I see of Asia, the more aware I am of the decadence of Western culture.

Many dark, naked children stare at us from poor hovels. Families squat around charcoal braziers, cooking fish.

The Cambodian dress is a long, transparent, tight-fitting gown worn over wide black silk trousers. The two split sides of the gown expose the black silk pants.

The people love poetry, music and dancing.

When my fountain pen leaked, the waiter brought me a perfumed finger bowl to wash my fingers.

The pool of the main temple was large enough to bathe 500 concubines.

People burn incense sticks before the statues. The worship of Buddha was preceded by the cult of the phallus, and a different invasion cut off the heads of the Buddhas; it was strange to see people burning incense before headless statues.

The tragedy of the temples was that although the large stones were imperishable, the roofs were made of wood, and as they crumbled the temples deteriorated and the jungle invaded them.

Long Sanskrit text is carved on the walls.

The first visitor was a Chinese ambassador, who made exact descriptions of what he saw and reconstructed the history of Angkor Wat.

The kings lived protected by the walls, and the people outside in unprotected huts. Artists engraved numbers on the stones so the French archaeologists were able to replace them in their proper sequence.

The alley of statues leading to the temple or palace entrance has, on the right, demons and, on the left, gods. The size of stones on the ground resembles those in Aztec pyramids or Inca structures. The height of the steps is twice that of ours. Some towers are in the shape of pine cones or pineapples. The capitals of a few of the columns in the shape of an open lotus. Many heads of cobras as ornaments.

A striking palm in the shape of an open fan. Chanting monks at night. Their orange robes against charcoal-gray stones. Traces of color inside the temples. One head of Buddha was sanded to show sculpture without verdigris or erosion. The natives believe the gods built the temples and then abandoned them, so at first they refused to excavate or restore.

In the middle of the ruins a young man is playing a one-stringed instrument with a violin bow. He plays well. He offers instruments for sale. Children sell flutes, jew's-harps, temple bells made of horn, and ferociously curved knives with handles carved out of elephant tusks. The natives live in bamboo huts on stilts. They sit out of doors around low tables, eating their lunch or selling fruit juice and Coca-Cola.

They are gentle. An old man is selling a bow and arrow. He looks noble. One would expect rather to meet him in battle.

Bodhisattvas: those human beings who, having arrived at perfect understanding, postpone out of love their entry into Nirvana, to help mankind to attain it.

Garanda is a mythical bird which appears frequently in decorative carvings.

Bangkok, Thailand.

The Oriental is the oldest and most famous hotel. I stay in the old wing where I love the teakwood rooms and the beautiful gardens sloping down to the river. Meals are served outside in the garden. I open my window and see the wide river glittering in the evening light. An Esso sign on the banks outshines the other lights. I had hoped to see Bangkok before its destruction by Western culture. I have often thought that the West is jealous of Asia and would like to destroy it. Asia contains the beauty, the ecstasies, the bliss and delights lost to the West. All the West had to do was to send an army of salesmen selling all the ugliness produced by technology—neon lights, signboards, and plastic; and television, to poor fishermen who own nothing else and sleep on the floor.

As in Venice, the motorboats not only disturb and unbalance the small sampans, but create dirt and noise, and endanger foundations. They carry hordes of tourists through the narrow canals, which are lined with small teakwood houses on stilts. Flowers made of silk. Mobiles of paper flying fish. A small sampan is attached to every house when not being paddled up and down the canals—"klongs"—selling fruit, fish, vegetables and cooked meals; one taking children to school; one for the postman; one loaded with water jugs. The river supplies the fish, the forest behind the houses supplies the fruit and vegetables. I watched people gathering watercress.

The houses are open. There is only one room. Families sit on the floor and eat the cooked food supplied by the sampan. Fish, bananas, corn, are cooked on braziers, the rice in vast cauldrons. They have very few possessions. One sees but one sarong hung on a nail, no furniture. A hammock. Photographs of relatives on the wall. Life is harmonious. They have enough to eat. They wash their sarongs in the river and hang them to dry on bushes around the house. A miniature duplicate of the lovely A-shaped houses is planted in the garden to house the spirits. Offerings of food and incense are placed before them.

The spirit house is called *chao ti*. A spirit must have his own house or he will haunt you.

Inside the open house I saw craftsmen at work, carving teakwood statuettes, masks, jade statuettes, miniature temples.

Paradoxically, it is the interest of the tourists which keeps the crafts and dances alive. It was an American, Mr. Thompson, who restored and revived silk weaving.

I saw a woman washing her long hair in the river. Women unloading bricks.

I saw boats being built, of teakwood. The royal barge was all gold and precious stones, with a giant gold swan at the prow.

The king's throne with its nine-tiered gold umbrella, the roofs in brilliant red with gold motifs like snowflakes. Near the throne there is a mirror, which has two interpretations—one realistic (the king is able to watch what goes on behind his back) ; the other mystical (he is able to contemplate his soul). A curtain is closed until the king is seated.

Precious stones are never stolen from temples because thieves fear the wrath of Buddha. Imagine our thieves afraid of God!

Religion seems to be at the bottom of the people's contentment. All they have to do to gain a place in heaven is to keep the monks' plates filled with food.

One morning I happened to awake early and to walk through the town. The door of the temple was open. I entered. A young man was taking the vows of a Buddhist monk. He was completely shaved and wore his white robe like a toga. He was very beautiful. He walked with his hands clasped around a lotus flower, his eyes lowered. His relatives carried a highly ornamented umbrella, red and gold with tassels and bells. Other relatives and friends followed the procession, carrying offerings of food artistically arranged in pyramids of colors and textures on painted baskets. This would be their last glimpse of the young man for three months. When he walked into the temple he would vanish into another world.

Cremation was born because of tribes moving, unable to carry their dead with them.

The East is a source of life. The West is a source of death. The East likes light, transparency.

Wind chimes and wind-bells are the voice of Buddha.

Possible link between mystic illumination and jewels. Jewels appear so often in LSD reveries.

Thai people say gold expresses joy, that it gives light even on gray days.

The entire open space in front of the imperial palace is given to the market—fruit, vegetables, fish, flowers. Dried snakes, live eels, guava jelly, cakes. Food neatly wrapped in banana leaves. Big banana leaves at the bottom of baskets keep fruit moist.

Singapore.

Singapore is a legend invented by Somerset Maugham.

The famous Raffles Hotel where Maugham sat at the bar gathering secondhand stories was typically English, formal and full of supercilious waiters.

Mixed races in the street could have been interesting but they were drowned in noise. Cars, rickshaws and bicycles jangle and compete, then the riders insult each other. Dirt. Open sewers. Open shops. Much hawking. The floor of my hotel room is tiled; doors reach only to the shoulder to let the breeze through, but they also let noise through from the street and the restaurant. The only thing I recognized from films of tropical places was the large overhead fan, as big as an airplane propeller, the overhead fan of Indian bungalows. And the monkey in the garden chained to a tree.

Many races living together makes for ruffled politics. Singapore's people are an amazing amalgam of many races and cultures—Chinese, Malay, Indonesian, Indian, British, Arab, Jewish. Native women wear kebayas from Malaysia; the Chinese women, their black chongsums; others, the Indian sari.

Penang, Malaysia.

At times it is difficult to separate the nature of a place from the atmosphere of the hotel where one is staying. In this case the hotel was overpoweringly and thoroughly English colonial. High ceilings, huge fans, shabby bathrooms, hard beds; somber and dignified. But there was a terrace for breakfast and one could see the Indian Ocean. One cannot swim there because the sewage empties into it.

But next day I discovered a beach of golden sand where one could swim and a pleasant hotel on the beach. Nature was sweet and rich with flowers.

I love the tropics with a passion. I'm physically attuned to the heat, the perfume, the lushness. The feeling of bathing in the Indian Ocean —just saying, This is the Indian Ocean—was so incredible. The effect of history and legend and literature so strong that it illumines and transforms. I think even with closed eyes I would have known I was swimming in the Indian Ocean. In old cultures they believe we live immersed in the souls of the past.

The beauty of the Malaysian women surpasses that of the Japanese, Cambodian and Thai, because added to a perfect, delicate and sensitive type is a tropical languor, a voluptuous motion. Waists very slender, breasts and hips full, lovely flawless skins and soft dazzling eyes. I watched a waitress moving about with her tray as if she were turning and undulating in bed on a hot afternoon, half dreaming, half prepared for caresses.

Manila, Philippines.

A modern city, white buildings surrounded by tropical jungle. Around and between the buildings, shacks of palm leaves and naked black children were the only appealing signs of native life. But the tour guides, salesmen, beggars attach themselves to you so you cannot go for a walk. Honking cars. Air conditioning now makes travel dangerous, to go from ninety degrees into an icebox and back again is a constant shock.

But two and a half hours away by car lie the genuine Philippines. Houses have sliding windows and doors like those of the Japanese, but instead of rice paper they use translucent mother-of-pearl. Dark smil-

33

ing children, water buffaloes washing or resting in their water holes. The Pagsanjan river magnificent, wide, with jungle flowers and vines trailing along the banks.

Pools filled with lotus and water lilies. Two native boys paddle us up the river in a long, very narrow canoe, like American Indians. When we come to rapids they get out into the water, leaping from rock to rock, pulling and pushing the canoe. Once the rapids are passed, they leap into the canoes again. We reached a high jungle forest, and a waterfall where the white water plunges 100 feet down from a jungle canopy. We left the canoe and sat on a sand bar. The native boys swam under the waterfall into caves. The trees carry long lianas. The birds are operatic. Coming down the rapids on the way back was easier than going up. Lunch in the forest under the trees was very simple and good—fried chicken and bananas.

People are poor. They earn one peso a day working in the fields.

Today the heart rending news of the fighting in Cambodia. Having just seen it, talked with the natives, it hurt me deeply.

After traveling through East Asia and finding it far more civilized than the West, the idea of America making war nauseates me. News of the hideous present catches up with you everywhere. You can no longer go into the past and forget the monstrous present.

[Fall, 1966]

When I returned from a fabulous, fairy-tale trip, I learned that Eve Miller had died. She was beautiful and talented. What happened? She took antibiotics for a cold with a whole bottle of gin. Did she want to die?

Oliver Evans gave me the manuscript of his book* to read on the plane. I was crushed by his lack of understanding. We exchanged bitter letters. I had let him interview me and had given him all the keys. He had all the collaboration he needed. But his point of view was Victorian and academic.

The Library of Congress asked me for a gift of the original diaries. I answered that this was my only capital. I had received recognition too late and royalties were barely enough to live on.

Nobuko [Uenishi] joins the Noh theater and writes and talks about its meaning. The inherited tradition of the Noh master, the incredibly severe discipline, broke down in America. The Noh master became an alcoholic and lost the tradition.

The past has not left me bitter or vengeful. I face the love, tributes I receive with pleasure. I am like a new woman, born with the publication of the Diary. This new woman is at ease in the world because whatever shyness is left over from the past is helped by the fact that when I enter a room or a lecture hall people know me already and they rush toward me. Their warmth creates a climate in which I can open, flower, respond, return their love.

I have problems with possessive friends. They magnify our friendship. I give beyond its genuine size. I hate to disappoint or hurt. I feel ungenerous not to be able to reciprocate in the same amount, at the same temperature.

* *Anaïs Nin* (Carbondale: Southern Illinois University Press, 1968).—Ed.

Roger Bloom, the prisoner with whom I corresponded, is free. Editing Volume Two of Diary. Meeting with Henry [Miller] to talk over what may concern him.

Meeting of the Otto Rank Association. I can measure how far I have traveled when I remember my rebellious and shallow attitude toward professional women. Today, I greatly admire Virginia Robinson and Anita Faatz. They are remarkable women. Their work for Rank is admirable, intelligent and self-effacing. After they finished their work at the Pennsylvania School of Social Work, they gave all their time to Otto Rank's work, to create a journal that would bring Rankians together, to see that his books were reprinted, that his papers given to Columbia University were translated (correspondence with Freud, his diary, poems and plays). Virginia has a remarkable history —her writings, her teaching, her courage.

Heard of Alan Swallow's death Thanksgiving Day. He died at his desk. Heart attack. Very affected by his death because he represented a unique attitude and integrity in publishing. He was a rare human being, a poet devoted to poets, a writer devoted to other writers. There was only one Alan Swallow. There are only a few human beings who cannot be replaced.

Visit from Varda. He came with three young women dancers, the Three Graces I called them. He looks ruddy and strong, although he had a stroke. He tells me this stroke delivered him of the fear of death. "I saw wonderful colors, like an LSD vision. It was beautiful. I had no sense of parting from the world, just dissolving in colors."

Met Dr. Félix Martí-Ibáñez, editor of *MD* magazine. The magazine wrote me up. I visited him and told him how much *MD* magazine had contributed to my education, as he writes on every conceivable subject.

He was wounded fighting against Franco. Exiled. Came to America. Practiced psychiatry. Evolved the clever, successful *MD* magazine, which is sent free to doctors. The advertisers pay. The magazine is full of articles on travel, biography, history, literature, history of medicine, essays on films and books, on personalities. I met his intelligent women assistants. I learned so much from *MD* about a thousand subjects.

Went to St. Mark's Church Parish Hall, where a few writers met to pay homage to Alan Swallow.

I read what I had written about him in the Diary.

Walter Lowenfels read poetry, Natalie Robbins too.

I talk with Marguerite Young, who complains of loneliness. But she lives in the watertight compartment of her self-created world. We are fictions. I am a fiction

I take Varda's latest drawings to a publisher who first showed interest and then reproached me for not telling him Varda was a West Coast artist, and therefore he was not interested.

I meet Nobuko for lunch. She wears a black sweater striped with emerald green and a velvet green bow in her hair. Ivan Morris has trapped her in a possessive, rigid marriage, into all that she was struggling to escape. I try to free her. "You can't grow with so many restrictions."

Lunch with Hiram Haydn. He behaved gallantly, but I cannot forget that in the spring when we met at the Algonquin and I brought him Karl Shapiro's beautiful review [of the Diary], all he could say was: "I wish someone would write like that about me."

I have dinner at Bettina Knapp's. She is writing a book about Artaud and also wrote about Louis Jouvet and Yvette Guilbert. She is a shrewd and meticulous biographer. It was Bettina, during her first visit to me, who solved the mystery of my quarrel with Artaud. I was telling her how it came about. I had returned from the south of France where I had celebrated my reunion with my father. I was telling Artaud about it when he burst into a tirade about the monstrosity of this love. A preacher's curse upon an unnatural love! I was offended by his moral judgment. At the time he was filled with his play about the Cencis, and, as Bettina said, he could only see what filled his own unconscious: Beatrice Cenci and incestuous love. He no longer saw me, but only Beatrice Cenci. Yes, I knew this, but I didn't know why this had caused such anger in me. For him, the unconscious *was* the truth. Clairvoyance. He read my unconscious, symbolic love.

Edmund Wilson said over the telephone that he was inspired by my Diary to begin editing his own. He also said he had enjoyed it very much but would give no written comment—he no longer gave comments to anyone.

At lunch Nobuko translated a beautiful letter from my Japanese translator, Mr. Nakada, and part of the long interview I had with Kenzaburō Oē, which was published in its entirety.

Barbara Turner working on script of *A Spy in the House of Love* for Robert Wise.

In the evening a visit from Jack Jones and Victor Lipton. I had been corresponding with Jack Jones, who is a specialist on Otto Rank, in response to his review of the Diary, in which he called me Lady Murasaki and which reached me just as I was sailing on the S.S.

Murasaki through the Inland Sea of Japan. Victor Lipton also had written a review I liked and we became friends. Jack Jones is deaf and has to read lips. He also has trouble with his eyes. But he is spirited, warm, dynamic, makes such great efforts to communicate. I am moved by his aliveness breaking through so many barriers. He types his letters in capitals. His friendship was Maxwell Geismar's only gift to me because when the Diary came out Geismar was silent, and it would have been his only chance to make up for his lack of understanding of the novels. I had sought a reconciliation after I was told he was pained by our quarrel and that he had been very ill. But when I asked him: "Why the silence?" he answered: "Because you have received too much praise."

Nobuko and I have lunch together. We discuss Ivan Morris's tyranny and possessiveness. For the first time the smooth ivory face betrays anxiety. Her ambiguities remain inviolable. But she says: "Anaïs, may I ask you a brutal question? How did you become free?"

I said: "Nobuko, may I ask you a brutal question?" (We are so Japanese together!) "Do you have a *grande passion* for Ivan Morris?"

"No, Anaïs."

"Well, then, to be imprisoned with a *grande passion* is pleasurable, bearable, but otherwise it will merely give you claustrophobia."

Before she married Ivan she asked him if she could get up at six A.M. to work on her novel. Ivan said no, no one could stir in the home until nine o'clock when he gets up. He wants her to give up her job with Toho, give up entertaining producers (part of her job is to effect interchange of plays and films with Japan), lecturing and teaching.

I took a bus to Princeton, and Anita Faatz met me and drove me to her home in Doylestown, Bucks County. She and Miss Robinson, who is eighty-three years old, retired from the Philadelphia school where Rank taught, and are devoting their time to the Rank Association. A neat, clean house in a clearing, overlooking a pond and a forest, a house filled with books. Rank's photograph on the table. Copies of the *Journal* in which they printed sections of the Diary referring to Rank. Talk about Rank—their memories and mine. Perhaps because of the habit of professional secrecy, we never talked about his friends or introduced them to one another. Many complications prevent his books from being reprinted. I felt bad because Anita and Miss Robinson were at the Cité Universitaire in Paris when I described the lectures as tiresome and said I would not continue attending them although Rank wanted me there. I felt I had been superficial in mocking the dullness of the meetings. I was not mature enough to appreciate the efforts of social workers.

The peace and scholarliness of the atmosphere pleased me, but I was depressed on the way back. It is sad to see people struggling to sustain a man's work, to keep his ideas alive. Perhaps I felt I should have sacrificed my life, my writing, to Rank's writing and his life.

It was a foggy night as I returned to New York. So many people, so many faces—no time to *see* a face. How often we make these circular journeys into the past, linking fragments of an incomplete puzzle, seeing a complete image. What emerges is the change in our vision, the changes in our character, the errors, the blind spots. As we make the return journey it is not only to pass judgment on our past selves, it is to crystallize, reinforce, consolidate what we have gained. I see today what I could not see in the 1930s, when intellectual life was ignored in favor of passion. I was more interested in love than in psychology. Now I can see the total work of Rank and join forces with Anita and Virginia. I worked with Rank for the moment only. They are working for his immortality.

But this fragment was not wasted. Rank's work was part of his seduction. It outlived the seduction. A life is then a composite which finally reveals its meaning, its purpose. It was not an error to be cast out. It became a synthesis worth keeping. So we pick up what looks like a stone, a broken shell on the edge of the sea, and on closer inspection it is a sculptured work of art.

Lunch with Hilda Lindley. She tells me not to expect star billing for the second volume of the Diary. "Second volumes never receive as much attention." What can we do to attract attention?

I suggest: "Let's have a party on a houseboat. In June it will be warm. The Gotham Book Mart will be hot and stuffy—not enough room."

Mrs. Lindley thought it was a wonderful idea. "But where will we find a houseboat?"

"I'll find one in the Yellow Pages!"

Our lunches are always lively. She feels it is easy to work with me. I do not have a prima donna's tantrums.

[January, 1967]

It is snowing. Saw the Chodoroffs. Stephen Chodoroff is brilliant. This generation is gifted and unconventional. He travels to Yugoslavia on an assignment, takes his wife and baby. They read widely and deeply. He is aware of past, present and future. He visits Ezra Pound. He reads the Diary with gusto. He does his job for "Camera Three" but dreams of many themes and subjects they do not let him do. It is so inevitable, this rigidity of the bosses, when they should be the ones most pliable to changing currents, to new tastes, new preoccupations, new interests. They always represent the immovable object, never aware of true happenings, of new waves, of explorations. They freeze. And so the media always lag behind the real interests, just as publishers are always behind.

I went to Marguerite's party. I was not in the mood. It seemed like a caricatural evening. Tom Harshman tells me how much he loves the Diary. I like him. I knew him first as a fairy-tale boy, young, transparent. Then the luminousness went out of his face. He became a successful designer. He wrote a novel about Haitian folk tales, he wrote another novel, he became Marguerite's student friend. But the light, where is the mysterious light which disappeared? What extinguishes it, what kills it? The Diary makes him feel an intimacy, a warmth. I would like to talk to the handsome priests from Fordham but I am blocked by a friend of Truman Capote's who is drunk, who sticks to me, and an angry woman who attacks me: "So you are Anaïs Nin. I hate women who tell all."

"Perhaps because you have nothing to tell, or may not know how to tell it."

I remember Proust's getting out of bed to visit a friend, to ask her what kind of flowers she wore on her hat twenty years earlier.

I am preoccupied with tracking down incomplete figures to round out a story, pursue a denouement. I'm only excited when I find a clue, which leads me to a new facet of someone's character, or a new version of an old story, or bringing my portraits up to date. I live for the Diary.

I love Marguerite and her apartment. It is like a child's room, the inside of a gypsy cart, of a wax museum, of all that a child dreams of —balloons, a merry-go-round horse, dolls, tin soldiers, sea shells, angels, chimes, crystal balls, dollhouses.

But tonight I could not communicate with people. There are times when the world I created and its personages seem more vivid than the ones before me.

Outside it is snowing. I walk very fast along Bleecker Street. Saturday night it is crowded, rowdy, half-bohemian, half criminal. The girls wear tight pants and high boots, and have long hair and heavily made-up eyes. The men in skin-tight pants and wide heavy belts; long hair also.

There came a time when Proust was no longer interested in life itself, but in completing his work. Have I reached this point? Or is this an intermittent watertight compartment in which I find myself only when the people are not congenial?

At Michael Field's masterpiece dinner I was completing my portrait of Leo Lerman.

I dressed up in my long skirt from Singapore. I dress up to cover my vulnerability, a pose in the world, to pretend I was not hurt when Leo said to me over the telephone on the day of the publication of *Ladders to Fire*: "You should lie low . . ."

When people talk about the drama of Sukarno, the drama is the same as all the other dramas: They all have their roots in the personal, a personal defeat, a personal humiliation. I study the personal and it applies to Sukarno, to Asia, to war, the world, leaders, bankers, to all. In the personal there is more hope of learning why; but never in history, because history is written by people with a personal prejudice. We are never able to get the truth of history. History lies. In the personal biography there is some hope of truth. To confuse the "I" of Proust with narcissism is absurd. The "I" is merely the "eye" of the microscope.

Marguerite said: "The Diary is an evolving whirlpool, tales within tales."

———————

Sara Berenson: "The Diary is a perfect balance to the novels—not that I felt they needed one when I read them, but the Diary does provide weight for them, anchors them in the world a bit more. And it made me go back to them and find them richer, just as they gave depth back to the Diary."

One night Louise Varèse called me up. She had just returned from a concert of [Edgar] Varèse's music perfectly played and was elated. She is writing about him. She talked about his death.

Strange that his last project was *House of Incest*. He was sensitive to the cry of anguish. He wanted voices which screamed the lines. He died before completing the music. Was his vision of hell like mine? Anxiety, the nightmare. Death turned us into statues.

The relationship we have to the dead is an entirely new one. Some traits which interfered with communion, with the flow of love, die with them. With my mother, it was her belligerence; with my father, his play-acting; with Varèse, his cynical mockery, which surrounded him like a constellation of bows and arrows. They flew out of him, from his bristling eyebrows, his thunderbolt eyes, his artistic dictatorship, his blasting opinions. With Rank (and that may have been the cause of my depression the day I visited his devoted followers), it was his desire to possess me, and he was the very one I came to for rescue.

With death, all these barbed wires, these alarm signals, these interferences in reception waves disappear and one hears the true self more distinctly.

Renate Druks's relationship to [her son] Peter was at first one of desperate guilt. She felt responsible for his death. Was she responsible first of all for depriving him of his father? He may have thought so. She caused the divorce. Was she responsible for his taking drugs, and before that for his conflict between art and science, between bohemianism and bourgeois life? When she went to Europe with John he felt deserted and was sullen and withdrawn. He tried bourgeois life with a family who wanted to adopt him and send him to college. He had said once to Renate that he would have liked a well-regulated life, but when he lived with the family he hated the meals at regular hours, the responsibilities in the organization, the rigidities of their life. He did walk through our parties, our masquerades, art games, happenings, like a ghost. But he drew, wrote poetry, and when I designed *Solar Barque* with his drawings I gave him the only fulfillment he had as an artist.

So at first Renate wailed and almost lost her reason. Two years later she discovered what she had given to Peter, from a girl Peter loved at age ten. The girl told Renate: "Peter and I were so close, almost married then, but his great worry was that I didn't believe in anything. He felt I should believe in something. He asked you to play the fairy godmother, to appear and grant my wishes." Renate dressed up as a spirit and came to the window at night and whispered: "Make a wish and it will be answered." The girl asked to be able to fly. The fulfillment of this wish was postponed, but meanwhile the apparition of Renate as a fulfiller of magic wishes made the girl believe.

Renate stirred Peter's imagination, encouraged his drawing and writing. At thirteen he asked her if he could not sleep with her. "I like you better than the little girls at school." Renate's answer was light and playful, not moralizing at all.

[Spring, 1967]

Marguerite Young spoke once of her visitors—Flaubert and Marcel Proust. It was because of Proust's allergy to real flowers that she used only paper flowers, I said.

Someone said about Louis and Bebe Barron's music: "A molecule that has stubbed its toes."

A lover once said, "I always need a double dose of medicine, I need twice as much LSD."
His friend replied, "That's why you chose Anaïs!"

All of February I worked on the third volume of the Diary.
The freedom of America is an illusion. Transplanted from Europe, I was fully aware of the opposite of freedom in the air, so much Puritan disapproval, so much of the spectator and the voyeur, watching one live and jealous of those who live. So much negative criticism, so much hidden hostility, like the hostilities of old maids locked in small towns who sent poison pen letters and persecuted lovers.
A sin to look inward, they feel, and yet that is why there is so much loss of identity. A sin to be personal, and yet that is why there is so much loneliness and alienation.

Much music this month. When I go to the Leightons I hear about projects for photographing the planets. Dr. Robert Leighton is a scientist at Cal Tech. He is the one who impressed me so much as the Ideal Father because he had built a treehouse for his children in a magnificent old tree. But the old tree showed signs of failing health, and Leighton was struggling to revive its vitality by all possible means.
At the Leightons I met the Ohnukis. Dr. Ohnuki is a biologist working on cancer, and Mrs. Ohnuki likes to translate Japanese works into English. She translated my interview done in Japan. She brought a friend, Kazuko Sugisaki, pale and self-effacing, who asked me how I had become free.
Hideo Aoki, editor at Kawade Shobo, came to visit and to meet

Henry Miller. Henry treated us to a cheerful dinner at an Italian restaurant. Miller is a great favorite in Japan. Japan, so suppressed, finds him liberating.

Kazuko Sugisaki came to my house to dance, framed by the pool and the lake. She appeared in a white kimono painted with red peonies—wistful eyes, the head bowed slightly like a rich flower. She carried two long muslin scarves sewn to fan handles. They were about three yards long and very light. She waved them in such a way that they undulated before, around and high over her head, sometimes slowly, sometimes swiftly, spirals in space—a river, she said, clouds, winds, breezes, waves filled with breath or trailing on the shore. Then she was still, holding the fan handles over her shoulder, the scarves hanging like a hierarchic cape. Meanwhile, as the head oscillated on her delicate porcelain neck, she arched backwards, holding her whole perfect body in graceful tension. Her body obeys a stylization, holds itself in control to design grace. When she bends her wistful face, she seems to be fragile and burdened. When she turns her back and half kneels, her neck looks tender and delicate, but her legs are strong as she holds the pose of a print. Her hands rest on the edge of an open umbrella for another dance, long fingers undulating harmoniously, free, but held reigned by the laws of the dance. Each dance is a song, a slow dream, a painting held long enough to be seen, suspended. The body serves the dream, is eloquent, fluid or static, free or fragile, in perfect obedience to the spirit.

Saw *Ulysses*, produced by Joseph Strick. Extremely well filmed; faithful script by Fred Haines; Irish actors superb.

Saw Edward Albee's play, *A Delicate Balance*. I do not respond to him—it is too abstract. How cruelly the news media has diminished Tennessee Williams, forgetting his past gifts to the theater and now greeting Albee with exaggerated praise.

Gave a lecture at conference of designers at Lake Arrowhead near Los Angeles. The designer before me spoke of the "intrinsic beauty" of billboards and neon signs in cities like Las Vegas; said they should be considered Pop Art. I spoke of the inhumanity of Kennedy Airport.

[Summer, 1967]

Eight hours from Los Angeles and you are in satori land [Tahiti]. Even at the airport, noise and bustle and all, what predominates is the caressing atmosphere, the scent of tiara flowers, the tinkle of shell necklaces, the beauty of the brown women. The atmosphere unties your nerves, opens the pores of your skin so that you feel like a flower opening to the dew. The shell necklaces are placed around your neck. The pareos worn by the women are printed with flower designs, so flowers and women are intertwined, their eyes like the black heart of the daisies, their skin like the velvet of lilies.

Everything I hear about the island—that there is plenty of water, that every plant is edible, that there are hundreds of species of each flower, that fish are abundant and not only savory but jewellike in appearance—all this seeps into my body like the very sun and makes it flower. The body flowers. The fruit falls and opens and spills its juices; the flowers grow out of breasts and thighs, out of the hair; flowers and fruit sprout from the hands and feet. The sea is rocking my body, the sun is melting it. Flesh, fruit and flowers are one—sap, gum, milk intermingle with the blood and veins. The light on the water radiates into the body. I feel the bird's light feet and flutter of wings, and they are asleep in my hair. Thousands and thousands of shades of green, from the deepest to the lightest gold green of certain palms and bamboos. A crown flower leans over our balcony into the room. A cup-of-gold vine and wild hibiscus are climbing over it. It would take a lifetime to paint all the colors, a lifetime to breathe the scent of every flower, to register the moods of the sea, of the lagoons, of the quiet coves and the fierce coves—the wildest one, a cave against which the waves hurl themselves with a hissing sound, like the furious breath of a giant. Strange to sit inside a bower of flowers as if we were the kernels, the eyes, the heart of them.

I visited the tomb of King Pomaré V, who, according to legend, insisted on being buried with all his bottles of Benedictine. He wanted the tomb opened yearly for people to drink Benedictine in his honor and place the empty bottles next to him.

Of course, in our history books much is said about King Pomaré V but little about Queen Pomaré, who became sovereign of Tahiti when her husband died. Her reign was long, spanning the Restoration, the reign of King Louis Philippe, the brief Second Republic, all of the Second Empire, and the seven years which saw President Thiers and Marshall McMahon in the Elysée Palace. But who today has heard of Queen Pomaré? The history of women remains to be written.

Eugene Burdick in *Blue of Capricorn* makes a startling statement—that man has such a need to dream of paradise that he refuses to see what is not paradisical about Tahiti. I looked but found nothing of this negative aspect of the island—except for the mosquitoes. It seemed to me that nature was generous. The tiny islands I could see from the mainland were never desert islands hostile to life. Coconuts fall off the trees, roll onto the beach, get carried away by the tide, float on the sea until they reach the island, and soon you have a coconut grove which supplies all that a human being needs to stay alive. The outer shell makes a bowl to eat from. The milk and white meat are both nourishing foods. Fiber from the hard shell can be woven into a body cover, and the young leaves can be plaited into baskets, hats and fans. The husk is used to make ropes and mats and to caulk canoes. Even broken skulls were mended with coconut shell.

I visited the pathetic Gauguin Museum. There are no Gauguin paintings; all are in museums elsewhere or private collections. But there are manuscripts, drawings, his copper plates and engraving tools. There are photographs of his early life here, of his Tahitian wife. And there are books about him, books which show his life as tragic. But the prize of the museum is Gauguin's diary. As I looked at the actual yellow pages and spidery French handwriting, I wondered if all our ink would fade and our paper crumble, our sketches vanish with time? Ostensibly Gauguin never knew the joy or ecstasy or satori of Tahiti. His Tahiti sheltered a suffering man. He was ill when he came, and poverty and starvation did not help. Was he denied all the joyous pleasures of Tahiti? Did he feel the soft breezes, the lulling songs and voices? He painted earthy Tahitians, resting on the earth with big, strong feet. He did not see the delicate bodies of the young girls. He carried his inferno within him and Tahiti could not cure him.

Nights in Tahiti are soft and lulling. All drive to activity, to work, is liquidated in the silken air. I could not understand my friends' anxieties and worries in their letters. They had lost (if they ever knew it) what the Tahitians kept so unalterable: the capacity to enjoy contemplation, to watch the sunset or sunrise, to enjoy the shape of a seashell, never to strive or will anything. The beauty of Tahiti is not only in its inhabitants, flowers, mountains, but in the subtle, insidious love of life which it imparts.

Eugene Burdick, who wrote so humanly and lyrically about the island, was building himself a house in Moorea to live in when he retired. He did not live to occupy it. To me this seems a message to carry out your dreams in the present . . . not in the future.

Back in Los Angeles, I visited Jerry Bick and his wife, the actress Louise Fletcher. Jerry is so well read, and she so gentle. He has done all he could for *A Spy in the House of Love*. The last script was a failure too. It sounded like *Ladies' Home Journal*.

At a cocktail party at the home of Dr. Haas of UCLA, I again ran into an editor of *Partisan Review*. The magazine became hostile to me years ago when I answered truthfully that I was not a relative of Andrés Nin, the anarchist and their hero. There are many Nins in Barcelona. They thought I repudiated him because he was a Trotsky man. Ridiculous. I was against Franco. Andrés Nin was a hero.

But I could not lie. From then on they sniped at me whenever possible. When I arrived in New York in 1940 the only thing that mattered was which political group you belonged to, and the hatred between groups was vicious. In the forties no one cared about writing, only propaganda. You were judged by your politics. I remembered a poor friend wanting to quit the Party because of her extreme ill health. She once sold *The Daily Worker* on street corners in the middle of the bitterest winter. Three rough-looking men came to see her, to intimidate her and tell her that no one could quit the Party.

It was at that time that Gonzalo reported often to the Party office and left me waiting for him in the street. My feeling at the time was that I was theoretically a sympathizer, but in actuality I was repulsed by the tactics and dehumanized authoritarianism. As soon as I saw cruelty, torture, tyranny, I ceased to believe in any party.

[Fall, 1967]

I have seen Deena Metzger often. We worked hard on the book about writing.* I had to leave to attend the Rank Association meeting. October 28 [in Doylestown, Pa.]. My difficulty there is that social workers see the destructive side of the young, and my work attracts the creative young, the talented, not the dropouts or the drug addicts. So we clash. Our interpretations clash. There was in the audience a long-haired, sensitive musician I had met on one of my trips. His wife was a painter. The social workers talked about the "bums with long hair." I had to defend my long-haired musician.

I spent Chanukah with Deena's family. It was a beautiful ritual. Deena had set two long tables, one for the family, one for the friends. The children read the history of the Jews. Each guest also read a section in turn. The little round caps worn by the men looked Oriental. Any ritual that unites a group of people as closely as we felt that evening is holy.

Lunch with Mako [Francis]. A repetition of Nobuko's story. The Japanese women expect to be liberated by marriage to an American. It does not liberate them. The American husband demands a Japanese wife.

Liberation comes from within. Mako's reproaches are vague, as vague as Japanese novels. Sam stayed out all night. To punish him she cuts off her beautiful long black hair. He goes to bed with a pile of art books. She is pregnant. She telephones me like a woman drowning. She does not like what pregnancy is doing to her body. "I feel like an animal, bloated and stagnant."

*The Novel of the Future (New York: Macmillan, 1968).—Ed.

I am nominated a daughter of Mark Twain.

My books are taught at Queens College in a course in avant-garde literature, along with Virginia Woolf, Joyce, Beckett, Ionesco and Robbe-Grillet.

I am invited to lecture at the Library of Congress.

Spoken Arts is bringing out a recording of my reading from the Diary.

I am translated into French, German, Italian, Swedish, Danish, Flemish, Catalonian and Japanese.

Three marvelous reviews of the Diary by Daniel Stern, Marianne Hauser* and Marguerite Young.

Dinner at Mary Wier's. Sutton Place South. Extreme luxury. Antiques, brocades, silver. Butler and maid. At dinner a pheasant displayed on a silver platter, feathers and all, beautiful wings spread, stuffed, holding a cherry in its beak. I could not eat. It ruined my evening.

I interpret Marguerite Young's obsession with drowning, submersion, as a plunge into oceanic unconscious. Dr. Bogner thought it was an obsession with the womb, the mother.

I call Los Angeles. The friend who cares for my house has just taken Piccolo for a walk in the mountains surrounding the house. The forest of eucalyptus and pine is now covered with wild flowers. Piccolo will return with blue bells clinging to his white lamb's hair, like a dog in Venetian court paintings.

Dream: The protesters against the draft are babies—five, six, seven years old. I look at them from a high place. People throw pieces of broken metal at them to cut them. I shelter them. I am waiting to see the doctor. I see a man horribly hacked, piece by piece, in agony.

* See *Studies in the Twentieth Century,* Fall 1968, no. 2, Troy, N.Y.—Ed.

I ask the doctor to put him out of his misery. I am desperate. The doctor tells me I have cancer.

Hippies in costumes from the past: Beardsley, beads, uniforms. The only creation is in sound and lights. I became obsessed with the beauty of light shows. Saw an interplay with my own work, which indicated a living, moving relation between the arts.

Book on writing now 300 pages—result of intensive six weeks. The peace, serenity, lack of interruptions in my Los Angeles home have been very conducive to reflective writing.

In contrast, in New York at the end of the day I play ostrich. I take a glass of beer or wine or a pill and go to sleep to have energy for the next day. This was the time I once gave to the Diary, to reflection. I am trying to recapture this moment, not to become submerged by the New York type of life.

From an introduction for a projected Japanese edition of *Under a Glass Bell*:

These stories were published in England after the war, at a most inauspicious time. There was not enough paper, the book looked prematurely aged and there were not enough reviewers or readers for a form of short story which was close to the poem and could not be classified. For certain books there are such out-of-time fatalities. We accept distillation to make liqueurs and perfumes, but the short story had never before been distilled, condensed. The only writer I felt an affinity with was Isak Dinesen. The affinity was in the acceptance of unusual events. But hers were situated in a past and in a country we did not know. Mine were distilled from the heart of life in Paris from 1930 to 1940. Many of the characters have since become well known, such as Antonin Artaud, Hans Reichel and Jean Carteret. The publication of the Diary gave the undistilled material and so completed and extended the stories.

Finished book on writing, *The Novel of the Future*.

The Imperial Hotel torn down. All of Japan tried to save it. I made a personal plea to the owner, Inumaru, when I stayed there, but he was determined to make more money by replacing one of the world's most beautiful buildings with a huge, faceless, plastic high-rise. At

53

least I'm grateful that I was able to live and entertain my publishers in it. Pathetically few parts will be moved to Meiji Village, to be shown like a movie set with famous buildings of the Meiji era.

Read a book on the Japanese mind by a psychiatrist who was there during the war. Japanese training in selflessness a problem. Repression a cause of disturbances. Obedience and order so strong that even in the insane asylums they need only paper partitions. They do not aggress on each other. Relatively low crime rate. They choose to commit suicide rather than to kill.

Reading at Poetry Center in New York was overflowing. But questions so pathetic and shallow.

Wayne McEvilly, Doctor of Philosophy and Eastern Religions, writes:
(The Buddha theme) " 'No one has ever said that I am a saint,' you [Anaïs] say. I will say it in my own way. Much scholarly data could be brought to bear on how close the diarist in Volume Two is to the Buddhist ideal of compassion, how close to so much of Mahayana, so much of the best of Zen."

Louise tells me Varèse said he was allergic to himself. He was ashamed of his rages (just like my father).

[Spring, 1968]

Letter to student:

I would like very much to help you with your thesis on Alan Swallow, but his letters are in a vault in Brooklyn and I have had the flu so I don't think I'll be able to do anything about it before I leave on a lecture tour.

As a factual contribution to the problems facing an independent publisher I have a lot to say. Alan Swallow's problem was mainly that of obtaining reviews from papers who would not review small-press books, or books which were not advertised, and this applies to the *New York Times* as well as others. He was up against this all the time. It was only when he or I made a friend of someone on a paper that a review might appear. And of course, he could not afford big advertising, and consequently the book shops also would not carry books which were not widely advertised or reviewed. The only papers who disregarded such crass commercialism were the underground papers, such as the *Village Voice,* the Los Angeles *Free Press,* and others.

We both collaborated on this, helping each other with new contacts, and new friends. . . .

Letter to Ronnie Knox, football player turned poet, who wished to write about me:

Here are some more concrete facts about the elusive Miss Nin! Names of trees: Canary Island pine (tall and languid); Juniper, twisted juniper or juniper torilosa (which means neurotic juniper, my favorite!); pittosporum (the bushes around the pool); bougainvillaea on the walls; eucalyptus, some blue gum, some red gum (I do love the names of trees); lippia is the ground covering, a green carpet, on which Piccolo likes to sit watching the birds. Ah, birds. I feed them. I really do. So I can watch them as they eat: doves, linnets, mocking birds, blue jays. The blue jays have a voice like Donald Duck and *demand* food, the ring-necked doves came from China, and they are gentle and coo. Some birds have black hoods around their heads; I don't know their name.

The little linnets have bright orange-red breasts and are great fun to watch. I can watch them as I write because the entire side of my house facing the garden is glass. I remember now, I used to sign the childhood Diary and some letters to my father "Linotte."* In French, this means "linnet," but I took my pen name from the expression *Tête de Linotte,* which means "featherhead" or "up in the air."

Love of costume was continued from early diary days. I brought back a Vietnamese dress, a Malaysian skirt, a Japanese kimono, and love to wear them. My favorite designer is Rudi Gernreich because he is imaginative. I like many things about California which the East does not have; the glass chapel of Lloyd Wright, son of Frank Lloyd Wright, the Watts Towers, which the surrealists would have loved.

One may think from the Diaries that I live in the past. Not so. Just as active with new experiences, new travels, new friends. Love light shows, and planning a reading with light show and paper dresses for Parsons School of Design. International friends, with a preference for Japan. On the Committee for Tea Ceremony School which is tied up with Zen. Love the hippies. Love underground films and student films. Best relationship of all is with the young. It is the young who read me and who visit me.

California ideal for a writer.

Nobuko is the opposite of Mako. Mako is free and living sincerely. Nobuko has become a woman of society and position and not free, or able to be herself at all because Ivan Morris is an Englishman. The English live on their persona, a conventional, artificial persona. I like them less and less. I was on a panel with an English poet, and he was all false modesty, false humility, false self-effacement. He could neither read nor talk without acute self-consciousness, seeking to obliterate himself, and the result was entirely negative.

Letter to Kazuko Sugisaki, who is translating *Collages*:

We had two days of summer. We heard the mockingbird sing wildly, and today fog again. Riots. War. . . .

How is your dancing? The chrysanthemum petals were a great success, did I tell you? I only served them to ourselves or very appreciative friends. They reminded me of a line I once wrote about the taste of fruit and the taste of the dawn, like eating poetry, eating flowers. We think of you and how wonderful it will be to see you. . . .

* The early diaries, covering the years 1914 to 1920, were published under the title *Linotte* by Harcourt Brace Jovanovich in 1978.—Ed.

The names [in *Collages*]: They are all half real and half invented. Not in *Who's Who*. Can names be translated? Could they be left as they are? Was Sabina translated? Varda is real, a Greek name (relative of Agnes Varda, the filmmaker). Renate is a real first name. Judith Sands is Djuna Barnes, writer, an invented name. Bruce is a pseudonym. Could they be left as they are? Nobuko of course is real. Those who consented to have their real names used I left in. The others I changed.

We all felt a shock when we found a pile of *Miss MacIntosh, My Darling* remaindered at Marboro for one dollar. The sight depressed Marguerite because most people misunderstand this and consider it is a proof of failure. So I called up Marguerite's friends and asked them to meet me at Marboro with shopping bags. We took the entire pile home. I sent many to college libraries, gave them to good reviewers. And thus Marguerite could walk head high along Eighth Street.

Editions Stock sent me a bad French translation of the Diary, Volume One. I refused it. Stock answered I would have to find my own translator and pay for the new translation. I wrote to Michel Fabré, who had first written to me to ask for more details about Richard Wright for his biography. We maintained a correspondence. He suggested a student of his teaching American literature at the Sorbonne: Marie-Claire Van der Elst. It was a lucky choice. She was excellent, both natural and exact.

Another visit from Jack Jones. Incredible courage against handicaps. Unfortunately too political. Considered Stalin's daughter important, whereas she was a fabrication of American publicity. She did not even know Stalin closely. Hardly saw him, had nothing to say.

At the death of Dr. Martin Luther King, Jr., I became hysterical. Could not bear the cruelty, the horror of it. Knew what a deep wound it would cause the black people. I never espoused a cause, but the cause of black people affects me deeply. I joined the vigil for Dr. King at Pershing Square in Los Angeles. That death was full of tragic meaning, humanly and politically. That it could happen was to me the darkest moment of American history.

At Dominguez Hills College I dedicated my talk to Dr. King and spoke of sensitivity versus toughness. Though I know it is too late for a cure.

Gave a manuscript to be auctioned off by Literary Auction for Peace.

[Summer, 1968]

Visit to Palomar Observatory, largest telescope in the world, en route to Mexico.

We saw the ancient pots and pans excavated during making of road for the Olympics. Many new schools but still too many poor Mexicans. They work on the roads in 120-degree heat from seven to six. Their wives bring a meager soup for lunch.

New motels along the road with swimming pools. The same gentle Mexican manners and the same arrogance from American tourists. The buses are more comfortable now—like our Greyhounds.

Visited caves, ruins, pyramids; learned the names of flowers, trees, birds. The whistling bird is monotonous—only one tone—like a young man whistling at a pretty girl.

Find it harder to write after driving all day.

In Acapulco, the road which led to Dr. Hernandez's house, a dirt road, dark and shadowy, on the left of the Hotel Mirador, is now a wide modern road along the sea with horrible jaundice-yellow sodium-vapor lights.

Drove up to the very mouth of a volcano near Hermosillo.

In Yucatán, using scuba divers, they found more treasures at the bottom of the famous cenote. And now the Mexicans value what they find and exhibit it well. Before, artifacts were always discovered by foreign archaeologists and taken out of the country.

The trip to Asia threw a completely new light on all I saw in Mexico. The connection with Asia becomes startling. Simple things like the *petate* on which they sleep identical to the Japanese tatami. The passion for flowers and birds, arrangement of fruits and vegetables in the market, a sense of design. The rituals of peyote. The Huichol Indians resemble the Tibetans, with tassels on their hats, prayer wheels, etc. The voices of the women in a group resemble the childlike voices of Japanese women.

The new archaeological museum in Chapultepec Park in Mexico City, one of the most beautiful museums in the world. This modernized expression of the grandeur of Aztec building gives the atmosphere of Indian life without the need of reproducing it. It is the artist who has survived the centuries to preserve an echo of the past. This is not a museum in the ordinary terms of crowded objects displayed without space or air. Here each room, with its high windows giving on the park, dramatizes a different period of Mexican history. The statues, the murals, the paintings are placed as in a theater, with space around them, against a background of red or orange.

There is continuity in the display, so that the history of Mexico unfolds not as dead objects but as living art. On the upper floor, above the artifacts of each period, the cultural life of that time is portrayed. A whole village will be shown in diagram. Then a life-size hut will be cut in half so you can see the construction of the hut and the way of life inside. Figures of clay represent the mother cooking, the child in its hammock crib, the father at his carving or weaving. Appropriate music brings it all to life.

Clay models under glass dramatize the archaeological finds. One could spend days gazing at the giant fan of green feathers worn by the rulers.

The tombs have painted murals, representing war and court scenes. A casket, probably commissioned by the invaders, is carved with exquisite care.

Every object projects a dignity, a pride, and an artfulness which the invaders were not able to annihilate completely.

Mike Steen, an actor I had met several times and now a neighbor [in California], told me Tennessee Williams had taken a house in the hills, and had invited us all for dinner. I had a strong desire not to go, remembering the Tennessee of parties, the artificial talk, the flippancy and hypocrisies. I had heard about his drinking, his depressions. I refused several invitations. Once Tennessee talked with me over the telephone, and he was drunk—"I need you desperately." Finally, last night, a friend and I drove up dark and tortuous mountain roads, looking at houses dug into the sides of steep canyons which expose only their garages and their cars and garbage cans. The air was pungent from damp earth and plants.

When we arrived, Mike opened the door. Mike is big and strong and at first one thinks he is merely an athlete. But he has soft eyes, and once at a party he was the only one who remembered to give Tavi (my cocker spaniel) water. He was also the only gentle and natural one at this party.

The last time I saw Tennessee was at a party after the opening of *The Milk Train Does Not Stop Here Anymore*. He was on his way to Italy. He seemed the same then as he had always been. Last night when I saw him standing by a table in an ivory embroidered Nehru suit, I received the full shock of the change. He looked small, soft, a mixture of old lady and child, the hands small and soft, the head round, full, the eyes slightly protruding—but all of it as if about to disintegrate. He was making an effort to hold himself together, offering me a red flower in a tiny glass holder. His lips were pursed, drawn into a tight bud. We embraced. His hair was longer and seemed so much thinner. His movement was not the lurching oscillation of drunkenness. It was the swimming underwater of someone drugged. He walked carefully. His eyes dissolved. There was a space between his words. "I can't see the beautiful aquamarine eyes in this light."

He spoke of the Diary. "So beautiful, so beautiful," he said. "I kept a diary too but it wasn't written."

"Show it to me, Tennessee. Read to us from it. You owe me that."

Mike and two young men sat talking. Tennessee and I sat together on the couch.

Suddenly what I saw reflected in him, in the dissolved face, the soft hands, was all the aging, desperate women he had portrayed.

He went into his bedroom to bring out three notebooks. He opened one and said, "No, these are notes for *Milk Train*." The second was "notes, too." The third was the diary. He read about a blackout—the one after the Japanese attack on Pearl Harbor. About feeling averse to making love after a scene of violence at the Claridge Hotel. He had not described the scene. He elaborated on it verbally. Two sailors had attacked him and a friend with knives and beaten them. Simple notations in pencil. A diary of facts—meetings, taking walks, seeing so-and-so—no revelation. He closed the notebook, though we wanted more. Then he talked about "the Gray Goose," who had come to see him. The Gray Goose was his mother, now eighty-four years old. He asked Mike to show us photographs. *La mère tigre*, who loved her sons more than her husband and destroyed the three children. "My sister is schizophrenic."

Of Mishima, he said: "He is a most *beautiful* man." The word "beautiful" was hissed as if uttered with hatred, lust, love. "He was in love with Frank. Did you know Frank? He died, you know. But I don't like his last book. It's too homosexual."

We sat at a formal dinner table. A stew cooked by the Argentine cleaning woman. All of us under tension to entertain Tennessee. The three young men were rather silent. Hypnosis came up because someone had put Tennessee into a trance for eighteen hours. Tennessee called him a guru; Mike called him a con queen. I was held by Tennessee's face. When he did not like the food it was that of an infant—spoiled. When he talked of Mishima it was one of lust. But at times his mouth seemed to become more prominent, as if he had difficulty in modulating words. His smile was a leer. There was theatrical puppetry, an unconscious show which did not match his words. His memory and sense of the present were at odds. The tender, soft, childlike expressions mingled with a wolflike grin.

On our way to the dining table he had stayed behind with my friend, and I could imagine him saying: "You are too beautiful to live with a woman." But what he did say was "Anaïs is so beautiful, take good care of her; you are so lucky!" He had said to me, "You are more beautiful than ever," and kissed me, but today I distrust the admiration of homosexuals. Why should I concern him? Yet I felt compassion. I saw him so vulnerably counting his loves. "Oliver was in love with me for so long." But the paranoia is there—"They want to kill me." And Ruby, the pug dog, worried him. "She whines. Her ears are icy cold." I put my ear to her nose and said: "She's wheezing. It's an allergy to smog. She is not ill."

"She is very, very ill."

Mike could not help saying: "You're projecting, Tennessee." He had to be reassured. I said, "We know a wonderful veterinarian who loves his animals. He once sheltered an old toothless pet lion the neighbors had reported because they were afraid. The lion was doing no one harm. He lived in a garage and when he roared his master spoke to him through the intercom and he would lie down and go to sleep."

We had seen Tennessee's film, *Boom*.

"A terrible film," he said. "They massacred the script. And when I first saw it, [Joseph] Losey had handled the camera like a bird—it swung, it flew here and there. At the opening all this was gone. I have never liked any of my films."

Between the words there were drugged pauses, fade-outs, meltings, silences. It was like sitting by a sick person having dreams and nightmares, and I suddenly understood how all these years we had been witnessing Tennessee's nightmares. He was given so much by the world, but the nightmares engulfed him. The last nightmare was about the dying old woman and the angel of death.

His face lay as it might in sleep—the eyes not seeing you but filled with ghostly visitors. At times, a grimace of lust, the tongue curling as if before a feast; or one of anguish; or a purse of lips seeking the small kisses of childhood.

He yawned. The pills and drink were affecting him. We left. Outside Mike said: "He must have taken a Seconal and one of Dr. Jacobson's injections. He is utterly dependent on them. He gives them to himself."

"Are you sure?"

Suddenly my last visit to Dr. Jacobson was clarified. I had been stunned by the change in him. He was bloated—an unhealthy fat, enormous. He did not know what he was doing. He faltered when giving me my injection. I could not understand. The nurse had to remind him there was a patient waiting.

I had once seen an item in a newspaper. The wife of an actor had reported to the police that her husband would get up in the middle of the night to get an injection from Jacobson.

What happened? Dr. Jacobson began with potent vitamins. He attracted people under stress—theater, concert, opera, movie and TV people—who *had* to perform. When did he begin to take drugs himself?

Mike's solicitude, his effort to bring around people who would understand and help Tennessee—all this was explained. It was this or a sanitorium. The damage to Tennessee; was it done by alcohol or drugs? Now Mike admits that Tennessee's associations are becoming secretive.

Why did he have to disguise himself in his writing as a woman—the woman who went mad, the woman who inhaled ether, the woman who howled for her dear love, the woman who had tantrums, the woman unloved by gigolos, the woman denied, outraged, used? I see the changing face of Tennessee, not the smiling face of the social Tennessee, but the baby-fat and the woman-fat softening, dissolving in the anguish of nightmares. The mask is shattered—Ruby moans; he moans. He does not want clear vision. He is flooded and invaded by his own theater of hysteria—with the poet's madness, at times inspired and at times infinitesimally small—a round-faced child.

Ivan Morris wanted me to review the *Pillow Book* for *Saturday Review*. They refused, although I did a good review of Dostoevsky's *Notebooks*.

[Fall, 1968]

Letter to Bettina Knapp:

I had so many frustrations with review of [Jean] Genêt that I did not want to write you. The *Village Voice* is overcrowded with reviews this season, so it would have had to wait. So I thought of *Open City* but it is now in censorship trouble. I wrote to *Free Press,* which, next to the *Village Voice,* has many readers. In the end I think it would be best for you if I did it for a university magazine like *Studies in the Twentieth Century* . . . Yesterday I mailed back the proofs of [my] Preface [to *Antonin Artaud: Man of Vision*]. . . . Someone recently wrote to me about the other book on Artaud and said it was very bad. I am sorry it came out first. But that is not important. I only hope you get a good review in the *Times.* It is terrible that a writer should depend on such a politically corrupt system as that of reviews. I am going through a depression as to the way things are run. Macmillan saying they ran out of review copies and omitting my loyal and friendly and selective list of reviewers, thirty or forty of them, and I having not only to buy the books but spending three days mailing them, an unprofessional gesture, a gift. Then Brown of *N.Y. Times* saying my Novel book was too much about French writers and not taking an *excerpt,* and then they let someone write about Cendrars who is not an expert on him, and gave Cendrars' book to review to nobody at all. . . . I wonder how they answered you at *Village Voice.* I am beginning to agree with the dropout hippies! I am detained here by film possibilities not yet concrete (options), have met Herbert Blau, a big theater man now in charge of Cal. Institute of the Arts. I have much work, but a feeling we are combating a Goliath Computer told to make money only, . . . but I know this will pass.

Letter to Robert Duncan:

Was glad to have your letter and now need your copy of Diary to make the changes. The original is with Gunther in New York, so please mail me those pages back. I wish we could have talked instead of writing. Yes, it is sad that the first contact and exchange did not bring any permanent alliance, but I believe that is the secret of people's inability to devote themselves to living influences or living writers. They feel they cannot attend to their personal growth unless there is much distance and perspective in the choice of relatives. Miller, Durrell and I went in totally opposite directions, too, but at least we had all the excitement of working together, which I never had again, but now have with those who understand what I am doing. So the circle is complete. Many things in your letter I did not understand. And you knew I would not. We *are* strangers to each other. I did not want anything in the portrait to sadden you. The Diary, you do not seem to understand, records ambivalences, changes, and my attitudes toward Patchen were painfully ambivalent. But where is there objectivity? In none of us. Each one has his particular vision of others. We are lucky if, by love, they come near matching. *Rashomon* is the only film which dealt with this theme. I am sure you saw me less well even than I you, because my concern was with understanding and seeing. The facts I jumbled in an effort to have some continuity in your life and which were told to me by you, do you have them in your diary? I do not think it is very important for example, whether you slept in a car in New York or Provincetown, except to a meticulous biographer, do you? I never understood why Harry Moore had to go to every hotel or inn D. H. Lawrence went to, every address he wrote from. I think you agree with me that is not necessarily a true portrait. Thank you for helping me to clarify what you did not want in. Send me the pages, as Diary is due at the printer's in two weeks, or less. Hiram wants to read it during the holidays.

Your letter has all the charm of the young Robert!

Letter to Laurens Vancrevel:

Here I sit in the house you know, trying to read your article on me [in Dutch], and unable to. To console myself I read your poem in French, and your letter. I found so interesting your concept of *dialectiques*. I have become increasingly aware of such dynamic interactions. In fact, the idea of connection and interrelation obsesses me. I am mailing you my book on the Novel. You will see how acute you are in detecting this in the early Diaries, when I thought I was merely suffering the hell of dualities. No, I was in Mexico before the violent and terrible events. It was in July, and there seemed only festive preparations for the Olympics. We stayed in Acapulco, which has suffered great changes from fishing village to Grand Hotel deluxe pool life. But the beauty is still there. I worked at dawn, from six to eight on revising Diary Three, then swam when the heat came. I had the same view I describe in *Seduction of the Minotaur*, swans and sunsets, same birds and same flowers. In Mexico City I saw the most beautiful museum in the world, the new archaeological museum, which is not only beautiful and noble and modern in architecture, but presents the history of man and of Mexico in a dramatic, living way. . . .

In New York it was the opposite. Three hundred and fifty people came to the Gotham Book Mart party for the new book. I hope you like it. Peter

Owen explained that in Holland so many people read English that the Diaries did not need to be translated.

I have heard of that bad book on Artaud. A good one is coming out soon by a friend of mine, Bettina Knapp; I will send it to you. The translation of your poems gives the sense of fluid images and subtle moods I expected from you. À la poursuite de mes yeux. What an image! What a marvelous welding of body and nature, of emotion and fragmentation, as in dream. There is a relative of Laura Huxley living in Holland. She is dying of loneliness. I may give you her address. I do not understand her prose (it may be due to her use of English), but you may. If I get her address from Laura I will send you her ms. and address. You have not joined with a publisher yet? The earning of a living. What a constant concern. And if one decides to let others be concerned for one, then like Henry Miller today one suffers from constant shame and guilt. He should not, but he does. All his *joie de vivre* is gone. He is only concerned with respect. The respect he imagines he lost by his way of life. *Etrange*. Strange. . . .

Preface to a Japanese edition of *House of Incest* and "Stella":

I am particularly proud and happy to be prefacing a book of mine to be read by the Japanese. It is only in the last few years that I discovered Japanese literature. If I had discovered it earlier it would have had an enormous influence on me. I feel it has all the qualities lacking in Western literature. It has poetry, subtlety, psychological depths, aesthetic style, and a preponderance of light in the sense of illumination from within. I like so much its emphasis on inner states, moods, feelings, and the fusion of moods with nature. I liked the sensitivity in the meticulous study of relationships, the care for nuances, the beauty of the physical descriptions, and its clear, uncluttered quality, like that of Japanese prints, stating only the essential and suggesting a forest by the study of a branch.

I read all I could find in translation: Ryunosuke Akutagawa's *Rashomon and Other Stories*, Yukio Mishima's *The Mask*, *The Golden Pavillion* and *The Sound of Waves*, Ogai Mori's *The Wild Geese*, Yasushi Inoue's *The Hunting Gun*, Tanisaki's *The Key*, Kobo Abe's *Woman of the Dunes*, Yasunari Kawabata's *Snow Country*. Of course I read *Tale of Genji* as often as I reread Proust. If this affinity for the vision of the emotions and the senses in perfect balance, the sensory apprehension of experience, the observation of quartertones in human relationships, the care and discipline of style, awareness by intuition, is shared by my Japanese readers, then it will be a reciprocated love and friendship.

When I finally made my trip to Japan this affinity was crystallized, and became very clear and defined. I stressed in various interviews the difficulties experienced by the sensitive or poetic writers of America, my regret that it was only the tough ones who were read and known outside as well as inside of the United States.

House of Incest took its inception from the words of Jung: "Proceed from the dream outward." In Paris in the 1930s Henry Miller and I began to keep a record of dreams. We wove them together and Henry Miller called his *Into the Night Life* and I called mine *House of Incest*. *House of Incest* was composed out of actual dreams later developed and harmonized and woven together. The dreams were the key to invention and improvisation and expansion. I dwelt on the theme of incest in its symbolic mythical sense, the love for those closest to us, our first love being enclosed within the family life; on the need to transcend these loves and transplant them outside of the family; on the prenatal memories of a place of tranquility and no pain, before human birth, a dream which the psychologists accepted as a memory of a time free of care and sorrow. The novels which followed *House of Incest* were a development and expansion of the same root themes: In dreams lay the secret of our character, destiny and experiences. A key phrase, like the phrase of a poem, was the genesis of the novel. The development of the novel was an interpretation of its meaning, its relation to life. When characters lost their way, became emotionally confused, they returned to the dream to find the way to their true nature and true desires. *House of Incest* was also a dream of birth in the oceanic unconscious, a surfacing into daylight and the conscious life. The legend of Atlantis is evoked because it was said to be the birthplace of music and of communication by way of intuition. The dream was thus always the genesis, the key to the mysteries of our destiny.

Having begun with a prose poem, and feeling it alone could express the unconscious, I felt I could no longer write heavily upholstered novels in the traditional sense, cluttered and stuffed with descriptions of objects and places not always a part of the inner drama. I felt a certain distillation was necessary, a discarding of nonessentials to take us more deeply into the subconscious dramas of our emotions, and to reach reality—in the words of the Talmud, "What we feel and not what we see." I felt that too many external trappings obscured our vision and dulled our awareness of what was happening.

The poem was like an emotional X-ray, and the expansion of the poem in a novel could only be achieved by a certain abstraction comparable to modern painting.

"Stella" was based on a real character. The style and form sought to match her physical appearance and her way of speaking. The myth extracted from it by this unrealistic approach was the inner conflict of actress and role, the love given to the actress distrusted by the woman, and the conflict of yielding and trusting illusion.

The action and tension in both works rest upon the conflict of dream and experience, and their interrelation, upon illusion and reality, as in so many Japanese novels.

Letter from a scientist:

CENTER FOR GENERALIZED NETWORKS AND MICROSYSTEMS
STANFORD ELECTRONICS LABORATORIES

"Only when the poet and the scientist work
in unison will we have living experiences
and knowledge of the marvels of the universe
as they are being discovered."

Anaïs Nin

Dear Miss Nin,

The other day I had good fortune—as you can see, your book *The Novel of the Future* is now in my possession. So I am trying out something. Will you mind if I use the above quote on my letterhead? (I have made a few copies in this form but will restrict its use to friends for now; this is the first one to go out—lucky you.)

For years I have believed in the tie between poetry and science; almost nobody in science seems to go along with me, as yet. But that is immaterial, for it is of the past and I think we have been able to pave the way for the future in science as do your works in literature. Perhaps you won't mind if I forward a copy of my technical work "Active Integrated Circuit Synthesis"; although it is technical (well into scientific research as well as engineering practice), perhaps it will give you a flavor for the actual potentialities latent in the quote I use above.

Too, I would comment on the truth of your views of women in literature being expressed badly by men; for this reason I have tried to encourage some of my women friends to write. Thus it was a pleasure recently to read your *Spy in the House of Love*.

Please pardon and forgive this intrusion into your life—I couldn't resist. *Je fais une sortie, mais je vous remercie pour l'art bien phrasé.*

Sincerely,
[signed] R. W. Newcomb
Associate Professor of
Electrical Engineering

Letter to R. W. Newcomb:

I was very proud of your letter. You understand my desire to relate to science. And of course you can quote me. You will have to be patient with me. I am not trained or prepared in any way. My only other friends in science are E. E. Epstein, astronomer, who heard me lecture and initiated me to his radar telescope at the Air Base, Aerospace Corp., and Dr. Robert Leighton of Cal Tech, in charge of photographing Mars.

I am not able to understand your "Transfer Function Design With Integrated Circuits"—but we both *want* to teach integrated circuits. I see or read science as a metaphor. . . .

I feel research in science uses the same elements of the creative artist—intuition, daring, imagination.

Letter to Wayne McEvilly:

Of course you would never offend me! We have a solid, well-anchored old friendship! When I don't write it is because I am drowned in work or very very weary! As a writer you sing your ballad, and suddenly when the world answers, it overwhelms you! I lecture and the students treat me like the Beatles! I'm swamped in correspondence. It is wonderful in one way, in another it is like the sorcerer's apprentice—he summons forces which he cannot control. I enjoy your letters and cannot always answer. Can do so today because I'm forced to be still to recover from two lectures, interviews and a hundred new friends at Berkeley University and Santa Barbara. When I went to Santa Barbara campus by the sea my Greek friend, who stirred up all this earthquake, warned me they were a sleepy, lethargic lot, too comfortable, dazed by the violence of events, and might not awaken. Awaken they did—We could have dialogued for the whole night.

There is a new generation of Americans nobody knows. They are caricatured as hippies—but that is not exact. They are enormously intelligent, loving and sensitive. America was too big a monster to fight (a monster Golem born of cupidity) and so they turned to the East. When I began my lecture a few hours ago I used the symbol of pouring teakwood oil on my spirit house from Thailand (the Thai people build a miniature duplicate of their home for the spirits to live in), and the young audience understood.

I asked a bookshop to mail you Henry's latest books. Did you receive them? Did Henry answer your letter? He will be in Paris in June for the filming of *Tropic of Cancer.*

Diary Three is in and will be published next September. What is keeping me busy is the excitement over *The Novel of the Future*.

You are quite right about eulogizing the living! It is not done enough. Why, I don't know. A mystery, the precipitation to praise the dead, and one word of praise can do so much for the living. Do we wish to deny them that pleasure? Recently an absurd editor thought it would be a joke to ask writers to write their own epitaphs. A stunt! I loved your surrealist eulogy, more like a perfect dream, a film, a *rêve éveillé*, full of cryptic meanings.

Summed up, you say what I like to hear:

> transformation
> transitions
> transmutations

UCLA first said they would not publish Carlos Castaneda's book [*The Teachings of Don Juan*]. It was not "academic" enough. I took it to Gunther. He was about to find a publisher when UCLA reversed its decision.

Deena brought Carlos Castaneda to lunch. He was fascinating, a mixture of primitive and academic. Anthropologist. Denies his Indian blood. Felt schizophrenic, divided.

I went to see the rushes of the documentary film on Henry Miller by Bob Snyder. He has been at work on it for a long time. I participated one afternoon, talking with Henry in the garden of his house at Pacific Palisades.

Bob's best quality is his enthusiasm. Nothing discourages him, deters him. When he left college, his first wish was to film Martha Graham. For this I like him. Other traits are discouraging: He is chaos personified. The rushes showed a kind of *cinéma vérité*—disconnected scenes, no coordination, none of the tensile strength of genuine free association.

But Henry was a perfect subject. He is natural, relaxed, humorous. The film was very faithful to Henry's changing moods, his storytelling, his recollections.

Bob took so much film (thirteen hours, I believe) that he asked me how one could edit such a quantity of images. I suggested that as he had begun in the style of *cinéma vérité*, he had to remain faithful to an unstructured, free-flowing assemblage.

We saw the film in many stages. It was not what Henry wanted.

Henry wanted a surrealist, Dadaist film. He did not want a plain, faithful documentary.

Letter to Bettina Knapp:

Your review [of *The Novel of the Future*] is *wonderful*. They [the *Village Voice*] may object to the warm tone of it. They like coolness. I like the interpretation and the way you developed it. Do you mind on page 2, line 16, leaving out *"particularly with the creatures of his fantasy,"* as it may be misunderstood. The bridge between human beings, their real secret selves, leads to greater reality in relationships. They have misunderstood this so much that I would rather not suggest people as *creations* of the imagination. Everything else is so right, and I know how difficult it is to analyze a book which is an analysis in itself. I like your ending about hope. I hope they take it. It sounds so warm they may suspect a friendship. I hope not. . . .

I have not given up on the Genêt review.

Letter to Wayne McEvilly:

I can feel in your letter that you have such a visionary way of looking at people (as I have) that they occasionally become transparent (I *closed* my eyes to see Henry), but at some point or other I felt this visionary life robbed me of the small things, or the earthy things. And I turned to the earthy people. Yes, balance. I know you have that, and are that. But more and more as an artist, I realize that the balance is there, but that the vast world the artist creates (or re-creates from small things, as the birds make nests with twigs, etc.) is not always in their lives and that much as one wants this world understood, appreciated, as you did Marguerite's, awe of it hurts both. Perhaps because of this my best friends were those who did not know anything about me, and liked me as a neighbor, as the one who took care of their children in a crisis, etc. Marguerite has much of the child too, her apartment is full of dolls and angels, and antiques, and a circus wooden horse, and tin soldiers, and old photos, and as long as one starts by loving her, not wounding her, she is the easiest person to know, to feel at home with, to relax with. It may be also why sometimes I protest the mysticism. I do not want it to rob me of my very human life. I want to be treated like anyone else. Probably because when I am not at work, not talking, not *inspired* (beautiful word), I love to swim, to walk with the dog, to walk on the beach, to go to the neighborhood movie, see a not-too-good film, anonymous. . . .

I am so deeply grateful for your understanding, your familiarity and response to the unconscious Anaïs, as [to] the unconscious Marguerite . . . but also love how you feel about snow, how you named your child, how you write about music, and how I imagine you are as a teacher. I have no doubt your students are fortunate. We three can liberate and set others creating. I just wanted you to enjoy Marguerite on one side of herself, after having loved the Big one. Our human life is small like an igloo in the North Pole, it is vulnerable like the birds I feed every day, or [my] dog, who never knows when I am coming back.

I telephone Eugene Epstein at the Aerospace Corporation to tell him I saw his Lumia machine at UCLA Light Show—the one similar to the first Lumia lightbox I saw at the Museum of Modern Art in the forties invented by Thomas Wilfred, a Dane, who died last year at seventy-nine, saddened by the awareness that he, the innovator, had not received as much recognition as those who developed the art into the light shows we admire today. Just the night before, at Venice, California, I had seen the light show by the "Single Wing Turquoise Bird." Like a thousand modern paintings flowing and sparkling, alive and dynamic, of incredible richness, a death blow to painting in frames, stills. (This after the show by Elias Romero.)

As we were talking, Eugene asked me to hold on for a moment; "I have to adjust the telescope."

I could hear the tuneless piano notes of computers through the phone. And my entire visit to the electronic art exhibit at UCLA came vividly to haunt me. I lacked the technical language with which to describe it.

Eugene had come to my lecture at UCLA on "The Influence of the Dream." I mentioned writers' lack of knowledge of science as a handicap to expansion. He invited me to visit the laboratory set up by the Air Force.

This is the place where "messages" from the stars, a certain pattern in their vibrations, were registered by sensitive instruments. I expected to hear these messages. I had my first lesson in transmutation. I was not to hear them *directly*. They were received by a giant white radar cup, oscillating and turning (mechanically) with the motions of the earth. We could walk around it, but it was not to serve us as a giant Ear listening to space. What it received was registered in countless intricate, mysterious computers. When we returned to the central switchboard after our walk on the roof, all the machines were working, tabulating, calculating what looked like cardiographs. Eugene talked, explaining, simplifying, pressing buttons. But even unbidden, the computers did their translations. Typewriter sounds, castanets.

The delicacy, subtlety, frailty of the instrument's parts, the miniaturization of the glass, of the knobs, beads, wires.

Although these processes were a mystery to me, I felt their pattern resembled the psychic radar's reportings. I could see my ear as large as the white radar, listening to a subtle change of voice—or storing up a memory. When Eugene said, "Hold on a moment, I have to adjust the telescope," and I heard the obedient shrapnel sound of electronic harmonizations, I was excited and registered this. A timid approach to science—and to Eugene, listening to me, knowing what I mean, owning a Lumia, which is the poetic expression of light and space. I was baffled not to be able to hear with my human ear the sounds denoting changes, alterations, pressures or temperatures in space.

So the machine had multiplied the power of my human ear, and achieved calculations which would wear out a human brain or hand!

In July 1968 I had seen a more dramatic, more gigantic setup—the Palomar telescope. There the magnitude of the Eye, the EYE surveying the stars, was greater than a cathedral—overwhelming. A new beauty, this steel and glass Eye, and its discoveries. The lonely vigils of astronomers. It is cold, for they cannot risk the effects of changing temperature on glass. And anyway, when the dome slides open and the Eye is naked in the night, on the mountain, a high place where no reflection of city lights will disturb the clarity of photographs, the vigil is out of doors. The photographs show nature's light show—sparks, nebulas, smoky trails, vaporous enigmas, fireworks, explosions, comets' tails, flying gold dust.

From Harold Norse's diary:

Anaïs, I read your diaries with speechless admiration. Who in his right mind could not read them this way? They are speleological reports from the caves of our psyche, exploring the dark areas with a blowtorch. They cut me to the bone, making me feel like the intuitive blind animal (as you describe

Henry and June). I am in the grip of my own specter. I have only flashes of insight that emerge like a fish thrusting its snout up from the unconscious ocean at brief intervals, then sink back into nothingness.

Letter to a reader:

I am glad you admitted me like an intimate friend into your night world—your moods, uncertainties and quests. They reminded me of my early journeys. I don't know if you were aware that you ended your description with the word *light*—the same with which I ended my first book. But I thought I had made clear that I was not luring anyone into the night life but into the richness of combining and fusing them. The two worlds are necessary to each other. One needs a strong core not to be destroyed by the pressures, despairs, chaos of the outer world. I spoke for this resistant inner core. Perhaps I did not make this clear. I wish you would read *The Novel of the Future*. It is hard to give everything in one talk. You caught the ephemeral quality of my talk but not its solidity or the solidity of my life based on interrelations between *all* worlds. You placed me only as a dreamer and not as I have been —dream in action. Not your way, you say. Let me know when you have found your way.

Robert Newcomb arranges a seminar at Stanford on "Integrated Circuits and the Poetry of Anaïs Nin"!

Visit with Pierre Brodin, who reviews all my books.

Julio Cortázar quotes me in *Hopscotch*. I receive reviews in Dutch, Hebrew and Russian.

I am invited to lecture at Rochester Institute of Technology and Clarion State College, Pa.

Work for *Voyages*, recommending poets, writers.

The books I printed have become collectors items. Sixty-five dollars for *This Hunger*.

University of Texas expresses interest in the original Diaries. I suggest they visit the vault.

Rediscoveries will be published with my essay on Marianne Hauser.

I try to interest Harry Moore in overlooked books: William Goyen, Marianne Hauser, Anna Kavan. Readers are catching up with them.

Daisy Aldan's interest in Rudolf Steiner alienated us. She sees everything through his eyes. God is back again in her poetry—an abstraction. It has removed her from human life and psychology. I feel as if in the presence of a Catholic dogmatist: every thought controlled by a theory. She translates a bad [Swiss] poet, Albert Steffen.

Visit from Nancy Durrell, Larry's first wife. No longer the slim ballet dancer I knew in Paris. Gray-haired and motherly, efficient, devoted to politics and humanism. Tells me wistfully: "When Larry and I were living in Greece, a couple came to visit and stayed with us for a while. It was while observing them together that I realized Larry did not love me."

Letter to Nobuko:

Morbid is not a valid criticism. One could apply that to Dostoevsky, Kafka, to present-day writers. Coming from *McCall's* it means nothing because they represent the middle class and are full of hypocrisies. Please pay no attention. Kawabata is morbid. I am at times. That is nothing to say about a writer: It is *how* a writer does it—how well. All children are obsessed with death at one time or other, we are all neurotic. Mailer is morbid (*American Dream*), Albee is morbid. Pay no attention to *McCall's* or you will achieve only a mediocre work. Be yourself, utterly sincere and truthful. I'm glad somebody will take care of the mechanics of your writing. When I sent my manuscripts to my publishers, they would say: "You can't say that in English." I would say: "Why not?" And today I am considered a stylist.

Notes on Marianne Hauser:

Sent to U.S. in 1937 as a columnist by Swiss newspaper. Has been here ever since. During this period she has been patiently refining the remarkable prose style of *Dark Dominion*. Spent her childhood in Strasbourg, Alsace. Her husband, concert pianist Frederic Kirschberger, was stationed in small towns in the South during the war. She now has a hippie poet son. She knew Rank and was analyzed.

William Young plans a deluxe edition of my selections from my work.

Letter to a friend:

You ask me about Eve Miller. She divorced Henry to marry a sculptor, a neighbor at Big Sur. I never met her but everyone said she was wonderful. She drank. She had a cold and drank a quart of gin with antibiotics—or sleeping pills. No one knows. Suicide? Accident? Henry does not know. He does not talk about her. All he said once when I said I had heard she was wonderful was: "When she drank she was the opposite of what she was sober."

June returned to New York, married the lover she had confessed having, . . . divorced, spent time in an asylum, became arthritic, rheumatoid, which ruined her beauty but stabilized the mental unbalance. She was cared for by a couple I know—[one of them] a psychiatrist. They became my friends . . . and helped me with the Diary so June would accept her portrait even though she has transferred all her hostility to me as having separated [her from Henry], which of course was not so. Their life together was hell—they were both trying to break. She sent Henry to Paris because she had a lover, and he went because he could not write when she was near. She is relatively well, holds a job in Welfare, but talks uncontrollably and as fancifully as before. She invents half of what she tells—Henry visited her a few years ago and ran away, shocked by her appearance and the sameness of her talk. She will not see me. I offered reconciliation. . . .

Letter to a reader:

Your letter touched me, and I like what you said about "much of the writing in depth is from asexual or presexual levels, from the common substrata of us all." I also agree about being one-to-one, and the talking to many people became a problem, and I still feel the difficulties. I decided I was after all talking to a few. I wrote a book on the novel hoping I would not have to talk anymore!

I'm in New York now and your letter took time to reach me, but I hope when I return to Los Angeles you'll pay a visit. I don't know where Orinda is (a beautiful name) but I hope not too far.

I turned in Volume Three two months ago and it may be out in October— not sure—but meanwhile Volume One is out in paperback with a hideous purple cover.*

Letter to Duane Schneider:

Although you came to interview me, I felt I became better acquainted with you. As in all these situations with limited time, one feels one has only begun to talk.

I wanted to talk more with you about the relation between literature and local welfare. So many people do not believe they are essentially connected.

About politics—even if the power-obsessed men win and not the good men (Eugene McCarthy or Dr. King), we still have to act, don't we—or it will be the Dark Ages. Power and money are stronger, but we still have to oppose them. Do you agree?

I enjoyed our talk. Next time let it be Duane Schneider who speaks.

Letter to Wayne McEvilly:

It was so strange last night. I was in bed with a fever, and I called up Marguerite to visit . . . she had talked with you for a long time, she said, and she told me a little, about Catholicism, about the wooden dog, about this or that—also remember she *beautifies*; don't let her overbeautify me, will you. Nobody can be as she says, it is part of her creation, invention. I don't want you disappointed. . . .

You're writing *books* in letters, and I'm deserting the Diary to write you, and today I thought this is the only correspondence which really counts, because it is free and deep. So I talked about you to a Chinese artist, Cy Roser; I told her I had been reading the History of China and that you were teaching me Zen. She will teach me how to handle the *I Ching*. It concerned me that you mentioned fragility of the chest—for that is the seat of emotion and after double pneumonia it became my weak point. So when I'm feverish I write on paper from Paris. I skip the present and ride into the future, for October 9 I will see Paris for one day—invited by my German publisher to attend book fair at Frankfurt. He is young, took great pains to find the best translator, and so the Germans responded en masse—and I have to dissociate the old Germany from the new I don't know at all. My father taught me to love its musicians—later I loved the Romantics, later still, ponderous, diffuse

* The cover was changed in the second printing.—Ed.

Jakob Wassermann (*Caspar Hauser, Kerkhoven,* etc.). But today? I only read *The Tin Drum*—no—but I hope you'll read *Snow Country* by Kawabata—the best Nobel Prize ever given.

Why does it hurt you to read Proust?

Letter to a reader:

Your letter was beautiful—and strangely came to heal that evening which I considered a failure. That particular evening made me wonder about the wisdom of seeking to share certain awareness with others—with the many. Or whether, as I once told Timothy Leary, all such sharing should be kept for the initiates, like a ritual—then after the fusion does take place, I feel it has failed, and then I get a letter like yours and feel that one person was worth the risks of exposure. So there was one person—that is a great deal. (I only write to friends on my collection of writing paper gathered while traveling.) There was so much in your letter. Music comes first, I gather, and I believe this too—and quite possibly I wrote to reach music because my father's severity barred the way to my becoming a musician. Writing as imagery—films—I love films. . . . Yes I understand what you say about Leary. I feared this from the first. At times I believed we should return to the concept of esoteric learning—clans.

About language—there is more to say—there is a language for all we feel. But it may never reach what we receive from music, or light shows. . . .

The establishment has remained rigid and indifferent to my work, but it has been a wonderful year for genuine friends, genuine fans, genuine critics.

Studies in the 20th Century with Marianne Hauser's review of Diary. Dazzling.

Cortázar writes me, announcing it will just be one letter because "it is agony for a writer to decide every day whether he is going to work on his book or answer letters!"

The writer writes his letter to the world. When the world answers, like the sorcerer's apprentice, he cannot control what he has summoned. I'm drowned in correspondence.

Well, the earthquake predicted by the hippies did not occur.

A friend tells me story of her child devoured by a wolf. Her first husband had a zoo for his own pleasure.

Why did Henry stop writing after the trilogy? Did he say all he wanted to say? Or was it the devastating criticism by Durrell at the end of their correspondence? "When will you stop lavatory writing?" Durrell really killed the father. Nobody noticed the assassination, not even Henry.

Correspondence with Harold Norse.

Correspondence with Jack Baron, who tried to compensate for evening of my lecture at Immaculate Heart, a failure.

Marie-Claire Van der Elst works on translating Volume One into French.

Legend of Lake Titicaca as Gonzalo told it to me destroyed by Jacques Cousteau's expedition. The fish dying, lake inhabited by big frogs the natives can't eat. No gold.

Marianne Greenwood—in a white cotton suit. Her Swedish eyes no lakes, no skies, no glaciers, but those of some Eskimo wolf dog, or fox. Intense—animal and mineral. Blond hair clasped at the back of her neck, cut in bangs over her eyes. Marianne fell in love with a parrot-fish in the aquarium of Monte Carlo. She went to visit him every day. He would swim directly toward her, flirtatiously, blinking his big eyes, fluttering his eyelashes. One day he was gone.

Later, she traveled on a Swedish boat to see America, as a seaman— a seaman? Swedish boats employ women as seamen. The cook, an alcoholic, was devoted to her. When he went ashore and bought fish for the boat, he always bought the best one for her. One night in her small, stifling cabin, she had a dream. The parrotfish was dead. She held him in her arms, rocked him, tried to bring him to life, breathed into his gills, felt the glistening body slipping from her. The next day the devoted cook served, with parsley and lemon juice, a parrotfish on a silver platter. For her the same fish. Metaphysically the same fish. Renate was skeptical. Renate does not follow others' stories too attentively. She is already formulating a story of her own. Marianne had an advantage. She was the active adventuress. She had gone, alone, into the jungle of Guatemala. She had been everywhere, known everyone —traveled as a seaman. A seaman! Did you cut your hair, wear pants?

No. She could look like a boy. She is tall. Her legs and arms are hermaphroditic. She is bold.

"I'm glad you didn't come to the party, Anaïs, to meet me. I behaved badly. I concentrated on a Japanese swordsman. But I must tell you, you did terribly disturbing things to me when I read the Diary. I was you whenever you described what you felt, but I was also June. Equally."

One of her husbands a gambler. Made a coup and disappeared. One son in England. Another somewhere else. *Audace.*

The *real* adventurer! I think of *The Wilder Shores of Love.*

Renate, not to be outshone by Marianne, tells the story of her first earrings brought by her father. During her childhood in Vienna, it was the fashion to pierce ears early (at six weeks) and insert a small gold earring. At seven she outgrew them and took them out but kept them in a tiny box. Much later she had a compulsion to look at everything through the microscope. She looked at the earrings, which had always appeared to be tiny gold loops with blue stones. But under the microscope she could see that each earring was actually a snake devouring its own tail. The magic snake, Uroboros. Jung's symbol for female. "No wonder . . ." Renate's mother murmured enigmatically. Renate never asked her what she meant.

Another story. John, a former love, on his way to the desert, stopped for the night knowing Renate had only one double bed. She refused to sleep in the same bed with a dead love, the skeleton of a passion. So she cut her air foam mattress in two and gave him his half to place on the floor. But John complained it was not half, it was only eighteen inches.

And now Max, the German who resembles her father. They are born under the same sign. Twin madness. Games. Disguises. Complicated courtship—no sensual fulfillment. They are fearful. He breaks his leg seriously, skiing. So Renate is now again—nurse, mother, cook. And a battle for domination.

Read Cortázar! I say to everyone.

Beatrice Blau gives masterful performance in Samuel Beckett's *Happy Days.*

Saw *My Uncle Yanko* by Agnes Varda.
Wayne McEvilly writes on *Seduction of the Minotaur* for the *New Mexico Quarterly*.
Tunnel of work on Volume Four.
Interview with Duane Schneider not good—my fault.

Letter to Frances Field:

Although I am drowning in letters, I want to write you. . . . The Ned Rorem diary had brilliant moments and he could have written a fascinating one, but remained on the surface . . . and also in spite of appearances, indiscreet but not open, not really. Some parts are striking. He never went fully into anything. He falls apart. Certainly his life is in shreds, and willfully superficial. Scattered. No courage and no core. A shame. I don't know his music. I am sure there was more there than he gave.

So, here I am, it is summer here with many flowers and the mockingbirds singing so wildly I want to record them for you, day and night. The pool smells of pittosporum, the weeping willow is languid and yielding as it should be, the life is structured. Up at seven to make breakfast. The hills are covered with mists as in Japanese prints. The coffee is Luziane with a little chicory in it. And at eight I am at my desk. . . .

Sometimes I take the bus to the post office. The morning is fresh and quiet but for the birds. Old people are gardening. It is serene. The neighbors . . . a sculptor, a painter, an ex-actress, an architect and a doctor, are relaxed and not too driven. The artists have opened a gallery which I am helping. It had a Varda show. Try to see a film called *My Uncle Yanko* by Agnes Varda, his niece. She went to Sausalito and filmed him. It is charming and enchanting. . . . The documentary on Henry Miller is great. Miller is a natural actor, he comes through as a tragic-comic clown, a monologuist, a complete egotist, warm to men and cold to women, naif, comic, warm, tender, schizophrenic, and without insight. It is worth seeing. His storytelling is at its best. It is Henry at his best. . . .

The *New York Times* never reviewed *The Novel of the Future*. But a beautiful number of *Studies in the 20th Century* came out from Russell College, Troy, N.Y., with three studies of the Diary. . . . And did I tell you I wrote to Cortázar, and he answered me the most beautiful fan letter you can imagine. That's more important than the *N.Y. Times*. I was so proud. And what else? We went to a love-in sit-in, invited by Sam Francis. For Easter. A picnic for 250 people. Carrying lilies.

Letter to Joaquin [Nin-Culmell]:

How is the Berkeley situation affecting you personally? I think of you but have been unable to catch up with my correspondence. Every morning at seven-thirty I unlock the briefcase containing Diary, letters to be answered, and work to be done. I am not writing a book at the moment yet I am busy all day. But the sun is shining, the pool smells of alyssum when I swim, the mockingbirds sing wildly day and night. . . . I am writing a preface for a Greek poetess, an introduction to a de luxe edition of my selected works by a rare book man in Boston, preparing for a seminar in the fall at Stanford University [on] "Electronic Integrated Circuits and Works of A.N." No kidding. Absolutely serious. Given by a Professor Newcomb, and I will appear in it. . . .

The paperback Diary is doing well but is still too expensive and no photos. I would like, like the Madwoman of Chaillot, to see all the oil men and businessmen and publishers go down the cellar and never return. A hippie world might not be as bad. The gypsies did it for centuries, stealing chickens. Why not we? . . .

When you feel tired, take a spoonful of honey after meals. It is not fattening and you'll be amazed at the effect.

You are right, it is futile to get angry at rudeness and stupidity, but every now and then one feels like teaching them a lesson. A wasted energy.

The revolution at Harvard surprised everyone. Do you want to know what the left radicals think? I am sending you a pamphlet. It is good to know how they see things, and some of the facts are rather startling. You probably have already read some of their assertions. Will you be going through New York in June? I will be there all of June.

Do you need any books? I'm sending you two copies of hardback for gifts you may need.

Try the honey.

Honey.

Introduction for William Young Co.'s deluxe edition of selections from my works:

A writer is often asked what is his favorite book. It is not easy to answer.
Sometimes I say it is the last one, the newest one, because it is nearer and fresher, like a new friendship, and the response of others is still a surprise,

and a mystery. At other times, when I am talking with writers, I think of the books I could not change, rewrite, revise in any way. Those are my favorites, I say.

Other times I think of writing as mountain climbing, and I am proudest of the highest peaks I reach, and this refers to the description of the most difficult, complex, or subtle states of mind, moods, reveries. The answer has many sides.

For this book I tried to select passages which answer all of these requisites. One short story I could not alter, for an expression of my love of humanity.

One passage from *The Four-Chambered Heart* for its expression of the poetry of love.

A passage from *Seduction of the Minotaur* because it expresses the beauty of nature and the possibility of fusing with it, becoming a part of it.

One of the most difficult things to write about is the dream, the waking dream or reveries which accompany our daily existence like background music. They are the most elusive.

Ultimately I look upon writing as wings. We are pedestrians, we walk along the earth; we may love the earth, but the moment of absolute magic is when our imagination allows us to take flights into vaster, more entrancing worlds.

Letter to a friend:

The film on Henry was wonderful, because he is first of all a natural actor, because it succeeded in capturing his personality, and even though you see him now, walking through Paris, Bob Snyder managed to re-create the past with the present. Henry is at his best in it, his personality really came through as he was, even though he talks about age, etc. The main thing which was captured was his humor and the sadness underneath which women respond to. But he prefers the cronies who only tune in on the comedy. . . . It was shown at University of Southern California. . . . Only disappointment was that Henry was not well enough to be there. He would have been mobbed. Naturally I'm glad you are writing to Anaïs of today. But perhaps in my concern I gave you a one-sided image of Henry today. If you came as a visitor you would not see the distress I described. He would be charming and open. You would see the conventional stucco house with pool of Hollywood standard pattern selected by Lepska. You would see all his books with all the translations orderly in the living room. His watercolors on the walls. His desk by the window. Piles of books and mail to answer. In the dining room there are collages of Varda's. In the game room there is a Ping-Pong table. His favorite pastime. In spite of his limp he can do that and until recently he could bicycle. People come in and out. All kinds of people. Hoki and her Japanese friends. An actor who appears in the film. His son is in Paris. His daughter lives elsewhere. Lepska is remarried.

Letter to Fred and Frances Haines in Paris:

I imagine Henry will be well by June. I hope he separates from Hoki, who is tormenting him with indifference. I have your script of *Day of the Locust* but have not met any interesting producers lately. Made friends with Herbert Blau. Beatrice, his wife, acts in a Beckett play at the Gallery. I wish I had loaned you my camera while you were in Paris. I thought of it afterward. Are we ever going to make a film together? In the Miller films appeared a photo by Brassai of cobblestones, just cobblestones in a circular pattern. Are there any left? Are the riverbanks ruined with traffic and no longer fit for lovers? One day when I was there in the sixties a painter who had been denied a gallery exhibited under a bridge, and had quite an audience, as well as a kindly gendarme watching his work when he went to lunch. Hung against the black smoky walls of the bridge. There was also a group of English boys pretending to be cowboys from the U.S.A. with guitars and appropriate costume. When they collected donations and were asked where they came from, they told the truth and then they asked: "Do you want your money back?"

Letter to Julio Cortázar:

I was elated by your letter all the more because I know better than anyone that these are stolen moments from work, but with *your* letter it is not a pause but a pattern woven into and with the work, flowing into the day, inciting the writing rather than interrupting it. I have mailed you the two Diaries, the novels, all but *Collages*, which I do not have but will send later. Curious your image of the unicorn. I was reading about it in a history of China. For the early Chinese it was a symbol of peace, and the day a hunter killed one, war began in the world. I cannot find anywhere *The Winner* of yours. They say it is out of print. I would like to have that; I can read French, Spanish or English equally. Volume Three [of the Diary] is coming out in October. Time played us a mischievous trick, for you could have been a part of the houseboat life easily. I can see you there. Much as I love the present and even more the future, that is one of the few periods I would love to relive. . . . For the moment a French company will film *A Spy in the House of Love* with Jeanne Moreau, but in New York and Canada. Filmmaking is now the next step, the next seduction . . . the next labyrinth. I would love to do

Collages . . . the people in it are beautiful and available all around me. Nobuko is married to Ivan Morris, one of the best translators of Japanese literature, recently of the *Pillow Book*. Renate is a filmmaker herself now, but poor. Agnes Varda just made a film of Varda I describe in *Collages* . . . *Yanko*. It is shown in France, I believe. It is a short. See it if you can. I give your books to everyone who comes to the house, a Lloyd Wright house overlooking a lake, with a pool. . . . This is in Los Angeles. In New York *en plein Village* . . . now rather sinister, never gay as our bohemian life was, but violent, mixed with crime, drugs, sadism, etc. How long were you in America that you could write so marvelously about Charlie Parker or jazz language and jazz life? Don't answer. Enjoy my letter and put it away. Do not add it to the pile invented by *l'apprenti sorcier!*

Notes:
Dr. Robert Leighton engaged in project to photograph Mars from satellite.

Danièle Suissa comes to Los Angeles from Paris to produce a film of *Spy*. She comes to my house every day and we work on script together. With a good script, she hopes to get financing from Hollywood!

George Wickes writes an inaccurate and absurd book on the Paris scene. Why did Henry let him edit the Miller-Durrell correspondence? His introduction of me at my lecture here at Immaculate Heart College was grotesque. I refuse to see him for an interview.

My publisher in Germany is Mathias Wegner.

I write about *Report from the Red Windmill* by Hiram Haydn for *Voyages*.

Two women write to each other as Alter Ego; they sign off Alter Ego. They sign a fan letter to me, A.E.

Age of absurdities:
In dress it is a masquerade. Nothing is new. The flower children wear their grandmothers' dresses out of trunks in the attics, or all the items of Oriental bazaars. Greek, Turkish, Spanish—a masquerade. Never *themselves*—always dressed as *somebody else*. Toreador. Gypsy. Swedish sailor. Guatemalan Indian.

Today I saw the 1969 Grotesque—a midget in a miniskirt!

There is about today's fashion something of the baby doll, the little girl, the adolescent. Nothing is invented. But Rudi Gernreich does invent with new textiles. I like the plastics, the new materials, the science fiction dress.

Letter to a friend:

First day of work [on script of *A Spy in the House of Love*] with Danièle on Monday. I was nervous about it. But it went extraordinarily well. After working with Jerry, with Tracey, with Barbara Lawrence, with Renate, I found suddenly that Danièle and I are on the same wavelength, but even better, we balance each other's weaknesses. She has a French logic within the irrational, she has continuity, and doggedness. She stands in the room and acts everything. A real actress. We wrote an outline, chronology, and solved the lie detector problem instantly. We type, or I type. . . . I have never had anyone who understood the book so well.

It will go quickly. She comes at ten in the morning from her motel. She rented a car. We work until we drop, around four. Then I swim, eat, and write letters or read. She has things to do in the evenings. She runs around with the son of Irene Selznick, Danny. She has friends. So I do not have to worry about her. She is quite a character. Quite thoughtful. . . . She is quite practical too. But now the sun refuses to come out and she told her family she came in part to sun and swim.

Letter to Pierre Brodin:

I was so pleased to see the shining and very modern-looking book of *Présences [Contemporaines]*. Read it with interest. I am always amazed at how you synthesize in such small space, cover the essentials. I was interested in your opinion of Sontag, of Mailer. Some names were new to me, and I learned about them. I think your study of Marguerite Young is very fine, very astute. What also amazes me is your objectivity, and even when you personally do not enjoy a certain writing, you convey its place, significance, in the total scheme of writing. The most characteristic quality of your criticism is its impartiality and fairness, which are unique today. A forgotten art, I would say. . . .

I was delighted with your tribute to [William] Goyen. How difficult it must be to choose, select, eliminate from so many . . . with all the other work you do.

For my work you have related Diaries and novels meticulously and subtly. The way you use the titles of the novels to indicate similarity of themes. *Villes intérieures de la femme,* etc. And how you combined Diaries, novels and the last book on the Novel with opinions of other writers. . . . I'm very proud and happy with this chapter. You will be the first to have studied my work in French. . . .

In our chaotic times your power of clarity and synthesis are valuable. I hope your book will be appreciated, and properly reviewed. Those who are not in it will be very sad.

Duane Schneider informs me my letters are selling for ten to thirty dollars each! His little book of excerpts from the Diary sells for twenty dollars—now a rare item.

Marguerite Young visits Wayne and Diane McEvilly. I wrote them what I felt would make her less intimidating. Wayne writes of her *Angel in the Forest*: This is "conversion of history into presence. . . ."

In New York I see Dr. Bogner.

In Los Angeles—work: correspondence, proofreading Diary Volume Three and French translation of Volume One. . . . Marie-Claire Van der Elst is doing a beautiful job. And play: I swim in my Tahitian pool two or three times a day to keep fit and because I love to swim—I like the feeling of the water, to escape from gravity. I go to the beach (Will Rogers State Beach, twenty minutes away) for sun and space.

Saw Albicocco's new film, *The Wanderer* (*Le Grand Meaulnes*). Beautifully done. His father, the cameraman, is the poet of his films.

Letter to Wayne McEvilly:

Marguerite sees all your gifts and suggests a plunge. I see your gifts and I don't know what to say, for I know you need your retreat like a snail shell, and you need a balance between your riches and its practice in a bigger world. The wounds can come from such little people. In the most sheltered corners. Among mountains, lakes, snows, flowers . . . a petty man in school, and there you are. Can I say do not be hurt? No, because one cannot be both sensitive and invulnerable. Being emotional you are doomed to vulnerability. . . . I have often encountered hostility, do not fear, in unexpected places . . . inexplicable, but to be faced. Only recently at Immaculate Heart one girl [in the audience] said out loud: "Dreams are boring." So do not be overprotective. Marguerite is more vulnerable because her writing is her whole world. Mine is not. My loves are there to give me strength. . . . She came last night for dinner. She was within her book. She was having dinner with

Ambrose Bierce, not so much with us. But all artists are obsessed this way; as in pregnancy, they cannot separate from their work. I wish I could help you at this moment. We are all, in turn, wounded, by someone, something. Yes, I feel as you do about the Power Men, Mailer, Vidal, Roth, hateful all . . . but invulnerable. Because they want power and get it. What we want is far rarer and more difficult. But in the end, in the end, power is ugly and never never wins love. Mailer never, in the end, received love; the adulation of the world, yes, but not love. Because only love begets love.

Letter to a friend:

Henry is gone to France. It is no wonder you are so dedicated and in love with his work. You are born under the same sign. And remember when I say he is lost, it is only what I read deep down in him, but he is not aware of it. . . . My vision of where he is now is not the one of the world, who thinks he has attained all he wanted, but if you said all this to him he would deny it. On film he appears as he does in his persona, alive and communicative and free. . . . What is the truth? People said after the film: He is so sincere, naive, so natural. The most natural man in the world kept his true self secret from himself and from others. What he wanted, a maternal love, a love that would be absorbed by him, what he most wanted, he could not have, because of the choice of women . . . because he remained at the stage of wanting a total devotion as I described in the Diary, to appease a neurotic need which could never be appeased by anyone . . . the whole love of the world could not fill that need, and the women who tried were soon, after seven or eight years, emptied—because, he admits in the film, he did not know how to love, how to refill or sustain the kind of love he wanted.

Notes on Morocco:

Having seen the eyes of Morocco many years ago, I never forgot them. I found them again in the men and in the women. The men's are like darts, daggers, the women's like burning coals. I love best the countries in which virility and tenderness coexist. America lacks the softness.

But first of all the arrival at Agadir was not like the arrival at Moorea. At Moorea, once off the plane, once on the boat, once landing in Moorea, you were in Tahiti. You heard Tahitian music, saw Tahitian faces. But in Agadir, at the Club Méditerranée, it was not Morocco. Yes, they had laid down a rug on the stairs and we were met by French girls holding copper trays with refreshments, dates and figs. But the music was not Moroccan. It was of provincial France— rock and roll on loudspeakers. The pool, the white walls, the architecture, the sea did not help. The bungalow was Moroccan in shape. The breeze came through open pipes placed transversally. The sea was beautiful, the village gay in color. But the sea was cold and foggy— and when I swam in the pool I had to hear loud and bad music.

The town of Agadir had been utterly destroyed by an earthquake. I remember hearing about this earthquake from Artur Lundkvist. He and his Danish wife had been close to divorce. They were in Agadir in the one modern hotel, on the highest floor. When the earthquake came the whole front wall of the hotel fell down. They were left in their room looking down at a shaking city, not knowing when the entire building would crumble. Death, its imminence, brought them close. They did not divorce.

So Agadir, the city, is new. Born anew, bridal white, and the soft gray of the burnoose. New market, and new shops.

At the celebration of the king's fortieth birthday I finally saw the people. Tents were erected on the boardwalk, beautiful white canvas tents with black designs. Rugs on the ground. The important personages of the town sat cross-legged before low tables. Copper trays and copper tea set. The townspeople crowded on the beach to see the Fantasia. The Moroccans, in white burnooses, rode their horses with spirit, galloped forward in unison and shot their muskets. Their thrust was as lively, as vivid as one had imagined and heard.

Veiled women in the back of the tent made bird sounds to signify approval of the horsemanship. The dancers were unveiled and dressed in satin and silk with an overlay of transparent muslin dotted with spangles. The women behind us gave the impression of a wall of silence and mystery.

Wives of officials sat on divans at the back. We sat on rugs. Tourist women offended the Arabs by their nakedness in bikinis and slovenly costumes.

The horseback riders rode on the beach with the sun and the sea behind them. The dancers, too, were outlined against the sky and sea. The men dancers all in white with an orange tassel and dagger holder hanging from the shoulder. They stamp their feet like Spanish gypsies. The women dancers in sea green, gold, rose, blue, gauzy dresses and many jewels and flat muslin turbans. The musicians sat next to the dignitaries—cross-legged. During the whole ceremony these dignitaries drank mint tea from their elaborate carved copper samovars. Silent.

Jellabas, burnooses of all colors. The wind curled and uncurled the red Moroccan flags. The riders leaped from the edge of the sea toward the terrace, shouting and shooting. The muskets were loud, startling.

The wild cavalcade so sharply outlined against blue sky and sea and sand—like an Eisenstein close-up of dark carved faces set in character and firmness. Hard codes, nobilities carve such faces. Bravery, tradition, order.

Tafraoute:

We cannot wait to get away from the fog, the loud rock music, the bourgeois French atmosphere of the Club Méditerranée at Agadir and into the desert. Our first tour is to Tafraoute in the Atlas Mountains at the northern edge of the Sahara. Our guide is François Camus, a radiant young Frenchman. He has green eyes, a transparent young-girl's skin, a soft smile and blond curly hair. Something so open to the senses. We travel in a Land Rover. The road is rough and narrow. It is predawn; we are not awake yet. The landscape is flat, all in sepia with a few tamarisk and palm trees. The mountain tops are wrapped in mist.

But when we arrive in Tafraoute, by contrast, we awaken to a sky so sharply, cleanly, so cloudlessly blue that the mountain peaks seem separated from it like a cardboard cutout—the purest blue I have ever seen. The village of red adobe cubes built into the base of the incredibly steep red sandstone cliffs reminded me of the American Indian villages in Arizona and New Mexico. The extraordinary quietness found only in the desert. One can hear the birds. Only the children are about, astonishingly beautiful. Enormous, sparkling, dark eyes; straight, pure features. Women in black jellabas fetch water from the fountains with earthen jars, as in biblical scenes. The men wear burnooses of gray, laundry-blue or black.

Our Berber guide is Ibrahim, a lean, finely carved man of about thirty, dressed in a blue burnoose with a white turban. Under his burnoose he wore a starched, high-collared shirt! He was unbelievably agile even in this costume. He climbed a very tall palm tree and came down unsoiled, unwrinkled, dustless, scratchless.

Grace. Calm. Patience. The tourists look disintegrated, graceless, discordant. Our Western culture.

At night I read the history of Morocco. Such a complex of cultures, Spanish, French, African—mostly Berber. But the history all battles, bloodshed and a constant struggle for independence. Treachery and exploitation by the French.

The women cannot be seen, but their eyes follow you intently, unblinkingly, steadily.

On the beach at Agadir, the young factory girls during their lunch hour remain veiled but slip off their clothes as they enter the sea. Men try to catch a glimpse of their figures. Saw a woman wading, breasts uncovered but veiled!

Do not photograph the women, said the guides. It offends them. Then what of the women in the postcards? Who unveiled them? Berber women were not veiled—only the dancers? Models? Prostitutes? Who?

Before dinner we gathered at the bar. Memory is so selective that the Club Méditerranée had no reality. Meals with people I could not distinguish or single out or remember. I want to forget Agadir. The beautiful meals by the pool marred by the bad, loud music. The French diarrhea of talk. Chatter. The waiters dressed as Moroccans—overworked and no time to smile or talk. But the Moroccan night came when we returned absolutely exhausted from a trip to Goulimine— and we found strength to dress, enjoy the voluptuous red tents, the lamb, the torches, the Fantasy on the beach at night.

Goulimine:

Up at five A.M. to drive to Goulimine, where the Atlas mountains meet the Sahara Desert, and arrive in time for the camel market. The area of the blue people. They favor a blue jellaba, and with the heat and sweat the blue finally tints their skin a gray-blue. Driving through the desert one remembers that the country of Morocco is "more earth than water."

There is a collective chant which says: "Only the eagle can assuage his desire for the sky."

On their wedding day couples are ducked in a well.

Notes on clothes:

Austere black cape (khnif) with a red diamond-shaped jewel at the hem.

Beni-mguild women: red and blue leggings—a full gown of wool.

Shocking pink on Berber sword.

Crimson embroidered waistcoat.

Torking ya—huge woollen haik.

Caftan—velvet trimmed with garnets.

In Fez, a vast robe of gold lamé.

Mood indigo of clothes and veils.

Kief—Eastern climate of contemplation.

Goulimine: What a word! *Goul*—sad, but *limine* seems made of light.

Plain of Oued Noun.

Desert nights were called *noches de terciopelo* [velvety nights] in Spanish Morocco.

Over the flat plains past earth-colored houses. Walls of dried mud, sometimes crenelated, sometimes built around a rose mosque, or a white one. The rose, strong when new, becomes with time the soft rose of the inside of sea shells. Veiled women sit side-saddle on don-

94

keys. Black cotton saris with white cotton face coverings. Children smile with beautiful teeth. Dogs. Herds of sheep and goats. In rocky desert land the hungry goats climb the argan trees to eat leaves and berries. Then the mountains. Always the heat like a furnace blast; the face burns as with a fever. The dust colors, punctuated by a blue jellaba. In the earth-colored plain walls a door of emerald green, or laundry-blue or a yellow or red design. A few small windows have iron grilles. Huge locks on doors, huge bolts. The silver jewelry of women also heavy and large.

A village on the way. Quietness. It climbs up the side of the mountain. Steps of stones. Closed doors. The men are at work in the fields. Only women, very old men and children left. Passageways making dark lairs for the animals, in dank shade. Smell of fodder. From inside of passageway the sun shines at the entrance like an unbearable diamond in the eye. The heat as one emerges strikes one down. The rays of the sun in 130-degree heat are concrete, like a blow of white-hot steel. Soon one is as thirsty and as parched as the desert sand, or a desert Arab. The whole body is thirsty—skin, hair, eyes. The gourds and goatskins the Arabs carry do not hold enough water for the extent and depth of one's thirst. It seems unquenchable.

The aspect of the villages is severe because of the heavy doors, walls and rare, small windows—often no windows—mere apertures in the wall. Born of dust—yet timeless, biblical.

The men are threshing wheat as in the past. Sometimes a row of horses tied to a post, egged on by chanting of the men, keep trampling the wheat in a circle. The chanting is rhythmic, a *mélopée*, as in a *cante jondo*. Clapping hands, singing, throwing the stalks back under the feet of the animal. Round and round.

In the still air, I hear a flute, or the prayer from the mosque. A bird call. Cicadas, loud and continuous buzzing. François and I are dipping our feet in a brook, a clear stream. A frog leaps out of the stream. François is talking about his ancestors in Anjou, related to George Sand.

After so much dust, rocks, citadels, walls, women in black cloth, which they hold before the face with one arm, as they balance a water jug on the head with the other; after all this dryness, in the middle of the plains—a patch of green palm trees, olive trees, tamarisk, fig trees, small fields of corn, mint, clover, and wheat, fruits and flowers, because of the water—an oasis. To feel an oasis, its greenness, humidity, one has to have crossed the desert—to have become a rock, an area of sand, of parched earth, with the skin of a turtle. An oasis! The music of the irrigation ditches, brooks, the music of water, soft, reflective, running alive like a silver fish. To feel its delight one has to have traveled over rocky roads, walked in the dust, in the sun, be tired, thirsty, with dusty feet and cracking lips. The oasis is shadowy, luxuriant. Everything in it is sweetened, softened, glistening from the mountain stream running through it.

We dip our feet in its coolness. The houses are closed, but some women peer at us from slightly opened doors, from roofs, or from behind grilled windows. The children rush forward in long jellabas, or just raggedy dresses. The little girls' hair is already braided into many small braids. At two or three years of age they have pierced ears and wear earrings. They are beautiful. Their eyes stun you. They are so charged with messages it is electrifying. They express the continuity of time. Religion gives them this unframed, unlimited cosmic flow—no beginning, no end. Their eyes hold all of the past, and we are not accustomed to eyes holding so much. At three or four years of age the children look at you as men, women, ageless, cosmic, ancient, powerful. The whole richness of the race is in them. The heat of the sun, the blackness of their nights, the concentration of their life has enriched their eyes as compression creates the precious stone.

Oases. And our sadness. Travel is seeking the lost paradise. It is the supreme illusion of love. It is not the love of the newborn country, its youth. It is the love of what it once created, the peak and culmination of maturity. I love the Arabs, their faces, the men's steely qualities, the women's secretiveness, but all this is lost to us forever.

We cannot recapture it. We are denied their faith in Allah, their tranquillity, their contemplation, their harmony with the pattern, the peace they have achieved with God, with nature, with themselves. Their bodies are alive. I love their silences, which are alive too. Traveling keeps romanticism and illusion alive.

By contrast, the tourists . . .

We see only the *ancient* Morocco.

We arrived at the camel market at Goulimine.

A wind-swept plain. The sand I thought gold is gray. The clouds it makes are dust gray, which the jellabas reproduce just as some of the little girls' dresses reproduce orange flowers. The market is enclosed by a wall. Groups of camels—brown, white. Papa and Mama and children. The baby camels still suckling. The Arabs are sunburned to an ash color. Their feet and ankles are gray and dry like leather. Their hands knotted. Never a flabby cheek, always a sharply carved face, lean, structured. Pointed vandyke beards, black or white. No women at the market. Two Arabs at the entrance sit on the ground. Using a big toe as a peg, they weave the pattern of hemp to be placed under the belly of the mother camel so the baby camel will not milk her dry. Some camels are free. Others bound together. In the old days you came here to buy your camels for a caravan—to find your guides and porters.

Some of the jellabas and burnooses are soiled and wrinkled. The Arabs sleep in them. Others are fresh, impeccable, like the one our guide at Tafraoute wore. Old men chatter. But most of the time the Arabs are silent, and their silence is graceful and beautiful. They squat, wait, dream.

Lunch at the oasis. Under trees. Bamboo trellis overhead. Rugs on the ground. Water for hands and faces. A sheep cooked on the spit served on a huge copper tray and eaten only with fingers. Plenty of red wine.

Hotel at Goulimine. Inner patio open to the sky. When I had to get up at four A.M. I saw the stars. I saw the sleeping village. There was a light in the mosque window.

The Moroccan men wear leather slippers. Easy to drop. They sit cross-legged like Japanese, backs very straight.

Our guide, the young François is twenty-three and in love with Morocco. He was born July 13. He is psychic and a dreamer. He is a subtle guide, choosing spots no one else would notice, commanding stops at semideserted squares at sundown because a few men are throwing wheat in the air with pitchforks, tying bundles in nets to place on patient donkeys. It is a golden sunset. It is quiet.

François is slender, indefatigable, kind, patient, equable. No irritation or impatience. We drank to his birthday at the hotel in Goulimine.

His birthday present, a cape, long, nude, with a hood. White muslin or heavy white wool with gray stripes.

The cherghi, blowing from the Sahara, is like a flame. It turns rocks black. It melts us. It gives an unquenchable thirst.

The argan tree bears a small bitter orange fruit which the goats like. They climb the trees to eat it. A tree may carry as many as five or six goats eating, while others chew standing on their hind legs.

Also known in Peru and New Zealand. The Arabs derive oil from it—an oil for beauty products.

We are repudiating all this. We travel, some of us forever, to seek other states, other lives, other souls. Lawrence's cry: "We cannot retrograde, we can only go forward."

We are outsiders.

By feeling we penetrate other lives.

Last night, inside of the red and green tent, sitting on a low bench, when they brought the lamb on a large copper platter, when the horsemen galloped on the beach and shot muskets in the air, when the torches snaked wildly, the fire under the meat burned red, when the dancers came, I wept as I did before the most exquisite of all Japanese soups. The wild beauty of the night by the beach. I am not only living my own life in Morocco, but that of Isabelle Eberhardt, of Jane Digby. I carry Lesley Blanch's book, *The Wilder Shores of Love*.

At one oasis, at the foot of a high canyon, a fortress called Agadir. After we had lunch in the cool shade of trees, the mules and donkeys were brought from the village across the Oued. I tried to go with the caravan, but the sun, the motion of the donkey were too brutal for me. My legs were not strong enough. I had to surrender and walk back over stones while an old Arab held my hand, urged the donkey on, and covered the distance in his bare feet. When I returned, I was flushed and trembling. I lay by the stream.

The Arab man is a great beauty. Tall, very dark, with regular features, the face always firm, set. Eyes bold. There is a style to his gestures.

I broke with my mail, the better to immerse myself in the life of Morocco.

Some exiles succeed in integrating with a foreign life. Isabelle Eberhardt did. Born February 17. Her horoscope was exact. She died by drowning in a flash flood in the desert.

When a saintly man dies the village places his body on a camel and lets the camel carry it where it will. Where it stops they build a marabout, a square building of either mud or stucco with a round dome and four columns. The body is buried wrapped in sheets, turned toward Mecca. There are marabouts for women saints, too.

At the market women wear their keys in a bunch pinned to their headgear. They braid beads into their hair.

Danse de la Guidra:

The dancers clap hands as in Spanish flamenco or play small cymbals held like castanets. They clap hands, shining against a dark sky. Saw this dance in the evening. A velvety night. A fire built to warm the drums. The women's dress, brocade and transparent muslin.

The musket shot is far louder than our gun. It is startling—dry and sharp.

On the way to Ouarzazate we visited village of Ait Ben-Haddow of the Aouch tribe. Undamaged, occupied—with carved roof tops and decorated walls.

The hotel of the Club Méditerranée in Ouarzazate, a most beautiful architecture inspired by native adobe—with towers—the modern adaptation not visible outside. Decorated windows of Moroccan woodwork frame a view of the village. Cool tiles, fountains. A swimming pool. Dedicated to the semiprecious stones found in the desert. Each room bears the name of a stone: Malachite, Quartz, Onyx, Hematite, Tourmaline, as in *House of Incest*. A baby gazelle came to greet the dusty, weary explorers. Dinner out of doors. Torches, charcoal grills, shishkebab.

The guttural chant of the women, in a circle, is started by one and followed and developed by the rest. The men play the drums. Cries, like American Indian cries. Bird cries.

The homes linked together, interdependent, within a protective wall. Gray or sepia, according to color of the earth.

Mint tea—at wayside cafés, in the home, at the market. The merchant offers it. The nomads make it over fires. You see fields of mint —children carrying armfuls.

Marrakesh:

The water sellers are dressed like Peruvian Indians—in red, covered with copper bells. They carry water in goatskin bags and dispense it in copper cups. They stand out in the crowd and the jingle warns you of their presence.

The snake charmer does not charm the snakes. They have an angry relationship. The snakes flare at him. It is an act to create terror in the spectator. He lets them touch his nose, his eyes, puts their heads in his mouth. One old charmer had two bites. It is an ugly sight. He slips them inside his trousers. He lets you hold them. People scream, move away.

T. E. Lawrence said about the Arabs: "They are too intelligent to work for others. Too intelligent and too proud."

A deaf queen arranged to have a black flag hung out during prayer time so that the deaf would know. When the prayer was over, a white flag appeared.

No markings on tombs—no names. Inscriptions, if any, are lines from the Koran.

El-Kamir Gate, Marrakesh.

From *The Arabs* by Anthony Nutting: "Overwhelming charm and humor, quick tempered, unstable. No Arab will ever forget a gesture of friendliness; likewise he will always remember an act of hostility. The Arabs, like probably no other people in the world except the Irish, are irrational and emotional to a point where they think only with their hearts, never with their heads."

Grand Palais de la Bahia. Rooms of the four legitimate wives. Room of the favorite—all in red—red, painted doors, red four-poster bed.

The *souks* enchanting but for the obstinate pestering by boys— fighting to guide you and fighting among themselves.

On the way back to Agadir, at Mogodor, I saw a van driven by Julian Beck, who founded the Living Theater in New York. He passed by our touring bus. I called him. Judith Malina came out, with a one-year-old girl. It was a surprise to meet the Becks. I was glad the bus was empty. The tourists were visiting the town; I was ashamed to be with them—French bourgeois, chattering every moment about trivialities, no deep interest in Morocco. And the hippies. They came for the hashish, but they fit in with the ragged Arabs.

Simplicity of the food. Couscous is delightful—a grain which tastes like something between rice, corn and wheat germ. This is flaky and dry and is served with a sauce flavored like Spanish rice—with vegetables and raisins. Often includes a piece of lamb and a piece of chicken. An intensely piquant sauce is served on the side.

The Arabs are multiraced, but achieve unity in dress, gestures and attitudes. The only great contrast is between the humility or weary attitude of the very poor and the haughty, proud carriage of the horsemen, dancers, and even of servants or guides. Nothing humble there—they address you as *tu*, are natural and friendly, at ease. The women are quiet behind their veils, but intensely curious. Their eyes are unbearably eloquent. Because of their expressiveness, their message could be interpreted as an invitation. If I were a man, I would be confused. The men's eyes, and even the boys', are so intimate, so personal, so alive, that the European, accustomed to feebler lights and nondescript eyes, is hypnotized. One boy looked so nakedly and fully like a man. One could write a book solely on eyes. Even the old eyes do not lose their light or depth.

Tomorrow, last day of motor tour of Greece—the classical tour. After Morocco, tame, monotonous, a museum of stones. Dead. Like the classics. Just a few stones on the ground, always the same column and the same face. Nothing as eloquent as Cambodia, as Mexico. Mild and uniform. Guide seeks to bring life but it is dead history, all surface and no depth. It is a convention to admire Greece, something dinned into scholar's ears. After seeing living places, with living villages, just to look at rubble and hear a lecture on mythology . . . Olympic games. Olympia. A vast field. Can you sit and dream there as you sit in front of a Zen garden? No, because it was a purely *physical* dream —like Los Angeles—or a film!

The only amusing touch, at lunch, under the grapevines—the wine was called "Blood of Hercules."

Only story touching upon some deeper roots was that of Asclepius, who cured the sick with herbs and theater. The theater was intended to make them dream and via the dream to find a cure! If they did not dream, there was a professional, official Dreamer who would do it for them.

On the ferryboat, on the way to Delphi. Nothing extraordinary about the landscape. People are impregnated with history. Without its history, Greece pales before Cambodia, Mexico, Japan—I had an intuition I would not respond to Greece.

A young couple recognized me and took my photograph. I tried to see Greece through their eyes. The young man was doing a photographic study of the statues.

The resounding names, legendary associations—Aegean Sea, Delphi. Through innocent, naked, unhistorical eyes, it looked like Italy or France . . . sweet at times, or harsh, but not as sharply harsh as Morocco.

After the ferryboat ride—and no lovely red sailing boats around—more bus driving, higher and higher, to Delphi.

Durrell, Miller and Caresse [Crosby].

Caresse's story of Delphi, where she sought to plant the flag of Citizens of the World on a mountain she bought. I asked about her mountain and went to see it in the early morning. Yes, the light was clear. The mountain's rim so sharp against a cloudless sky that it seemed cut out, and one is aware of the space, the clarity.

So Caresse bought a mountain and placed a plaque of the Citizens of the World on it. Whereupon a humorless government ordered her to be arrested, as an invader—a colonizer? An aggressor? The village people knew her well. The young soldiers recruited from the village had to obey their government, but they managed to express both loyalties. They placed flowers in their guns' mouths! And escorted her to Athens—trials and tribulations of an idealist!

After Greece I went to the Club Méditerranée in Izmir, Turkey. Just as in Agadir I immediately felt I was in a French pension. The people of Izmir were not allowed inside and the atmosphere was French, not Turkish. The only Turkish corner was the patio, with rugs and pillows, the copper samovar, and the big copper trays piled with fruit. The bungalows were built native-style with open tiles to let the breeze through. But to my dismay, I found that the bungalow was equipped with a loudspeaker which could not be turned off and which blared the same loud rock music we had in Agadir.

Izmir was cold, the sea icy cold. So cold that a woman who taught Yoga exercises and breathing for the club and who insisted on meditating while floating in the sea (though she had been warned of the effects of the cold water) finally drowned while meditating.

Because of the change of name—Smyrna (Greek) to Izmir (Turkish)—I did not realize I was in the birthplace of Yanko Varda.

No Turkish music with dinner, amateur rock and roll.

I was glad when it was time to leave.

On the way to the station I had some extra time and visited the little fishing village of Izmir. The houses all of stone, the street cobblestoned, the women in black, the men looking as if they had spent their life on the sea. The little shops, street cafés, were all simple and bare.

At the station I felt a renewed regret not to have known that Izmir was once called Smyrna. Not to have imagined Varda in the little village, building boats (his first profession) until a tourist brought a ballet company to Izmir and Varda was asked to paint the sets. He did this with such color and fantasy that the group took him to Paris to study. Izmir was then under the rule of the Greeks. Now it was Turkish. I must confess that after becoming familiar with the story of T. E. Lawrence, I took a dislike to the Turks. Their dark eyes, dark hair and very tight belts gave them an air of conquistadors, which did not appeal to me.

I had dreamed of going to Constantinople (now Istanbul) and of visiting the Greek Islands. But I had to abruptly end my travels and hurry back to New York to care for a friend who had just had emergency surgery on both eyes.

On the way back, flying from Turkey to Paris, our plane ran into a flock of sea gulls and had to land at Athens. While we waited overnight for another plane, I wrote the story "My Turkish Grandmother."*

* Later included in the collection *In Favor of the Sensitive Man and Other Essays* (New York: Harcourt Brace Jovanovich, 1976).—Ed.

Dreams:

A white cat is pursuing some kind of insects—shaped like diminutive gorillas, pink like cooked shrimp, and poisonous. He catches them and bites them to death. I hear the crackling of the shell-like skin. But one of them bites him and he dies of the venom. (Frances Steloff has white cats. They came to my party.)

I am typing, writing a book *with* someone. Perfect collaboration. When we are finished he embraces me (not amorously but whole-heartedly). He sits in same armchair very close. There are others there. Durrell is there, but I pay no attention. Friends drinking. By the sea, a very murky sea, with undertow. I swim naked. People disapprove. They want to go and drink—visit a Montparnasse character. I do not know where to take them.

Written for book-signing party at Books in Review Bookshop, Los Angeles:

The reading of books is in itself the most beautiful education of all. Because of reading I became acquainted with the entire world, physical, intellectual, historical, scientific. My life was expanded. The knowledge of what existed in the world, in other countries, of the possibilities and potentialities of life, prepared me for experience, for the unknown, for unfamiliar situations. Only by reading does one possess such a power to travel, to visit all the lands, to make friends with characters of all periods, so that one learns to observe the riches of the present and the possible loves and friendships around us. Through books I discovered everything to be loved, explored, visited, communed with. I was enriched and given all the blueprints to a marvelous life, I was consoled in adversity, I was prepared for both joys and sorrows, I acquired one of the most precious sources of strength of all: an understanding of human beings, insight into their motivations. I also learned from books how to enhance what needed to be enhanced, by understanding, and by aesthetics. Books are the greatest companions, confessors, confidantes, tutors, a source of pleasure, a cure for loneliness, and to find one, in the middle of an island in Tahiti, in the heart of the Moroccan desert, or at an airport where one is stranded for a night, is to find the friend who reminds us we are not alone.

Letter to Daisy Aldan:

I hope your summer was an antidote to New York. One needs an antidote to a poisonous life. . . . I received a call from Danièle that [Jeanne] Moreau was in Hollywood and we should see her, become acquainted, discuss *Spy*. It was quite a beautiful meeting. She is an Aquarian, and so well read and intelligent, as we could tell from her acting. She is Sabina. But with awareness. We had two evenings together. Dinner last night at the home she rented while making a film here. She is rejuvenated by America. In her the extremes of gaiety and anxiety are appealing. So here we are. Diary Three will be out in November . . . I will be back in October. The 9th to the Book Fair in Germany. I am trying to learn a few words in German with recordings. . . . Read so much during August . . . biographies mostly. Moreau can't read fiction anymore. The trip was a mixture. I was utterly bored with Greece, a monotonous and shallow culture. One design, one statue, and shallow gods. Turkey the same. Live in the past but with so little of the past visible. And the present shabby. After Cambodia, and Mexico and Japan, Greece seemed tame, mild and superficial. I am afraid the scholars are responsible for sustaining this dead culture in which (as my Zen teacher says so poetically) history is not made *presence*. In Morocco history was made presence. It is alive in the people. The theme of the trip I took from his line, which he used to describe Marguerite's *Angel in the Forest*. Well, may New York be kind to you.

Letter to Wayne McEvilly:

Our meeting was perfect. You are like your writing, like your letters and like everything you read, say, and there was a perfect welding. No inconsistencies. We talked as we wrote, in perfect confidence. I was only concerned that you would be put off by our frivolities, our interest in little things, birthdays and little things of life. At times when we talked alone, I felt no going away, but when we were with Marguerite and the others, I saw you going away, in your eyes I saw the departures, the absences. I hope you were happy. Was it a strain? Were you disappointed? Marguerite distressed me by saying: "Life will always be a disappointment to Wayne, for he is a romantic." A dreamer, yes. I know that. I hope we did not damage your dream. I was not altogether free to give my time to you as I would have liked, for walks, talks, etc. Finally I wanted to write you immediately but remembered you would not be home for a week. Then when I came to Los Angeles I found that Jeanne Moreau and my producer took all my time. Moreau is a fascinating woman, soft, strong, intelligent, the actress with intuition. She is frightened of Sabina. "It is *me*. And I would have to make a journey to the end of myself." She lives Sabina. She is afraid to look at her. Act her out. So we talk. It was only last night, being wakeful at four A.M. that I was able to read what you wrote on *Seduction*. And it was beautiful, and extraordinarily profound. Yes, you go to the depths easily. That may be why you find it difficult to live on the surface. I was the same way, but I learned. When Danièle could not get a firm written commitment from Moreau and agonized, she refused to participate in the dinner Moreau gave, to relax from her actress life, interviews, tensions. She could not turn away. Moreau wanted to rest, to play with her dog, to go and listen to a folk singer. I could do that, but Danièle could not. I have learned to turn away from my own submarine journeys. . . . I hope Marguerite is not right and that you were not disappointed. Among the depths you never lose your way. I think your study of *Seduction* is outstanding. I want it to be an introduction so more people will read it. I am writing to Swallow about it. I am going to include it with the book now.

Letter to Danièle Suissa:

I was a little sad tonight, pasting and collecting letters for the June Diary, to find your loving letters. I feel you are less close to me than when we were working together. I feel a shadow. I feel perhaps you still think I lacked faith in *you* when I never swerved from the statement I made in my letter to your father. It is the businessmen I have no faith in. I felt there were only two ways open: Only when one has independent means can one do everything one wishes. The New Wave was created by three or four filmmakers who had independent means. I believe you highly gifted in many directions, but what I said to you over the telephone was that I was anxious that distributors and bankers would not give money without strings. That was not lack of faith in you but in the system. I know also you were deeply disappointed not to be working with an actress of your generation. I hope the shadow I feel, your sudden irritations, were not due to anything between us. Reread my letter to your father. The very first time I realized you were not independent and mentioned studios and distributors, you remember I expressed my feeling that everything wonderful was done in spite of the bankers, alas.

All I meant over the phone was that. . . .

Well, Monday we will know. Much of this shadow may have been due to a year of stress and overwork and overtravel—I hope so—because I have not changed.

My publisher asked me to write a few pages on the problems of editing the Diary:

When I began editing the Diary, I was faced with problems which are not solved by ambiguous legal definitions. An editor must ultimately set his own rules.

The law speaks of damage, but how do you tell the truth without injuring the lives of others, and how do you define injury when this damage varies with each person portrayed, with each situation, with each period of time? We had to study each case separately. If the person was alive we consulted with him. The law entitles a living person to excise himself completely from the Diary or to erase damaging lines. We had remarkably few characters bowing out and very few erasures. I believe this was due to the basic motivation of my portraits. I am concerned with *understanding*, with knowing, exploring, rather than with judgments. I made the portraits very full, in depth as well as in range, allowed everyone to speak for himself by way of letters and conversations. In the end, all the elements are there and a balance is achieved, which is an approximation of justice. If a man is big enough he can support his frailties. I was faithful to motivations. I never began with an intent to caricature, to mock, to judge or to distort. But I did not glamorize or retouch either. It was the basic intent to understand which guided the selections and made the ultimate portrait acceptable.

When I dramatized Dr. [René] Allendy's limitations as a psychoanalyst, I also made it clear that this limitation was only in relation to me, as an artist. I included his own revelations about his personal difficulties, a description of his positive achievements, his pioneer work in the French courts (he was the first one to bring psychoanalysis as a factor in the trial of a criminal), his role in the exploration of new ideas. It shocked me when someone said I should have turned in anger against Dr. Allendy. What right had I to judge him only because of his error in my case when I understood his personal traumas, the origin of his fallacies, and I knew his contribution in other fields?

A personality only emerges truthfully when all aspects are included.

Everyone has an image of himself which conflicts with the image held by others. People have been shocked to hear their voices on tape;

it is never the voice they imagined they had. They have been shocked to see their faces for the first time on film. How much more shocked they are by others' portraits. But if these are made without intent to damage, they are usually not damaging. It is possible to tell the truth without committing character assassination if one's motive is not to ridicule or disparage. The desire to be faithful has to be stronger than the desire to expose faults.

Truth remains relative, but a knowledge of psychoanalysis helps to reveal motivations. A listing of incidents and anecdotes does not add up to a faithful portrait, but familiarity with the inner man gives the key to his acts, which is more important. To study a person in depth is more important than to catalogue his actions. If one is deaf to the vulnerabilities of a human being, one also has no ear for the more subtle recording of his sensitive wavelengths. Giving all the facts, all the incidents, all the anecdotes, rather than a meaningful selection of them in order of their importance and accompanied by clarification, very often leads to a petty, shrunken portrait. If a full psychological portrait is given, and if it is accurate enough, one can infer the rest, fill in, read between the lines, as with a close friend, or a member of one's family. To seize upon the basic, essential lines of a character is more important than details. Nothing essential to a portrait was left out of the Diary.

Sacking and invading privacy belongs to war, not peace. Anyone filled with aggression, hostility and venom makes a very poor portraitist and reveals more about himself than about others, for people intuitively rarely disclose themselves to the enemy. Insensitivity usually causes a human being to lock up his secrets.

The portrait of the diarist has to be included as well, to balance as indicator, receptor, barometer. "I am a camera." You, the reader, have the right to know the brand, range, quality of the diarist-camera. For the Diary's truth is ultimately an alchemy of portrayer and portrayed. People relate to a presence. Many manifestations of the personality only bloom in the presence of love or friendship. More is revealed by interrelation than by so-called objectivity.

By objectivity I never meant impersonality. We learn more about others from relationships than from objective scrutiny. People only unmask themselves in the privacy of love or friendship. But such revelations impose noblesse oblige. One has to treat them with care to keep them alive and warm. A human being who reveals himself should be treated with the same care we accord to a unique discovery in science or nature. He is unique, and we may never see another like him. We must protect him from injury if we are to share his life. Only a long-lasting friendship will give a continuous portrait. To offend, insult, humiliate as some diarists do, is simply to cut all lines of communication with human beings.

I am not claiming that I have avoided all the pitfalls. I may have offended certain susceptibilities, because one cannot always know what they are. I have not changed anything in the Diary, only omitted, and the greater part of what was left out was repetition. Repetitions are inevitable in a diary, but they have to be eliminated. The very process of the diary resembles that of a painter making a series of sketches each day in preparation for a final portrait. This portrait is made only by cumulative effect because the diary never ends. As the diarist does not know the future, he reaches no conclusion, no synthesis, which is an artificial product of the intellect. The Diary is true to becoming and to continuum. I could not make conclusions which even death does not make. The portrait of Dr. Otto Rank did not end with his death. I am making new discoveries about him, revising some of my opinions because of new information.

If the diarist has no humanity, no psychological insight, no ethics, the portrait will lack these dimensions too. It will read like a vivisection. Many portraits have been acts of hatred or revenge, others are so shallow that the characters pass like shadows with names pinned to their lapels. Some resemble the voodoo hexing ceremonies during which a vengeful native sticks pins in a doll as a substitute for the original.

I remind myself that as a diarist I can create a prejudiced view of my model. I once introduced a letter thus: "His war letter from a safe place was a monument of egotism." This statement was prejudicial to the defendant. I crossed it out and quoted the letter itself, allowing the person to make his own portrait.

The solution to the negative consequences of truth lies in the fullness and richness of the portrait so that all sides are heard, all aspects considered, and in such organic development lies a possibility of balance.

The writer is not limited to painting one aspect of the personality. He is able to include all of them. The sum is achieved by completeness. A selection of the major traits takes the place of a petty accumulation of anecdotes, which may resemble snapshots taken by an unprofessional photographer when they are told without their proper interpretation or out of context.

The destructive element of truth is neutralized by a deep probing into motivation which makes you understand a character beyond appearances. What is understood is not judged. Psychoanalysis was my invaluable teacher in the study of motivation and interpretation. Understanding creates compassion and suspends judgment.

Today we live by a savage code: that the life of one man is always to be sacrificed for the benefit of the many, that a public figure belongs to history, that we have a right to know all. But we never stop to realize that a great part of this curiosity has nothing to do with history or psychological progress, that it is often on a par with the curiosity of gossipers, and we must draw a boundary line indicating where respect for the life of a human being is more important than the satisfaction of a sensation-seeker.

Writers have given an example of ruthless invasion instead of a lesson in the creative possibilities of intimate portraits. This becomes very crucial in an age which is repudiating the disguises of the novel because it lives through TV and films, closer to actuality and the reality of personalities.

If our age is noted for alienation, it is largely because we treat each other without tact or sensitivity, because we have lost our faith in our confidants and can trust no one to deal humanely with the truth. Diarists have given examples of sniping, if not outright murder. Respect for the vulnerability of human beings is a necessary part of telling the truth, because no truth will be wrested from a callous vision or callous handling.

Letter to Richard Centing, Librarian at Ohio State University:

I think the idea of a newsletter is wonderful as there is so much activity and news and development and expansion not only in my literary life but in that of all the people I was and am related to, extending to all parts of the world. There will be much to write about, many brilliant contributors we can count on. The newspapers and book reviews are so much divided into conventional routines that much material of great interest is not used and could go into the newsletter. I will collaborate in every way I can and put you in touch with the old group (Miller, Durrell, etc., as well as the contemporary ones). Gerald Robitaille, the writer-artist-secretary of Henry Miller, can keep us in touch, and when you are ready I can give you names of writers and reviewers and publishers and articles which will make interesting reading. Let me know. In Los Angeles I will have more time to give you a detailed list of potential collaborators.

Pan American flight on the way to Frankfurt Book Fair. A beautiful day for flying.

The letters from my German publisher, Dr. Mathias Wegner, were so insistent, Diary One so wonderfully translated, Diary Two appearing for the Fair—all this persuaded me to accept.

Strange double journey, for my Diary continues to be for me the secret confessional, while at the same time half of it has been made public. Half is private, secret, it is still carried to the vault, volume by volume, but 1930 to 1939 is open for all to see. Why? Because at a certain moment I became aware that the characters I was writing about had become influences in the present, woven into contemporary life, that returning to them was like investigating the sources of the Nile—the sources of today: Miller and sexual revolution, Otto Rank and psychological training of welfare workers, surrealism leading to Pop Art, and Artaud's influence on the theater. No nostalgia for the past, no desire to go backward in time. No. It was not that. At a certain moment characters seemed historical, not personal. The transition Proust spoke of had taken place. It was made by time. I wrote at the instant happening, but time situated us outside of the personal. Not venerable statues in parks covered by autumn leaves and pigeons, but active. Henry watching *Tropic of Cancer* being filmed in Paris. Otto Rank kept alive by the Otto Rank Association. Artaud's work out in six volumes edited by Paule Thévenin at Gallimard and subject of Bettina Knapp's book prefaced by me. Surrealism everywhere, in films, novels, theater, taking Artaud's name in vain. And curiously, three rebels—Henry against puritanism, Rank against dogmatic Freudianism, Artaud against dogmatic surrealism.

Germany, its warring shadow cast over my childhood, Nazism's specter, froze my heart, and I had to discuss this with Dr. Bogner. Bogner was born in Germany. She gave me *Weimar Culture* [by Peter Gay] to read. We talked about the two faces of Germany—Bach, Beethoven, Brahms, the mystic Novalis, Kafka and the Romantics, Paul Klee and the other painters I loved. I had to see beyond the Germany of invaders and sadists.

The élan which throws me into adventure . . . an adventuress always looking back at the peaceful moments.

But I'm on a plane, going to a country I do not know. The tightness is gone.

October 10. I arrived at midnight. A quiet airport. Two or three people at the gate waiting. I divined which one was Dr. Wegner—tall, thin, refined, blond, with glasses, a sensitive face. Between thirty and forty. With his beautiful young wife, Christine. His smile is charming, sincere. We get into his sports car. There is a fog. We get lost on the freeway. When we reach the hotel where a room has been reserved, we find Dr. Wegner's secretary has made a mistake. It was reserved for October 6 and when I did not arrive they rented it to someone else. Frankfurt was so crowded that the bed of the housekeeper had been dragged to the middle of the foyer, and as a joke an artificial rose and a bottle of beer lay on the pillow. This amused me, and I had to lighten the disappointment of Dr. Wegner. We drove to his hotel. He told his story to the desk clerk, who called the housekeeper. I had stayed in the car. They came to tell me she offered to take me to her house. She had a guest room. Tomorrow I would have a room in Dr. Wegner's hotel. So Dr. Wegner went off and the housekeeper, plump and maternal, drove me in her little Volkswagen into the fog. A deeper and deeper fog. She knew no English. I know no German. But a sympathy was instantly established through the ordeal. The white guiding lines disappeared. It was a long ride. It was two o'clock when we arrived before a neat white, plain tract home—like any middle-class home in America, clean, orderly, full of homely details. The light was on. As we entered the living room, in an alcove which may have been the dining room, a man lay in a double bed. "*Mein Mann*," she said. He spoke a little English. He was partly sitting up. He explained he had been paralyzed since the war. On the table was a glass of beer. We talked. They offered me food. I asked for beer. Then she took me up to her bedroom—the best room. She opened a wardrobe and chose from a neat pile of nightgowns her wedding nightgown! It was strange and touching, to enter Germany through its simplest working people, a workman's house. I slept. I took a bath in a meticulous bathroom. I had breakfast with them. I will never forget her carrying her husband, his legs dangling, to his armchair by the window. . . .

She drove me to the hotel Hessischer Hof. At ten A.M. in the lounge I had my first interview with the *Münchner Merkur,* with Monika Schubert. And with Kurt Zimmermann of the Hessische Fernsehen. Then I met the young woman who was going to make my entire stay a delight—Monika Kruttke. Monika looked like a young Marlene Dietrich with short hair and a turned-up nose. She was to interpret for me, watch over me. She had a lovely voice like Marlene, and was bright, gay. She took me to a temporary hotel where she was staying.

At three o'clock I was at an elegant bookstore signing books—piles of books. People came endlessly, carrying the two Diary volumes. A few said beautiful things in faltering English, but most of the time I found myself reading faces intently, all my antennae out, all my receptivity alert. What I read was warmth, admiration, respect, response. Without language! Monika helped me with the spelling of difficult names. So much respect for the writer. So much love of literature.

At 8:30 P.M. a reception for me in the editor's office of *Der Monat.* Three rooms and hallway absolutely packed. Twice as many people as expected. Newspapermen, two TV cameras and at least ten photographers. Dr. Wegner was amazed because at the Frankfurt Fair there are so many events going on at the same time. But until midnight I greeted people, was photographed, offered flowers, interviewed for television. Champagne! At one moment I was overwhelmed—the fulfillment of a fantasy, to be received unanimously, admiringly, for my writing. So much awe and admiration that I almost wept. It was impossible to speak. Dr. Wegner gave a quiet introduction. I saw hundreds of people. Emotional faces. Luise Rainer was there with her publisher husband, [John] Knittel. The salient quality of the atmosphere was sincerity.

October 11. Monika, Dr. Wegner and I drove (forty minutes by freeway) to Darmstadt where at eleven A.M. I signed books at the Darmstädter Bücherstube. Again a wonderful crowd. A young actress read vitally and warmly from the Diaries (her own selections) in such beautiful German I almost understood. Then a talk-discussion. The owner of the bookshop made a speech translated by Monika: "I was so nervous at meeting a famous writer, but you cured me. Now I feel relaxed." We laughed. I began my talk saying I knew they wanted to know all that was *not* in the Diary.

At four o'clock I was at the Fair signing books in the booth of Wegner Verlag in front of enlarged photographs of the Diary covers. Again I was televised and interviewed. Who should turn up at the Fair but Fred and Frances Haines with the producer of Fred's next project, Hermann Hesse's *Steppenwolf,* and Robert Snyder, who was promoting his documentary film, *The Henry Miller Odyssey.* Monika listened intently to Fred talking about Carlos Castaneda's *Teachings of Don Juan.* Dr. Wegner was interested in the film of *Steppenwolf.* He wants to publish Tim Leary's *Politics of Ecstasy.* They helped me to move (again) and I invited them to dinner as they all looked seedy and tired. Fred and Frances looked absolutely ill—yellow. Dr. Wegner joined us at dinner. We discussed why American youth should be interested in Hesse—an old classic for the Germans. I had to find my own explanation. They had lost body and spirit in the American soil. They were searching for both. They relied on adopted religions: Buddhism, Zen, religions from India—on venerable classics: Hesse, the *Tibetan Book of the Dead.* They wore costumes of other times and other countries. They were living out their romantic period.

My idea of Germany is totally changed. They are so well read and so unashamedly serious and deep. I always become neurotic when I am caught between two cultures. The good manners of the Germans made me feel European again and alienated from America.

The whole city is full of banners with book titles. The interviews are intelligent and meaningful. I have rediscovered the Germany of great composers and literature.

Flowers in my room. Hand kissing!

October 13. I took the train to Munich because of the fog. I stayed at the Regina Palast Hotel on Maximilian Platz with Dr. Wegner and his wife. Christine is beautiful. She wanted to talk to me intimately but we could not find the opportunity. At three I had to sign books at another bookshop. And in the evening there was a reception at a literary club.

A lovely red-haired actress, Eva Berthold, read from the Diary. Difficult moment when a handsome young man rose and protested the formality (people sitting around dining table), the stage, the loudspeaker, and challenged me to come down from the stage and talk more intimately. I was taken by surprise and caught by not wanting to offend my publisher, the club which invited me. At this collision of two worlds I was anguished rather than skillful. The student insisted later on my coming out to a café, but the club had planned sitting around in the hotel bar.

October 14. Stuttgart. A lovely lovely city, trees, parks, hills. The hotel is next to a park. There are flowers in my room. Miss Teurer, who runs a bookshop, offers me a book on the city. It is all clean, cheerful, soigné. Even a little paper collar around the wine bottle!

At three I talk to the [German] American Women's Club. A dud. They buy no books. They chatter about their household problems. Coldness.

At five cocktails and a beautiful dinner with Miss Teurer. Evening at Amerika Haus—a different crowd. Full house. Discussion. An actress reads from the Diary.

It made me sad to see Americans occupying Stuttgart. The center of the city was bombed, so they turned it into a park.

Hair washed for TV tomorrow. Interviews. Sitting alone in the restaurant, as I must go to bed early to work all day for a German TV film, equivalent of "Camera Three," which goes all over Germany. Tired and cold, but had to accept for sake of my publisher.

October 18. First day of filming. For the set they chose a historic mansion—winter cold—eighteenth-century furniture. But for the bitter cold, I would have enjoyed it . . . talking . . . walking. Statues. Parquet floor. Formality. That is how they saw me—looking Louveciennes. I talk, and after a moment what I say will be spoken in German.

Second day—they placed me at the head of a very very long dining table (like the one in the film *Darling*)—camera at the other end. I played a scene reminiscent of Ionesco's *Chairs*. I spoke about my invisible guests from Paris on the right and from America on the left. I mentioned Miller, Durrell. Lloyd Wright, Varèse. At the foot of the table were the not famous ones: Millicent, the scientists, the hippies, the men in jail, the black writers. *Comédie humaine*. . . . Came back at four, frozen, no lunch. Went to bed with *Glühwein* (hot grog) ordered by Monika, to hope for best tomorrow. They are not finished but don't know if I can do any more. My publisher has been so sincere and devoted. . . . I hope my body will hold out one more day.

Monika deserves special attention—the charm of her manner, warm, spontaneous. She took charge of me, organizing, deciding, but always gaily and thoughtfully. I enjoyed her presence. I let her make decisions, translate, help me inscribe books. For the film, she wanted to interview me in place of the woman who had been assigned. She was the luminous paint. She and Dr. Wegner, whom I didn't feel like calling "Mathias" (because one doesn't use first names in Germany).

Monika's father had died in the war. He was a doctor. Monika was now twenty-eight and unmarried. She had too absolute a concept of marriage—she frightened herself, as I told her. She took me to dinner at a beautiful small restaurant, all wood, beams, fireplaces, antiques. Low ceiling, intimate. Small lamps, as in a country home. And the music came from a music box—a big music box with large copper disks with holes for the cylinder to follow. The last night, another small, smoky woody place. I saw Monika's apartment—all white, clean, modern, a big picture window facing trees. She put on records. She fixed a salad. Her young man came from Berlin. She gave me a list of books to read. We talked a great deal. She wanted to know why politics did not play a major role in my writing, and I answered because politics were not a cure for war. I put my faith in the cure of individual hostilities. I turned my whole attention to psychology as a cure for hostility.

Watch me making my alliance with Germany, combating in myself a past image, a past trauma (the war, Nazism), watch me connecting with deep, serious, intelligent Germans.

Of course, I was receiving love and homage, and my impressions were colored by this. In the park, when we were filming and Monika asked a German Sunday stroller not to come down the path I was going to take, he refused angrily and looked contemptuously at the cameras.

Such beautiful cities—parks, rivers, trees, grass, repose, air. Even the freeways are planted, fringed with trees. No signs, billboards, neglect—no unkempt spots. Politeness and love of nature almost like Japan.

The formality is old-fashioned but full of exquisite thoughtfulness, really the opposite of the caricature of the German, more like the German officer pianist in the film *So Little Time*, or Oskar Werner in his earlier days. The contrast between our ruthless military and their intelligentsia is almost as sharp as that between samurai and tea ceremony—or paper houses! At first they liked me as part of Henry Miller's life—but with the second volume it is for myself. I speak spontaneously all day, and every evening. The young do not have the power, the freedom, the voice that they have in USA. They are steeped in tradition, like the Japanese. But they are 100 percent political—and leave literature to parents. As a result of sending only best-sellers, America has a poor reputation. I should come back to talk about American writers.

Ideal driving country—lots of little cozy inns. It's tiring—people, people, people—but my aptitude for reading faces, expressions stands me in good stead.

Hildegard Knef sings and acts on TV now. The good German films now all made for TV. Here, TV has commercials only for a short period each day—and that is all!

Dr. Wegner believes he will sell as many Diaries here as in America. The publisher who kept me waiting four years and then said no to Diaries is astonished. Miller's *Letters to Anaïs Nin* sold little.

I'm glad people encouraged me to come to Germany. It has been a wonderful experience. The attitude toward my work has been overwhelmingly warm and deep. How they treat their writers! Like movie stars. My hand has been kissed to shreds. Flowers in the room. Such response to the Diaries. My publisher took Diary because he loved it, said it might not sell but he did not care. But it is selling, and the press has been wonderful. I'm a little dazed, but grateful for the genuine love of the Germans. They read deeply, seriously. They ask about America. Why not more writers like you? America sent [Jacqueline] Susann of *Valley of the Dolls*.

It's so relaxing to deal with a high level of journalism. I have been very spontaneous. When they asked if Paris was the peak of my life, I said no, the peak is the present. Monika was afraid of what I might have become. She was glad to see me alive and happy in the present.

Paris: My publisher has reserved a room for me at the Pont Royal. I like the hotel. It is small. My window opens upon a huge stained-glass window of a church. Flowers from Danièle. Telephone messages. A journalist is waiting downstairs. In the evening, dinner at M. Charles Orengo's, the head of Editions Stock, my French publisher. He is vital, positive and incisive. When I arrive, Dominique Aury tells me how much she loves Diary One. Mme. Jacqueline Piatier of *Le Monde* too. André Bay says he is surprised the young like it, he had thought it would touch only those who lived through that period. Maurice Nadeau arrives and says nothing. But Orengo regrets that the photographs were not used, and the titles of my many books.

The next day at his apartment—elegant and refined. I meet Robert Kanters. But after Germany I feel depressed. The intelligence is dry and heartless. Intellectual piranhas. It is all too clever, too quick, and too abstract. Suddenly my dream of France is shattered. Refined, affected, artificial.

I prefer my publicity girl—Danièle Mazingarbe. She is in her twenties. We talk sincerely. She has organized my time. I cannot see my friends.

Journalists.

They are all writers and we can talk. They come with tape recorders. I go to radio studios, all new and sterile as in New York.

My Swedish interviewer, Walter Edenrud, with camera and tape recorder. I took my only walk—along Pont Royal, down the stairs where the houseboat was. No change here. The clock of the Gare d'Orsay, which timed lovemaking, love meetings, love partings, is dead. On the opposite quai, cars drive along a freeway to decongest traffic. The sun is out. The weather is mild. The beauty of Paris moves me as always—these islands of peace in the heart of a city—trees—water—the arrows of cathedrals, the homogeneity, harmonies, symmetries. My Swedish interviewer, with whom I have had a sporadic correspondence, is so affected by our meeting that he swallows pills for his heart. He looks tall, strong, in his prime, but has had a heart attack. So we walk slowly, sit on a bench. At the hotel again, over a coffee, he tells me he believes women can reconstruct the world; he is writing a book about remarkable women!

A lunch at Danièle's father's house. Luxury. Servants. Formality. He is a clever businessman; swollen ego, no father. He dwarfs Danièle. Jeanne Moreau, dressed by Cardin, in a suit suggesting astronauts—plastic—but soft, relaxed, eating a pomegranate a cell at a time—leisurely, *gourmande*, her skin fresh, her fawn eyes clear, her smile sudden and absolute. The color of her skin is beautiful, slightly golden.

Paris has refined Danièle's father, but not enough to prevent him from boasting of all the important people he knows, also that he can never be taken in—he is too shrewd.

Dinner chez Marie-Claire's family on Boulevard St. Germain. Clan. Visit to great grandmother. Proustian atmosphere. Aunt a specialist on Proust. Empire furniture. Young people quiet.

Lunch at Jeanne Moreau's. She arrived in a pageboy blouse of red wool and shiny pants and a black cape. Her apartment is in an old house but modernized. The old nana was there to cook. For the dining room Jeanne had chosen a sort of melon color evoking south of France; a big mineral stone in the center of the table. Alain Resnais was to come but he had a liver crisis. After four years of therapy Jeanne wants to be independently creative, free. She wants to write and direct her own script. I was very happy at this because she would act Sabina as I had intended her to. Men always judge Sabina and portray her as a nymphomaniac: a free woman is a whore.

A dinner with a Dutch journalist, blond, sensual and luminous but tormented, psychologically blind, overpowered by a failed marriage, telling me of her wild love affair with a strange writer. A painful, harrowing obsession, with a sudden break on his part. She had interviewed Cortázar. Described him. He was not in Paris.

My mind was on my task—to explain, fill out the Diary's interstices with my presence, cease the wild speculations of the journalists on missing parts. The Virgin and the Gypsy says one, *House of Incest* says the other. Instead of reading simple passion between the lines, they invent myths.

I left before the reviews and interviews came out.

I arrived in New York worn out. I opened my mail and found this delightful message from Richard Centing to greet me:

Good news! Final approval for the newsletter! [*Under the Sign of Pisces*] I enclose a contribution from B. Franklin, who will supply bibliographic articles concerning publications of your work, works about you and the Circle, etc.

You and your friend-contributors will produce the new fire that will light up the newsletter academic world.

Next day early rise to get to Doylestown, Pa., for the Otto Rank Association lecture. I persuaded doorman to drive me. Arrived at ten

A.M. Historic house left to town for lectures, perfect setting for *Under a Glass Bell*. Lectures, discussions on the novel not good. I was disturbed by negativity of Miriam Waddington. When my time came to speak, I delivered a spontaneous, impassioned talk on the subjectivity of our reading (what we lack, need to nourish us) and gave them my recent experience.

I felt powerful and alive and it was contagious. Tired as I was, I overflowed with life, faith, new currents.

People responded to the aliveness.

Worn out from trip. Fighting sinus infection.

Telegram from Lili Bita:

THIS MOMENT I FINISHED THE TRANSLATION OF SPY IN THE HOUSE OF LOVE STOP MAD AND DELIRIOUS STOP CANT BELIEVE IT STOP WORKED 8–10 HOURS A DAY ALL MONTH STOP ZITO STOP TONIGHT IN THE TAVERNA WE WILL DRINK TO YOUR HEALTH AND BEAUTY AND SUCCESS IN GREECE STOP WILL WRITE MORE FROM ATHENS STOP

SABINA THE GREEK

From the transcript of my talk to the Otto Rank Association:

When I heard so much today about the death of the novel, I wanted to say that what is dying is the false novel, the psychologically unreal novel. The usefulness of the Diary as a document was that when I wrote fiction it was a development, an expansion, a symbolization based on observation of the true workings of human beings. What discouraged the young from reading was unreality. American literature suffered from two taboos: one Puritanism, the other inherited from England, a false shame about the self, about subjective reality. Fortunately Dr. Rank and a study of psychology supported my belief that this absence of the self was hypocritical, its denial dangerous, and that the so-called objective novel caused alienation. We know that even our reading is subjective: We read what we need, what nourishes us . . .

What is dying is the novel which refuses to acknowledge depth psychology as a science of human growth as well as creative growth. The young are not reading because the taboo on the subjective, analytical novel of insight has deprived them of what they most needed, an understanding of themselves.

The taboo on the individual deprived them of that inner quest for values embodied in a human being, a search for identity, for self-discovery and self-understanding. So-called objectivity gave them a sense of alienation which came not from others but from their own self. Psychology supported the claim that our unconscious was the root of all problems. Psychology asked us to look within for the sources of distortions, hostilities and prejudices. The second volume of the Diary ended with a reminder that we were each individually responsible for war as long as we warred with ourselves, with our families, children, husbands, wives.

So I may say, all the Diaries are a tribute to psychology and to Dr. Rank, because they are a story of growth, and there seems to be no growth without confrontations with the unconscious and a unification of conscious and unconscious.

Letter to *Los Angeles Times* critic, Robert Kirsch:

I was on a lecture tour when your review [of Diary Two] caught up with me, and I must confess for the first time I could not respond and answer immediately. I was stunned as one is when one reaches the fulfillment of a wish and finds it suddenly granted beyond one's imagination. Of all the things which have been said, written about the Diaries, you wrote what has the deepest meaning for me—you answered as only someone who *is* a writer *and* a critic and a *human* being could.

You stressed not only the whole of the work but what most mattered to me, the human rapport with all experience. Being as sensitive as you are, you must know what it means in human terms for the child of an unpraising artist to attain to the understanding of a person I can respect. Very few times does this happen in life. As I expressed it when I first read your review: "I have really been answered, a writer cannot wish for more. . . ."

I hear rumors you like Europe—and of course I'm glad. I did find the selected critics I met in Paris this time, though kind to me, overcritical, harsh to writers, all in the head as D. H. Lawrence would say.

Letter to Wayne McEvilly:

I never want to impress my beliefs on anyone, but while traveling through Germany and France, and facing the world, hundreds of people, journalists, cameras, and TV, I was obliged to say to myself: I could not have surmounted life in America, its hardness, I could not have flowered and expanded, I would not have had the courage to publish the Diary, I could not be open to love and response after so many harsh blows, but for psychoanalysis. No religion, no love, no friendship could rescue me. Panic before the camera . . . that was only a symptom. I would by now be a recluse . . . and would not have done my work or my loving. Now, we need something of the spirit to give us strength and repair the shattered vision or shattered faith. . . . So when I once said I was glad you had Zen, just as I was glad my brother had Catholicism, I meant I was glad religion gave you that unifying strength, that healing confessional that psychoanalysis gave me. I never lost my faith in it. It made me metaphysical, it made me human, it made me live, love and write. When I care about someone, this is my secret advice. Sometimes I have forced my friends into psychoanalysis. . . . I no longer do that.

Letter to Harry Moore:

Your letter on Diary Three was beautiful. I am very proud of it. I particularly like that you stress the portraits, the *illumining of life,* as many seem to misunderstand the necessity of my being there not as ego but as receptor, and not as mirror but interpreter. I know your heavy working schedule, but I cannot help hoping you will be able to review the Diary, once more. I like your point of view, your vision of it which sets things straight.

Perhaps I was right to withdraw (a little) from the personal giving of myself and work, as now the Diary seems to be used: by a psychiatrist as a study of growth for his patients, as a lesson in autobiography by Harvard, as the subject of a seminar on the Poetics of Science. . . .

You will receive notice of a newsletter from University of Ohio library, on A.N. and her Circle, which will enable us to follow the activities of our friends. So please tell me if there is anything you want commented on, what you are working on, what you wish highlighted.

May I quote your letter on illuminating life? Thank you warmly for your understanding.

Letter from Frances Field:

I was so pleased that you wanted me to have the third volume of your Diary! Like the other two, which I also have, it is a window onto an unfamiliar landscape that would seem infinitely remote but for your presence there.

Whenever we have come together, over the years, you appear to me little altered from the shy, ethereal girl of my earliest memory. It is in accordance with that picture of you that your Diary should have been a sanctuary for the exploration of your inner being, the unassailable retreat from which you regarded the storm and stress and strivings of those who lived outside in a world you never made.

But once again, as I read this latest volume, I am struck by the dualism I would have barely glimpsed but for the Diary: the girl and woman who has given herself with such passion and generosity to life, to complex—and often terribly demanding—relationships; to the fanning of the creative spark perceived in others; to the guidance of the lost and confused through the labyrinth of self; to filling material needs when her own were as urgent; to the struggle to bring what she herself had created into the light of day. This is the other aspect of the Anaïs I thought I knew. Together they make of both the inner and the external life a work of art.

I know I'm not the first to have been impressed by this mutually creative duality, but perhaps for me it has a special force because my myopic picture of the private, contemplative Anaïs was a personal, rather than a literary conception. . . .

It has seemed quite natural that you should have given to me to read at this time the volume which ends with the years that saw the end of my marriage and the beginning of my own long, fumbling voyage toward self-knowledge. As I read how Martha Jaeger had illuminated a stage of that journey for you, I realized—I think for the first time—how much you were offering me when you suggested that I take my pain and confusion to her. I was too impatient and impermeable then to be able to undergo analysis—and when I read what you have written, I can't help comparing my own half-lived life with yours, seeing you as one of the rare individuals who has fully realized her potential, and recognizing how long, how arduous—and how productive—was your struggle to know yourself, without which, I believe, that realization could not have come about.

Thank you again for thinking of me. How fortunate I am to have a friend I can meet, and meet again in her books even though time, space, and divergent lives keep us apart!

I accepted Dr. Newcomb's invitation to meet with the Stanford students because we had corresponded on the relations between art and science. I was interested in finding in science new metaphors, new symbols as equivalents to psychic and psychological discoveries. I cannot say I understood the principles of integrated circuits, but I was fascinated with the concept of miniaturization, the amazing reduction of powerful conduits to so small a size that one needed a magnifying glass to see them. I was amazed by the jewel beauty and intricacy of integrated circuits. The equivalent idea of compression and condensation in writing had been an obsession with me, how to match writing to new forms and new rhythms of thought, and new dimensions. This is the theme I expected to thrash out with the students. But somehow the connections were not made. They questioned me on the creative process. We did agree that in science as well as in creation there comes a moment when the old formulas and calculations cannot help you. You have to make the leap into the unknown, and there begins invention and creativity in science. Someone always dares to make this leap beyond acknowledged methods. I do not know whether the science students feel that they can only discuss integrated circuits with scientifically equipped, trained technicians, and whether the principles could be related to the principles of creation in writing. All I know is that the concrete existence of this unbelievable reduction of power and connecting links is an inspiration to modern writers. That these new forms, structures and almost invisible creations must have their effect on language. The subject was left in suspense.

Letter to Marguerite Rebois:

I can hardly believe myself that I spent three days in Paris inside the Hôtel Pont Royal constantly interrogated by journalists. I went out only with my publicity agent to my publisher's home to meet more critics or to go to the radio station. If I had called you to say I could not see my friends I would have felt worse. . . . Personal friendships, home life sacrificed to public life— but as this is against what I believe, I will learn to control it. I am not fond of public life—as you know. But I am so happy that I have received all a writer can dream of—all the love I gave has been returned. Because of the response to Diary One the second [volume in French] will come out in March. It is *vitally important* that you tell me now what I asked you a long time ago: shall I change Jean Carteret's name? Is there anything in Volume Two that would injure him? I have no desire to hurt anyone. If you do not wish to contact Jean, please give me his address. I will write to him.

As I remember, your last letter was a happy one.

Who would have thought the only walk I would take along the houseboat's place on the Seine would be with a journalist carrying a tape recorder and a camera!

This is not good for the real artist—and it is the danger of succeeding. One has to have the courage to refuse it and return to work and privacy.

Fortunately I have no taste for it.

One of the longest jobs I had to do was to talk with Pierre Lhoste at "Radio France Culture." If you hear any of it let me know. It took hours—all morning in fact. In Germany they made a one-hour television show—it took two days.

The lectures are frustrating. They are the opposite of personal and intimate friendship. Only a passing glimpse of persons you would like to know better. The public life is the opposite of what I believe in.

This year was all life in the world, and I long for quiet to work on Volume Four.

I feel I can no longer be prevented from communicating with the world by destructive criticism.

Psychologist Sarnoff Mednick of Michigan University developed a test for creativity based on ability to make association between things which might not appear related at first thought. Drive toward novelty creative. Aversion to novelty anticreative.

Children named after me.

"But your special gift to the reader is a rare articulation of what the nerves feel."

Beginning friendship with Sharon Spencer.

From a letter to a university that exhibited my personal letters without permission:

It was kind of you to write me. . . . Let me explain my attitude: If a friend or a publisher sells my letters during our association and while we are still corresponding, without having the courtesy to advise me so that I may place a restriction on them, I consider it a breach of friendship, and I cease all correspondence. Such actions may ultimately deprive libraries of the very material they wish to collect.

Among writers just now there is much talk about not writing any more letters. . . .

If a stranger sells you a letter, I cannot control that, but I expect to be protected by the ethics of librarians. It is a matter of ecology. If we lose confidence in our librarians, we will stop writing letters. One has to create a climate favorable to the new crops. . . .

It seems important to me that all of you should protect your writers from damage if you wish to benefit from their productivity. For the sake of the very works we give you, the books we write, we need confidence, trust and peace of mind. Otherwise you damage the very source of the works. . . .

Ian Hugo's latest film is called *Apertura*.

From an underwater grotto the "guru" arrives to preside over birth from a mineral cave, then to guide the newborn, first through endless doors and corridors, then monstrous jaws and barricades that cause the fragmentation of the woman. Then she emerges from the test by fire, saved and made whole again by water and the guru, who continues on through the final apertura.

The newsletter edited by Richard Centing arrived. It is titled *Under the Sign of Pisces*. It is a neat blue-green pamphlet. It contains reviews, news of publications, articles by McEvilly and Laurens Vancrevel, a description of the documentary film on Henry Miller. It announces Benjamin Franklin's bibliography of my work. It is intended to give news which includes the activities of my friends. I call it "the Café in Space." I hope it makes a link between all of us who have common interests. Writers are invited to contribute. Some reviews are quoted in part.

Richard Centing invites correspondence, information on publications, films, lectures. Later, I hope, we can have photographs and dedicate each number to a different writer. Special events like celebrations, commencement talks, famous visitors, will be described.

It is so difficult to sustain links between us because of great geographic distances. We do not have time to write long letters. But many friendships have formed around my work, many connections.

Richard is a very meticulous librarian, very precise and well informed. He will make a good editor.

Letter to John Pearson:

I was told today that I have a tumor which is too dangerous to operate on and they will try radiation. This means I have to curtail all my activities, conserve my energy, and cannot keep my promise for January 15. Forgive me! I was only told today. I was looking forward to seeing you, to seeing Dr. Stone and the others. . . .

Radiation means reduced energy and intermittent stays at hospital. This detailed letter is for you. Officially say only what is necessary to explain my absence.

Letter to Jean Chalon:

Shocked to hear of the death of Louise de Vilmorin through your praise of her. I knew her well at one time, admired her, and tried to see her the first time I went to Paris. Because we could not meet I disguised her name in the Diary. You will find her in *Under a Glass Bell* and in *House of Incest,* which I am sending you today. Strange that when I met you [in Paris], it was of the *lignée* of Giraudoux and of Louise I thought. I meant to ask you if you knew her. She must have loved your writing as much as you did hers—what separated us was not knowing how she felt about my descriptions—not hearing from her, and fearing her displeasure, for one never knows how one's portraits affect others. In a way it was sweeter to hear of her death through your poetry than in any other way, for she deserved such a salute.

Letter to Richard Centing:

Born [under the rising sign of] Libra (!)—justice—I get concerned about those who *need* to be written about—for instance Rank's *Journal* and his books more than Henry Miller's magazine, *The Booster,* and for example the Poverty Theater in Dallas, Texas, who are doing a dramatic reading of Volume One. People are a little tired of the Miller-Durrell-Nin triangle—and we have other configurations!

I'm deluged with news.

Grolier Book Shop at Harvard—Gordon Cairnie—very aged now and ill—

was like Gotham Book Mart's Frances Steloff. Carried my books from the very beginning. In honor of his birthday in August, *Antioch Review* is bringing out a number about the Grolier Book Shop with photographs and a page written by all his writers—so perhaps we could comment on that. Elsa Dorfman came today to take photographs for that and for a collection of poets and writers being completed by Dr. Walter Grossman for Boston University Library. Robert Creely, Allan Ginsberg, Denise Levertov, Robert Lowell, Charles Olson, etc. It is Mr. Cairnie's seventy-fifth birthday.

It all began after New Year's with moderate bleeding. I went to the Kaiser Clinic for a checkup. One checkup led to another, and Friday the 23rd I knew they found a large tumor in the uterus. The alternatives were radiology or high-mortality surgery which would leave disfiguration.

What kind of disfiguration?

"You would be left with two open holes and a bag for evacuation."

I hurried the doctor because a friend was calling for me and I didn't want him to hear. I met him in the hall. I didn't tell him all. (Disfiguration—a cripple—end of my life.) But when we got home I did weep.

When I arrived in New York Sunday night I felt doomed. But when I saw Dr. Parks, the gynecologist who operated on me a few years ago, I felt more hopeful. He said the tumor was small, contained; my general health good, no loss of weight or fatigue. I had 75 percent chance of getting the tumor healed by radiotherapy. Slowly, I grew calmer. My spirits rose. I saw Dr. Bogner. We discussed illness and my image of the tumor as "worry" or "irritation." I said my psychological state was so good, it would help. I keep busy responding to correspondence, all of it loving and giving me strength.

When I arrive at the Presbyterian Hospital it is the baby hospital in whose cellar the X-ray machine is located, so I suffer to see children in wheelchairs, heads shaved, with black pencil marks indicating where the radiation must be focused—for tumors—cancers, etc. I pass beds being wheeled to the radiology department, old, sick, infirm people who look near death.

At 9:15 I enter the radiation treatment room. It is a yellow room.

The machine is huge. The nurse cheerfully focuses it on my pelvis. Then she turns it on. It is deafening. From the first day I decided to close my eyes and help the radiation. I achieved what I call spiritual radiation. As I lay there in the bright yellow room, under the huge yellow machine, and it started the loud noise I had been warned about, I closed my eyes and began seeing scenes of beautiful, happy, joyous moments of pleasure. The noise became the exaggerated whirring of a projector.

Scene One:

My phantom lover takes me in his Ford Model A up along Riverside to look at a silver birch tree. He is thin, agile, intensely alive.

My lover and I are driving through the canyons, stop by the Colorado River—and plant a small tree by its shore. We make love on its sand. We make love on the desert.

My lover lands in Acapulco, the early Acapulco. The planes land on the beach. There is no airport. We live in a small house on top of a rock where grand hotels are built now, with a dazzling view.

We drive through the jungles of Mexico.

We visit Chichén-Itzá.

We swim.

We build a house.

The six minutes are up.

Tuesday, I am in Cambodia, in the courtyard of the hotel, having coffee, when the elephants walk in. I walk through Angkor Wat. The green of the moss, the white of mildew, the bone-gray roots, the wet and damp stones, the brittle dry stones, the dancers at night, the shower at the end of the show, the dancers in the bus, laughing. The smell of ripe fruit, of stagnant water, jungle—the quietness.

Not one image to discard—all of Cambodia—*all* of Japan except Tokyo.

The six minutes are up. I was hoping I would not run out of images. Every day, six minutes, for three weeks.

Today: Tahiti—all of Tahiti except one moment—when my lover forced me into an outrigger canoe, and we spilled, and I had to walk to shore on sharp coral.

Cut—return to fiestas—Tahitian fiestas—Mexican fiestas—Moroccan fiestas. Save Morocco for tomorrow!

The mail pours in. It is all love, praise or learned interpretations. *Space, Time and Structure in the Modern Novel* by Sharon Spencer. A book in Spanish from Cortázar. Books. Manuscripts to read.

My phantom lover spoke of how he would die if I did—that we must die together—on a plane, while traveling.

The wintry taxi ride to 168th Street: Presbyterian Hospital. Every morning at 8:30 the taxi waits for me. I see the big ships anchored. They are beautiful. Some all white, and some black and red. But the buildings on the right are ugly, and the highway is cluttered with discarded cars left to disintegrate. Burned, twisted or merely abandoned to scavengers.

The radiation was weakening me. Each day I felt less strong. But the film lasted. The South of France, the Italian Riviera, Portofino. . . . Sun. Water. Dancing. Swimming. Tahiti I dwelt on—always with my phantom lover.

On MacDougal Street I found long Indian velvet dresses of beautiful colors, blue and aubergine. They made the weakened body seem less ill. I see few visitors. The [Michel] Fabrés because they came from France and were only in New York for a day. Marianne Hauser, Marguerite Young.

I have to give up appearing at Erika Freeman's class at Bennington. She is using the Diary to teach.

Each time I return to New York, I tell Dr. Bogner the same thing: "I want one life."

February, the month of hospital visits. Each patient clear in my mind. The sullen river. The noisy machine. The cheerful nurse. Dr. Trotter, whom I annoy a little with my impatience to leave for Los Angeles, but she was trained at UCLA so she believes it is the sun.

At eight I am dressing—white boots, white stockings, white wool dress, white beret, white coat. I go down for mail. The mail is almost always interesting. The usual amount of "read my enclosed poems, read my story"—but also letters from new readers, love letters and better and better reviews. I take them with me. A taxi comes every day and takes me on the speedway to the hospital.

It is not the Yellow Submarine—it is the Yellow Machine. I looked at it this morning, at the wires, plastic cones, at the funnel and the buttons, questioning the nature of its healing powers. When I lie there and the noise starts, the reverie (*rêve dirigé*) is not all beauty, love, sun; there are shadows. The end of it this morning was the phrase: T. is a desperate woman.

Dr. Bogner picks this up—ever alert—ever aware. Why T.? T. the failure, failed to become a movie star, failed in marriage and love affairs, no longer young—accident prone—car accidents, freak accidents.

A.N.: But my life is just the opposite!

DR. B.: Yes. Precisely because of that do you feel guilt toward the failure—guilty for succeeding.

A.N.: When the tumor happened I thought: Why *now*, when all my wishes are fulfilled?

DR. B.: You compared them—success, tumor.

To help the radiation I cast out irritation—shadows—but I thought of T.

Worked on filing reviews—on scrapbooks. Correspond with Orville Clark, friend of Wayne McEvilly teaching at Missoula, Mont. Letter from Beatrice Harris.

Writing to console an unhappy love: I found every sorrow dealt by love superior always to nonlove.

Outward facts differ, but *feelings* are similar, the women write me.

Volume Two out in paperback.

Swallow Press wants preface to novels.

I do not need to be introduced anymore. And people are getting tired of the same names. Neither Miller nor Durrell understands the novels. I have younger and more penetrating critics.

Correspondence with Laurens Vancrevel.

I am responding to X-ray treatment and hope soon to be back in L.A.

Letter to Frances Field:

Because of ill health I cannot attend your memorial service for Caresse Crosby, but I am enclosing one of Caresse's last letters, a few days before her death, showing her pleasure at the tribute I paid her. I feel it is in this way she wanted to be remembered. I wish some of this portrait could be read to maintain her forever young.

Letter from a French painter:

One night living seemed so difficult, so painful, that death, the only forgetting, the only rest, seemed the only solution. I returned to Geneva with this serenity which comes when body and soul have howled too long and nothing else is possible. One must either push upward violently like the deep-sea diver to rise to the surface, or else drown. I started on the second choice. I had bought your Diary two days earlier. I opened it and began to read, and from the very first lines, your thirst for life, your passion for life warmed me. You were there in the room. I did not finish the bottle of sleeping pills I intended to finish. . . .

Letter to Richard Centing:

About psychoanalysis. *Yes*—it is the spiritual discipline of today, more important than any religion, it is the only way for us to achieve wholeness and growth, to relate conscious and unconscious as they once were by faith. It is our modern way to faith. I believe in it as a philosophy and metaphysics. What violence could never achieve, understanding does. It is not a luxury. It is a matter of finding the right person (as we once had to find the right guru, or priest, or wise man). There are clinics. I consider it the most beautiful of experiences next to love, the key to all other experiences. . . .

The treatment was over. I was examined. Dr. Parks and Dr. Trotter were satisfied. But it was not over. In three or four weeks I must return to have a capsule of radiation inserted in the vagina. For that I have to stay in the hospital a week.

[Spring, 1970]

Los Angeles at last. Convalescence, with the beautiful view before
my eyes, the hills, the lake, the mountains. Dr. Weston comes faithfully
to give me injections. Slow recovery.

Letter to Henry Miller:

All those meditations and mantras must have been effective, for I am on
the way to recovery and by April may be all well. Thank you for helping
radiations. While under X-ray machine with a fearsome noise six minutes a
day I was able to pretend it was a projector, close my eyes and run a film of
only beautiful or happy images.

Don't you remember we read *The Bright Messenger* in the forties? I called
the young astrologer that (the one in the Diary).

I'll have to send good radiations for your problems now!

I wrote for *Merian,* a German magazine:

The characteristic aspect of the women of New York is that they are in
motion, perpetually active, and that one would have to photograph them at
a speed used for ballet dancers or athletes. Coming from above, say a helicopter, we see first on the twenty-fourth floor of one of the highest glass buildings facing the United Nations, Mrs. Millie Johnstone, who initiated the first
Japanese Tea Ceremony School in New York to counterbalance the hectic,
frenzied activity. In her apartment, one of the most beautiful in New York,
decorated with some of her own tapestries evoking the Bethlehem Steel Works
of her husband, with collages by Varda, with wool rugs from Peru, and with
a view of the Hudson which seems like a view from a transatlantic plane,
one room is shuttered by a trellis of wood and frosted glass, subdued and
simple: It is a Japanese room, in the austere classical Japanese tradition.
A low couch, filtered light, a platform covered by tatamis for the tea ceremony, the utensils, the pot, the cup, the brush, the spoon, the napkin, the
wafer. She dispenses the calm and serenity of the ritual in a blue kimono.
Having been a dancer she is very graceful, and her New England profile
melts into the formal design expected of an Oriental stylization. She feels
that modern man and woman need to learn repose and meditation to sustain
themselves in a city of frenzy.

Uptown, in a private house, in an apartment which opens on a backyard as some of the private houses still do in New York, sits a chic, slim, attractive woman, Dr. Inge Bogner. Sitting in a deep, modern plastic black and white chair, knitting, speaking in a soft voice, with lively, keen expression and the most outstanding knowledge of semantics, she wields an influence over the life of New York on two levels which throw their cumulative power in a widening circle difficult to measure. She treats the neurosis spawned by the city, every day, every hour, creating a circle of sanity, of renewed strength, for the city of New York is like a vast computer, ruthless to human beings. She advises young men in trouble with their draft board, parents who do not know how to be parents, creative people defeated by commercialism, the confused, the lost, the discouraged.

She was born in a small town in Bavaria. Her father was a doctor reputed for his liberalism. Her second activity is in politics, so that her teachings, her psychological insights are not only applied in her office, individually, but she acts out the commitments they point to. Not theory but practice. She has participated in marches, has walked the streets of her neighborhood seeking votes. She is a woman in action, in harmony with her insights.

Now we travel to the Village, west on notorious Bleecker Street, beyond the cafés and the rock and roll nightclubs, where the antique shops begin, arts and crafts boutiques. We are visiting America's greatest writer, Marguerite Young. Art is the night life of the people. Marguerite Young is the describer of the American subconscious, just as James Joyce was of his own race. She is totally committed to the pursuit of this oceanic unconscious night life. Her apartment is all in red and filled with collections of dolls, angels, tin soldiers, a circus horse, mementos, sea shells, Indian necklaces, a children's paradise. The walls are covered with books. Already celebrated for the classic *Miss MacIntosh, My Darling,* she is modest, continues to teach, eats at drugstores, converses with anyone at all, lives most intensely within the book she is writing so that you are taken into the world she is exploring at the moment, its associative infinities. This earthy-looking, plain-spoken Middle Western American wafts you into spatial semantic games, elasticities of wildest imagination. For America who only looks at its day-action face, this oceanographer of the deeps is a phenomenon. When she works, the pages cover all her floors, furniture, bookcases, divans, couch, chairs. One day they will fall over the city of New York, outshining the paper rain for the astronauts.

A professional pianist is practicing for a concert in a studio in New York. She is a tall and handsome woman. But she is best known as Xavore Pové, the woman who writes about astrology for *Harper's Bazaar* every month. The monthly horoscopes are written with imagination and poetry, and even when they do not necessarily fit the person, one wishes they did. It is a destiny, a life designed by an artist and preferable to reality, for its ambiguity allows for surprises.

On New Year's Eve she is the only one who practices spilling melted lead into cold water and reading the modern sculpture hieroglyphs, as predictions. She has studied minerals, herbs, health foods, and relates astrology to other knowledge, music, chemicals, jewels. I would trust her portrait of anyone, for like the lover, she sees the potential self. She is herself born in the sign of our age so should be able to read its intentions.

In another penthouse lives an even more symbolic figure of New York women, for she lives in luxury without serenity, and writes books of poems between telephone calls, hairdresser and dressmaker appointments, frivolities, social activities. She is young and beautiful, graces the pages of *Harper's Bazaar,* is restless, whirling, hectic, paying attention only for sixty seconds, starting a hundred new lives a day, wishing to live in an orange grove in California, to be back in Hong Kong or Cambodia, seeing everyone who has a name, dropping in on her little girl with her governess while they take air in the park, saying she cannot write poems all day, so she studies Chinese exercises and writes about them, about sea shells, is everywhere, knows everyone, never rests anywhere, like a female hummingbird whose hum, the poem, she must write how and when? One does not know. When she calls up it is a cry of distress, typical of New York too, for it is repetitious: New York is a poison (ambition), one cannot believe in friendship. Life is not real (in New York)—"I am lonely!" everyone admits over the telephone, behind the gusto, the glitter, the metallic surface, the glamour, the activity. The poem comes out smiling, witty. It is a sport to smile, glide, propelled by what? whom?

John Pearson prepares a beautiful book, *Kiss the Joy as It Flies* (quote from Blake), of his photographs and quotations from my work and from Loren Eiseley, whom I admire.

A long interview for *Mademoiselle* with Susan Edmiston.

Working on editing Diary Four, which is concerned with my faith in the young.

Letter to a French reader:

I have been so long away from France it is easier for me to write in English. I hope you can read English. I want to thank you for your letter, which only illness prevented me from answering sooner. I am grateful for your appreciation of the Diary and hope you will like Volume Two as well. I liked your saying *"la nostalgie du premier âge, du premier soleil."* . . .

It is difficult to know what to leave out, too much editing might spoil the spontaneity. No, I do not wish to convert the Diary into a *memoire*, because immediate impressions have a life which memory cannot re-create. I never tamper with what I felt at the time. It would falsify everything. I hope my editing will grow wiser with each volume. Are you a writer that you know so much about pruning? I like your saying I seek transparence rather than the truth.

Answers to questions sent to me by an interviewer:

The problem is not to separate masculine or feminine traits. It is to find out who and what we are. Some women have more of what we once called masculine traits than others. Some men have gifts for what we once called feminine. It would be good to eliminate these terms and use psychological ones. Some personalities will always be dependent; some men think irrationally, some women are combative. I don't think we should blame social mores or men for our predicament. The professional inequalities are true enough, but if we attack man, when so many men have helped women, we are in danger of losing the love of man. I love man. I have found as many men helpful to me as I have found selfish, egotistical men. I have also found destructive women, and my file of "bitchy" distorted, hostile reviews is equally divided between men and women. If we stopped using masculine-feminine, we might come closer to the truth about ourselves. I think the most courageous thing to do today is to conquer ourselves from within—not blaming others.

I do not believe in erasing differences. It makes for monotony. I believe in the couple—in two people, man and woman, or man and man, woman and woman, who set out to find a balance between each other so as to meet the problems of life. For this they have to accept not *fixed* qualities but the quality of sensitive fluctuations. Men and women have days of courage, days of weakness, days of dynamism and days of confusion. We need interdependence. Whenever any *one* person has attained too much power, we can see the imbalance (leaders), and they cease to live *with* others. We have to work out our liberation through love and mutual effort. There is already too much hostility and aggression in the world. I wish women would stop giving birth while there are starving children in the world.

Weakness, dependency, inability to think rationally, are clichés equally applicable to men. But women have not had the problems our culture caused in man, which is the linking of his power as a man to his sexuality. This is what has caused his "ego." Woman does not feel she is a failure as a woman if she fails professionally.

I do not consider dress or homemaking a feminine attribute. I like men who care for their dress as much as women. To deny our need of beauty is to add to the ugliness of the world. I like to do anything that gives pleasure to the eye. I also like the men who design, who decorate, who paint, who are artists.

We must not eradicate any quality just because it is associated with femininity. We have to live by our own standards. That is liberation. Real liberation is being true to what one is.

The current feminine movement is not yet clearly defined. I don't believe in separatism or violence.

My answer is all through the Diary: psychoanalysis as the only way to remove cultural patterns, childhood brainwashing, and to know one's self.

As for devotion: There is no difference between my helping of artists or any handicapped oppressed people. I am for creation and will always help creation wherever I see it. Today I see it in woman. I was always identified with the black revolution as well.

I do not regret the efforts I spent on Miller. They were a symbol of what the world should do if they expect creativity to survive. Not helping anyone, which was the attitude of the Establishment, and still is, is what created the young's hatred of competitive, selfish commercial goals.

It is the young who understand me.

There is no possibility of fulfillment or liberation by war. I will not declare war against man any more than against other races. We can only be liberated by joining forces.

Plenty of women have abused their attributes of beauty, as plenty of men have abused their power in the world. But we will widen the chasm of misunderstanding when we should be annihilating it.

Woman's difficulties have been her own responsibility. She did not express herself as a woman. She did not learn to win over man to become an ally rather than a tyrant. The problem of liberation is not woman's alone, it is racial, universal, man's as well as woman's.

Someone said: "The job of being man is a hard one. If we have no sympathy for his problems, he will not have any for ours. We have to gain man's understanding."

Letter to Dr. Martí-Ibáñez:

As I worried you, writing during a night of insomnia, I must tell you I am well again. X-rays worked and soon I will have my energy again. Two months wasted on illness! I know how impatient you must get with your eyes, as you love to read and write. I hope your eyes are better. I heard you highly praised by a Dr. Otto Neurath who spoke of your vast learning, the beauty of *MD* magazine, the incredible scope of your books. Did I tell you I read all of your history of medicine? I never would have read this written by someone else, but your gift as a writer makes history colorful, with all the themes you weave around medicine, such as the chapter on Maurice Utrillo—or literary men. Today I think you are the only Renaissance man I know. How do you find time for all this learning and practice as well? Now I have to work on Volume Four—I am way behind.

Just wanted to wish you all blessings and admiration.

[Summer, 1970]

My French publisher asked me to come to Paris for the publication of Diary Two. My English publisher also wanted me for the English publication of Volume Three, and offered to share expenses, so I went to London first.

Peter Owen and his wife, Wendy: He wears a yellow lace shirt and a tie embroidered with bangles. She came to the airport wearing a red feather boa in the style of Clara Bow. They drink until I fear they will disintegrate before my eyes. Wendy said in a genuine cockney accent: "You're a laidy. Peter should have married a laidy like you."

He wants to be at every interview to be sure I mention his publishing house. The interviewers do not like that. When the B.B.C. sent a car to my hotel to fetch me for an interview, Peter was waiting at the door of my hotel and came along.

The photographers are long-haired hippies, very much like those at home, and I get along well with them.

But the interviewers are as brutal and malicious as in the States. It was a woman who wrote the most hostile review. Cold, bitter, cynical. Because it was cold and I put my hands in my cape for the photographer, she said I was hiding my freckles to appear younger. The entire review full of venom.

At the Press Club, women were not allowed until a few months ago. I was met at the door by a man so old I was afraid he would die before my eyes. He said in a quavering voice: "You must realize this is a privilege, not a *right*."

I found the feminist women fiercer than the Americans because they have less freedom. Because I listened to his wife's griefs with sympathy, one critic wrote that I was a fierce liberationist.

The drinking is staggering. The interviewer who took me to lunch drank until he could no longer control the tape recorder. He wanted to know if Henry Miller was as good a lover as he purported to be in his novels.

Journalist at 10:45. Press conference at 12:00. Journalist at 3:00 P.M. Television at 9:00 P.M.

Yesterday a reception at 8:00 P.M. I lost my voice. And I heard about the death of Anna Kavan, who was all dressed to come to the reception and died holding a heroin needle after giving herself an overdose.

But my intuition is that the English in general do not understand or like my work. I met some exceptional young people from Cambridge and there we harmonized. The young are natural, warm and spontaneous. I met a young woman who worked for R. D. Laing. I would have liked to meet him.

Left London feeling it was the most hostile place for my work.

So grateful for Saturday in Paris because no one knew I was there and I was able to sleep, rest, walk along the quays looking at books.

I received direct praise from awesome people like Dominique Aury, for years a powerful figure at Gallimard, editor of *Nouvelle Revue Française*; from Mme. Piatier of *Combat*; from very experienced old journalists like Pierre Lhoste of "Radio France Culture." It was all serious and on a high level, the level I remembered and romanticized during my exile from France. The high quality of French criticism was of great help to writers.

At M. Charles Orengo's dinner, however, I experienced the same fear of that piercing critical ability. They passed all the recent writers in review with a severity which astounded me. Not just with the personal, insulting style of illiterate American journalists, but with a truly expert, learned dissection.

The next two days I spent with a French television crew, four young men. The sound technician, the cameraman, the makeup man, the director. They told me they were usually bored with the interviews. This time they listened and we became friends. We had a gay lunch at the Coupole. The makeup man took extra care, came on his own to make me up for the *Elle* photographer the next day. They asked for Diaries.

A cocktail party at Comte Christian de Bartillat. A modern salon. I met Jacqueline Barthe, who makes or breaks writers; the American representative of *Publishers Weekly*; an editor of *Combat*, and the editor of *L'Observateur*.

"Your diary is at my bedside table," says the young woman from *Votre Beauté*, Mme. d'Albray. All my dreams fulfilled. Yes, somewhere I have roots, I can talk about Bachelard, about Pierre Jean Jouve.

Coming out of the restaurant Closerie des Lilas on this summer evening and seeing people sit outside under the trees evokes a sense of sweetness of life, a moment of repose, relaxation. Those who sat there in the soft evening were alive in the prison, not driven by ambition.

Success in France has another meaning for me. I have carried for many years the love of French literature and the French way of life. To be ignored as a writer in France meant to be ignored by my intellectual and literary motherland. To be ignored in America was to be ignored by a foreign country. So when success came, my reaction was emotional: You can go home again.

Marie-Claire's family gave a party for me. Her mother, her aunt, her brothers, are all brilliant. The mother, widowed by the war, raised her three children. Very often Marie-Claire brings her translating problems to the dining table and the entire family collaborates. Their conversation is witty and sprightly. Her aunt is a specialist on Proust. Another aunt is head of the costume museum. The background is the one Proust's parents would have lived in. It was the style of rich textures, like heavy brocade curtains, glints of gold on the furniture, tapestry, an atmosphere of warmth.

They are delicious as a family. In my own mind I called them my French family.

When I was in my teens, shy and lacking in self-confidence, the *esprit français* frightened me. But this time, the renewal of my link with France proved I was no longer timid. I can parry, discuss, talk on any subject.

In an interview I described myself as a detective of the unconscious. Myself as a guinea pig, the "I" of Proust is also the "I" of others. The point of view of the woman is always combined with empathy for the point of view of others. I have no nostalgia for the past. The recording is simply a loving desire to preserve. For memory is the least reliable of all recorders.

Jean Chalon is a charming young man I met for an interview. We became friends. He was a close friend of Louise de Vilmorin. His books are witty and light-hearted. He writes for *Le Figaro*.

For two days, working with a German television company, directed by Georg Troller. The camera filmed me sitting at a café writing, at the side of the barge, walking the streets of Paris, walking through Louveciennes. Jeanne Moreau joined us, and she and I walked through the Bois and talked. We sat on a bench next to the lake. There was a mother duck with six baby ducks floating near us. Jeanne and I reached a point in our talk when we mentioned psychoanalysis. At that very moment, as soon as we had said the word, the mother duck fled in a panic, her six little ducks following her hysterically. Quack, quack, quack, quack. We laughed uncontrollably, and the camera slipped in between us and caught the laughter.

In Louveciennes we ran into trouble. I went to visit the owner of what was once my house. She now lives next door. The only one who was French in our crew came with me. I summoned all the charm I could and asked permission to enter, to film the house and the garden. I reminded her that I had lived there for years. It was locked and neglected. The iron gate was rusty and corroded. The old lady became furious, said she would never allow us in, that this is the new way places are burglarized by so-called television groups. So we had to stay outside, photographing me at the gate, and what we could see of the house. The shutters of the old lady's house were closed. Suddenly they opened and the old lady, as in a puppet show, sprang out and said if we did not leave immediately she would inform the mayor. The young Frenchman answered that he had seen the mayor and that the mayor knew I was a famous writer and should be allowed to visit the house. But the morning was spoiled. We walked through the streets of Louveciennes which have not changed, saw the old castle in which I had wanted to live, surrounded by a moat filled with swans.

We returned to Paris and drove to Villa Seurat (street of Henry Miller's studio). There memories assailed me. I remembered that Chana Orloff lived in the corner studio. That she made a sculpture of my head and gave it to Rank. That her studio was full of pregnant women, that she wanted a child so much, her sculpture finally seemed to induce one, to become a reality. With this obsessional expression of

143

maternity, the irony was that when it was fulfilled the child turned out to be a cripple in a wheelchair and her maternity could only be expressed in nursing.

I walked along the cobblestones to the end of the impasse where we found Henry's studio (the studio I found for him in 1934). This, too, we were not allowed to visit. He had a large room with a window which spanned two floors. The balcony was used by painters as storage space. The bedroom gave on the street. I was photographed in front of the door, or on the way out. It was a famous street. Chaim Soutine lived there once.

We walked around the Place Clichy, but I could not find the street on which Henry had rented a workman's apartment, small, new and clean.

Troller had invited Michel Simon to meet us by the Seine. A scene took place which was unrehearsed. Michel Simon was the one I had rented the houseboat from. He had cut a big coal barge in two, topped half of it with a glass studio which gave a complete view of the Seine, but the monkeys he loved so much escaped along the quays and he had to move to the country. I rented the houseboat for ten dollars a month. During our conversation about the past, I asked Michel Simon if he knew what had happened to the houseboat during the war. I had tried very hard to find it, had gone up to the place described as the cemetery of houseboats.

Michel Simon answered: "During the war the Germans amused themselves by shooting it full of holes until it sank." The scene caused me pain which showed in my face.

I sit at the Café du Dôme writing while the German television camera photographs me from the sidewalk. I have never written in cafés. But Troller thought it would be a good atmosphere. So I wrote: "Twenty years later, or thirty years later, I am walking the streets of Paris not with Henry or Rango or Artaud, but with a television équipe. At that time I wrote every day. That is no longer so because of my activities. I always wrote without premeditation, free association. On the bus, or on the plane, the Diary, which everyone is reading. No longer secret. It has the opposite effect of *Werther*, it prevents suicides. But the Diary will never be finished.

"I am thinking of Michel Simon, who does not believe women love him, who by this method extracts great declarations of love: Of course I love you. And when he has had enough assurance of love, he looks happy, tender, romantic. The women do love him.

"Will I ever return to Paris? I feel at home in Paris. Their over-criticalness, which frightened me in my thirties, no longer frightens me."

Nothing crossed out, no regrets, no desire to return to the past.

I never saw the film. I made so many television interviews, but the only one who presented me with a copy was the Canadian Broadcasting Corporation. I never saw the one made in Germany during the Frankfurt Book Fair. I would have loved to have a print of the scene at the long table in the historic mansion.

It gives one a very sad feeling of ephemeral creation when one works so hard for two or three days and has nothing to show for it.

The journey back. As soon as I am alone in the airplane I find my real self again. I am not happy in public roles.

Letter to a French friend:

I do feel I escaped the danger that the Diary should be, as you say, *"qu'en fonction de Henry Miller."* Some critics, fanatical about Henry, . . . were biased—but others . . . seemed to treat it as more than that.

Letter to Richard Centing:

What a coincidence and what the surrealists called concordance. You take an interest in Anna Kavan and write wonderfully about her. I go to London and hear about her death. I talk with [her publisher] Peter Owen. I meet a man who has written a fascinating portrait of her, her life, her work. We are too late to dedicate a number of the newsletter to her, but your article sounds marvelous—and I'm so pleased you are writing. . . .

I am not surprised at the English review. They have always been obtuse about my work (as they are about woman in general) and I met there the ugliest of all women journalists. Even my visit did not dispel my impression except for the young again—a young man from *Cambridge* magazine and young underground paper—a different breed. I don't drive anymore and I hate automobiling, so I'm in sympathy with you. I love walking.

Letter to Renate Druks in Maui, Hawaii:

I was delighted with your letter describing voyage to the volcano, delighted with your new cycle—new story.

Was sorry you did not leave your film in care of someone in L.A. We all felt helpless. Raven [Harwood] called me. She has not yet found a distributor. I suggested Grove Press.

As soon as I came back from Europe, I went to work on Volume Four. I feel well. A big success in France—genuine—the critics, the mature and the young. Diaries going into paperback. But London as petty and peevish as ever—*avare*—that is what they are, stingy with everything, words, love, etc. The young are wonderful— . . . the men are old maids. But France! Walking the streets for two days, with television camera, to houseboats, cafés, Villa Seurat—all so lovely. Beautiful summer day.

Piccolo died suddenly and painlessly of bleeding ulcer at eleven—very old for a poodle—while I was away. I cried for two days. But a friend immediately found a baby Piccolo, four weeks old, who looks like his child. I call him Piccolino.

Letter to a reader:

When I'm working hard as I am on Volume Four, I usually give up letters and write only notes, but your long letters deserve an answer. Yes, I understand dualities in love, yes, I understand multilevels and multifacets—yes to all you say, to LSD, to wonder, to what gives you faith in America—the music—the young. I will someday give you a full description of LSD experience. It's coming soon, in the Diary. A writer only becomes miserly when he is working. I wrote part of LSD experience in *Collages,* gave it to Varda's daughter. So much to say—I understand your life, your moods, your loves, your enthusiasms. . . . No, you do not appear literary or philosophic—you always balance your human life, love, moods, reading ideas well mixed—yes, lyrical, and alive—the texture is good, fertile.

Letter to Charles Champlin, film critic of the *Los Angeles Times*:

I have always liked your articles on films, but I was moved to write you about your last one on *Myra Breckenridge* and *Beyond the Valley of the Dolls.*

146

It is the first time someone has come out boldly with intelligent distinctions between vulgarity and quality in erotic films. You have succeeded in expressing this difference, in exposing the profit motive underlying the trashy one. Everything you say is true and can be quoted whenever this subject is discussed. "Freedom involves responsibility, and fouling your own nest is classically irresponsible." I like your stressing the destructive consequences of burlesque, of baring monotonous clinical exhibits. I admire you for taking this stand which demonstrates that there are values and evaluations to make. I liked your comments on *Women in Love* and *Brotherly Love.*

Letter to a British critic:

I was very moved by your essay on Anna Kavan. It is written with insight and sympathy. It is well balanced, giving all the aspects and elements. It was fascinating for me. What you pointed out so well, what attracted me from the first, was the early control of the dream material (*Asylum Pieces* and *House of Sleep*), the surrealist quality. You studied her deeply and humanly, too—a fine portrait. By an ironic twist, when I was struggling to bring surrealism into American literature and I lectured and read examples, I had erroneously included her among American writers. But for years I mentioned her name and made people read her. Your study is very valuable and should appear uncut. Would you mind if I sent it to magazines I know?—Alas, not the best-paying ones. If you want me to do this, let me know. Otherwise I will return your carbon regretfully.

I liked your relating the work to the life, the life to the need of drugs, leaving in question whether drugs enhanced or enriched the source of images. How strange it is that drugless as I am, the dream literature has made me appreciate her writing as I have. You suggest *Asylum Pieces* was written before the drug habit—and *House of Sleep* also.

I have a great admiration for your understanding.

Letter to a reader:

I do not want to leave your letter unanswered, but I cannot write as fully as you wish me to because I am working. The answers to your questions lie in the Diaries—did you read only One? Shall I send you Two and Three? That is why I give all I have to the work. You *can* tell if the psychoanalyst is good. Analysis is not *all* painful. One discovers the *knot,* unties it, feels relieved and in control of one's destiny. Sure there are other hurts. After several sessions you should be clearer about what you are and feel. People do not will themselves into madness—madness is the illness. But neurosis is another matter. If all you expected was ·protection, care or love from analysis, it will not give you strength, it is true. Most of the effort is *yours* to make in order to achieve independence.

You are in a state of ambivalence as you well describe . . . but your effort is important even in finding the right way (person?).

Your letter was sincere and that is why I answered. But no one but you can give certain answers. And there are no general rules. Examine your choice. In your choice of analyst you may be trying to prove analysis is useless too or that you may not pass its test. Have faith. Please read the Diaries as progressions—fears, negativities, struggle to conquer them, a step forward, errors, but always forward. When you allow yourself to be negative, you add to the burdens of the world—and we owe all of us the effort to create ourselves.

Letter to Monika Kruttke:

When I was in Paris recently I expected every morning to hear a lovely voice say: "Hellooooooo . . . are you ready to meet the journalist?" I expected you to be downstairs, smiling and fresh and ready to translate and be patient with my dedications in books. Alas, no Monika. And Stock kept me so busy that I did not see my friends or even my cousin who lives there.

We did a television show, though, walking through Paris and embracing houseboats, sitting in [a] café and visiting Villa Seurat, which took two days and reminded me of our two days of television. Do please tell me how it came out, honestly, as I know you can do. Also I am concerned as to whether Mathias Wegner was satisfied with the page I wrote in such a hurry; was it what he wanted? Am I really a fan of his?—I did not want it to show too much. Paris and London were successful. I did a television [show] in London and another in Montreal, in French. And now I am working on Volume Four. I hope my books are going well, not only for myself but for all the trouble Dr. Wegner took. . . .

Personal interviews are the same everywhere, they always misquote you, and I do not know what good they do. I had a four-hour talk with [Jacques] Lanzman, the close friend of Sartre, for *Elle*. Our talk was most interesting but the final result (on tape, cut) did not seem so. . . .

If I had not been kept so unbelievably busy even Saturday and Sunday I would have telephoned you. . . . Do you have the women's liberation movement in Germany? It was strong in London. Hardly any in Paris. Do give me news. . . .

Robert Snyder says Germany liked the Henry Miller film very much. Is

that really so? Now he wants to make one of me, and I do not know quite
how to avoid it.

Letter to a French friend:

I wish we had had more time to talk together. I thought of so many things
after you left. Now while working on Volume Four I thought again of your
dislike of Rango-Gonzalo. I was wondering then if the role of certain personages does not play in my life the part of the shadow, as Jung called it, the
dark unconscious that one does not allow to be lived out (overly repressed).

I described this stifling and imprisoning goodness in *The Four-Chambered
Heart*. The only way out of it, the Catholic rigidities, was to associate with
the free ones—free to destroy, to take, to use, to rebel—doing it for you,
exorcising the devils, as it were. Rank acknowledged this possibility. Do you
remember *Four-Chambered Heart*? I am sending it to you just in case. . . .
Destructive rebellion. Of course that was a phase, but it is also a phase which
is taking place in the young here. They feel their life is ruled by such powerful Big Business tyranny, such immensely powerful economic interests, that
they get desperate and they burn a bank. I do not think we have had this
kind of rebellion in France. America incites it because it is the triumph of
power and money which drives the young to desperate means. I do understand your not liking Rango-Gonzalo. I feel you yourself are such an independent, such a free-within-yourself woman (am I right?), that you needed
no dark shadow to exorcise your imprisoned rebel. We only began to talk.

I hope you received *Art and Artist*. Let it be a gift. My agent tells me
several of Otto Rank's books are coming out in France. I was glad to hear
that. . . . I wanted to ask you more about the new critique. Otto Rank in
the last *Journal* is quoted as calling himself a "philosopher psychologist."
This kind of criticism seems naturally due. I wanted to ask you more about
France's phase of turning its back on psychology. Even prejudice against
psychoanalysis. The two are not inseparable. Psychology as philosophy is what
is permanent and not fallible. A way of understanding and interpreting even if
you wish to deny its therapeutic effects. Do you agree? Did you receive the
last Otto Rank *Journal*?

My trip to Paris was successful. I did a television program . . . with Jean
Chalon, walking to various spots and sitting at cafés. I hope it was good. *Elle*
will publish *Under a Glass Bell* story which was written about the Vilmorin
family, inspired by Louise, as was Isolina in *House of Incest*. I changed her
name in the Diary but have now written to her brother André to see if he has
any objection to my naming her. When I was in Paris I was told her life was
not a mystery.

The daughter of Robert and Gracia Aiken is baptized "Anaïs" in a Greek Orthodox church in Los Angeles. Lovely ritual, old bearded men dressed like Catholic bishops, tiaras, gold and red capes. The baby is bathed all naked in holy water, and the old women in black chanting as they have done for hundreds of years. The church white and blue. The phrase uttered: "Now you are illumined, now you are a child of light."

By choice I would not have elected to have another dog. But once I saw him, looking just like Piccolo, I was done for. Only Piccolino is not a pedigreed dog, he has no distinguished history, and for that very reason seems sturdier. I do not remember what age Piccolo was when I got him. He seemed the same size as Piccolino, but I do not remember that he chewed shoes, electric wires, snails, branches, rugs, pillows; nor that he decided where he wanted to sleep, either on my bed or among the shoes; nor that he asked for his breakfast, lunch and dinner at regular hours.

He is one big job, has to be watched every minute. I am glad when he is napping. The kennel though, far better than the New York shop, gave me a typed page of instructions. He gets a frozen meat loaf, which has wheat germ and soy sauce, and vitamins, and I am thinking of exchanging diet with him. He also gets drops of vitamins in his water. He is so full of pep; he chases butterflies, leaps in the air with imaginary games, chases birds, cats, is alert to every sound. He is so small, the garden seems like a jungle. I take him out to the movies. He cannot bark yet. His teeth are beautiful; he cocks his head when he is puzzled.

Letter to a reader:

I want to reassure you that I am the same, that I was able to survive, to work, to find love and communications with the world—one can. What you felt in Three was the difficulties. A friend called Volume Three "Survival." Everything survived: values, a certain kind of life and quality in my friends. So you will too. I know from the tone of your letters—you have an inner world, and that is the secret, to resist outer pressures. Someday we'll meet— when I'm in New York and you feel you want me to see your writing. New

York today is grimmer than in the Forties but all depends on friends, activities. It can be rich.

Thank you for writing me what you felt.

Letter to a reader:

I liked all you said about yourself and the Diaries. I was sorry you tore up your own diary; you express your thoughts and feelings clearly. I hope you will begin it again. I'm glad you feel I'm an affirmation of woman. This is a critical period for women, and never was it more important for them to have a firm core, an inner strength to avoid what more belligerent women are bringing on, revolution and war against man! That is why I'm hurrying with Diaries—as this may turn out to be the main theme, the growth of woman without loss of love.

Letter to a reader:

You are so right when you say: "narcissism which is but self-doubt." This argument always comes up with the Diary and I always refute it. A woman psychologist said it was the most exigent, demanding narcissism she had ever seen, striving for growth—and now because of letters like yours, I know it is useful to others!

Letter to Sharon Spencer:

To be absolutely truthful, when I first dreamed of converting the Diaries into a fictionalized form, I felt I had failed. The greater success of the Diaries, and the silence which greeted the novels, convinced me I was a failure as a novelist.

Analysis had made me so much more interested in the intimate knowledge of human beings; the novel seemed unable to achieve that. But the Diaries did. Do you know the Gaelic word *furrawn*? It means the kind of talk that brings strangers to intimacy. In that sense, I did not feel the novels conveyed such revelations, but I am happy that you think they do. Yes, I am terribly sorry I did not know you during the difficult years, also for your sake because I know in New York the most remarkable woman analyst, who is responsible for my expansion, and you could have known her. She is intelligent, sensitive, and has never made an error. We will talk about her. She enabled me to balance and integrate impossible extremes.

No, *Collages* does not represent a new direction. It was a game, a playful book. Not deep. Not developed in depth but in color and impressionism. . . .

No, I had no preconceived notion about the novels. All I knew was that the Diary could not be published, that the characters I described might be fictionalized to make publication possible, and that they became composites. The books evolved like the endless house of an architect whose name I cannot remember now—organically. When I finished one a new theme evolved, prolongations, I suppose really growing as the diary grew. . . .

Yes, it is the right time for women to be recognized. They have been kept in the shadow.

Not only women as writers, but women characters treated by men novelists. We have a great deal to talk about.

Letter to a reader:

Dreams. They are the key to the secret, unconscious life. . . . I am mailing you a book, *Collages,* in which I gathered up the dreamers I knew, those who could not share their dreams with others, or those who had gone too far in to carry them out, for as you know, I also believe in carrying them out. Have you read my *Novel of the Future?* There is a lot about dreams there. I can see from your letter that you are a pure dreamer, and I hope you listen to them, and live them out, and sometimes as one lives them out others begin to see what they mean (dream of houseboat, of the printing press, of contacting the world as a writer—all became action). Sometimes I make errors. I romanticize a character. It turns out ugly. But it is their loss, not mine. I am not poisoned by error. They are poisoned by their betrayal of their potential. Errors do not matter. We love. To love we need to see all of a human being and sometimes more than [he] can achieve. Then human love begins. We accept the defeat of the dreamer. It is important to sustain this faith that in [dreams] lies our secret, imbedded, concealed and most vital self.

Letter from Marguerite Young, writing as Esther Longtree, the character in *Miss MacIntosh, My Darling:*

Deer Anise,

Im sow glade ewe got my letter and enjoyed it. Iye toll wain ewe would not because wew wood knot now how tew understan my ornitheslogg (spelling, knot bird watching as ewe thing). Eye wirk sow hard like a dawg all day lung, all night lung, riting this missal tew ewe is my only relagsation. Eye hop ewe will forgive and forget it—like the old saying gows, it mustnot not disturb yore peace, bitt it's wat happened tew me, Eye am gone, the time was tew shirt to learn to rite, you sea, and yet eye tried. Ow, if only Eye was living in Gall-o-way in Northern Scottland with mists where the dead walk, eye wood bee happy, or if I was living in Cairo, or maybe in Tite Street whare you wood comb to see me with yore strawberry kolored hare like Ellen Terry, or else we wood both call on Oskar and take our english additore with us, also his wife, ore wee could go call on Alexander Pope sum afternon, push him in his sedan, and that is what is rong with this world all the way from Wapping to Wapping, we can't but eye thing I would bee happy if I could meet them awl over thare, am sure there is no wonderfull world like that, but thare shed bee when this whirled has gone, there were not enoff people in it, sow I don't belief in the populasion eggsplosion they are always tucking about, dew ewe? Well, Anaise, this be my lace letter for a lung time, so rest in peece. Sweets to the sweet, it will be riten on your tombstone.

Letter from Yanko Varda:

Chère Muse Horizon
Known in this vulgar
Planète as Anaïs
Excuse delay.

A group of 4 dancers, admirers of yours implore me to bring them and throw them at your feet. I ask 17 minutes of your time for the consecration. May I???

I am amazed by your diary. The more *"vous mettez votre coeur à nu,"* the more the innermost core is veiled.

You have been a high priestess of the Eleusinian mysteries in a previous life. . . .

Please let me know if this is possible.

Letter to Bebe Herring:

I could not write before. The Diary takes all my energy. And now September 3 I must go to Paris for television appearances. New York, September 17. Then back here [Los Angeles] where my peace and happiness are. Yes, California can still give trees, mocking birds, passionflowers, lakes, and pools . . . and sun. I understand the passage in your diary about need of the hero. If not the hero (the classicist is the one who conquers life, the romantic is the one who is conquered by life), at least the person who represents what you wish to become. As June was the free woman for me, and until then my freedom came from books, D. H. Lawrence. I am so happy he is being faithfully filmed. *Women in Love* is beautiful. *The Fox* was well done, but not as subtle. And now *The Virgin and the Gipsy*. I understand someone filmed *The Princess*. I hope you can see them. . . . When you have time, send me the definition of "Furrawn" again. I love the word and use it but do not remember exactly how you defined it. I want to write it on a card on my wall. I think that is the overall title of the Diaries . . . "Love."

[Fall, 1970]

Was greeted in Paris by a beautiful review in *Le Monde*. Françoise Wegener, who reviews foreign books, is a very attractive person, international, articulate, and full of insight.

Met with my French translator, Marie-Claire Van der Elst, who has Volume Three ready, and I will see her, her family and the translation Monday. Had a wish today that the books should sell without the help of publicity, and that I could stay at home to write quietly. Meeting the world is a strange challenge which I impose on myself to prevent my inclination to isolate myself. It has its rewards—marvelous friendships, such as meeting Françoise Wegener—but I resemble the soldier who is frightened of war and throws himself into battle to overcome his fear.

I rehearsed for a TV show and visited my relatives Count and Countess de la Taille. They live on the rue Henri Heine, where my father lived at number 27. So I passed by the house and was assailed by painful memories.

When I returned in the evening the Tuileries were having a *son et lumière*. The fountains were flowering and people were listening to classical music on the loudspeakers. It was a soft night. The beauty of Paris is indestructible. Now I am resting for a few minutes in my little room before going to Editions Stock and a TV show, see my translator, read the translation.

At Stock I found that Diaries are selling well and that they are planning to do other books.

Dinner with André Bay to plan for the future. Meanwhile I am reading translation and helping with phrases not clear to Marie-Claire, such as "What Patchen knows about sex fits in a thimble."

Had a nightmare that the sea drowned my house.

This is the quiet hour of my day from nine to ten A.M. Nobody goes to work before ten. Interviews succeed each other.

Swiss TV interview: We walk through all the old haunts.

I see John McLean, who put on a play based on the Diary in Dallas.

My room is full of flowers like that of an opera diva. The book shops lend me books, will not let me buy them, so I read the diary of Georges Simenon. Surprised at his reticence.

Letter to a reader:

Your question touched me—about affinities with France. I never lost mine because of the literature. I love Proust, Bachelard the philosopher, Cendrars, etc. I think it is a loss to be uprooted, but a loss which *can* expand our life, that is, instead of just being French, or American, you become all artist, a writer and international. Yes, if I were you I would *live* out all your French affinities which are in your blood—read all you can that is translated. It can only enrich you. To be of one country only today is not enough. I hope someday you can see France, Mauritius, Senegal. The more one explores countries which have formed our unconscious, the richer. My deepest affinity today, however, are the young Americans—the new generation. I have a deep faith in them. Yes, of course, send me your novel when you feel ready.

How French? I have a faint accent—I can talk and read French but no longer write it, and as you will see by *The Novel of the Future,* I think they are the best writers in the world (but that is a prejudice!).

Letter to Richard Centing:

I want to explain the matter of "executive." As my husband asked to be left out of the Diary, the times I talked about economic difficulties seem like a falsehood to those who find the connection. I cannot explain how this came to pass (the ups and down), but the legend of wealth (started by hippie friends in France for whom having a house, a car and a maid was "wealth") was such a falsehood that I never was able to extricate myself from its destructiveness. The house was rented, the maid cost ten dollars a month, the car was a small French car to go to work with, but to the eyes of Miller it was munificence and also, let us face it, a wish fulfillment. Marguerite Young's fantasy made me the Lady Bountiful who will take care of her when she is old and sick. She dreamed up this situation. Because of the Diary this seems like a paradox. Thus I am trying to dissipate this destructive myth. I know you will help me in any way you can. You have been very thoughtful and tactful and I do not want to make your editor's task difficult.

Letter to a reader:

I am overworking and so cannot answer your letter fully, but I appreciate your writing, and you have understood what I meant about liberation being very much from within, even under handicapped circumstances. My husband demanded not to be in Diary. He cannot bear publicity. It was not my choice. Yes, there is a difference between men and women, and it should be maintained or else it will be very monotonous. Woman is closer to her unconscious, but men who are analyzed or familiar with the unconscious can understand her better. Men are not logical, they rationalize their irrational impulses and make them sound logical. I am sure your husband would agree with that. No, I only practiced lay analysis for five months but I kept my interest in it and my only utopia is a belief that hostility and war could be modified by psychology. Nothing else worked! . . .

The self-direction came from an early consciousness of an inner life, which developed and became my direction. Our American culture was all extroverted and never encouraged this inner life. . . . Today I feel the climate is propitious for this inner journey because the extroverted one failed us.

Letter to a reader:

I understand how you feel about the Diaries and Paris. I must always have had a need not to see the ugly side of any place or person. I must always have created my own world and selected those who fitted in. But you know there *was* unhappiness in the Diary, too. Your life does sound difficult. Don't you think every experience has a dual aspect? I have known many selfish artists—and many unselfish women willing to play the role of audience, inspirer, protector. Soon you'll find out who you are and perhaps love a different person.

Of course I'm not the same Anaïs. I haven't changed basically, but now I'm a full-time writer, and when I'm not working, I'm traveling at the invitation of a publisher, or lecturing, or talking with students who find in the Diaries a key to their inner world. Yes, the conflict between political action and literature is always there. For me, it was answered when the Diary became useful to others. Unlike [Goethe's] *Werther,* it stopped two people from committing suicide. You'll find your own most useful role. But start with yourself as an individual and then you'll be effective in action. I hope you find yourself in Paris. It is easier there because people are not ashamed to attend to their growth—and this might make a better world.

If my activities are different now, I am the same in placing emphasis on intimacy, personal relationships, on understanding and nonviolence. I hope Paris gives you what it gave me.

Letter to a reader:

You are getting your own press. That's marvelous for poetry. For prose it grew too heavy and arduous a work. It took me eight months to hand-set *Winter of Artifice*. I wish Ohio Libraries could afford a different cover, by various artists [for the newsletter] . . . the monotony is disturbing and so many of my friends can draw, engrave or do lithography, and would do a cover. Perhaps later. . . .

Yes, I am interested, naturally, in the liberation of women, but the few I have met are warriors, and I can't work with them. More concerned with expressing hostility toward men. I would like more emphasis on the marvelous women we can admire and support, writers, artists.

Recently a woman, Bess Myerson Grant, spoke uniquely on war, exposing every company working for war, giving hard figures (she worked in Washington, she had the budgets), asking that we should not buy their products, from General Electric to Alcoa, Bulova, etc. I sent for a reprint and will send you a copy. She was beautiful on TV, serious and powerful. When I suggest on campus that they read women writers, I feel they will not do it. They prefer to waste ammunition on Miller, Mailer, and unjustly on D. H. Lawrence, who has to be placed in his time.

Letter to a reader:

It is not the love that people cannot respond to, it is anxiety and desperation within the love which people feel like the grasp of a drowning person. When I suffered such anxieties and fears people felt it and were fearful of it. The love, the quiet, sure, unpossessive love they can respond to. This excess is what I wish you had been helped with. I know what it is, and I know it destroys love. I hint at it in the volume I just turned in. Anxiety, I say, is love's greatest killer. It stifles it. . . .

So, like a good chemist, extract *anxiety* from love and you will have a happy reciprocated love. Separate the fear from the love. Examine what caused the fear and anxiety. You'll win. You're a beautiful and lovely person, you know that.

Letter to Sharon Spencer:

You are sensitive to my underlying moods! Yes, I seem to be going through a depression. It may be physical, fatigue, reaction to all that happened. Before

I came to New York I had been in the hospital ten days. I had a teaching engagement to fulfill. I turned in Volume Four. . . .

I am so glad you saw Dr. Bogner. She is an island of wisdom in a maddening world. The story of Mishima shocked me. I have read him, and could not detect the madness which threw him back into a Japan of the Middle Ages. . . .

I am just winding up photographs of the architecture of Lloyd Wright. Volume Four is again prophetic. I run away from New York toward nature (ecology) and meet two artists of stature, one giving beauty, the other joy. And then Mexico. Somehow, I have come to feel the city is poisonous to human beings. Not only physically but in other more subtle ways.

Letter to Harry Moore:

When one is in danger, one becomes aware of certain facts one does not consider at other times. Among them is how persistently America has denied me any recognition in spite of such good critical appreciation from people like yourself. It seems to me I have done enough work, yet I have nothing to show for it. At sixty-seven should I not be considered by the National Institute of Arts?*

Letter to a teacher:

All these beautiful letters from you, like smoke issuing from the fires of the book itself. No, your letters do not cheat the Diary because it is the same world. A continuity. It is merely the bulk of my mail, with such personal, intimate letters which cannot be neglected. At one moment, you speak of that moment reached in Fez, happening only when the external life matches or harmonizes with the inner one. Fez did. It matched the dreams, so I was able to unite them. That is why it is so important to create the outer life to match one's inner longings, so that they reach a marriage. Diary is being given at College of Psychologists as a map to inner journey. But even if that is true, people forget how much I struggled to make the outer world conform to my dream or image, discarding what did not belong and whoever did not belong, in order to create a harmonious world. It also explains why I often shut the door on TV and newspapers, the pollution by the press, which dwells only on the criminal side of human nature.

Received a beautiful letter from Orville Clark, actively teaching my books,

* Anaïs Nin was elected to the Institute in 1974.—Ed.

as well as others, as you are. What lucky students, to roam so freely through what you and Orville think the best rather than the dusty lists made a hundred years ago. It [was] not an end to introspection, I thought, it was the bridge between inner and outer. This I had trouble conveying to students recently at Philadelphia. They can only see either/or, and erect barriers. It is when the circulation is established that miracles happen.

[Winter, 1970-1971]

My publisher insists upon permissions for the portraits I make. So I asked to see Edmund Wilson and he gave me a rendezvous at the Princeton Club. Imagine the setting of another period. We met in the cocktail room, under a dim lamp. He looked pale and frail. He told me he had had a heart attack and his activities were limited. I went through the ritual I invented. I gave him a pencil and said: "You can cross out whatever distresses you. If you cross out too much, I leave out the portrait altogether." He chuckled as he read parts I thought would anger him. He said: "I didn't realize you looked upon me as a father." He only crossed out references to Mary McCarthy because, he said, "she can make a terrible fuss."

I was beginning to feel compassion for his age and illness. I knew my portrait was harsh and I felt he was generous and mellow. I was surprised. The rest of the time we spent on lively talk about a French writer he admired, about his illness and his editing of his diary, which is appearing in the *New Yorker*. He wrote me a letter that he had forgotten how charming and stimulating my company was! Of course, I never asked him why, after praising *Under a Glass Bell*, he never mentioned me again.

While in Paris, I had sent Gore [Vidal] a telegram, suggesting we meet and explaining why. He came from London. We sat at the bar of the Pont Royal Hotel, familiar to him. I offered him a sharpened pencil and the usual words: "You can cross out whatever distresses you. If you cut out too much I take the portrait out altogether." He began to erase hesitantly. He crossed out the names of the writers he admired in his teens. He crossed out all references to his mother "because she would make trouble." They were all statements made by him, so I could not see how she would make trouble for me.

I was shocked by his appearance. He is only forty or forty-five but looked older, dissipated, worn. His smile is forced, a rictus. He has lost all his beauty because his expression is cold, malicious, strained. He is playing roles. He is false. I let him talk because it was the talk of a madman, so full of hatred toward everyone. No matter who I mentioned to make conversation, he would tear apart, find the worst thing to say about them. It was repellent.

I had refused to have dinner with him because I knew I would choke over my food listening to his venomous remarks. As he had told everyone I had been his mistress, was he afraid I would say it was not true? His venom showed in his face, all charm gone, only mockery and tension. Life showered success on him, wealth, best-sellers, his books were filmed. But he is bitter and destructive. He spoke of how he enjoyed destroying writers in his articles. I was appalled.

Letter to Jean-Michel Fossey:

I would be very happy if you recommended the Diaries to a Spanish publisher, but I am afraid that Volume Two, being against Franco, might be censored. It might be best to recommend it to South America or to Mexico. I am sending you a review which came out in Spain. Do you need critiques etc.? I have tons of them. Essays, evaluations, etc. Let me know. Perhaps your word will be enough. I am sentimentally keen on being read in Spanish, although so many Spanish people read French.

I hope Désiré was not too malicious about me. She was in love with "Rango" (Gonzalo in American Diary). I was helping Rango to print things for Spain, against Franco, but she did not believe me, because my father was on the other side, yet this happened to so many families. As I was always behind the scenes, the misunderstanding of my situation was extensive. I never made a public declaration of my sympathies. But the Diary tells the story. I was not politically an activist then. I am now. But the issues here are more direct. You are for the Negro, the Indian, the Latin, the Mexican, or for the oppressive Anglo-Saxons. The choice is simple. I do not know when we will talk, as I cannot for the moment face the grinding, overwhelming publicity Stock exposes me to, the intense public life when I like intimate life, friends, etc. For the moment I am resisting the idea of coming in May for Volume Three and facing an avalanche. The strain, stress, and pressure spoils the flowering of friendship.

Letter to Gore Vidal:

On page 203 you overlooked a statement: "He had wanted his mother to die." I imagine you want that out too.

I hope you are aware that by erasing your mother you have erased the only alibi you have for your destructiveness toward human beings, your lack of compassion and understanding. I had hoped to make you less hated.

For recording in the Diary I would like to know what prompted you to spatter me with your venom when I was one of the few people who once had faith in you.

My portrait of you shows that. You chose to fulfill your mother's predictions rather than mine: "You are full of venom."

Letter to Jean-Michel Fossey:

First I want to explain a delicate matter which is typical of American life. Magazines are divided into two classes: the paying ones, which are Establishment, and which totally ignore me, and the nonpaying ones, the literary, underground, independent, genuine ones which accept what I recommend, beg for articles, etc. There is nothing in between. That is why I cannot help you. Your article belongs with the noncommercial ones. The commercial ones take only best-sellers, big names, selling names, etc. I will make one attempt with the *Los Angeles Times*, which pays thirty-five dollars an article, . . . where I know someone. This is one of the realities of American life, the sharp dividing line between quality and commercialism. . . .

I have no letters of Artaud's other than those I published in the Diary. Yes, the attitude of Désiré is the same as the Negro has now in the United States. He no longer believes in the white man, even in the ones who help him. They want to liberate themselves by themselves.

Your letter makes me aware how little interest American journalism has in French or Latin American writers. All the little magazines would welcome your articles, or the underground newspapers, which are an extreme of vulgarity, pornographic illustrations, and articles on Artaud, etc. One can never describe the "chaos" of America, the confused and mixed elements which are thrown together. I may send you samples. It took me six years to get Louise Varèse's translation of [Henri Michaux's] *Miserable Miracle* published. Yes, I remember Antonio Galvez. A friend had talked a great deal about him and sent me a photo he made of Cortázar. But I will remain on the alert if I can possibly connect you with a worthwhile magazine.

I gave your name to the two Belgian poets who had wanted to plan an *hommage* number but do not have the means, and tried to interest Stock in the project, but failed. They are now concentrating on a deluxe translation of *House of Incest*.

Never hesitate, as the *"bavardage"* of your letter, as you call it, is not *bavardage* to me but interesting activity, taking the place of the talks we might have had. I like the multifaceted energy you show, and I hope I can be of help to you as a writer.

Letter to Fred Haines:

I read the script [of Hermann Hesse's *Steppenwolf*]. I know it is a difficult book to do. And I know scripts change as one goes along. I know the atmosphere will come from your directing. I thought you did an *excellent* job and yet, as a lover of Hesse, I fear people will feel as I do, that it could be more faithful to Hesse's night world. I felt, and I must be honest with you, you colloquialized the dialogue, and it ceased to be Hesse. There is nothing more dangerous than to Americanize the language, to update it. It immediately destroys the spirit, banalizes it. I want to be an honest friend. . . . I feel those who love Hesse like its transposition, they do not want it made familiar to the ear. I wish we had talked about this. I feel strongly about it. It was the dialogue which worked against the atmosphere you created in description. People who read Hesse do not date it. It is timeless. But to be timeless, you cannot have contemporary expression in talk. That dates it. It makes it today, here, now, and certainly not Hesse. It is as vital as music. A tone, a note, a certain accent . . . it is all part of the integrity of timelessness. That was my only negative reaction.

If you have time and would like to write about Hesse for the newsletter, what you wrote to me was interesting but I know you went deeper into the relation to *Steppenwolf*. I am very happy you will be allowed to direct, and I know it will be a fine film, like your *Ulysses*. If Hesse has a son, relatives, why is his life so little known (his intimate life)? Perhaps you will find out more. I thought you solved the theater exceedingly well. I wish you all the luck and backing in the world.

Even in analysis I was not able to fathom the Christmas neurosis. Even though it is common and almost a joke now, it is so universal. But one evening this week I finally unraveled the labyrinth. It has to do with faith and illusion. The illusion of Xmas. That is the first one. It vanishes. It is tied to the family and illusion of stability and unity and harmony and magic. *Bon.* One grows up. But more and more illusions have to be dispelled as you mature. Corruption in politics. Injustice. Buying useless expensive planes and cutting down on Medicare. The treachery of politicians. The cruelty of history. (Just read about the useless killing of a million Frenchmen at Sedan.) The irrationality of leaders and our helplessness. Anyway! Loss of faith, in religion, in history, in science too as it achieves destruction (all the bombs, gas, germ warfare, etc.), in the goodness and humanity of people (crime and so on). Somehow, this first loss of faith (in Xmas) was associated with all the phony rituals, bells, Santa Claus, begging in the streets, Salvation Army, Mr. Ronald Reagan trimming his Xmas tree hypocritically after destroying the budget for education. It all became one theme of loss of faith (food is contaminated, drugs are harmful, everybody cheats, steals, spies, etc.). A black picture. I know the positive side, the good, the heroic, the creative, etc. But they are defeated, killed (Dr. King). I admire Ralph Nader. But the twinkling lights, songs, sentimentality, gifts, sicken me, literally. I now have *nausea* in the shops. Cards. People who never write you all year and then send a card. Gestures. Empty gestures. Sending cards for business reasons. Anyway, at Xmas I get a sickness which has to do with a child's loss of innocence and faith, the awareness of fraud, of social shallowness, etc. Ecology, idealism, all of it became one theme: Illusion and loss of illusion. The rest of the year I can bear because I am busy. But I refuse to join the celebrations and thanks and wishes when reality is so dark and fearsome.

Perhaps because I do not have children, I think of holidays as something to forget quickly because they only remind me of lost parents and scattered families.

Gerald Robitaille betrays all of us and writes a cruel book about Henry.

From an article on women's liberation for the newsletter:

Naturally I want the liberation of woman, but to be consistent with my personal convictions I must emphasize the psychological liberation, the liberation from within, which has to begin with a study of our cultural, racial, family, or psychological patterns. Some of the handicaps and pressures do come from the outside, but many also come from ourselves. It is important to examine this formation before we blame others for the traps in which we find ourselves.

In my Diaries I carefully recorded the conflicts, superstitions, the concepts which handicapped women, and how to transcend them organically, step by step, how to involve men in this growth. . . .

I know many men who are deeply touched by the dilemma of women. I never believed we could overcome these conflicts by becoming men, by declaring war on them or by erasing distinctions. Transvestism is no solution. We can only win recognition and equal rights by quality, skills and discipline, with wisdom, intelligence and a total vision of the problems. Nothing will be gained by a mere exchange of roles, any more than by a change of system. We have to deal with human nature, its fears, its anxieties. Some of women's difficulties have come from a blind acceptance of mores, ideologies, and concepts. She did not express herself as a woman. Men and women have a greater chance of understanding each other today because of our common knowledge that most of our acts stem from antiquated and primitive patterns, and that deep down in the unconscious we are more alike than on the conscious level.

I believe in the couple. We can meet the problems of life by balancing each other, by sensitive fluctuations. We have to work out our liberation through love and joined efforts. There is already too much hostility and aggression in the world. A willful seizing of power will not liberate us. Liberation is a state of mind, of being. It has to be achieved from within, and then it becomes an influence, it radiates outwardly, it achieves its energy and its aims creatively.

Letter to Professor Bob Fichter:

I probably have more faith and interest in the Academy because I only think of it in terms of people like you and my other thirty-year-old professors, of Zen, of science, etc. I always take my "rating" from the top level! All I understood from the article you sent me is that computers are counter-intuitive. Funny because these scientists who invited me [to Stanford] were trying to find a link between surrealism and integrated circuits. But the inventive, creative scientists are intuitive and jump into the unknown as the artist does.

Don't worry about [my visiting] Radcliffe. I overextended myself last year and I am glad to be less active this year.

This was the Year of the Letters. And what do you think all my French poets, journalists, painters, etc., write me? They want to come and live in the hippie communes! They think young Americans have solved the bohemian life. And we know they haven't. I have to deter an invasion of penniless Europeans. I have to get some information on the communes. There is little to be had and some French journalist has been painting them as havens.

So I'm in the role of antiromantic!

And all my American friends are slipping over into France.

I would love to hear about your analysis, if possible. It is my only "utopia."
As society deprived us of the capacity to create a world, analysis can give us
back our autonomy, and potentialities.

Letter to a friend:

Of course I'm not angry. You sent me pages of your diary and I wanted
to answer fully and I couldn't. Recognition has come this year with a tidal
wave of letters, lectures, work. I work from seven A.M. to midnight! A new
kind of trap—fame! Rejoice in your freedom. Please never interpret silence
as bad, or forgetfulness. The demands on me this year are overwhelming—
and my energy is less. I am unutterably tired. I am reminded of Dreiser's
story. A king found a way to turn everything to gold. The crowd surged
around him to have him perform the miracle. They surged and surged—and
stifled him! I am not stifled yet. But I cannot do what Miller does—throw
all the mail in the wastebasket. So please understand. I know you mean to
share and give your writing—but I can no longer answer as fully.

Read at Town Hall, New York, for Poets for Peace. A record was
made of this reading by Spoken Arts.

Lectured at University of North Carolina, Chapel Hill.

Lectured at University of California, Santa Barbara.

Lectured at Temple University, Philadelphia.

Lectured at Otto Rank Association, Doylestown, Pa.

Lectured at University of California, Berkeley, on "Dreams and
Literature."

Lectured at Wesleyan College on "Artaud and Theater of Cruelty."

Lectured at Stanford University, for Electronic Laboratories on
"Integrated Circuits and Surrealism," Dr. Robert Newcomb, author of
Integrated Circuits.

Lectured at American Designers' Association, Arrowhead Lake,
California.

Lectured at Star Lake Writers' Workshop, State University College,
Potsdam, N.Y.

Invited to lecture by Dr. Robert Haas, Director of Arts and Human-
ities Extension, UCLA.

Talked with Freudian analysts from Los Angeles Hospital at one of their home conferences and discussion meetings.

Discussion with Extension Course in short-story writing, UCLA.

Lectured at Berkeley University, Rochester, Ill.

Lectured at Long Island University and Brooklyn College.

Lectured at Library of Congress, invited by Dr. Basler, Washington, D.C.

Lectured at Immaculate Heart College, Los Angeles.

Lectured at Smith College, Mass.

Lectured at Clarion College, Rochester, Pa.

Lectured at Barnard College, New York City.

Lectured at Philadelphia Art Alliance.

Lectured at Pennsylvania University, Philadelphia.

Presented Snyder film, *Henry Miller Odyssey,* at Harvard.

Lectured at University of California, Santa Cruz.

Invited to Book Fair at Frankfurt, Germany.

Writing on the plane to Los Angeles:

A year of recognition, of flowers, loving letters, crowded lecture halls, of faces coming very close and conveying love, of interviews and television appearances, and visitors.

Whenever I was asked if I still wrote in the Diary, I answered automatically, "Of course." But one day I realized this was not true. I was binding 1970 together and found many letters, photographs, testimonies, programs, clippings, but no Diary.

A letter to my father, a letter to the world, an answer to my letters to the world, and then my answer to the answers. And I cannot write merely from memory unless it is an accidental recall. So it is all gone. Is it in the letters? I read some of them. No, it is not in the letters.

It was not for lack of what to write. So many sorrowful moments, so many beautiful moments, so many joys, and dreams and nightmares.

New York at six A.M. It is dark. I can see across the way the lights of insomniacs. If I lie in bed I can only see the sky. At seven, looking out of the window I see the tenants walking their dogs on the grass. A few taxis. Delivery trucks. A fire engine. The hideous Johnson library at NYU hiding part of Washington Square.

It snows. I will not go out. I file reviews, miscellaneous articles, interviews, a box for each country. I have various states of edited Diary, first version, second version, fan letters. I bind the 1970 Diary. File photographs and notes for future diaries.

I talk with Marguerite, who loves the telephone, and with Marianne Hauser. Visited Frances [Field], whose marriage is a series of crises. Michael overworks, he is driven by the American illness of the Big Deal. Success and fame, as the best cook in the U.S., but no fortune yet and more debts than riches. He needs many assistants, assistant cooks, assistant research workers. The reality is that he overworks to the point of breakdown and cannot reach what he wants. Frances gave up her painting to help him. She runs the cooking school, she has become one of the assistants. *Life* and *Time* sent them to Morocco to describe Moroccan cooking, but they clock them so they do not have one hour for themselves to enjoy the city. Michael has the illusion of being on stage, but wealth eludes him. Frances dreams of a simple life in the Village, a return to her painting, of less strain and stress. Michael is absent, always ready to leave, never still, haunted by the American Big Shot idea. Their anxiety is connected with achievement and a security which is an illusion.

I lectured at Sharon's college [Jersey City State] because her book *Space, Time and Structure in the Modern Novel* is a discovery in criticism, an innovation, a profound book which could create a new school of criticism. She studied with Anna Balakian.

From an interview with Judy Oringer for *Ramparts:*

J.O.: In your Diaries you record the life you led in Paris and New York in the thirties and forties in the company of Henry Miller, Antonin Artaud, Otto Rank, Lawrence Durrell and other male writers and artists. What did it feel like being a woman in this circle?

A.N.: First of all, I was shy and didn't say too much in the cafés. But I was a personal friend of Miller, Artaud and the others. We were all writers and they respected me as an artist and a woman. You see, at that time Miller and Artaud considered themselves *ratés* [failures], there was no such thing as success. We just knew each other, and talked to each other about art and writing. We talked, just the way you and I are talking now.

169

J.O.: Women in America are avidly reading the Diaries and identifying tremendously with them.

A.N.: I receive between two hundred and three hundred letters a week (mostly) from women who are reading the Diaries. They're confessional, on many levels, some from women who don't understand exactly what I was trying to say but who felt something from them. I suppose that I was able to articulate my feelings and emotions. Most women have felt what I have felt, but not all have actually been able to articulate it. The hardest things to write about are your emotions and intuitions. The strange thing is that women have accused me of keeping part of my personal life out of the Diaries. When I wrote them I thought people would want to know about Henry Miller, Artaud. I never thought they would identify so strongly with me.

J.O.: You've written a number of novels as well. What were the advantages of writing the Diaries?

A.N.: In the Diaries I was the most honest, I revealed myself in the greatest depth. And by writing the Diaries I was exercising my art and disciplining myself, which helped me in the novels, and the novels reinforced the Diaries. The only thing is that one is always tempted to get to the end, but I insisted on maintaining the chronology of my life. I recorded my growth, development, the germination of ideas and my relationship with other people organically, step by step.

J.O.: You seem to have a romantic vision of the world, searching for the liberation of the individual as if he or she lived an isolated, contained existence.

A.N.: No. However, I do believe in the psychological and emotional liberation of people. Very often we fall into traps we set for ourselves, blaming our situation for our failure to act. We must become self-aware and self-honest so that we can deal with ourselves. But I'm not talking about liberation in an isolated way. People think that introspection as well means withdrawing into oneself. On the contrary, it means delving into one's own unique sensitivities and patterns so that one is able to relate to others. I think liberation is then a collective effort. Of course, it's true that many of our limitations, frustrations, are caused by external circumstances, but we must deal with ourselves first and then tackle the outside world.

J.O.: Kate Millett in *Sexual Politics* has taken Henry Miller and Norman Mailer to task as "male chauvinist pigs," anti-woman, et cetera. Do you think Henry Miller is anti-woman?

A.N.: First of all, I make the distinction between Miller's life and his work.

170

There is no doubt that Miller writes about women as sexual objects in his novels. But Miller did a lot for sex by writing about it in a lusty, possible way. I think women are wasting their energies, however, by trying to decide which male writers have debased women. They should be creating, not destroying. . . .

J.O.: What have your contacts been with women involved in the women's liberation movement?

A.N.: Some of the women have attacked me for being apolitical. They don't realize that only through my own personal liberation, and my fulfillment as an artist, have I been able to contribute as a woman. . . .

J.O.: How do you react to exploitative sexist commercials on television? Do you get angry?

A.N.: No. I used to get angry for a long time at not being treated at all as a sexual object. As you know, America inherited a large dose of Puritanism from England. It seems a strange coincidence in timing that now that American men are first beginning to approach women sexually, women have become hostile and are declaring war on them. American men and women are really in a dangerous position. I have the feeling that women don't appreciate enough that both women and men are victims of the same system, that men, oppressed by the extremely competitive aggressive outside world, oppressed their women at home, oppressed the only beings they were able to. Women really have a double role—to liberate themselves and to seduce, attract their men into working for their liberation as well. Only by working together can they truly liberate themselves. I always involved the men I was with in my liberation so that we collaborated in our combined liberation.

J.O.: You seem to be talking about preserving the polarity between men and women, as opposed to many feminists who encourage unisexual trends.

A.N.: I want to preserve polarity, if that is the word, but not between men and women, between any two people. I don't believe in men or women having traits which limit them as "masculine" and "feminine." My mother, for example, had extreme physical courage, she wasn't afraid of anything. There's no reason why people should feel themselves bound to outdated, stereotyped characteristics of masculinity and femininity.

J.O.: Along with the sexual revolution has come a new self-image for homosexuals. The gay liberation movement is encouraging male and female homosexuals into acting aggressively and openly. What do you think?

A.N.: I think gay people in becoming aggressive and demanding have only responded to the harsh repression with which they have been treated. I certainly think that homosexuality is as "normal" and "natural" as

171

anything else. Men should live with men, women with women, if that's what they want. Of course, it is much harder for lesbians to come out. But fortunately I don't think they'll have to go through the stage that male homosexuals have been going through: that is, constant focus on sexuality, terrible insecurity and loneliness. Lesbians seem to form more permanent love relationships.

J.O.: We were talking before about women artists, women writers.

A.N.: Yes, I would like to see women creating in all the arts, to see women film directors—that would be interesting—women painters, et cetera. But we have to be careful. Women have been conditioned to think like men for so long that some women don't realize that they are copying men's standards for women. For example, Marguerite Duras was adapting my novel *A Spy in the House of Love* into a screenplay. In the book Sabina is a female Don Juan, a woman who has hangups but is sexually liberated. Marguerite Duras portrayed her instead as a whore—which she wasn't at all. She was just sexually liberated, as any man is allowed to be. . . .

J.O.: During those years in Paris . . . did you know Zelda Fitzgerald, for example, or Gertrude Stein?

A.N.: I only met Gertrude Stein once, and I didn't like her personally because she insisted on dominating everyone she was with. Zelda Fitzgerald lived in Paris a generation before me, in the twenties. I didn't know her. . . .

J.O.: Simone de Beauvoir is another woman writer who is very popular in this country. What is your opinion of her work?

A.N.: I respect Simone de Beauvoir as an artist, and partly because she managed to overcome the limitations of a narrow background. I find *The Second Sex* old-fashioned. . . . In a way I've always thought of Simone de Beauvoir as the shadow of Sartre. In accepting Sartre's existentialism, she seems to be denying, like him, her emotions, her intuitions. That's why her women in her novels are false, unreal for me. But her autobiography is more authentic.

J.O.: Do you ever regret not being a mother?

A.N.: Not at all. I had a stillbirth, and found I was physically unable to have a child because of surgery I had had when I was nine. But I've never regretted it. I've created books, been a mother to people I have known, such as my students. I certainly don't think that every woman should have children, nor that women who aren't mothers are "unfeminine." Women shouldn't have to feel obligated to fulfill some obsolete definition of what a woman should be.

J.O.: Probably one of the reasons for the development of the women's movement in America has been the American obsession with virility and aggressiveness in business carrying over to personal relations.

A.N.: Yes, men here have always had this fear of showing their emotions. They were afraid to accept the definition . . . that we all have in us "the man, woman, and child." American men were always afraid that by revealing their sensitivity, their emotions, they were "feminine." European men never had that fear. Frenchmen, for example, are always very conscious of aesthetics, of design. Fortunately in America this is changing significantly. Younger men are ridding themselves of this notion of fear of not expressing their emotions and so on.

J.O.: What about women in America? Don't you agree that they are in fact more oppressed than their European sisters?

A.N.: Yes. The strange thing is that European women have always thought of the American woman as freer, more independent. As we know, American women lead much more alienated existences, and their so-called independence is limited to feeling isolated in a plastic suburban environment.

J.O.: Of course we're talking about white middle-class women who feel their lives are meaningless. What about black women, chicana women?

A.N.: Naturally I'm for the liberation of all women. I feel my role is that of a woman artist, who might be a symbol for other women of any type or class. When they see that I accomplished a certain amount in my art, they might take courage from that knowledge that another woman demanded self-expression.

Letter to Marcel Moreau:

I hope you don't mind my writing you in English. I can't write in French anymore. But years ago . . . I read your first book in translation and was quite bedazzled by its imaginative flights of thought and language. I have not yet received your new book, but it may be waiting for me in New York. I'll write you again. This time it is only to tell you I'm proud that you liked my work. I always admired those who let their nightmares free. Most of mine I kept secret in the Diary, not always willing to share the doubts, fears, visions, in my eagerness to overcome and conquer them for the sake of a passionate affirmation. I never let them carry me into delirium but I do *understand* those voyages. *Les cavernes de Pluton. Les saisons en enfer.* I let you carry me off in your first book. I never hold back when another holds the reins. Why is it some of us hold back on the brink of madness as Artaud refused to do? You are braver than I. I metamorphose my nightmares into lands of fertile loves and friendships. Salvation. Do I think it is the role of woman to disarm the demons? You have lived much for me in your book.

Letter to Henry Miller:

Thank you for your advice on Japan. How have you fared?

I wanted to tell you that I had an hour interview on television here with Keith Berwick. To my great surprise, he was like a European interviewer, gentle, tactful, intelligent, well read, mellow and human. The entire interview was a pleasure. I was relaxed and at my best. Of course he admires you, and for the first time I felt here is someone you would be at ease with. He has the gift to make one feel eloquent! I wish you would let him visit you. He lives near you. He is married to an Italian. He teaches history at UCLA but there is no hint of the academic in him. Trust my intuition. I know how you feel about most interviewers, and rightly so! But to enjoy an interview is a new experience for me. It was like talking to a friend.

Letter from Henry Miller:

I was delighted to see you on TV last night. This is the first time I've heard you in public, aside from the bits in the *Odyssey*. You were extremely lucid, spoke clearly and loudly enough to be heard (which was a surprise to me) and seemed to be in perfect command of yourself. Quite a treat!

I thought Berwick was very good with you, but am not so sure I would hit it off with him so well. He was soft and suave, as you said. But he still seems like the college professor in many ways. However, I'll arrange to meet him and then decide if I want an interview. I really loathe these interviews. There are very few persons who can make you sing a new tune. I always feel that the interview should only begin (on TV) after one has talked for an hour or so and both are warmed up. Otherwise they are like TV dinners.

There was one moment when I thought you were really thrown, or stumped for an answer, and that was when he mentioned "ambivalence." I lost both of you there.

I never knew either that you had read so many Japanese novelists. You know, of course, that their language is admittedly vague, sometimes they don't even understand one another—that's why you so often hear them say, "What's that?" or "Is it not so?" I am trying to write now about Mishima's death— my reaction to it. He's very difficult to follow, I find, when he explains things. Even the Japanese agree to this.

About the "Insomnia" book. I don't think you grasped the purpose of it.

If you read between the lines you will see what I mean. However, even if it was as you "imagine," should I be reproached?

I was surprised to hear you say that perhaps only one or two more volumes of the Diary will be published. I still believe the early ones, starting from the very beginning would enchant your readers.* Be good to yourself!

From a program note:

Ian Hugo made another film called *Aphrodisiac*. An abstract expression of human sensuality, created with female forms, color, light and the gemlike plastic and metal sculptures of Feliciano Bejar. The rhythmic pattern bridges the stream of sensation that floats through other levels of consciousness. In creating this hauntingly beautiful film, Ian Hugo displays a unique sensitivity to the female experience. The results transcend the visual and aural senses to evoke memories of rhythmic contractions and releases, involuntary moldings of pleasure and pain.

Letter to a reader:

The answer to your question lies in the Diaries themselves. Yes, fighting anxiety is a great drain on one's energy; that is why I never hesitated to resort to professional help. I put my faith in therapy as others do in religion, or philosophy. Did you read Volume Three? In every volume, at every crisis of negativity, I turned to therapy, unashamed and proud of my belief in it. Today it is no longer a luxury, it is available to all, and what is needed is the courage to confront one's fears and find out what they are and conquer them. Other writers who would not believe this, either stopped creating or repeated themselves, for neurosis is not a source of strength or inspiration as some artists believe; one creates in spite of it, and far better without it, as you leave your obsessions behind you and evolve into other themes, other experiences.

Invited to new house (in Los Angeles) of Daniel and Gloria Stern to listen to chamber music (string quartets and piano quartets). It is

---

* *Linotte: The Early Diary of Anaïs Nin, 1914–1920,* was published in 1978. A complete edition of the French original was published in two volumes in 1979 by Editions Stock, Paris.—Ed.

only while listening to music that I become almost ecstatically aware that I reached in my life the beauty of music—its flow, rhythms, variations, emotional tempos, quietness and fury, passion and pulse, liquid forces unified. I can find my blood as impetuous as the bows, the pedal, the vibrations as keen as the strings, and the great pulsations each time miraculously unified.

Do you still write the Diary?

Perhaps I do, invisibly now. The voice, the melody has become multiple. How did I arrive simultaneously at the perfection of an intimate life and the perfection of a cosmic consciousness in public, so that I felt at one with people in France, Germany, America—anywhere—Mexico, Tahiti, even Japan where I did not know the language? Why can I look at the faces which come toward me and love them and know them instantly?

At twenty to seven, Piccolino, who lies on the bed, seems heavier, and he wakes me. I turn on the heat and go back to bed until the house is warm. Then I wash my mouth and eyes and comb my hair and go to the kitchen to make coffee, toast and eggs. At seven-thirty I am in my cozy study at the typewriter. The lake is always still in the morning.

Except one morning in early February when I was awakened at six A.M. by a tremendous earthquake! The bed shook and trembled. Waves splashed back and forth in the pool, inundating the garden. The huge pane of glass in the center of the house vibrated and shook and rattled, a horrendous sound like the death rattle of the world. Suddenly the dark house was illuminated with a lightninglike flash of white light. Such a light could only come from an atomic bomb. Quietly I went out into the garden to observe the end of the world. There was an incredible stillness. Nothing was to be seen of the atomic bomb or the end of the world.

I came back into the house to find Piccolino hiding under the couch. He refused to come out. As I made coffee I learned from the radio news that it was a major earthquake. A new hospital near the center of the earthquake had collapsed, the upper floors falling on the lower, and many were dead or injured. The great flash of light came from the power station nearby, where the earthquake shorted out lines carrying all the electric power from Boulder Dam to Los Angeles. My house was undamaged, thanks to the Wright design, even though it contains so much glass and stone.

Minor quakes followed, oscillations called aftershocks. It seemed like the ultimate instability after constant war, unemployment and the attempt of the government to save money on the poor, the old, the sick.

For most people it seemed a perfect external match to anxieties, fears—a matching of tremors. To a mother tormented by her three drug-addicted sons, to men out of work, to war veterans in hospitals. Never had the world seemed more terrifying. The blacks desperately violent. Women restless and revolutionary for themselves. All the revolutions simultaneous, infectious.

How can one celebrate, at such a moment, the culmination of a life's work? I wrote somewhere that the artist keeps an individual rhythm. This year I became aware that I was helping women flower, that I was read widely and with the same feelings I poured into the lives of those I loved. Suddenly every word I wrote was heard, and a young woman wrote to me: "There is a new consciousness and you are its poet laureate."

I am not spoiled by the letters which come because they are emotional, human. They are not flatteries. Some are very saddening. They are deep responses, secret confessions.

[Spring, 1971]

When I was still suffering from the effects of radiation treatments, I received the Prix Sévigné for the first two Diaries in France. It gave me pleasure but at the same time I felt: Why so late?

From France I receive letters from outstanding poets: Marcel Moreau and Claude Louis-Combet. Both, in a sense, *"poètes maudits,"* extraordinary writers. Louis-Combet has many affinities with *House of Incest*. Moreau is like a human bomb, anti-intellectual, anarchic, powerful.

Met a gentle and beautiful poet, Elliott Coleman, at Johns Hopkins University. He introduced me with subtlety and care.

I had to refuse invitation to Festival du Livre at Nice. Felt tired and overworked and dislike such official events. Could imagine the banquets, the speeches.

I reviewed Jacques Henri Lartigue's photographs for the *New York Times*—a delightful, humorous book of photographs. The same day the review appears I receive a letter from him, very much like Varda's letters, on many-colored papers, full of fantasy. He had been reading the Diary! Such a coincidence.

An avalanche of letters and lectures. Activities for the newsletter.

Sale of paperback Diaries exceeds expectations.

Letter to André Bay:

I'm very happy about the prize [Prix Sévigné] and proud that my first prize came from France. Please tell me more about it as my friends here do not know what it represents.

I hope you are not disappointed about my not coming in May. I have been working too hard. I have given six lectures in two weeks, suffered from Irving Penn's photograph in *Vogue*, the ugliest photo ever taken of me. It was strange that the minute he stepped into my apartment I had the intuition this cold man *did not see me*. I should have had the courage to send him away. If one could always act according to one's intuition! The stationery store woman who sold me the magazine and saw the photograph, looked at me and said: "What have they done to you, poor thing." How I would have liked to be in Paris to enjoy the prize. Did you read Regis Durand's essay on *House of Incest* in *Langues Modernes*?

Letter to Cyril Clemens:

To answer your question: I read Mark Twain at fifteen when I was reading everything I could find in the public library. Mark Twain's *Joan of Arc* was read aloud to the graduating class of New York Public School 9 as we sewed our graduation clothes. But the person who revived my interest by his enthusiasm and devotion to Mark Twain was Dr. Otto Rank, the psychiatrist, who read into Twain's books more meaning than most people. I am sending your *Journal* to the Otto Rank Association because I am sure someday comments on Mark Twain will be found among Rank's papers. The work of translating his papers is going on now. They were left to Columbia University.

I suppose you have read my Diaries with allusions to Rank's love of Mark Twain. If not, I will gladly send them to you.

Sincerely,
Daughter of Mark Twain

From letters to readers:

Yes, I know many questions are left unanswered by psychoanalysis, but I have kept my faith in its essence and have avoided the dogmatic aspect. I still refer to it as a way of *connaissance* and recently consulted it again on the problem of women's liberation, to find my exact position in it, my own integrity. It is still the only way for self-knowledge and guidance. I live in a confused, chaotic country where one has extra need of awareness.

Recognition is a new kind of trap I have yet to learn to free myself from. For all is lost if one has no time for friends.

So glad you wrote me as you did, for your letter made you a vivid presence and made me feel I know you. I couldn't see anyone the last weeks as I am between books. I said yes to lectures and they have accumulated.

Strange, your going from prose to poetry, but then I feel we need poetry in prose so much, we need the poet! If only the world had answered a little sooner when I had more time and more energy!

I was in Japan too, for six weeks. I fell in love with it, of course, and read all the novels I could find beginning with *Tale of Genji*. And then the novels made me realize they have no Self, and you can never know how they feel or come close (I have several Japanese friends). So I lost my first love of the country and it remains now an aesthetic love. . . .

If you want to know the good changes in America, read *The Greening of America*. Yes, there is a new consciousness. The press only tunes in on the ugly. There is a beautiful America.

Your note on the television interview with Keith Berwick pleased me so much. These talks are usually so dependent on the interviewer, and he was so probing and so helpful that I forgot the camera. I am glad I talked truthfully. I missed the show as I was lecturing at Queens College in New York that night. So your comment helped me. It is not always easy to be authentic in artificial situations.

More lectures. At the Feminist meeting at Cambridge, Mass., I was subjected to outlandish attacks by aggressive women because I did not talk about the child-care center or equality in salary. I explained I was seeking to liberate them first of all psychologically so that they could produce the effective changes they wanted. The hostility and vulgarity of the attacks turned the public against them. They were hooted out, and the rest of the crowd gave me a long ovation. After the lecture they surrounded me. We sat down to continue the interrupted talk. The angry women want war, declarations of war against man. They are only adding to the misery and fragmentation of the world. They do not know how to work in harmony.

The next morning I met with the women who had invited me and we had a balanced, intelligent interview which was published in *Second Wave* magazine. We remained friends. And the lecture raised enough money for the magazine. The church was overflowing.

Letter from a Cambridge feminist:

I have written to you before when I was in a softer mood—at that time I spoke of masks, the poet, the self. Now I write out of anger. Several weeks ago you spoke at the Old Cambridge Baptist Church. You were beautiful, strong, your face set like a cameo, you did not flounder. I knew how difficult it was for you. And then came the question period. How can you stand it? The inane, bitter, hostile, insipid remarks hurled at you were not even worthy of any response, yet you handled even that well. I was so furious with my sisters for being so blind. Why can't they see beyond the thin political veil? Why can't they sense beyond the immediate "women's movement" to the true revolution of liberation for us all, once we learn to like ourselves? I just had

Anaïs Nin with manuscript volumes of the diary, 1966

Rupert Pole

Japan, 1966

Cambodia, 1966

Rupert Pole

Cambodia, 1966

Tahiti, 1967

Morocco, 1969

Los Angeles, 1970

At the Berkeley Celebration, 1971

Donna Emerson

Lecturing, in the 1970s

Phillip Citrin

In Paris, being photographed for German television, 1971; above, with
Jeanne Moreau; below, with Michel Simon; right, in Louveciennes

Giving a talk in St. Clement's Church, New York, 1972

With students, at home in Los Angeles, 1973

Rupert Pole

At an Esalen Institute seminar, 1972

Left and above, at home in Los Angeles, with Piccolino, 1972

New York, 1971

Puerto Vallarta, Mexico, 1973

At Dartmouth College, with Justice William O. Douglas, 1974

With Henry Miller, Pacific Palisades, 1974

Rupert Pole

Bali, 1974

Rupert Pole

Bali, 1974

to write and tell you how frustrated I was. I wanted to speak to you of dreams and colors and visions, and more concretely of lying and being small and being true to oneself. But the words turned to tears when I heard the heated remarks, the circus that had nothing to do with you, or with them! I am growing, I am suffering, but often I am learning to be happy and free. Where are they leading themselves? Haven't they seen enough futile hostility wrought by men? Must they emulate the worst of men and ignore the best?

It is out now. I'm sorry to have troubled you. I would rather have spoken in my soft voice. But this was a time for screaming. You seemed to excuse them, understand them. I cannot. Maybe this is something I must grow into also.

Do not ever falter from the dream. Someday they will understand.

Letters to Cambridge feminists:

Yes, Cambridge was difficult, but then the women's movement has in it the same element I disliked in the forties—the narrow, bigoted robots mouthing slogans. But even though they did not let me finish what I had to say and failed to see the bridge I was making, I felt I had more friends than enemies. I had the same experience in Los Angeles with women artists; we were prevented from talking together by two parrots with closed minds.

Don't worry. I do not have this with students.

I am glad you wrote me after Cambridge. I could not measure the degree of hostility or misunderstanding as well as you did. I thought I could be useful to the liberation of women, but I wonder. Those who understood were those who knew the work. I hope some of the issues will be cleared in the long interview I had the next morning. But I must confess I am ashamed of some women's behavior. They will only add to the war, ugliness and despair; they bring only their psychotic angers. I don't know if my effort to mitigate hatred and war was effective.

Who has brainwashed so many women, programming them to follow the worst theories of man, not the best, and add more war and hatred to a war-filled world?

I liked so much your saying: "There are parts of some women that stay secret and hidden and you seemed to address yourself in writing to those parts and make them secret no longer." The new public role thrust on me (I have liberated women in a different way) may be impossible because the militant

181

women do not believe that working on raising the quality of human beings would take care of the social evils.

Anyway, my effort was worthwhile if it connected with a person like yourself and gave you the pleasure of a presence.

The Diaries have swallowed all my energy. I may only return to fiction when I am through editing, and I don't know when that will be.

Letter to Judy Chicago:

I'm discouraged about the women's movement. At Harvard, three hostile, aggressive women prevented me from finishing my talk. Really psychotic! I was ashamed of them. The public hissed them out! And half the audience stayed on until twelve—long past the lecture.

Letter to a Filipino feminist:

I understand how you feel. The American women's movement is confused too. It is split between the militant, violent, old-fashioned Marxists and more intelligent, individualistic women who know if we develop a higher type of human being, we will solve the other inequalities.

Joaquin was commissioned to write the mass for the dedication of the new St. Mary's Cathedral Church in San Francisco. The novelty was that it would be sung in English.

The day came and the cathedral opened its doors for the first time. It was very beautiful and gave the ritual grandeur. In the high vaulted ceiling, the vast space, music always has a sonorous, a powerful amplification. I did not listen to the words because in English they lack mystery and lyrical power. But when Joaquin's music began, it was like a shower of gold. It was dramatic. It filled the vast space of the cathedral so that you felt inside the music. His interpretation was brilliantly alive. The most detached listener was engulfed and possessed by the vast themes, the variations from joy to pain, the spirit of celebration and royal ascension. The sorrow and pain was contrasted with ecstasy. The music was certainly the language of the gods. No words could convey the depth of the drama. Yes, the cathedral must be immense to contain man's effort to reach divinity.

Joaquin had the necessary elevation and infinite expansion. Every nook and cranny was overflowing with the colors, the eloquence, the brilliance of the notes, matching the candlelight, the shower of crystal which was the central light.

Musically he expressed transcendence and the infinite.

People outside carried placards: "The wealth spent on this cathedral should be spent on the poor." True—but as well as bread, we needed to have a building for ceremonies which expressed the depth and grandeur our feelings could reach.

Robert Snyder began to talk about how many shots of me he had taken during his filming of Henry. So much left over that it would take little work to do a documentary of me. He made it sound like something that would not take too long or too much work. So we began. Whenever I had a free day, or whenever Bob was free we gathered at my house, set up the cameras, and Bob, while not appearing on the screen, incited me to talk.

I never liked documentaries which focused exclusively on the central figure, never moving from one room, and with endless talk. I wanted to include going out to the friends I was interested in, wanted to show the whole world I lived in, the artists I admired, who had an influence on me. So the film began to go beyond my just talking and you saw Harry Partch, Martha Graham, Isamu Noguchi, a light show, the string quartet that plays here every week. We worked for many hours—stopping only for sandwiches. The cameraman, Baylis Glascock, was exceptionally good, the sound men (there were several) exceptionally bad. Bob was handicapped by lack of money, so he accepted inexperienced sound men.

Letter to a reader:

Dreams are always true; we are childhood friends! I am happy at your finding yourself in the Diaries and at your response. I feel differently about America because of this new generation in whom I have great faith, the young who read me and write to me and I meet in colleges. They are beautiful and sensitive, and I only hope the other America, the empty, power-greedy, destructive one does not harm them. I see the country as dual—the greatest evil and the greatest goodness—and I don't know how these young people could be born here and develop such humanity and tenderness. I feel it is the similarity of feeling and vision that brings us close, with a true kind of col-

lective consciousness we recognize in each other, so we can say from a letter
—this is a friend. . . .

Yes, you have a much more difficult task than I had, to keep this new awareness and change America. I think you have changed the unconscious—but the results will take time. You are fighting giants! Let us stay close and then remain true to our dream.

Letter to Sharon Spencer:

I have several suggestions about warming up for writing!

Try writing about what is *closest* to your preoccupation as if you were talking to Dr. Bogner. Sometimes putting the lid on the immediate interferes with the objective story. Bring it nearer. Even on the theme you write me about, we can misspend our energy seeking to reverse a negative trend. Turn away from the negative into your own work.

Another suggestion is to write something other than you had planned to write, to get away from the directed plan—a whim, an emotional theme, anything—just to flow again. You may need to come closer to your unconscious concerns.

Letter to a friend:

I reread the diaries [you sent] carefully. As you know, it is difficult for me to be objective about you because of our closeness, and naturally I would find your diary interesting because it is you, your story, your life. But as *writing* I must say, as I said before—in photography you are in direct contact with life, there is no distance, there is love enjoyment. But in the writing there is a self-consciousness. You are telling *about,* you are not at one with the medium. Now this does not mean that by continuing to write you may not suddenly be *inside* of your feelings, as you are inside of the camera. I was interested in your ideas, your longings, your experiences, your reaction to paintings and books and people, your plans, projects. Naturally, I would be. May I suggest one thing. Stand in front of an impression, or sensation, or experience for a long time—as you would making a study—*dwell* on it at length, make a total portrait, a dream. Perhaps in the diary you are running too fast. Take pleasure in the words until their magic registers, until you get high with words to match the experience. How you feel but also how it feels to feel. No one watching over your shoulder, including yourself.

Letter to a French friend:

It makes me sad to hear of France reading the most ordinary American best-sellers! *Love Story*—we all recoil from it—we say corny, cliché, *vulgaire, ordinaire! Last Exit to Brooklyn de même!* I cannot believe this.

Letter to a reader:

I only write to ask you to keep faith in psychiatry. The Eastern religions have compounded an evil born of our culture, which is passivity. The only way to reawaken the creative will and the will to live is through understanding of our experiences. Too much unprofessional analysis is bad; but professional analysis restores us to the flow of life. As a friend, I can only beg you to understand your experiences; only then can they benefit your growth.

[Summer, 1971]

Lectures are not only a way to earn a living but far more than that. The students are the majority of my readers and we have a rapport. They crowd around me; we sit on the floor and we talk freely and intimately. The professors had warned me that they would not talk. I attract the best of them. They come with gifts made with their own hands, and we express tenderness and love. It is a lively relationship which sometimes is continued by correspondence.

Men exist who respond and collaborate with women. We have to seek them and we have to know how to create intimacy. Some women's groups who invited me refused to let the male students in.

At every lecture in California I saw the same young woman carrying flowers. She had enormous green eyes. She did not speak. She simply held out flowers. It is to her, Claudia Cranston, that I owe the knowledge of H. F. Peter's biography of Lou Andreas-Salomé [*My Sister, My Spouse*]. We became friends.

Walter Lippmann: "The discontent that is shaking this world cannot be dealt with by politics or on the periphery of life, but must be got closer to the central and intimate places of personalities . . . what has been wrecked cannot be restored by some new political gadget."

A while ago, I met Gloria Vanderbilt, who had asked a friend to arrange a meeting with me as her birthday present, because we have the same birthday. She is a beautiful and sensitive person, an artist. She suffers from her wealth because it is difficult for her to prove that she is an artist. Her husband described her better than I could, stressing the flower quality of her character. She talked about her nightmares. We felt a strong bond of empathy. Every now and then I receive a word from her, a catalogue of her painting, collages. We only met twice and would have liked to meet again.

We agreed that we had to design a new woman instead of fighting man and society. We can create in individual worlds, each one of us, and then they will connect and form a growing, larger world of quality and meaning.

A cyclone of work, visited sixteen colleges, gave two commencement talks, answered tons of mail.

The women are going through a great crisis as they enter the larger world of man, fearing they must give up being a woman. They make me talk, but they refuse to acknowledge that some problems are personal, psychological, emotional, not all political.

I am limited in my editing of the Diary by many human, ethical constrictions.

The Frenchwomen who wrote openly about sex, Violette Leduc, Christiane Rochefort, are treated like lepers. When I asked to meet Françoise d'Eaubonne I was told she was impossible and would not care for someone like me.

Women's fears are the real obstacles to inner freedom.

Liberation is a work of one's own. Political problems can be solved only when we are ready from within, well oriented and self-respecting.

Evelyn Hinz's *The Mirror and the Garden: Realism and Reality in the Writings of Anaïs Nin* is ready for printing.

Letter to a reader:

All I wish is that my Diaries give you courage to edit yours. It *is* difficult, because of human considerations, people's susceptibilities, ethical reasons, having to think of consequences. It is an intricate task. But I was ready for it when I finally did it. No one was hurt. But what complexities! Much of mine will have to wait. But I hope yours may not be as difficult. I was afraid to unmask myself, expose myself. I had a dream of opening my door and receiving fatal radiation! Instead, it was mostly love, and I feel richly compensated by a reciprocated love.

About allowing myself to be used. Yes, I know that was my weakness because I identified with others' needs. I still have to fight that, for today the majority of my readers are the young students, and they would fill my house. But I have learned to protect my work and my energy. I live quietly in Los Angeles when writing—frenziedly when I am lecturing or traveling.

Letter to a friend:

I was so glad to hear from you. Sometimes when I am riding along freeways (which I dislike), I make myself think of something beautiful; and a few days ago, when you were writing your letter, I thought of all the thoughtful and poetic and magical giving you did, every episode. It made me so sad that I was not free to return such imaginative, generous friendship merely because I had become a public figure. What a sad happening, carrying on a love affair with the world as an artist, which really destroys one's intimate friendships. I am learning to *make* time now, but the first year of being a public figure was overwhelming; and that plus the illness (I found out it was cancer) made me feel so ungenerous, ungiving toward many lovely persons.

I am resting in Los Angeles. The fall will be hectic again with Volume Four coming out. I'm a best-seller in France after the Prix Sévigné. Give Paris my love. And believe in mine for you.

Letter from Henry Miller:

I am very slowly getting my strength back but am in bed more than out.

Before I went to the hospital you wrote me about several things. I never noticed Wickes' book in the Pisces—I read very little of magazines and no college papers at all. I got a book [*The Life of Fraenkel's Death*] about [Michael] Fraenkel (by [Walter] Lowenfels & [Howard] McCord) months ago but I never read it. I don't care about reviews or reviewers—they can do as they like. I've become immune to adverse criticisms, lies, distortions. How can you prevent them?

I probably never did a portrait of a woman artist because I never knew any intimately. Is it necessary to do one just to prove one is not antifeminist? I don't pay any attention to women's lib or their detractors or defenders. I read only what interests me. I find it useless and silly to try to defend oneself—you simply waste your energy.

I wrote a thirty-three-page article on Mishima just before entering the hospital. Japs took it immediately and paid well. Now I am trying to place it with an American magazine.

Must stop. Will take several weeks, I feel, to get back to normal.

Hawaii:

I saw a volcano before flying back. This one presents a vast terrain of smoking earth. The rain falls and meets with heated lava and exudes this steam. You walk over lava paths, and around the immense crater.

It is a scene of incredible desolateness. One path is poetically called Desolation Trail. The trees are burned clear of leaves, left as white bleached skeletons. They look like [Yves] Tanguy paintings. The ground is cooled lava through which flowers persist in growing. But it is the very image of death itself. This volcano is still erupting and being studied. One photographer was busy taking photographs of a lava flow when a new one started behind him. He was a forester and had a radio transmitter in his car. A helicopter flew out and rescued him, but his car is still there, half buried in lava.

I saw moving pictures of volcanoes in action and it is like a child's idea of Hell as described by the Catholics. Not one, but rows of fountains of fire. In this case of Desolation Trail, the lava overran a road which led to the black sand beach. The scientific American mind has it all organized, with drawings, maps, little lights flashing on to study how the earth is formed. I never realized that most islands are formed of eruptions from the sea. The lava accumulates and adds to the mountain each time. The last one added thousands of acres to Hawaii. Things grow again. The real estate people come and plant their "For Sale" signs on the still-smoking lava. To look into the heart of a volcano is terrifying. It smells of sulfur.

I wrote for Rochelle Holt's collection of poems, *Eidolons*:

Ascending towards Kilauea volcano in Hawaii, the trees, flowers, bushes, fruit, birds grew rarer and finally there were none at all. Where the soft earth was, the grass paths, the weathered fences, there was only a black lava, not shining as it does when wet and erupting, but the dead color of the blackest ash. It hardened. It burned trees to bone-white skeletons. Approaching it, it smoked still, ready for other eruptions. It was a vast crater. One could walk on its rim looking down at the infernal pit. It smelled of sulfur. There was a silence, a suspense, for everyone who leaned over knew what had come before, a wild, incredible explosion, fountains of fire, rocks propelled in the air. Perhaps because I had been near death several times in my life, I recoiled from the volcano. It was a landscape of death. I hated the black void, the black expanse of emptiness. I wanted to return to the flowers, the rain forest, and I felt the deepest admiration not for the gaping angry volcano but for the small yellow flowers which persisted in growing among the black rocks of fury. I saw only the devastating explosion until a poet from Australia said: "But it is the energy of fire which created our world."

[Fall, 1971]

It was the year of letters. The Diary became an exchange of letters. It was an avalanche of letters, all of them personal, intimate and like the demands of a friend. The Diary became answers to letters. At six or seven A.M., whether in New York or in Los Angeles, I open the black plastic briefcase, six inches deep, and take letters out to be answered. In the early morning light I make an effort to see and hear the person who writes to me. Sometimes they send photographs, sometimes I make a note on a card: "poetic letter, fascinating letter, photographer, artist, sculptress, musician. Sent bad poems, sent a beautiful engraving. Friends." Instantaneous friends because they respond to the Diary by similar revelations. They confess, they describe their intimate life. I am taken into their life. A young couple in Switzerland studying at the Jung Institute: He is a painter and she talks to me in fourteen pages. A young Frenchman, a cultural attaché in the Near East, is a painter and writer. But he does not bring me the essence of Baghdad. He does not love it. He brings me his love affairs and his introspection. Claude Louis-Combet sends me two dazzlingly poetic books, sensuous and perverse. Marcel Moreau writes a letter which reminds me of Artaud in its vehemence. Rochelle Holt in Sioux City buys a press and prints her poems, as well as those of others. Beatrice Harris, like a nondestructive June, voluptuous in body and brilliantly lucid in mind, writes me lovingly and full of awareness. Frances Field, in her widowhood, turns to writing, not painting. Newly discovered Spanish relatives, Comtesse de la Taille (Paloma) and her sister in Madrid, send me a fan. Letters from unknowns. A woman from Austria sends me photographs of Greece.

Gerald Robitaille writes a vicious book about Henry. Why did Henry trust him for four years? As a parting gift he gave Gerald $5,000 so he could get started in France.

Letter from John Pearson planning an Anaïs Nin celebration in Berkeley. The young German woman photographer who took photographs during the making of television program generously sends me copies in color of Louveciennes, Villa Seurat, Michel Simon. Letters from Daisy Aldan enclosed in her Rudolf Steiner dogma. As soon as you enclose yourself in a dogma, life becomes narrow and restricted. Letters of distress, letters expressing the need to see me, to talk with me. One letter describes the Diaries as a "natural high." Letters asking for interviews. More poetry than I can read. Isel Rivero from Austria describes a trip with Cortázar, and a kiss from him, in a poem. Letter from Fossey, who put together the *Cahiers des amis d'Anaïs Nin*. He is a Latin American journalist, poet, novelist. Letters from Henry on small matters. From my publisher on publication problems. Piles of novels from publishers asking for a comment. A book by Erika Freeman on Theodor Reik, proving he is old-fashioned and conventional.

Did I write that while talking to Dr. Raymond Weston I discovered it was cancer I had and that Dr. Parks in New York had not told me? "Miraculous recovery," said Dr. Weston, who now takes care of me. But it made me take rest seriously.

The Diary reflected only what I saw and heard. The death of Michael Field came as a shock to everyone. It happened while I was in Virginia, so I only received the second vibration. No one believed it at first. Michael in his fifties was at the peak of his popularity. He was working on several books at once, everyone sought him out. He had vast dreams of reforming airline food, of being televised like Julia Child. He worked for Time-Life.

I was familiar with his speed, restlessness, breathlessness. He received a sign, he broke down, he was exhausted. His dreams, his expectations were a strain, he was always under pressure, lively, tense, anxious. Frances was concerned. The trip for *Time* to the Orient was clocked, rushed. No time to rest or enjoy. The American way of non-living. Frances wanted to write the books while he recorded the recipes, so as to be able to spend more time with him. But he was a public figure who liked his audience, and Frances was given only the exhausted human being. One evening he complained of fatigue and lay down, and was killed by a massive heart attack. At his burial his publisher admitted: "We killed him." Frances was submerged in the complications brought on by his death and had hardly time to grieve. At his funeral service they played a piano recording of his. His new friends did not know the marvelous pianist he had been until deafness obliged him to take up his hobby, cooking, as a professional occupation. I saw the struggle, the murderous rivalries, agents, percentages, exploitation of his gifts, the inhuman pressures. This and his own natural extravagance created a constant struggle. When Frances demanded a rest from public life, a slowing down, a more human, intimate life, she was instinctively seeking to save his life. But he could not rest. He was enslaved by the American dream; wealth alone would bring freedom.

Perhaps because he was so intensely alive I cannot accept his death. He left a resonance of music, of dinners which were works of art, of his renaissance spirit. Another one who does not die in my mind's vision is Varèse. He does not fade. When I think of him, he appears exactly alive in all his detail. Strange how some of the dead do not fade and others slip away into the void.

The reading of Van Gogh's letters made me aware of the undertow of depression which lies at the bottom of my life, ever ready to suck me down. I fight it. When it greets me early in the morning, I rush to the pool and the swim heals me. And then the letters, a furnace of love and a thousand connections. But it is there, and when I read the biographies of those who succumbed to it, I am aware of it. Wayne McEvilly wrote about Volume Four: "The refusal to despair."

How I strain the ugly and choose to remember only the mayfly and the lunar moth out of *The Hellstrom Chronicle,* a science film of magnified insects which depicts all the horrors invented by nature.

Up to the time I met Oliver Evans I wrote my lectures and read them to the audience. And even then I was nervous, cold. One day Oliver asked me to come and talk informally with his class, which usually consisted of fifteen or sixteen students, and I arrived without notes. I was ushered into a full auditorium of two or three hundred persons. I had to talk. And I did. For three-quarters of an hour. Having done this well, I lost my fear and from then on I talked spontaneously, even without notes. My confidence grew. I finally could talk at Reed College commencement without preparation.

I discovered that this spontaneous talk with the students affected them more than a written lecture.

I sincerely believe I have liberated more women than the angry women's libbers. Another one came up to me at the Gotham Book Mart, somber bloodless face, big wide-brimmed hat, and said: "How could you relate to a chauvinist pig like Miller?"

Dr. Bogner suggested I do not respond emotionally but study my defenses quietly and be ready for the fray.

Hatred and war never won anything.

Letter to a young poet:

It is true that I am overburdened and overworked and I cannot read manuscripts. I am enclosing a letter which will explain the situation. I did look over your poems. They have great beauty and are truly expressive. But alas, nature turns things around; I have the wish but not the energy anymore to help others. Last year I had a bout with cancer, and though cured, have less energy. So please do not be disappointed. In poetry I have never been able to get any of my poet friends published. Years ago I showed editors the best poetry sent to me. My best poets are publishing their own work. The writer is not all powerful in America as he is in other countries. But please go on writing; as Miller said, in the end it pushes its way like the plants. I wrote for twenty years in a void, and I learned patience. So did Miller. Just keep writing. You are definitely a poet, and you have a sense of meaning and richness.

[Winter, 1971-1972]

Winter. Los Angeles. Frost on the ground in the morning but the sun melts it. The weeping willow has shed its leaves but not the other trees. The birds are quiet. They come to feed and to bathe in the pool. I sit at my desk at seven A.M. I work on pages on ostracism as a writer, surgery, LSD, portrait of Cornelia Runyon, Renate Druks, Paul Mathiesen, Jim Herlihy, Peter Loomer, Peggy Glanville-Hicks, the Barrons, Huxley, Alan Watts.

The love of Mexico.

The growing detachment from New York.

Nature.

In Sierra Madre one day I went to the post office and there was no mail at all. I felt desolate. Today my mail is enormous and I can hardly keep up with it. I have to answer with cards or short notes. I get books from publishers asking for comments. Books from friends. Watercolors, engravings, photographs. Requests to talk here, there. Reviews, interviews, visitors. I cannot see all the people who want to see me.

John Pearson arranged a celebration in my honor at Berkeley. He did it with so much lightness, casualness, joyfulness, that the atmosphere of thousands of people seemed to be that of a small, informal intimate meeting. It was so warm, so harmonious. John had invited women I suggested who were good writers but not known: Sharon Spencer, Evelyn Hinz, Lynn Sukenick, Deena Metzger. He also invited Richard Centing as editor of the newsletter; Harold Norse, the poet; and Robert Snyder, who was to show a roughly edited documentary film. There was a feeling of love and fraternity. Toward the end John brought to the stage a young man, Richard Stoltzman, who played on his clarinet Olivier Messiaen's "Flight of a Bird," a piece he composed in a German prisoner-of-war camp. He played with incredible finesse, it made one fly into space, the crowd left elated by the music. A perfect ending.

Judy Chicago reproached me for not taking this opportunity to talk about women's problems, child care, clinics, equality of salary, etc. I answered that there were women better equipped to do this, that my work consisted of freeing woman psychologically.

Each one of us must do what he does best.

The letters I received were full of recognition that this evening had given them the desire to live, to pursue their talents, had filled them with hope and joy.

When I first met Judy Chicago I was impressed with her honesty, directness, boldness. I asked her to come and see me. We sat beside the pool, cooling our feet. She gave me her tender and vulnerable side. The persona dropped off immediately. A warm, admiring friendship developed. Even though our ideas were different, they were good for each other. It was a salutary difference. I grew very fond of her. I encouraged her to write so she would not give so much time to teaching and lecturing. A book would take care of that. She must preserve her time for work. She brought out my own strength.

I admired "Womanhouse," a prodigious feat.

It was a shock to me when she criticized the Berkeley Celebration.

Letter to Judy Chicago:

I'm trying to put in a letter how I felt about the women who criticized the celebration.

I suffered twenty years of criticism for being apolitical. Now I am getting the same treatment from radical women.

The Diaries show I found another route to liberation. I will no longer accept criticism. And I feel it is not clever of the political women to alienate me (as the political men did) because I have a great influence on women who do not respond to *them,* and I bring into the movement women they could never reach.

Because I respect the way you work, I want you to respect the way I work. I inspire women. I do not propagandize. It is not wise to split the women now when we need each other. I am fully aware of their hostility, and I am also aware that it is patterned after men's methods in the forties during the dogmatic phase of Marxism. So let me work in my own way. I was generous to your activities; I can be helpful; I have a name. But I demand the same freedom. I will not be subjected to dogmatic, narrow tactics. If the radical women continue to harass me, they will lose all that women could gain by not imitating men's political bigotry.

I thought the comments which were quoted in the San Francisco *Chronicle* petty and unintelligent. The comment on Varda was absurd. Women have courted men and there is nothing offensive about Varda's courting of women. The celebration was in part to introduce unknown women writers and to inspire women to create. It was not a political meeting. The radical women have lost all sense of reality, of proportion, of fairness. The celebration was planned by a man, John Pearson. The attitude of radical women alienates both men and women.

You don't seriously believe I would adopt their tactics when all my life and work have been devoted to helping human beings understand each other, to avoid aggressivity, hostility, hatred.

Do you think that if I held out against men's political obsessions for thirty years and accepted persecution from them, I will yield now to women's imitation of revolutionary tactics?

Those who come to my gatherings come because of my work. My work liberated them. Why do the radical political women come? I have made it clear I am not political. Mine are not political meetings. No one invited political women. I find their tactics ineffectual and self-destructive. They are destructive in their narrowness and fanaticism.

Nona Balakian. A tender face, soft dark eyes, a warm smile. Her whole life dedicated to literature. She is in the review section of the *New York Times*. Her desk is a mountain of books which she has to assign to the proper reviewer. She treats her writers with gentleness. She has acuity of judgment. I enjoy our lunch together because we can talk about writers without cruelty.

Her sister Anna teaches French literature at NYU. Has written several dazzling books on symbolism and surrealism and a biography of André Breton. Anna's apartment overflows with books. Her two children are beautiful, brilliant and fine musicians. It is my favorite place to spend an evening. Anna's husband adds to the atmosphere of love. He has the splendid Armenian eyes which I have only seen in Arab children. An atmosphere of liveliness and tenderness I find in few American homes. An evening with them is a feast of music and literature and human warmth.

Read at the Poetry Center [in New York]. Overcrowded. Atmosphere of utter receptivity. While I receive the vibrations from the crowd and messages from certain faces, I read with delight. But the disillusion comes with the questions. I never could find out if it is always the one who does not hear me or understand me who asks the questions, while the sensitive are silent, because after each lecture I receive letters full of understanding from those who did not ask questions. Most questions make me feel I have talked to the deaf and blind. But then this is mitigated by the letters.

After this reading I went to lecture at Westbrook College, Portland, Maine, because of my friendship with Steve Halpert, which was born in a strange way.

I received a letter from a businessman who had made enough money so that he could retire and give all his time to his first love: writing. He looked to me to help him get started, he looked to me for the first spark. He found it difficult. His letters revealed a physical weakness which I did not realize was due to leukemia. He died of it. His son read our letters and came to see me. He felt I had given his father his dream of being a writer. Steve was a professor of literature, a sensitive and attractive young man, but it shocked me to hear him say, as his father did: "My dream is to be a writer." But now there was the teaching, a wife and three children. So the correspondence of encouragement continued, similar to the one with his father, and I feared a repetition of his father's pattern.

I have never experienced obstacles and difficulties in writing. Perhaps because I began so early (at eight years of age).

More lectures, television interviews, seminars at Esalen, Santa Clara, Cal Arts, Sacramento, St. John's College. Celebration.

Ian Hugo made a new film which he called *Levitation*. Inspired by my words: "The poet teaches levitation."

A man is watching birds flying high above his head, and after some failures and in spite of a woman's terror, succeeds in flying. She then joins him and they fly together. He escapes from a marine prison in which he has been transformed into a bird, swims out of this and joins her again in a watery blue ballet from which he detaches himself to penetrate black totem figures of fierce, menacing birds. In the end, standing above all these, he appears half bird, half man.

Beatrice. A very beautiful woman, with long black hair, large eyes, a voluptuous body. Magnetic. She is a psychiatrist and a scientist. She bears some resemblance to June except that in June sensuality ruled whereas in Beatrice the intellect dominates. She is so beautiful in a sensual way that she reawakened the question which was never answered: my love of woman, which reaches up to the sensual frontier and no further. But it stirs in the depth of my unconscious, aware that it nearly asserted itself. The question was never answered because June did not initiate me at the time when I might have been awakened. It has remained like a small area unlived in my life, in fact the only one.

If I were thirty Beatrice would have disturbed me. Now with my love entirely focused on man, I can admire, love, enjoy the friendship of women, draw very close to them without any sensual vibration. It is a happy state because I can love them naturally, deeply, and without ambivalence.

At Sharon's house, with a beautiful South American woman at the piano, I had a reverie of what might happen if I were granted a second life; I might enjoy the one delight I missed.

Letter to a friend:

On my way to Goddard College. Your letter makes me hesitate to see you in Chicago for fear of disappointing you. I must explain that public life is not of my own choosing. The lectures are my way of earning a living. Long ago I found that the public event and the personal life were in conflict. I would catch glimpses of friends I wanted to spend time with. But without lectures I would not even have a glimpse of them. My friends understand. But you expect me to be free, to shake off the work, to cancel meetings with students and to take the day off, carefree and playful. This I cannot do. You seem to take my work as a refusal; you are overly sensitive, and feel I should not give in to the pressures. Well, this year the pressure to work is there. I love my work. I love communing with the world. During this period I can only have friends who do not make me feel I am neglecting or ignoring them. How you manage to have a life of absolute leisure I don't know. You criticize my public, but there is nothing wrong with my public, they are aggregates of writers like yourself, well worth talking to.

Whenever I have a free day and Bob Snyder can gather together his crew, they come to work on the documentary. Bob does not direct, he begins by talking a great deal as if to create an animation. He asks me questions, prods me. Certain subjects inspire me to improvise. We work in the little room in which I write. I talk about Varda. The quartet comes to play and I write while they play, which shocked Henry, but for years I have written during the quartet's playing, inspired by the music.

We seek pieces of film about Partch, Caresse Crosby, from Maya Deren's film, from Kenneth Anger's film. I did not want the focus on me only but outgoing, including the other artists who interested me.

The house, the pool, the weeping willow tree, all made ideal setting.

Letter to a person who writes me a charming letter:

How could I become disillusioned with the world and people when I get a letter like yours? Yes, terrible things are happening in the world, but also marvelous things. Because of the marvelous side, I have remained open and not angry. Some of the students reproach me for not being angry. Anger is toxic!

Having been told so often how wrong it was to write about one's self—how I should take the self out of the diary—I never expected the consequences. Because I gave of myself, many women felt I spoke for them, liberated them from secrecy and reticence. I did not expect to get letters from women working in offices, on farms, married and lonely in little towns, nurses, librarians, students, runaways, dropouts, pregnant women without husbands, women doctors, women in the middle of a divorce. Suddenly I was discovering a world.

The dominant theme of the letters was loneliness and lack of confidence in whatever the writers undertook. The miracle was that my diary made them eloquent, confessional. I became a friend you could talk to, ask questions. I heard from women who had exiled themselves in Greece, in France. One wrote from Tibet where she was assisting her husband with his filmmaking. I discovered women with talents never used before. One woman sent me her first drawing made after reading the Diary. The Diary cured depression, opened secret chambers.

There was no ego in the Diary, there was only a voice which spoke for thousands, made links, bonds, friendships. All the clichés about self-absorption were destroyed. There was no *one* self. We were all *one*. The more I developed *my* self, the less mine it became. If all of us were as willing to expose this self, we would feel neither alone nor unique. I was so tired of the platitudes hurled at me. The two most misinterpreted words in the world: narcissism and ego. The simple truth was that some of us recognized the need to develop, grow, expand—occupations which are the opposite of those two words. To desire to grow means you are not satisfied with the self as it is, and the ego is exacting, not indulgent.

"You speak rain words which fill the saucer eye of a parched insomniac."

"Thank you for helping me to learn the passageways."

Letters. Voices. Women and men enter my life. Persons I never knew existed. In exchange for my Diary they write intimate letters: "I am nineteen and live in a very small town which does not even have a library. I feel I am going mad with loneliness. But now I have your Diary as a companion, and to discover that you felt as I did makes me feel less lonely."

A black girl stops me in the street: "I am a night nurse; I could not have lived through those long nights but as I read the Diaries I felt I was not immobilized but living a hundred lives."

A woman of sixty: "I thought I had died and was just waiting for the final departure, but the Diaries wakened me, made me relive my life, enjoy it, find new aspects to dream about; you gave me a second life."

A woman with eight children on a farm: "I write a diary at night. That way I keep my two selves alive, the early me who wanted to be a writer and the one who is attached to the farm."

"Through the Diaries I have uncovered the seeds of my own ability to dream."

"My world is richer because you have given me yours."

"When I read the Diary, it took wings! All was transcended. Like some immense swan, it took me on its back lifting me into the air— that now familiar air of your vision which I draw in like strength, like purity, like invisible draughts of growth."

"May you know whom you have touched, awakened, raised from the dead. May you know the legacy you have already left, the soil you have watered, the seeds planted, all the solar barques you have launched toward the sun."

"You are the fringe of a new humanity that is moving through flesh to the psychic as spirit and matter develop simultaneously in a spiral ebb and flow of eternity."

"Reading your Diary is like reading by lightning."

"Your Diary restored hope in me of a world that is possible if one has the courage to make it."

From a grandmother: "I did not believe I could ever uncover all the treasures hidden away in the nooks and crannies of me. But there they are, sprung back to life, with all the nostalgia alive again."

"A great hunger in me was being fed."

"Your Diary has drawn up what I thought I had lost, it was so deeply hidden within. It was a surprise to read my feelings and thoughts in your words. After a long period when I read only feminist propaganda and fiction, it was a clear day and cool air to read your Diary."

"The Diaries are my helpmate. Because they're so personal and honest, I know that you have been through everything I go through in my own struggle to find my full humanity."

"I read your Diaries and because of your incredible courage and your creation of yourself, I began to grow inside myself the woman that had been buried in my fantasies and imaginings. I thank you for giving me this faith—to believe that I could be what I imagined myself to be."

"You gave me the courage to embark on my self-discovery."

"How reassuring to know that you were in my backpack ready to read whenever I needed inspiration."

"You taught me to be a woman of tenderness, affection and independence."

"When I read your books—when I feel your faith in yourself—in dreams, in art—I truly feel an inner strength, an inner burning, a desire to touch the hearts of others no matter how long it takes."

"I even went as far as trying to fashion my life after yours. That of course was wrong and disastrous. It was just that I loved you and I wanted to be close to you. Your writings, your honesty, helped me accept myself as a person, a woman, an artist."

"You have made a difference in my life. You have confirmed my belief that miracles are possible in life when it seemed that everyone else wanted only to break me of that belief. You have given me strength to pursue my ideas and dreams."

"I will never forget holding it and reading the first lines—I had found my opium. Your life challenged me to live beyond myself, to make a dream and a palace from each day. Your works sustained me through high school and even now I turn to the Diary to beautify my life."

"You made me want to write because through your writings I could see that the detailed account of one woman's life, an extraordinary life, yes, but also an ordinary one—such an account had a great deal of meaning for the rest of us."

"Your Diary nourishes me. Not that I am like you. The feelings you write of are not mine. But there are moments, when you describe what you have seen, that I know you have been here with me. I am understood, loved and reassured. In the past, I jumped from airplanes to at once dissociate and reconnect myself to the earth. Having read your words, such acts are no longer necessary."

"There are women who roar and demand to be heard. You are so much more effective because you whisper in our ears and by so doing touch our very souls."

"Your life and work have been a reaffirmation of what is positive. In a way there is no beginning and no end to your work, and this must be the highest form of compliment. To me, it has been a spiritual document, for it is the 'livingness' of it (feeling), like music, that is so sustaining and inspiring."

"I was still a little amazed that words could be found to express those things I had thought were inexpressible because I could only say them with music."

"You have revived the intuitive, caring woman in me and I feel I'll be a better therapist for it."

"By living constantly in and through the very essence of people, in the world of feeling and imagination, you have killed not only ugliness but time itself—no aging—yet a constant evolution towards the summit, or rather the 'center,' the depths."

"I read you and I hear myself think. You describe so clearly what I feel every second of my waking and dream existence."

"Because of you my writing and my painting have improved enormously, and the pains of this journey through darkness are soothed by knowing that you are my comrade and fellow traveler."

"These books are not only self-expression but also are a dialogue in which you speak and the reader answers."

"There is a recurrence of this desire or sensation of being between conscious and unconscious and the whole conflict associated with it which is so vividly described."

"You renew in me the determination and courage to be true to myself (even at nineteen, these things have been threatened!). Through the Diaries I have uncovered the seeds of my own abilities to dream, to live the dream, and the strength to create an expanded, open world, a livable world, through art. What a joyous beginning you have given me!"

"I would like to say it was your honesty, or your intellect, or your creativity that I responded to. It is, rather, your wholeness. The unity of properties that comes from a centered being."

"Parts of myself long ago put to sleep have been gently wakened."

"My world is richer because you have given me yours."

"You are the fringe of a new humanity that is moving through flesh to the psychic."

"You are writing my life also."

"In evoking something eternal, you escape the fate of topical writing."

"Your writing reaches deep inside of me and tells me things about myself that I only know in the dream."

"You create for us the world in which we would like to live."

"The Diary is better than hashish or LSD."

"I am sometimes afraid that my own personal growth will stop the moment your writing does."

"My responses are so strong, I can only read a few pages at a time! Your work truly is the nourishment dreams and joy are born of."

"The discovery of your Diaries was as monumental an experience as my discovery of Proust."

"I am not the same person I was when I began them."

"Thank you for sharing yourself, for destroying loneliness."

"I was lost. The Diary was magic, lightning, an injection of mystical energy that filled me with new worlds."

"I am sixteen. In your Diaries I see the person I am and the person I want to be."

"The concept that life needs joy—and that when there is no longer joy, there must be change—enabled me to change my life."

"I felt that I was reading about myself, as though a voice from inside was articulating for me all the conflicts I felt so that I could begin to understand them. You have taught me more about how we understand and misunderstand ourselves and others than any other artist, philosopher or scientist."

"More important than the psychological insights in your work was the subtle essence of spirituality that touched my soul."

"You have put down in writing my life and thoughts. It was a strange experience to read of myself like that."

"Your works affect me as magnificent music—every nerve vibrates, I soar to great heights and then go limp. Never before have I responded thus to the written word. Your complete candor about yourself is beautiful, having the cleansing effect of a mountain spring washing over my skin, particularly in a world over-full of people concerned with creating an 'image.'"

"You have done as you wished to do—you have written as a woman and not as a copy of a man. And it is frightening to first see and read and feel and think that for so long we have been misled and deluded in our most loved books. Language has been man's, and only now with your work do I see the difference that can be when a woman writes as a woman. Damn you, Anaïs Nin, damn you. You make me think and feel as a woman, and you put it down on paper. It isn't fair, and it is very strange and not a little frightening. Now I have to grow, now I have to become what I have been hiding beneath intellect."

"Through your words, your refractions of experience, I have come upon the thresholds of my soul."

"It is a real shimmering of light on water."

"Your Diary is like a long-drawn-out blood transfusion, each volume bringing new life and joy and love and healing."

"What I feel awakening in me is my nature as woman. I find in your work life itself, the original union between woman and life."
All the love I have given is now coming back to me.

Letter to Marianne Greenwood:

How bad I felt at your description of malaria and your loss of weight. I both suffer and enjoy your adventures. Sometimes I would like to change lives with you, the perpetual wanderer, roaming the world, homeless but with a thousand friends. I am trapped in what I call the "Sorcerer's Apprentice." Like all writers, I wanted my love and my work answered and now it is too much, and I am submerged in work. Every college wants me. A hundred and thirty letters awaited me when I came back from my tour of Chicago, Milwaukee, Vermont and New York. Soon I shall have to say: enough! and go in hiding. I read the letters and wonder which ones deserve an answer. They all do. They are all beautiful.

Last night I had two interesting visitors: Dory Previn, poet and singer, who is writing a play, and Georg Troller, the director of the German television documentary I made in Paris. He is filming Dory Previn, has already filmed Daniel Ellsberg, and is looking for César Chavez—our heroes. But Chavez is hard to find; he has to hide.

We visited "Womanhouse." An old, huge mansion which was about to be torn down. Judy Chicago asked if she could use it for a month or two. She gathered fifteen young women artists, her students, and gave each one a room to decorate as the room of their dream. They created the most surrealist and original effects. One of the most striking ones was done by a young woman who was given the staircase. At the top of the stair, against the wall, she placed a mannequin dressed as a bride. The bride's train spread down the stairs to the bottom. At this point the figure of the bride disappeared into the wall, half of her was drowned and ceased to exist. One young woman decorated a room in the most chaotic, neglected way. The bed was a mattress on the floor, there were empty beer bottles strewn around, everything was dusty, grimy, books and records on the floor, clothes piled up in a corner. Then, within this room she built a small bower, the walls covered with delicate pink textile, the lamp dimmed, a beautiful lot of cushions strewn about, a place for dreaming.

Letter to Claude Louis-Combet:

I am very proud that you dedicated your book to me [*Miroir de Leda*]. I do not need to see it, as I know it is written by one of the most poetic writers of France. I admire the depths to which your work reaches, the daring and the psychological innovation. When the skill of the poet, the complete mastery of language is matched to the willingness to go into the depths, there is nothing to equal it. Your lyricism and your sense of imagery are so strong and so controlled at the same time, the depths never reach chaos.

After a lecture Ruth Barati placed a beautiful necklace around my throat. It was a sculptured moon, which followed the roundness of the neck, with a glowing sun hanging on it. I wrote her a letter. She told me that George Barati, her husband, composer and orchestra conductor, intended to put some of my text to music. She sent me a recording of his music.

Was on a television program with the Russian poet Yevtushenko. He was vain, arrogant, unpoetic. He disparages woman, said no diary could ever be truthful, and I, who already had discovered he was a bad poet, remained detached. The poem which was read by his translator was mediocre, a cliché.

Letter to a questioner:

The questions you ask are not possible for me to answer. Any study that seeks to go further into the Diaries than I was able to share is not fair to the diary work. It is not by choice that I avoided certain subjects but out of respect for others' vulnerabilities. My sharing all I could should inspire respect for what I could not share. You are free to interpret the Diaries as you wish but not to seek more than I was able to give. Beyond that is truly not understanding that the Diary is a balance between revelation and not violating others' feelings. As you know, each portrait had to be released by the person portrayed. I ask you to respect the boundaries I set. If I violated this, as so many writers do, I would not be the kind of person people confide secrets to.

Everyone wants me to lecture. Everyone wants to see me. Media has produced so many fakes that people need to know I am real, that I *am* my work. When I tell them it is all in the work, they do not quite accept that. They want to see me in the flesh.

––––––––

From a report by James Campoccio:

[Anaïs Nin] culminated her stay with a personal appearance, the night after her televised program with Yevtushenko. The setting was San Francisco's First Unitarian Church.

She walked in and confronted her crowd. Her face was carved from pain. But it was as if a thoughtful sculptor had finished his work—with a moist coating clay of compassion and understanding. You could tell her features came from the same dramatic mold as Antonin Artaud's, and the other strong artists who, with her, shaped the future of surrealism and existentialism. . . .

The audience began to stare shyly at her physical form. It was garbed in a beautiful red gown, and it spoke with a voice that had a melody.

Miss Nin announced a decision to assume the job of full-time correspondent to the world, now that her self-correspondence, her diaries, were complete. She would extrovert fully, and share the knowledge of her life.

Throughout her words, she demonstrated a rare compassion; it seemed to go out to each listener. And sometimes the people addressing questions to her felt they had to bolster their stance, with large words and complexities. They did not realize, that in addressing a self-realized being, nothing is needed—save simplicity.

Jokingly, the authoress mentioned the first hours spent in the company of Durrell and Miller. "At first we wrote only for each other; public acknowledgment was not there . . . and perhaps now in the audience next to 'you' is the famous writer of tomorrow."

And then, not trapped in false humility, she said, "After all, am 'I' to be the only good writer?" The audience laughed and respected her all the more.

Agreed to write a preface for *Harvard Advocate*'s number on "Women's Writing" only if they included Marguerite Young, Marianne Hauser, Anna Balakian, Sharon Spencer and Bettina Knapp.

Letter to Marcel Moreau:

I have two marvelous letters from you and the manuscript of *Les Epileptions*. Because your writing produces exactly the reverie, the *ivresse*, the dizziness you wish it would, I sometimes find it difficult to answer. It is as if it plunged me into depths where I wish to remain, and where my life at present and other writers do not allow me to stay. It is as if I felt only from there can I answer, and what has happened to me is what you do not wish, that I have been pulled into the surface of the limelight, to appear in the limelight, to perform as an incarnation of what I write, because the young of America are so fearful of being once more deceived, by words or acts, as they have been, and so they wish to see me.

But I was immensely touched first by the letter in which you imagine our friendship in the pages of the Diary as it might have been, and then share with me the incredible vertiginous pages of manuscript. They silence one like a drug. For the first time I feel writing as being a drug, something (as you once wrote) to drink and consume. It is written with body and nerves and blood, and I would say that such a potion is almost more than human beings can bear. If you feel I have inhabited the depths, I feel that you bring into language sensations and experiences I once thought indescribable. In a sense, the metamorphosis of flesh into words, and words into flesh, is what you accomplish. It is a prodigious feat. I have not abandoned my efforts, as you will see from this letter. I offered to preface the book. I am writing to my English publisher to see if he will do it in England. It is not because I want to draw you out of the obscurity in which you are at ease (and more favorable to writing than my surfacing); it is because I feel people need the drug you offer, the vision and the genuine heaven and hell you dispense.

But why imagine the friendship in the past? It is taking place today. I am as ready today to spiral into labyrinths, yours, or to partake of nightfevers. These journeys are dangerous to take alone, are they not? Someone has to listen. So I do. Someone has to prove the drug is potent and awakens dreams and rebellions, and angers never awakened before. *"D'où l'écriture en tant qu'insulte à la sobriété?"*

Beautiful letters, and extraordinary life, lived in dimensions rarely reached. It makes the voyage to the moon dull. But at times I tremble for you as much as for that moment on the burning ship, simply because there are labyrinths one enters in which there are no echoes of other human beings and one no longer knows if one is still in life, as I felt when I wrote *House of Incest*. But in this case I may say that I understand every word . . . *"la rose des voix intérieures."* . . .

Letter to J. C. Travis:

Even though I am on a strenuous and continuous lecture tour I want to answer your most beautiful and eloquent letter. Nothing makes me happier than to hear the Diaries restore us to life and faith, because I have so often known anxiety and depression and discouragement and if out of all that I made a potion which heals, I am happy. I know so well the feeling of being oppressed by events, and then finding something in a book which is like a transfusion. I owe many writers so much. Yes, I have known the mists and clouds and fogs around the plane, and sudden clearing, and also the strange fact that people only draw close together in danger, as you say men do in wartime. Thank you for understanding condensation. Yes, and Tolstoy, though there is no direct influence. I have not read Amiel since my teens. I should reread him. But when?

Miller (on his eightieth birthday) and I said wistfully: "What happened to our leisure?" We had so much time to live in France. Is overwork our vice? Is it the culture which makes us work and not allow for leisure? This year I had new responsibilities, so I had to say yes to all the lectures. In the summer I must work on Volume Five. I am glad you say you have to have time for sloth. I can only achieve this now by running away, and it must be the tropics so I can become a nature woman. . . .

Yes, your patients are like my students I love so much, but they eat me, and it is all giving. They send poems and manuscripts to read. They want, they need, they ask, and my mail is staggering. You are right to fear for my safety and quiet. We will meet.

Letter to a young writer:

I am very touched by your article. It has all the warmth, the understanding, the human approach which I had sensed in you. You captured all kinds of things no one else did, the things to laugh at, the mood of the lecture, the students, and I can't help feeling that this is a new kind of journalism, lacking the cold detachment, the looking for the flaw, of which we are all so tired. I can only say you were overgenerous, but this is so rare nowadays, in what someone called our "bitchy society," that people must find it a novelty, a relief. . . . At last no caricature, no put down. You covered a lot of unexplored territory. I hope this article does you good, if this is what you will do for a living until you write other things. I am personally grateful that my sense of friendship was justified.

Reading your article, I wondered what would develop with your writing, what you want from it, where it will go. Just now, I imagine, being a portraitist may enrich it with people.

I always daydreamed about being a "roving editor" (the "roving" part was essential). French writers won't teach; they feel even badly paid journalism, as it is in France, is more variable and less monotonous and enriching. Is that how you feel? Do you want more books for your Nin shelf? Incidentally, for your own information, my books are taught in fifty-two colleges. Adoptions, they call it. That is how the lectures began, through young professors teaching the books.

Letter to Marcel Moreau:

Your book is dazzling and utterly amazing. The realm you have uncovered, explored, is, up to now, obscurely felt and never expressed. Only with such astounding poetry could you go so deep into the senses, into the endless ramifications of sensation. You confirm what I believed, that only with poetry can you *transmit* a life of the senses which is otherwise indescribable. I feel it is immensely bold, and new, and may frighten some. But for me it was a revelation, an extension into illimitable experience of the senses. I recognize its veracity, its accuracy.

I think it is not only the ultimate expression of sensual love, but that it stirs in all of us remembered sensations which may be sought again, hopelessly, in other loves. I don't know of anything like it in literature. You have gone deeper than anyone could go in prose, because you are able, by some miraculous skill, to expand, to develop as an ultimate flowering, all the senses we possess, but with such a depth of knowledge and daring granted few poets. Illimitable dimensions. Illimitable explorations. The beauty of expression is so contagious, it appeals directly to this unconscious you enter, it throws tentacles and awakens dormant knowledge. As a poet, you have advanced into layers of experience the psychologists whispered about and most of us did not believe. But I believe, and I am deeply impressed, both as a poet and as a woman. It is not a book to be read, it is a new life to be lived; as if as plants, we did not know until now how many tentacles, how many leaves, how many pistils, how many perfumes there were in our bodies. It is a book which expands one's being, and takes him further into his own responses than he has ever been. The true revealer. I cannot tell you how subtle, how at once sensual and psychic a language you have developed, to make both body and psyche respond and traverse the paths you open.

Dory Previn. The voice of a poet and the voice of a woman with depths, ironies and humor, profoundly moving. She sings from the depth of her own feelings. Human depth and wit.

My publisher received a cable from a woman with the following message: "Please tell Anaïs Nin I am going to commit suicide." She gave her name and address. She was a French Canadian. I took up the telephone and called her. I had no idea of what I was going to say. A very delicate voice answered me. She was stunned by my call. I asked her: "Will you wait until I come to New York and we will have a good talk."

Her answer was a very resigned "I will wait."

Two or three weeks later we met in New York. She was a soft, gentle person; married, with a daughter. Therapy had not helped her. She wanted to be a writer. Every now and then she would plunge into such depressions that she felt death was preferable. We talked for several hours and then I took her to Dr. Bogner. She went back to Montreal with a new strength. We corresponded. She came for another visit and was exposed to an evening at the Balakians' and their warmth.

Then, for the sake of seeing me again, she organized two lectures in Montreal, one at a French college, one at an English college. Because the feeling between the French and the English is hostile, the French students insisted I translate whatever I said in English into French. This included the questions and answers. At the end I was utterly exhausted.

My friendship with the one I playfully called "my suicide" was warm and tender. She was not completely well but the depressions were not as deep.

Letter to Orville Clark:

Here you see a writer at loss for words. Your essay "Studies in the New Erotology,"* was so beautiful, and said for the first time something I had felt

* See also *A Casebook on Anaïs Nin*, edited by Robert Zaller (New York: Meridian Books, 1974).

but not expressed to myself, something I had wished someone would say, something I myself had obscurely sought but did not know consciously I had achieved. It is perfectly expressed and completely original. I can see why you were not satisfied with anything else that was written. Of course, no one caught the desire for fusion, the effort at fusion, and then when you say it was attained, it is like receiving the Nobel Prize, only even better because the Nobel is not always given wisely. I was at once grateful, admiring of the work, the writing, and the concept. I am immensely proud of your essay. . . .

It is strange how, at times, one is brought to fly low in order to answer human questions and one is in danger of flying too low, and then someone comes to remind you of your proper route, and your course is set right again. Anyway, I am touched and happy.

MAGIC CIRCLE WEEKEND—APRIL 28–30
WAINRIGHT HOUSE, RYE, NEW YORK:

The drive with Beatrice Harris to Rye; Beatrice who has such a deft sense of direction even while we talk of subtle subjects. We want to redefine the much distorted use of narcissism and ego. The isolation which strikes the neurotic at the first shock of destructive experience is not narcissism. It is not a willful isolation and has nothing to do with self-love. It is a withdrawal to rescue what is left of a shattered self. In the same way, self-development and a quest for self-awareness and identity are not ego trips.

We talk about our lives, our friends, but it is always to find the meaning of our lives, our friendships. She has that rare mixture of sensuous presence with intelligence and insight which add luminosity and vibrancy to all she does and says.

The house at Rye with its stately beauty reminded me of the house of *The Wanderer,* of Alain-Fournier, of times when people had a sense of living space.

The garden was peaceful and led down to Long Island Sound. It is a home, I thought, in which we arrive as guests, and Adele Aldridge and Valerie Harms, standing in the entrance hall to receive us, make it seem like the hospitality of friends. They were offering champagne, and the fairy-tale clothes of Sas Colby were displayed on mannequins, setting a mood of color and fantasy.

We are distributed to our rooms by Mr. Hewitt who acts as if he is personally interested in our comfort. I can see the Sound from my window. I can feel the presence of the trees.

Adele has placed on my bed a gift of her book illustrating the *I Ching*. A beautiful book with bold and vivid designs, each one a different mood, emotionally appealing. Her work reminded me of the mediaeval expression "illuminated manuscript," a lost art, but this was an illuminated manuscript giving the words of the *I Ching* a face. The large sea-turquoise eyes of Adele see more than other eyes, she sees dreams as clearly as others see the trees and the Sound.

As I come downstairs I see faces which will later become the faces of those I was corresponding with, whose inner faces I knew, and it was my turn to seek the faces of the letters as others seek the face of the Diaries, to discover the physical presence of my letter writers. Some were friends already: Daisy Aldan with her ever-youthful voice and laughter, Evelyn Hinz with her deep, dark eyes which convey all the depth and thoughtfulness of her being, Jeffery Mundy with his airy grace and elusive words, Frances Steloff with her candid blue eyes and white hair glowing like a pearl.

Others whose letters had such vivid accents of distress and solitude: Bebe Herring, tall and beautiful, all eyes too, and Alex Crocker, with his warm, open face and eloquent silences. Lex came from Texas where he is studying philosophy. His letters were moving and deep with feeling.

Bebe Herring gave me the word *furrawn*, which she had discovered in Joyce and would be the title of her novel. The Welsh word meant "talk that leads to intimacy." It had inspired all my lectures this year.

Elaine Marks, teacher of French at Amherst, wrote a biography of Colette and spoke to me in French. Later she stood out in my mind, sitting in the front row when Anna Balakian read her essay on my work, nodding her head in approval of Anna's dazzling study.

Trew Bennett, the potter who had written me such spontaneous and confiding letters about her work and her inner journey, now stood before me as beautiful as her letters, whole, with perfect features, open and tinged with a sadness which never turned to anger or bitterness. The sadness cast her features in a firm, well-balanced beauty. She bears the mark of sorrow without distortion; it is a mark of courage, of complete sincerity. Her work is strong and rich in color.

Jeffery delights in juggling words, in mystifying, in eluding finite meaning. He and his brother seem like two aspects of the same being, both handsome, Jeffery more tenuous, more vaporous, James more grounded, more present, not so prone to taking flights in space.

Nadine [Daily] is silent, but in her silences conveys thoughtfulness, inner activity, and one is curious to know her world. But I knew it would take time, and the weekend was so full and rich it did not allow me to stay with any one person long enough. I was making a superhuman effort of memory, to fuse the person standing before me with the letters received, to reconstruct the exchange that I want to renew and continue. I do not know why I feel that recognizing others, hearing them, sensing them, is so important to life. Too many of us pass in anonymity, invisible, unheard, and I wanted so much to receive all of them. I feel like a gardener concerned with the thirst of flowers, the leaf in danger of withering, the fruit torn off the tree by the wind.

Human beings appear vulnerable, and with great needs. My antennae were spinning furiously to catch all the messages and leave none unheard, but there were so many that I am sure I failed. I read their eyes. I notice when Evelyn sits alone and wonder if she feels isolated, has not found a friend yet. I want to hear every word and receive every message.

Our first evening in the library, when I wanted so much to know them, and they talked about the effect of my work, I felt wistful. The role of the writer forces him to speak for others, and I wanted to hear *their* voices. I had to accept that my Diary was theirs, that they found themselves in it, their voice, and that they were speaking through my work, making revelations about themselves.

I am moved by the response to my work, the statements made about its significance at crucial moments of their lives. I wanted them to introduce themselves, and what they told me was of their encounter with my work, and its impact, so I have to speak about their revealing themselves to me through my words, and my being their voice.

Happenings begin. The walls are covered with paintings. I notice some large, blue sea and sky paintings. I notice masks of iron, abstract and very modern. The face and the cagelike mask interplay, part face, part mask. The sculptress Suzanne Benton is there, and later she will talk about the masks while we try them on and see ourselves transformed. The hand-printed books are in a glass cabinet, and we will talk about them later.

Valerie effaced herself. She was attentive to the flow and continuity, and to the forming of links. She was protective and receptive, asking nothing for herself, running through her slides too quickly for us to seize the intention of her book, a study of the fears which hamper women artists.

At times the whole weekend appeared like a ballet. Everyone brought charms, skills, richness, and we moved about discovering each other. We discovered each other's struggles, evolutions, achievements. We touched, contacted. But I could not select one and go off for a walk, or select two and talk all night; I had a more difficult task, which was to respond to all. With my passion for knowing others, I sought, in the few moments given us, to perceive a whole life, a whole person. I talked with Trew Bennett, with Lex Crocker, with Bebe, with William Claire, with Georgiana Peacher, who is designing and writing a beautiful book, with Helen Bidwell, with Lele Stephens, and others.

The next morning (I was the only one whose body refused to stay up all night) I was up early, at six A.M. I saw Trew sitting out by the water's edge, writing, and I wanted to go out and talk with her, but I had manuscripts to read, Jeffery's poetry, Bebe Herring's novel, poems.

As I came down the curved stairway, Bebe was sitting in a nook, in the sun-drenched stairs, with her large, questioning eyes. We talked about her novel, her struggle to fuse fiction and non-fiction. Dressed in a long flower-colored dress, she seemed like part of the garden, a nymph.

During the talk in the library on women's liberation, Beatrice brought her skill at balancing contradictory and extreme generalizations. She brought symmetry and harmony to ideas carelessly incomplete.

It was then that Larry Sheehan spoke movingly and humanly. He said that it was concern for his daughter's future which made him open to the efforts of women to change women's status. He became aware that his daughter might live in a better world. It was a human and humble and touching concept.

Frances Steloff sat gazing at a yellow daisy, her white hair luminous, her eyes down, looking into the heart of the flower while telling her story of courage and audacity.

She told the whole story of the birth of the Gotham Book Mart, with a capital of $100. She came away with a new awareness of the importance of the Gotham Book Mart in the literary history of America. Every story we told during the weekend ended with: "We took our work to the Gotham Book Mart and Frances Steloff agreed to sell it."

William Claire told the story of *Voyages,* that of a man occupied by a full-time job, writing poetry on yellow pads during interminable conferences and persisting in publishing only what he liked. He had the courage to turn down a bad poem by a famous poet, something very few editors are capable of.

Color and playfulness were given by Sas Colby. We all tried on her capes, skirts, masks, but they came to a life of their own when she put them on, with her pixie face and blond hair, acting out a semidance, skits of her own making, brief airy lines, humorous and in harmony with her clothes.

Anna Balakian read a penetrating essay on my work. By way of symbolism and surrealism, she developed the genesis of the work and its ultimate significance. She opened the very heart of the work. Everyone gasped and begged for a copy. I was close to tears at her understanding and evaluation.

Saturday evening was an evening of slides and films.

The evolutions of friendships, of exchanges, of communication through one's work, were warm and continuous. Everyone was writing; I found manuscripts at my door, poems and letters on my bed. The happenings were necessary to our knowledge of each other's work, but after that was done, we could have lived together for many weekends and not exhausted all we had to say to each other. Most of them had suffered (as I had before the Diaries were published) from isolation and loneliness. This was a banquet. I love the French expression *"liant,"* which means "connecting," like the branches of ivy. In French they say a woman is *liante* or not *liante*. Liana, a beautiful word. It could have been the keyword of the weekend. An atmosphere was created by Valerie and Adele and Larry, of faith and appreciation and encouragement and response. I felt joyful that my work had made the links, and that I could lie back and enjoy the miracle. They were writing, they were walking together, talking together, they were exchanging books, they were living and I could rest as after giving birth. I was being thanked. But I did not want to rest. I wanted to talk at length with everyone, to read all the writing. I couldn't. My body could not. At midnight I was asleep. The life current was strong. It belongs to them now. There was in me a wistful relinquishing dictated by the body, but the receptivity never ceases, as if I were responsible for sustaining the life force. I could sleep. I felt I was inside of my Diaries, enclosing new friends, new faces.

There was another beautiful young woman who had come to me at Green Bay in tears. Moira Griffin. She is here, clear-eyed, graceful.

I was reminded of my envy of the life of George Sand, when distances by carriage were so great from Paris to country homes that friends visited for long periods. They wrote books, put on plays, worked all day, but gathered in the evenings, and I thought how wonderful then to have such long deep days with others when modern life makes our meetings brief and fleeting and travel disperses us.

Here we just had time to begin friendships, to give each other courage. They gave me courage. I was moved when Joan Anacreon stood up during one of the dinners and read with great emotion a poem saying YES YES YES.

I may have been the catalyst, but the radiations of the circle extended far, and each circle gained momentum from the contributions of others. Jeffery shed light and charm, Nadine read her music-filled novel, Beatrice clarified tangled thoughts and left confirmed of her own desire to write.

I came away convinced I had found a way to sustain life and creation, and this selection of people proved it; it was filled with talent, skills, beauty.

Everything I ever gave was returned to me. We gave birth to each other.

Letter to someone who could not attend the Rye weekend:

Your letter did bring your presence to the circle, and I feel as if you had paid me a visit. The weekend was beautiful, so many friendships were born, and so much inspiration. People are lonely in this too-vast land of America— so lonely they came from Texas, Illinois, Indiana, etc.! How much kinder small Paris and café life was to lonely ones! I can write you today because I do seem to generate this unifying principle but at the cost of great exhaustion, so today I am in bed and can answer letters.

Spoke at Chicago Psychoanalytical Society on creativity, invited by Kate Ollendorf. A vicious newspaperman wrecked the good feeling I had established with the women by inventing and lying, putting words in my mouth.

It was also very obvious that the men came to the lunch but left the hall when I began to speak. The director was particularly patronizing and told me he was writing a book about the relationships of famous writers to their fathers. I asked him why he did not include women writers.

At this meeting it was the first time I was made to feel the disparaging attitude of men toward women in the same profession. Not having worked for anyone before, I had never experienced the lack of respect of men in professional situations.

Letter to a participant in the Chicago forum:

The honesty of your letter deserves an answer. You evidently knew much more about the seamy side of Chicago life. I have the happy faculty of tuning in only to the positive or creative side of people and totally disregarding the hostile, the fake and the hypocritical. It is my formula for not despairing.

Your image of that lunch is repulsive. But which one is the true one? As against what you describe, I experience only those who come up to me and are utterly genuine and sincere. The others do not matter. If a few only were in harmony with me, they are the ones who count. You were very genuine and faithful to what I said and intended. Then you saw the other side, which I simply do not wish to live with, or contemplate or explore. My whole effort has been to turn the negative into positive. The students have had enough of a mirror catching only the ugly face of Nixon, etc. Why can we not tune in and stress the deep, the human and the beautiful? Do we always have to register the hostile ones, the destructive ones? They get all the attention.

You explain how you want to be aware of the total picture, the black and the white, an objective synthesis. But you know, from your quote of Durrell, that there is no objective image of the world. We tune in on one aspect or the other according to our temperament. I was not disappointed by your attitude toward me at all. But I did not want those who had read me, those who had waited for years to meet me, to be lumped in one category with the others you had reason to despise.

It is true that the men analysts did not come, but they never come to these luncheons. That is their loss. Other analysts here are giving the Diaries to read to future psychologists, and I have talked with many psychology groups in colleges, and perhaps future psychoanalysts will come to respect what I have done for the science under fire.

My reward, if there is one, is that my work only attracts people I can love in return. The fringe of hostile or indifferent or mocking ones should not be given such rapt attention unless our business happens to be to fight them, as Ralph Nader does so magnificently. I admire those who fight the destructive forces, like Daniel Ellsberg, and Nader. But there are various ways of fighting them. There is also a concentration on affirmations which my genuine readers respond to.

Barry Jones was the only one who thought of giving the Diary back to me in the form of a tempting blank book. It reminded me I was losing it, that I had not written in it for a long time, that this year everyone pulled me away from it. I gave it away to the world. It was open and shared. The response was love and friendship, and like all lovers and friends: "Come and see me," "Be with me," "Answer my letter," "Come to *my* houseboat," "Come and talk to us for commencement," "Come and visit," "Let us visit you"; and I was imperceptibly drawn out, outward, flying to this college, on trains, on planes, in cars, talking—oh, talking from the moment I landed to the moment I left— my life's summation a bouquet of talk, talk in interviews, talk on the radio, on television, over breakfast in college cafeterias, over formal lunch at the Psychoanalytical Institute, at dinner with Loren Eiseley; and answering letters, letters from Baghdad, India, Italy, Germany, France; and reading clippings, reviews, essays.

As I was criticized for once noting in Volume One the praise or compliments friends expressed, considered narcissism, I felt I could not tell the story of this year because all of it was response, praise, thanks, not in the form of flattery but in the form of love and friendship. I felt I could not tell the story because this time it was "Thanks, Anaïs, you saved my life"; "thanks, Anaïs, the Diaries gave me strength, gave me faith, made me want to live and create." All the feeling I had for human beings, all the love, all the friendships, were returned to me.

How could I record that? I could only accept it because it was given with genuine feeling, sometimes with tears, sometimes with muteness, fumbling words, an embrace. I received countless kisses at times and no words. I received thousands of confessional, intimate and very beautiful letters. I discovered thousands of persons I could love. My faith in America was established firmly. If I had left then, I would be leaving the most sensitive, the most intelligent of people in a great deep process of change. Miraculously we were in tune, we synchronized. I was no longer the outsider, the foreigner, or chronologically in the past, not the present. Young women laughed at the editor who did not want to do another *nostalgic* piece! Nostalgic! I was called out by women's liberation, asked to be active, to appear at festivals of women of the arts, at symposiums, at Esalen seminars.

A million integrated circuits, an image from electronics which seduced me.

It is 6:30 A.M. I slept in a student's room in a prefabricated house at Amherst, where I was invited in 1946 when *Ladders to Fire* appeared. I was invited to give the commencement address at Hampshire College, and we had our commencement in the sun, on the lawn. I was the only woman among the tall black-robed faculty.

Timothy Landfield invited me.

"Thank you. And I look forward to dancing with you sometime."

I was lecturing too much. I was tired. I felt myself growing empty because it was all given away in talk, but the invitations to dance I could not refuse! I said yes. And Spring decided to be festive. By a slender fruit tree in blossom, after commencement, stood three or four young women in long dresses, flowerlike and in all colors of the palette, with their long hair floating, *Les jeunes filles en fleur*, the modern romantics; I looked at them and felt the elation I felt before Botticelli's graceful, festive figures in green landscapes.

Soon someone will awaken and make coffee. Soon Evelyn Hinz and John Teunissen will come to drive me to the airport.

All the themes of my work were *talked* this year—relationships, creation, the creation of self, the creation of an inner world—and my only enemies were the militant women with ready-made slogans and hatred of man. And the betrayal by Gore Vidal, accepting his portrait and then seeking to destroy the Diary by lies and yellow journalism.

Small assassinations which I survived. What predominated was the power to convert destruction into creation. I was practicing with Gonzalo and Helba. I was in training for this role and when I found the students disillusioned and passive, I knew what to say and I said it yesterday again giving them the key to my secret for the refusal to despair—the key to my conquering of fear, timidity, helplessness, distrust, traumatic breaks, confusions and conflicts.

I can face an audience of two thousand persons as if I were talking to one person; each one feels I am addressing him directly. I have no notes. The talk springs from the deep well of feeling and conviction. I use the metaphor of integrated circuits, the image of the spirit house from Thailand, a duplicate in miniature of one's own house to be inhabited by the spirit.

So much richness offered me which ironically I cannot take time to enjoy because the work makes inexorable demands. When Editions Stock invites me to France, pays my hotel and my trip, they meet me with a schedule and for two weeks I am the prisoner of appointments, of journalists, television, radio, documentary films and official dinners.

I recall the day Georg Troller, the director of the documentary, brought Michel Simon and we embraced like old friends. He is effusive, full of love, and had asked Henry Miller many times if he could meet me. We stood on the quays talking about the fate of *La Belle Aurore*. His eyes have the same intense expression as the eyes of a mute animal seeking to convey messages far beyond the power of words, the same pleading intent look of dog's eyes transmitting a love or distress or anxiety we cannot always understand. Another day I spent in the Bois with Jeanne Moreau. But talk with her is peripheral and not deep; evasive and unfocused. She once identified too much with Sabina and was frightened. Now, years later, she is self-assured (analysis) and dreaming of being a writer. I felt no contact with her. She is not direct or open immediately, or perhaps is so only with her close friends.

In Los Angeles when there was a possibility of her acting in *A Spy in the House of Love*, she invited us to dinner with Henry Miller and his Japanese wife, Hoki. During dinner I mentioned Jeanne's having played a record of Hoki's singing (Henry met her when she was performing at a Hollywood Japanese restaurant) and what a lovely voice she had. Henry said spontaneously and devastatingly, "Yes and I thought she was like her voice. . . ."

Knowing Hoki's hard-boiled and calculating nature, I was amazed by Henry's romantic statement.

Everyone knows now that I have at least half of the feminist women behind me, and many more who are not feminists but consider me a pioneer in independence, a heroine, a legend, a model, etc.

At seven A.M. Timothy Landfield comes to say good-bye. He is a dancer with a fine-bred, sensitive face, Botticellian hair around his face. He will teach theater and acting. When he received his graduation papers he turned to me and was about to kiss my hand but I embraced him. The long fraternal embrace is part of the modern romantics. They set their own graduation rituals, no formal speeches; they wore Moroccan jellabas of various colors, they played electronic music, they read poems. The black-robed men were tolerant and natural. A conquest over formality and decorum.

I remembered the anarchy of Reed College students. I was the first woman invited to give their commencement address. The year before, obliged to wear the dark robes, they wore them with nothing on underneath and at a dramatic moment took them off. So the year I came, they were allowed to design their own costumes.

Among the many struggles against the mania for classification and filing is the theme of chronological age which Americans use to divide thought and creativity. Your birth date determines where you belong, as your race, religion or class determines it. A theme to explore. All of it is a part of a divisional mania, generation gap, generalizations about parents or even birthplaces.

The most difficult task was to dissipate the taboo on introspection and the inner journey. To cast doubt on group psychology, group thinking, group rebellion. To point to the danger of collective nonthinking, brainwashing, imitation and contagion.

Virginia Garlick wrote poetic letters and then appeared yesterday with pale, fair hair and a poetic face. Barry Jones also appeared, a black student from Dartmouth, working on a thesis on my work, handing me this book, which at first I expected to be filled by him. I have received diaries—from beautiful Virginia Heffron, who died recently of lung cancer at forty, from a young woman in Berkeley who deposited them on Joaquin's doorstep.

I sit on the TWA airplane waiting for the right-wing engine to be repaired. When we leave Hartford, in twenty-five minutes I will be in New York, and tomorrow in Los Angeles. Then work on Volume Five in the small cell-like room I work in, all books and files. A friend asked for an overdue sabbatical to help me. He sees me drowned in correspondence, some of it with colleges, planning lectures, dates, flights. He can also edit the Diary. He is meticulous and has a finely tuned ear for the English language inherited from his Cambridge-bred father and his actress mother's fine English delivery; and from the Wright family's respect for language, even when old-fashioned, certainly classical, as one can see in the books by Frank Lloyd Wright.

It would be an adventure to visit all my correspondents, in Holland, Baghdad, Belgium, Switzerland, Germany, Japan.

Since my break with Catholicism I seldom visited churches; once, with Gonzalo, as a romantic regression to our early faith, we haunted Notre Dame to kiss in dark corners, more perhaps to indulge in a sense of sacrilege for the forbidden sensuality so oppressed by the Catholics. Also perhaps for the very sensual atmosphere of incense, candlelight and music. I visited another church at the time of my mother's death, out of respect for Joaquin's faith and need of his sustenance, and out of gratitude because this faith had given my mother a serene old age, an acceptance of death.

But two Sundays ago, Father Monick of Saint Clement's Church on New York's West Side, in the Puerto Rican quarter, persuaded me to talk and I found myself at a ritual so relaxed, so informal, so democratic, that I was touched. Instead of a sermon he presented films, dance, a reading of my "Birth" story. I talked with ease about the spirit house from Thailand. There was such spontaneity and harmony. The congregation not only clapped but stamped the wooden floor with delight. I remember Father Monick praying for whoever asked to be prayed for and saying after my talk: "You said just what I needed and wanted to hear. I am on my way to the Jung Institute at Zurich in quest of what you described."

We opened the ritual with meditation. He was dressed like a Catholic priest but without the solemn unctuousness. There was only a table with a cross in the middle and two candlesticks. Women won their plea to be allowed priesthood. They run the church. They read from the Bible. They revolutionized the church. I was reminded of the Mexican church in Acapulco at which I attended a wedding. It was filled with beggars, wandering children, dogs, mothers carrying their crying babies and suckling them, prostitutes in their silk dresses, noise, chatter. No solemnity or silence.

These evolutions delight me, just as the destructive ones shock and hurt me: war, bombs, anarchists, holdups, crimes, muggings, drug addicts, hijacking of airplanes.

Ours was named by some the "bitchy society." It was prophesied by me in Volume Three. The price, not as they believe for social injustice, but for the taboo on feeling and sensitivity, the taboos on art, on self-development and reflectiveness, on analysis and all that would make each one responsible for the fate of every human being. By great collective abstractions, political theories, they achieved nothing but the incredible savagery of war and crime.

I was right to situate the source of both evil and creation within each one of us, and the power to redress, and create.

Anaïs, what have you become? Where are you? Have you become a teacher, a guru? Just speaking the accumulated experience because so many needed an end to loneliness, a new faith, a rediscovery of human values. Lending my presence because so many wanted to ascertain that I am real, ascertain if I had the voice of my words, the body of my words, the face of my words. They have been so often cheated and betrayed by the media, by their heroes, they fear to believe and want to confirm this belief in the words. Even before I speak, they give me standing ovations at Harvard, at Berkeley, at this college, so it is the work they respond to, and then I speak from the heart of the work. I who felt always that the written word was more eloquent, more subtle, more meaningful than speech, and who said in Berkeley: "I hope you find everything in the work because there will come a day when I will not be present."

I never expected my love returned. I believed in personal love, but I never imagined or envisaged a universal love. That is why this year I abandoned my solitary chant and answered letters. "Yes," I respond, "I am happy you felt it was your diary." They bring me new words. One wrote: "The freedom women demand which they can create for themselves."

A student said: "You once wrote that you wanted to live only for the marvelous moments. How does this talk with us fit into that?" I answered, "It is also a marvelous moment. Our talk together was a marvelous moment." It was. A group of strangers suddenly thrust into warm communication. In one moment I can detect a friend. A letter will confirm this.

When a friend asked me to telephone a well-known actress, who was threatening suicide, all I could think of was: "Do you wish to kill your children as Medea did? For if you kill yourself, you are killing them too, remember that." And the image of Medea murdering her children did affect her.

And those who wish to come as disciples, to help me, type for me, or cook, or garden, live in my presence.

A symbol. So, Anaïs, you are a symbol. Even if I pointed out the way the struggle was accomplished, they do not seek the discipline of psychoanalysis to rescue themselves by a spiritual effort. They want to receive it with love and friendship from me, like the group in St. Clement's Church who ate real bread, big, round peasant bread, and drank real wine.

TWA Flight 5 from New York.

At 3:30 we will land in Los Angeles. Past the Mojave Desert in that lovely champagne color, past the mountains enveloped in smog. I think of the Magic Circle Weekend. Beatrice Harris, and Barry Jones and Virginia Garlick, my new friends. Jeffery and James Mundy both tall and handsome, Jeffery more of a dreamer, a body with wings, James near and more physical, but they seem to complete each other.

Evelyn Clark and Nancy Williamson had caused me uneasiness because I knew they were grounded in politics and I feared they would repudiate a total devotion to creation. We discussed it over the telephone. Are you sure you want to come? The atmosphere of politics is always depressing, dogmatic and puritanical. But they came and it lifted their spirits. Nancy read from her diary, her discovery of lesbianism. Evelyn read Trotsky's comments on the value and influence of literature (but we all know how dictatorial Russia has become and how it oppresses and persecutes its intellectuals).

The iron masks by Suzanne Benton were original, a modern version of the Iron Mask, more like abstract cages in which the head participates in the design and is altered by the design. The paintings were skillful and varied.

I had corresponded with Bebe Herring. She brought a half-finished novel. She was beautiful, tall, with distressed eyes, and we tried to say in a few moments what it takes years for a friendship to exchange.

From a farewell sermon at St. Clement's by the Reverend E. A. Monick:

This spring I met Anaïs Nin here in this church when she came to speak at one of these services, and I will not forget that day ever. It was a personal event of the highest order. Nin was to me a fragile queen from whose lips came the words that brought life to me—strong and uncompromising words—that told . . . the story of my own transformation. In so many words she said that what had made the difference in her life was the development of her interior being—and with that a sense of the diminishing importance of the exterior.

Afterward we embraced each other, and I told her that she had explained perfectly why I was going to Zurich. She was lovely. She said, "You do not need Zurich, you already have what Zurich will give to you."

Letter from Nancy Williamson:

The weekend at Rye was one of the most exciting, inspiring and positive experiences of my life. I am glad we didn't give in to our fears and not attend. It was a delightful moment for me and one that occurs rarely.

Letter from Bebe Herring:

I was not going to write you again for a long time because I imagine you are always struggling up a hill, weighed down by reams and reams of letters, all bearing one sentence: "I love you." Those letters one cannot discard or ignore, not if one is Anaïs. I wish I might help you, somehow, assume your identity in some way that would enable me to answer your mail (letters like mine). I fear that with exposure to so many of us who come to celebrations such as the one at Rye, to touch the hem of your robe, you will lose your final and complete submersion in character. We, the Bebes and Jefferys and Lisas, will stop your writing. The ink and energy you spend with us could be poured into another story, another diary. Anaïs, I shall always hear your voice, each trembling r, each smile molded yes. I could not speak with you. I was afraid my loudness, my little troubles might somehow crease you. You told me that I have no self-confidence and I cried. And that conversation was never finished.

Letter from Lex Crocker:

I do not want to bother you, but I only want to tell you that I have lived in pain and conflict most of my life and that you (sweet magic being that you are) have done much to give me hope and direction. It is hard for me to express my love for others, but your writings have revealed to me that this is all that is important in one's life, and I am trying on my own to become free of all my silent pains. So I only want to tell you now that I love you sincerely and tenderly even if it is difficult to write these feelings in physical reality.

I spoke at commencement exercises at Hampshire College and was able to spend an evening with Evelyn Hinz and John Teunissen.

It was at Hampshire that I met Barry Jones. We had been corresponding. He presented me with a hardcover notebook, in which I began to write the next morning at six A.M. after having neglected my Diary for a long time.

Barry Jones was like his letters, colorful, sensitive, exuding joyousness and love. His black eyes so warm, his smile so winning. He had all the qualities of his black race, aliveness, beautiful voice, spiritedness, and besides that a tremendous culture, having studied at the Sorbonne, at Oxford, and graduated from Dartmouth. He has a faculty for attracting friends.

The lectures are impossible to describe. Different cities, different atmospheres, different reactions. Most of the time they had read me well and so received me with an ovation. Always one or two students became friends. As I was leaving the hall of Chicago University a young woman embraced me and slipped a beautiful carved ring on my finger, saying: "You wrote in your Diary that you always gave away the thing you most cared about, and I am giving you a ring I loved the most." If she ever reads these lines she will know how touched I was. In Green Bay College a man embraced me so fervently and with so much strength. I would like to have known his name. Different mental and physical climates. The young women at Smith College lifeless, knitting as they listened, indifferent. Snow and ice at Smith College. Summer heat in North Carolina. Smith was the only college I could not warm and bring to life.

The journalists ask me if I am still writing in the Diary.

I answered yes automatically, but one day I realized it was not true. The Diary has become a correspondence with the world.

Was this what I really wanted?

Evelyn Hinz persuaded me that a biography would supply a factual, objective completion of the Diary, which sometimes does not cover all the ground. If I agree, it will be for the Diary as well, to fill in.

Letter to Valerie Harms:

I am a little embarrassed to be called a heroine. I was always extremely stubborn, but not heroic. Could we find another title for the description of our celebration? A title which would include all of us, all the artists. I even prefer "Magic Circle." This describes all the good we enjoyed. What do you think? I think I was not the heroine but merely the catalyzer for us all.

Letter to Barry Jones:

It was a joy to meet you, to place a face and smile upon the pages of your letters. I must tell you what was born of our meeting. You were the only one who thought of the Diary, and your thoughtfulness in presenting me with a book to write in, rather than some of your own work, had a powerful effect. I had neglected the Diary this year to answer letters, and I felt the difficulty in returning to it, but your beautiful book with its empty pages tempted me and I awakened at six A.M. the next morning and began to write again. I wrote in the plane too, and on my way to Los Angeles. That was your gift to me. At first you remember I said: "Is this your diary? You owe me a filled book with your own work," but afterward I was touched and understood your message. You have a smile which fills the world, and is so open and loving. I am sorry our meeting was short, but some encounters no matter how short can create a friendship.

Letter to Bill Henderson:

After visiting twenty-six colleges, and speaking at various commencements, I thought I could never sit and write the history of my press. . . .

But here it is, and I was struck by the irony that Doubleday was the most consistent of my rejecters, even when Edmund Wilson introduced me there. . . . Your attitude and plan for the book* is very much needed at this time when the young get so easily discouraged. They lack the stubbornness and persistence we had. I would like to hear about your self-publishing. These stories give them courage, which they badly need.

Letter to Dr. Bogner:

I want to tell you last night's dream. I arrived at your place one hour late and you could not see me professionally, but you invited me to go on errands with you. We were in a very light mood. You shopped for some brilliant, colorful scarves, and I bought one too, yellow and gold. It was snowing. You took my arm and we slid over the snow as children do. You held my arm and I let myself be led. I had a feeling you were sustaining me, but it was like two children at play. You visited some patients, a family, but not too long. I was happy to have attained this mood. You said to me: "It is the first time I have been able to feel free and playful with a patient," as if you too felt the doctor-and-patient separation was over. The mood was gay and confident.

I don't know what it means, but it must convey some feeling of harmony. One factor is that I recovered very quickly from the fatigue of the lectures. I am working well on Volume Five. I feel *smooth*. I thought it would please you that we had such a good time together.

* *The Publish-It-Yourself Handbook* (Yonkers, N.Y.: Pushcart Book Press, 1973).

Los Angeles.

Ever since I came home I have been at work on Volume Five. Part of it difficult because I suddenly decided to be timeless and not date anything.

Working here is a pleasure. I tape the singing of the mockingbirds. It is amazingly varied and colorful.

The death of Violette Leduc hurt me as if I had known her well. She was the most honest of all writers, honest to the point of making herself appear repellent as a character. I admired her courage, her marvelous style, her extraordinary honesty.

Evelyn Hinz has started the editing of my lectures taken from tapes.*

Robert Zaller puts the *Casebook* together, and it was accepted for publication.

Parents ask me to write to their sons at war.

Will I have the strength to respond to all that is offered me, and to do all I must do?

Last night we went to Henry Miller's home. He limps and he is in pain, but he hesitates to undergo surgery. His mood was good. He wanted to see the work in progress on the documentary film on me being made by Robert Snyder. Henry was critical; he had wanted his own film more surrealist, more dadaist. He wanted Snyder to treat me poetically. "Anaïs is a legend. You must get that." Of course, we both carry in our minds images from the past. I always see him dynamic, walking forever all through Paris, joyous. He always sees me as I was, lively, a dancer. Of course the film cannot catch that. Henry's Japanese ex-wife was there. She never loved him; for this I dislike her. The walls are covered with his watercolors. Over the mantelpiece, one of Varda's

* *A Woman Speaks* (Chicago: Swallow Press, 1975).

best collages. On one wall the shelves are filled with translations of his books in fifteen or twenty languages.

Letter to a writer:

You should have told me that your editor had a specific preface in mind, hers, and I would have refused to do it. I have never written to order. When I sign my name it is something I feel, believe, and part of my integrity. Her suggestions are petty, cliché, and unacceptable. When my name is used to sell a book it has to be my preface, not manufactured by someone else.

I will not change a word. You are free not to use it, but I have to be paid for the time I spent reading the huge manuscript and time spent on the preface when I'm already overworked.

I am too much a symbol of integrity and independence to write according to another's mind. Your editor was evidently insensitive to the fact that the respect I command is due precisely to my never writing what I was asked by editors.

As soon as I came home, I relaxed. The house gives me peace and beauty. The swimming restores me. I sit at my desk at seven-thirty. I work until lunchtime. At four I go to the post office. There I face an avalanche of letters, manuscripts, books from publishers ("Please comment"). I have to return manuscripts unread. I answer letters with a card. Correspondence with colleges where I have to send posters, photographs, announcements before lectures. And I must edit all the Diaries because no one else can do it. In Volume Five I stopped dating. And as I lived so fast, I often made notes which I have to develop and expand. So much I want to do. Diary of Japan I would like to publish with many photographs in color, little writing. I want to do a diary of letters received.

The letters are an important part of my life now. Most of them are interesting, revealing, putting me in touch with so many lives, all ages, all kinds of places and atmosphere. Teachers, students, mature readers, feminists, young men artists, poets, psychologists, novelists. Far-off places. All the letters are sincere, sometimes scholarly, sometimes illiterate, but always emotional and genuine. An authentic current, revealing an America I did not know. Each one isolated, without the benefit of rich friendships. One or two are suicidal. They suffer from loneliness; I suffer from overabundance.

Last night another lecture. I hated to tear myself away from Silverlake house, pool and garden. It was University of Northern Illinois at De Kalb. Difficult at first. Summer students not prepared with knowledge of my work. But warming toward the end. And faithful friends there. And then unexpectedly I met someone who was at the Sorbonne two years and attended Bachelard's lectures. His description of the lectures magnificent, lectures like his books. He talked about the high quality he never encountered in America, because of the ingrained concern for the inadequate, the retarded students. Bachelard addressed his peers. And left. It was up to the students to climb the ladder to reach his vision. He began one lecture this way: "On your way here, did you look only straight ahead of you, or did you look up at the sky, and at the left of you, and at the right, and behind you? Next time I want you to do this on your way."

Here, because of the irrelevant questions, they can clip your wings. You are made aware of the ones who cannot follow, the ones who make no effort. Our staying behind them to keep them company does not help them. It is not a real democratic interpretation. We should, those who can, run ahead and be an example. The students are inert. They expect you to make the effort to translate all you say in mediocre, corny terms.

I am weary of public life even though I love the contact with the few exceptional ones. And talk always seems to me to fall below the level of the writing.

Fell asleep reading Rank's *Volonté du Bonheur*. It helps me. How much we owe to others we absorb unconsciously. Surrealism and Rank. Unrecognized depth. Delayed acknowledgment.

Dr. Staff said in 1947: "Analysis is like a spiral. The crises grow smaller, less violent."

Life heals you if you allow it to flow, if you do not allow it to trap you.

Freedom means that no one is able to destroy you, enslave you, paralyze you.

In July I spoke to raise money for a women's clinic in Los Angeles. The place was so crowded some listeners had to stay in the outer rooms used for painting exhibits. Judy Chicago introduced me warmly. Toward the end of the talk, during the question-and-answer period a tall, lean young woman asked aggressively: "Do you consider yourself a liberated woman?" I said yes, I did. "You are not a liberated woman because you are not a lesbian."

I met Mrs. Verraux who called me up a few days later to recommend a film I would like very much. I trusted her and I went to see *A Safe Place* by Henry Jaglom. It made me weep. I spoke with him. The next morning at seven A.M. I wrote a review of the film* which Jaglom liked so much he gave it to the *Free Press* because the *Los Angeles Times* had already reviewed it badly. He then took the review of the *Free Press* and bought a whole page of the *L.A. Times* as an advertisement. We became friends.

Blurbs written for the film *A Safe Place*:

All the subtle dreams and fantasies which color our experience are captured here. The inner world of a young woman becomes as vivid as her outer world. Here is a dimension left out of other films. A new vision, more encompassing, of feeling, tenderness and humor.

For the first time a description of the mixture we live by, this interweaving of dream, childhood wishes for magic power, fantasy interfering with experience, the constant transformation of reality by illusion.

Great tenderness and understanding of the power of the dream, a marvelous skill in seizing upon its subtle influence, a great daring in erasing the boundaries to immerse you in the very heart of it.

This film communicates freedom: It fulfills my concept that the poet teaches us levitation. The gift for depicting our inner life is liberating. The real magician here is the writer director, Henry Jaglom, because our fantasy for the first time is set free.

A film which seizes the multidimensions of our experience. A life directed by a childhood wish for magic power.

* See "Henry Jaglom: Magician of the Film," in *In Favor of the Sensitive Man and Other Essays* (New York: Harcourt Brace Jovanovich, 1976).

Letter to Anne Metzger:

I hesitated to write you because I feared that André Bay would disappoint you again, but now he writes me he is enthusiastic about your translation and he sent me a copy.* I like it and feel it is faithful to the mood and color of the book. It is not an easy book to translate and I am aware of the difficulties. I think you understood it and transposed it exceedingly well. I am keeping it awhile for very small details, small things such as "fool's gold." It is a word which does not exist in French because it was born of the Gold Rush in the West when men took pyrite for gold and it was called "fool's gold." In such cases of untranslatable expression I feel it is best to leave it out because *l'or de la folie* does not convey the fraud. But there are details. In the lyrical passages, the most difficult of all, you caught the rhythm and the mood. . . .

Do write me about yourself. I never heard of Romain Gary again, or Lesley Blanch. My favorite book of his besides *Les Couleurs de Jour* was *La Promesse de l'Aube*. The rest I find insincere.

From a review for the C. G. Jung Foundation for Analytical Psychology:

Doctor Esther Harding's book *Woman's Mysteries* has just been reprinted. I admired it when it first came out, but did not realize it would stand the test of time and become important to women today. This was because Dr. Harding was probing into the inner nature of modern woman, and because when she studied the mythology of the past, she analyzed its meaning in modern terms, she translated the myths into psychological insights. We are all concerned now with the myths which originally created the concept of women; we wish to challenge and examine these myths which have shaped the thinking of both men and women. . . .

There is a great amount of misunderstanding about psychology stemming from the Marxian prejudice against it. Many women have accepted the trite generality that psychoanalysis, being practiced by men,

---

* Anne Metzger's translation, *La Séduction du Minotaure,* was published in 1974. Previously, she had translated *Une Espionne dans la Maison de l'Amour* (1964), and *Les Miroirs dans le Jardin* (1962), i.e., *Ladders to Fire.*

forced women to conform to bourgeois standards. In the first place many distinguished women have practiced psychology in all its ramifications. Those who espouse this prejudice are the ones who never studied the development of it beyond Freud. Ultimately it has been, for many women, a system of discovery of the self and a dissolution of guilts created by social taboos. Dr. Harding examines all this with clarity and balance. Those who do not wish to study myths and symbols need only to read her analysis of these myths and symbols in modern terms.

Each one has a nature which seeks for love and relationship, and also there is imbedded in everyone the necessity to strive for impersonal truth. These opposing tendencies are expressions of the duality of human nature which is both objective and subjective. In all human beings such opposition is at work and leads inevitably to conflict. In the Western world of today this conflict is most severe and bears hardest upon woman because Western civilization lays especial emphasis on the value of the outer, and this fits in more nearly with man's nature than with woman's. The feminine spirit is more subjective, more concerned with feelings and relationships than with the laws and principles of the outer world. And so it happens that the conflict between outer and inner is usually more devastating for women than for men.

Aware of woman's evolution, Dr. Harding writes:

The recent awakening of woman from her long apathy has brought to the fore latent powers which, naturally enough, she is eager to develop and apply in life, both for her own satisfaction and advantages and to increase her contribution to the life of the group.

Aware of woman's restlessness, she observes that "For no human life consists only in the personal."

Aware of the need of woman to become aware of herself, she comments: "She has no conscious understanding of herself, and is for that reason totally unable to explain herself to man."

This is why I have consistently asked of women that they do not give up this probing and journey into the self in order to achieve the very expansion they wish for.

The depreciatory attitude which many a man takes towards woman is an unconscious attempt to control a situation in which he feels himself at a dis-

235

advantage, or he seeks to undercut the dreaded power of woman by inducing her to act towards him as a mother. In this way he is released in large measure from his fear, for in this relation to his mother nearly every man has experienced the positive aspect of a woman's love. Even so, he is not entirely free from apprehension, because in making the woman a mother, he at the same time makes himself a child, and is thus in danger of falling into his own childishness.

About the theme of masculine and feminine Dr. Harding comments:

No individual is entirely male or entirely female. Each is made up of a composite of both elements . . . until this personal aspect of the problem is resolved, the individual man or woman will not be able to find a solution of the external difficulty in his relationships, for he will inevitably project the less conscious, less disciplined part of his own psyche upon his partner.

I have only chosen a few salient themes, but the entire book is full of this fascinating relation of old myths to modern woman's problems. It is essential to woman because the influence of these myths has not yet been erased from our subconscious.

Lee Potts works on her dissertation on Rank's concept of creativity and my work.

Met Pamela Fiori, editor of *Travel & Leisure*. She is a friend of Sharon's. We had a wonderful warm afternoon. She offered me an assignment on any subject I liked and assured me I could write it in any way I please.

I write a preface for Judy Chicago's book *Through the Flower*. We have remained good friends in spite of opposite ways of thinking. I admire her as an artist, I admire her courage, her effort to liberate women. She has two selves, one very belligerent and aggressive, another tender and loving. I forgave her her criticism of the Berkeley Celebration. She makes me aware of the situation of women, and I gently draw her back into her art. Otherwise she would give her whole life to teaching women who deep down resent leaders and models.

Our first meeting was very interesting. I was intimidated by her powerful personality. She was intimidated by the lady of the Diaries.

236

She told in public how shocked she was that I should offer to squeeze orange juice for her. "Those hands which . . ." But what happened is that we immediately felt tenderness and recognized that we needed each other. I encouraged her to write so that she would not have to lecture as much. Both of us incited each other to stick to our work, which would have ultimately more influence than lectures.

On elitism: "There is no such thing," I said [to Judy Chicago]. "Every human being should push his development and skills and creativity as far as possible, as only then does one become valuable to the community, valuable to others. It is wrong to hold people back to remain on the level with the herd. We need explorers, adventurers, pathfinders, models, inventors. The real democracy is to develop yourself as much as possible, for then you can teach and help others."

Every day a surprise. A painter brings me her paintings all the way from Berkeley, and leaves one as a gift.

Joaquin came, read the new Diary volume and revised sections concerning my mother. He asked for fair and just revisions in the Diary. Mother was not *brutally* honest, for example. She did not *endanger* my life. My father was twenty-two when he married, not twenty.

The quartet is playing while I write in the Diary. The empty cello case looks like a Henry Moore sculpture.
Music is part of my writing. I often wished I could write the equivalent of a sonata.
The days when I am happy are the days when I hear music in everything.
Days of rhythm.
My childhood was nourished on music.
I love to write to music. I wrote *A Spy in the House of Love* to music.

My three weeks in New York were filled with activity. Three days spent with Radio Canada while they photographed a one-hour documentary. France l'Abbé, my interviewer, was an interesting woman, steeped in my work, and we talked endlessly about her too. The *équipe* was wonderful, sensitive and individual. We enjoyed each other's company. It was work, to prepare the Diaries and books for display and talk. To walk in the park. To walk in the Village. To talk from ten A.M. to four P.M. But the work was made enjoyable by their personalities and we ended up friends.

Two-day interview and photographs for the Canadian magazine *Châtelaine*. Also from ten to four. Helene Fecteau intelligent and cool, but also ending in friendship. I feel the most miraculous sense of contact with others. Perhaps knowledge of the Diary sets the level for intimacy. I feel as if every cell in my body is alert and responsive.

Trip to the vault to get all the Diaries for Volume Five because I found I needed the originals to work from. They contain letters, programs, photographs not in the typed copies, clues to dates.

Dinner with John Ferrone. I feel a great affection for him. Our friendship dates from the day the first paperback of Volume One arrived with a hideous drawing of a hard-faced woman on the cover. I went to his office to protest. As I entered he said: "I see what you mean."

He had them change the cover. We work well together; he is intelligent, sensitive, well read. A beautiful person, emotional and tender.

I receive an assignment from *Travel & Leisure*, to go to Fez. How late this has come! When Durrell's first book appeared in the U.S. he was asked to write for *Holiday* magazine immediately.

I see Frances [Field] and encourage her to write.

I see Sylvia [Spencer], who was gravely ill and awaits her portrait in the Diary eagerly.

I talk with Millicent [Fredericks] over the telephone about her new false teeth which hurt her, and her tired heart.

I see Beatrice, so sensually attractive but with a watchful intellect. At this point her qualities are balanced. I hope the intellect does not control the body and face created for passion. In September she becomes "Dr." Beatrice Harris, one of a new generation of analysts.

And then the dream:

I am watching my house in Los Angeles being battered by a storm.

The sea is there. I am aware the house was not built for such a violent assault. There is a landslide. I enter when the storm abates and find under the bed is a hole created by suction, where the earth crumbled.

[Fall, 1972]

Dream: Dr. Bogner wears glasses. She looks different.

I have to climb a strange mountain made of cement. One path is painted in vivid colors. I choose to follow that one.

I am walking over a bridge with Alice Rahon. She falls between the planks, a bad fall.

I have nightmares every night. One night I dreamed I was to lecture and had forgotten to put on my dress.

Underlying melancholy, though my life is beautiful. Hundreds of loving letters. Interesting visitors. Work on the film. A warm pool, an enchanting playful dog. The sun. Indian cotton dresses in the closet.

Age, yes. At last detectable in photographs. Inevitable now, a paradox because I do not feel as I look. I feel fresh and dewy and relaxed and not old. Freckles on the hands, wrinkles. How strange, when nothing in my emotions corresponds to that. The feelings are crystal clear, perfect melodies, never strident or rough like the voice of the old.

A psychic youthfulness. When I swim in the morning I am grateful for another dawn. So strange those hours of writing, so much like a spider web, but one in which people love to be caught and start their own web of human connections. The letters stir me, touch me. I am broken-hearted when I have to return huge piles of manuscripts. I receive books of interest, Ira Progoff, the Rank *Journal*, *Dream Power* by Anne Faraday. And bad novels.

I spoke at Tiburon [Marin County] for "Women on the Move." Stayed overnight with Anne and Alexis Tellis, friends of Varda's. Their house was so close to the Bay that I had the feeling of staying in a boat. They are charming and gay. We enjoyed being together. When they drove me to the Teachers' Conference at Pacific Grove, they took one look at the cafeteria and whisked me away for another gourmet dinner and joyous talk. We hated to part.

At the Teachers' Conference I was asked how I coped with my waning energies. I answered with foolish pride that the problem had not confronted me yet. A partial truth because the truth is I am exhausted after every lecture. And sometimes in my hotel room alone, I weep with fatigue.

Letter to Ira Progoff:

I am so glad I followed up my first curiosity about you when I heard friends talk about the intensive journal, for thanks to that I have discovered your book, *The Death and Rebirth of Psychology*. It is not only a very vital, necessary book, it is the best integration of psychological concepts I have read. I wrote to Anita Faatz and Virginia Robinson about it. They direct the Rank Association, edit a journal, work at translating his works and keeping them in print. I am sure they will review your book with much interest. I have maintained a constant interest in the development of psychology, but you seem to be developing it in a direction which I admire. Thank you for inviting me to one of your gatherings. I will certainly come. As you may know, I will be able to talk about Frances Steloff at Skidmore College when she receives her doctorate.

I thought you might like to know that Rank did write plays, poems, novels and a diary. Have you read my Diaries? May I send them to you? There is much about Rank in them.

I will myself get your other books. I am sorry the intensive journal is only available to those who engage in the seminars, as my overwork, constant writing and lecturing will make it impossible for me to join them.

Letter to a friend in Australia:

I was so pleased to hear from you. When I gave up my writing because of overwork, I always felt now I am losing a friend. But no—here he is, quite changed. I don't really believe money needs to corrupt one. It is the guilt we have for possessing some which harms us. We all have dual wishes, dual selves. A flashy side which wants to be noticed and famous, and a quiet side which only wants to be left alone in peace to work. My resolution was always: Do it all, they are all you, embrace them all. So now I do both—the public and the private. I must confess I prefer the quiet writing life to the public life, but the public life gives me the reason to be free, to move. As a young man you wanted to get free, and Miller's way was not freedom (debts!). So now you are free of concern over making a living. It is one kind of freedom.

The last two years were years of fame and discovery—a new segment of America, a new generation. Suddenly we were in harmony. I just finished Volume Five. Now I begin lectures at colleges. . . .

From the tone of your letter I would say you have not lost anything of your sensitive and dreaming selves. They *all* have to live in peace with each other, all our selves! I notice one gain . . . your focus is clearer, what you want, are, think, etc.

I sit writing you during the only evenings when I can write letters—when the musicians come and play quartets. One husband designed the cameras for the satellite which photographed Mars, one wife knits, and I can write letters. . . . Henry asked where was all that time we had in Paris, to talk all night, walk about, read! . . .

So enjoy your life as it is! Though you too do not seem to have much leisure.

About balancing analysis and action and all the other balances which cause us pain: They will soon fuse into one harmonious whole—one becomes adept at balancing like a seal!

Viveca Lindfors, a beautiful and most gifted actress, created and acted a one-woman show of quotes from women's writing called "I Am a Woman." She included some sections from *Under a Glass Bell* and from Diary One.

The producer of *The Yellow Submarine* asked me to write the screenplay for a full-length cartoon based on *Alice in Wonderland.* The artist was to be Peter Max and the feature film would be "a light, funny phantasy aimed at a fairly sophisticated, intelligent college audience." Or course, it was the kind of "Hollywood" project that never bore fruit, but I was delighted to be asked and had fun planning how I would do it.

Leopard dream. Reading van der Post. Leopard suggests fear. I tease Piccolino when he barks too much and tell him: "The bushman's dog does not bark. The leopard will get you." Then I dreamed a beautiful sleek leopard slept next to me, alongside me, just like a contented cat.

───────

Just before lectures I feel a resistance to them. In spite of constant success, constant effectiveness, my power to move people, I have a short moment of fear as if the gift of speech now acquired, spontaneous, inspirational, could suddenly leave me.

Where is Anaïs?

On a plane on the way to Chicago University, writing letters. In a car driving to Skidmore College with Frances Steloff, impressed by the flowering of her life, her life story. On my way to Dartmouth where Barry Jones awaits me; he gave me this diary notebook I am writing in now. Everywhere long, warm ovations. I speak well now. I improvise. The women and the men who come up to me later truly reach me; there is a moment of intimacy in this vast sea of loneliness. I quote Baudelaire: "In each one of us there is a man, a woman and a child." And I add, "The child is always an orphan!" I think I have drawn toward me all the orphans of the world. They weep when they come close; we embrace when they cannot find words.

But after visiting so many colleges, I found I was repeating myself and I was in despair. It is not that it is insincere but that it has become an actress's performance. Dory Previn and I understand each other. She does not want to sing her songs every night. I want to create something new each time. The record company wants her to go on the road. On the road I am grateful for the love I receive, but I cannot keep the same feeling after a thousand exchanges. So Anaïs is now an actress (not insincere, says Bogner, not at all). I step on the stage of the Edison Theater holding a metal mask before my face, sculpted by Suzanne Benton. I say to the audience: "For centuries woman has worn a mask and played many roles. Today she is unmasking herself and showing her true face." And I removed the mask and read from the Diaries. I am uneasy about this new phase. Now at home, listening to the quartet play Brahms, I know how deeply I feel, how deeply I feel the distress, the emotion on the faces I see. I remember them out of a crowd at Douglass College. I singled out Diane Northern, a black girl; we linked hands and her face was clear to me. Later she read me a moving poem over the telephone; she was crying. Her warmth touched me. I have rarely encountered such intensity. It captured me. I spent an afternoon with her and her husband. She gave me her diary.

Barry Jones, with his enthusiasm and pixie way, his blue denim grab bag made by his mother filled with books and his camera, hitchhiking to hear me talk, bringing gifts always.

I have let loose a great force of love. I feel it flowing from me and catching fire from others' response. This is my sincerity—that I do love these faces, these letters, these messages I receive, the poems, the paintings, the drawings, the student at Chicago who gave me a ring, the young woman at the Teachers' Conference at Carmel who asked me to walk on the beach at seven A.M., the one who appears at every lecture with flowers and whom I call my recurrent dream. So many lovely women; so many tender men. Why can I not relive my life? Now it is full to the brim, overrich! What if all this had come into the void of Louveciennes before Henry came?

The only time I feel power and enjoy my power is when I can praise a film such as Henry Jaglom's *A Safe Place*. My review brought a crowd. So Anaïs is performing, yes, the art of presence, but the feeling is there intact. I have not changed, lost my responsiveness. "I have a million daughters," I said in an interview.

Hidden moments, when the music fills me, pushes me. Didn't I write long ago about orchestration? Why should I be concerned that one of my selves has been projected into public life if it is part of unifying all of us by feeling?

I began these pages with a doubt. Can one multiply, share, expand without loss of substance? And I answered my own question. Yes, if you can extend feeling into all you do, say, write. If in one minute spent with a stranger you can create the annihilation of strangeness.

Just as when I read van der Post's book he becomes a part of my life, his total way of experiencing—poet, man of action, psychologist—and he then writes me he is working seven hours a day but he can read the Diaries because they run parallel to his writing, do not cut the current. So I have come out, but the blood is no thinner, the split did not take place. How could I have felt so weak and so passive at twenty and feel so strong now? It is so wonderful.

———

A woman attacked my talk at Douglass College. "I work fifty-five hours a week; I have no time for an inner journey."

She came right up to where I stood, raised her sleeves like a pugilist, was fat and gross and aggressive.

I let her rant and rave and then said coolly: "I didn't hear you very well. But I work fifty-five hours a week and I find time for the inner journey."

Letter to a reader:

You made me painfully aware of what one loses when one tries to give, respond [to] and contact too many: You lose the precious individuals you discover, by dispersion. Names are erased, love fragmented. I singled you out because your presence is beautiful and meaningful. Yet I had lost you to pressures and dispersed energies. It was a lesson and I will act on it.

[Winter, 1972–1973]

Barry arranged for me to lecture at Dartmouth College. We were all so depressed by the victory of Nixon that I had to gear my talk to awaken courage for the ordeals to come. I had to console, to indicate ways to bear this catastrophe.

Barry took me to the apartment he shares with two other students. We talked for a long time. Todd is going to be a brilliant lawyer. During the long drive to the airport I became aware of his uncanny insights.

Barry is loved by his friends. He has a big family in Virginia, farmers who sent all their children to college.

He is always high, joyous, takes everything lightheartedly. We became very close friends. He is sensitive and lively.

Dream: I am helping someone with her manuscript. The pages are in disorder, and she is distracted and confused. I finally organize them. I give them to her and say: "Now they are organized. There is a continuity." She takes the manuscript and runs into the open country. She is playfully wrestling with a man, and the pages are scattered. I feel that she is happy and that it does not matter, but when we begin to look for the manuscript, we can't find it. I am on a bicycle. She and the man are waiting for a bus. I am afraid I won't find my way back. The man gives me directions. I was also about to teach school. I was nervous and unprepared. I finally decided I didn't want to be tied down. The man (principal) was very well equipped. The mood of dream was of fogginess and effort to clarify. I was nursing someone. The same woman whose manuscript I worked on. Everything was gray.

Dream last night: The son of Gonzalo comes and we are in a perfect sensual and emotional harmony. I feel joy and fulfillment. We are one. But when I mention Gonzalo he is hostile and says: "My father was a slob." I am shocked. I have the same feeling as when I defend the hippies, a guitar player a welfare woman called a bum at the Rank Society meeting.

Being famous is only destructive if taken as a narcissistic appraisal, but creative if taken as means of discovery of other people, other lands, other ideas, other artists. I discover others who come to me. More doors are opened. It is not a static pose to accept tribute but a means to explore and discover.

The praise is not the essential element of my visits to colleges. Overflowing crowd, standing ovations, stifling crowds surrounding me afterward. I look for faces I can love, friends, daughters, a moment of contact, of intimacy, of revelation. That is what I love and seek.

This year I had to reconcile the public and the personal, make them one as sincere as the other, not in conflict. Every year we have to make a new synthesis. Conflict only if the public self is different from the private one. If it becomes a role. If one believes in what the public tells you you are. I have not done that. My image of myself is stable. It is not susceptible to flattery. I take it like flowers, cut flowers, but which have no permanent influence on my work or on myself. There is no conflict if I appear in public as I truly am, do not accept their image of me, maintain my values and my severities toward myself.

Ian Hugo's film, *Aphrodisiac*:

At the end of a long prismatic tunnel a woman drops her robe and is immediately whirled into orbit, then turned in ecstasy. Her inner physical sensations are progressively expanded and transformed, culminating in the rich images of a filmic painting.

Frances Field wrote her own description of the film:

Mysteriously yet awesomely familiar, the film's intent dawns only slowly and where I least expect it. Magically fantasy configurations on a screen can evoke body memories of rhythmic contractions and releases, involuntary moldings of pleasure and pleasurable pain. In my mind's eyes I see again these images: droplets of moisture, translucent globules floating and joining, golden warmth in well-like depths, sudden collapses and growing tensions. Is this the work of one male artist who has revealed his own unique sensibility to woman's experience?

His films create a kind of mobile impressionism, and his images—many of them shot through mirrors, glass, or water—build to a descriptive poetry of the unconscious, a surreal domain between light and shadow, waking world and dream.

247

Discussed with Bogner my distress at attacks from militant women. They are trained in Maoism, they mouth platitudes, they make war on man, on psychology, on introspection and individuality. When I talked in depth about the way to attain psychological liberation, they responded with tremendous hostility, demanding I discuss the problems in political terms. It startled me to be attacked by women. Until now I had only talked with students of writing, with literary people, with psychologists. It startled me to be faced with hatred. I always felt a fraternity with women, an impulse to collaborate. Also it was such a prejudiced, narrow attitude: Varda's courtship of women was a crime, they felt. From the very beginning of my lecture I would state my point of view, that my efforts were in the direction of liberating women emotionally, psychologically, so they could cope with the practical problems.

Bogner understood the shock I felt seeing a woman distorted with anger asserting all the political clichés.

They hated the way I dress and the soft way I spoke.

They attacked the shadowy parts of the Diary and showed all the inhumanity of revolutionaries, the kind which guillotined anyone with clean nails.

Out of a crowd at Reed College I had singled out Claudia Cranston. She came to every lecture, always with flowers, and large, intense, distressed eyes. She came to visit me yesterday. Tragic childhood. Tragic love life.

Her visit made me aware of the dissolving power of public life. I recovered the concentration on one human being which I value. Not lost. We talked like very old friends. Deeply. About her life. I hope my life at the moment, so lovely and rich, will heal her.

In spite of everything good, I awaken depressed but convinced it is physical because I have constant digestive troubles since the radiation treatment. I have to watch my diet. On lecture tours I live on tea and toast because I can't risk restaurant food. One glass of wine can give me pains and insomnia. So all is not well with the body. But I throw it all off when I enter my work room, read letters, acknowledge gifts, renew friendship with James Leo Herlihy, undamaged by a long separation while he lived in Florida and in Pennsylvania.

John Pearson introduced me to Laurens van der Post and I began to read all his books. I love the mixture of an active adventurous life matched by philosophy and psychological awareness. He has wisdom and humanity. He writes well. He reminds me of Antoine de Saint-Exupéry, but his life has been richer, fuller, and he has encompassed more experience.

From *Venture to the Interior* (1953):

The African belongs to the night. He is a child of darkness, he has a certain wisdom, he knows the secrets of the dark. He goes to the night as if to a friend, enters the darkness as if it were his home, as if the black curve of the night were the dome of his hut. How the ghosts of the European mind are warmed with memories of the African's response to the night. He does not really care for the day. He finds his way through it with reluctant, perfunctory feet. But when the sun is down, a profound change comes over him. He lights his fire, he is at once happy and almost content. He sings and drums until far into the morning. All would be well if there were not still this hunger. And what should he do about it? We could tell him, we who have too much of the light and not enough of the night and wisdom of the dark. We could, but we will not because we are split against ourselves, we are infinitely prejudiced against the night. Half the love we give ourselves would do for him, half of our bright morning selves and half for him. It is enough for both. Listen to his drum and listen to his wail, look how he goes with people like Michael and myself, cheerful, staunch, friendly and strong, on a journey he does not understand, to a place he distrusts. He would go anywhere we ask for half our love. There is no problem there. It is an irony so characteristic of our basic unreality to blame the problem on him, to shoulder him with our fears and our sin, to call it a black, a native, an African problem. It is a striking, an effective, a plausible irony. But it is not true. The problem is ours; it is in us, in our split and divided heart; it is white, it is bright with day. We hate the native in ourselves; we scorn and despise the night in which we have our being, the base degree by which we ascend into the day. The wholeness and the split, both are within us. But we have come dangerously late to this new awareness. We do not understand that we cannot do to others what we do not do to ourselves. We cannot kill and murder outside without murdering and killing within. We turn our hate on the native, the dark people of the world, from Tokyo to Tierra del Fuego, because we have trampled on our own dark natures. We have added to our unreality, made ourselves less than human so that that dark side of ourselves, our shadowy twin, has to murder or be murdered. If we could but make friends with our inner selves, come to terms with our own darkness, then there would be no trouble from without. But before we can close our split natures, we must forgive ourselves, we must forgive our European selves for what we have done to the African within us.

Letter to Marcel Moreau:

I was so happy and so proud to receive your book [*L'Ivre Livre*]. I think you will do for writing all that you wanted writing to be—something alive, drinkable, edible, a *philtre*—a magic potion. The intensity and savage power of the words make other books fall into ashes. I fear for you, for the opaque and sullen reactions. Isn't it strange how people fear to be resuscitated? For that is what your book does; it annihilates the false and the shabby and the props—it calls forth that dark side of ourselves which we have buried, what Laurens van der Post writing about Africa calls our African soul, our continent which we try to destroy.

Like all those who tried to transform by gentleness, by love, and often failed, I love those capable of storms and cyclones, and scourges for inanimate flesh. I hope you are impervious to misunderstanding. The power of words! When everyone here is persuaded by a sterile McLuhan that words have lost their power, what they should be saying is that people have lost the power to feel, to be angry, to cry out, to protest, to feel and therefore [the power] of words. I admire your book as the human bomb D. H. Lawrence wished for. I understand the allegory, the metaphor which is no longer allegory or metaphor but a direct lashing statement of long lost verities. Yes, I do listen to every word—as to some elemental attack upon facades and cowardices. You are brave, and I hope people won't stone you for it.

Letter to a French friend:

There is another book written about my work by Oliver Evans which I don't like at all. He did not have any of the keys. His point of view takes the eighteenth-century novel as a standard! No surrealism, no psychology, no poetry. I learned a great deal about the poetic novel from Djuna Barnes's *Nightwood* and [Jean] Giraudoux's *Choix des Elus*.

I have a deep and intense dislike of Norman Mailer, who is the symbol of everything hateful in American life to me and to my readers and all sensitive Americans (the new generation).

I do not believe in marriage as a dogmatic law-infested structure with lawyers meddling with divorce, the church and all other institutions having sway over its laws, etc. It will have to be freed of all that.

I have not read [Simone] de Beauvoir's last book. The one on aging seems to me to overlook all the ways by which we transcend the human condition. . . .

Letter to Peggy Glanville-Hicks, who cut from my portrait of her the difficulties she experienced as a woman composer:

Whatever cuts you made are your privilege. . . . I did not hesitate to describe the twenty years of either silence or destructiveness. It is good for young artists to know what they are up against and it is a pity to erase the difficulties, the obstacles, the problems, and to present only the climax, apogee. Later I can state all the good things. The shame is not yours but the art world's. It is like Henry Miller erasing how badly Hollywood treated him when he was unknown, because now they fawn over him. History should include the dark ages. I rejoice over your present fulfillment. Yours came earlier than mine. Mine only came when the Diaries were published—and I'm sixty-nine! This is the first year I am earning a good living!

I'm delighted to have all the news. You earned all you are receiving. I do remember your feeling that being a woman composer was part of the problem.

Letter to June Singer:

It was a *deep* pleasure to read your book, *Boundaries of the Soul*. It has an extraordinary clarity on subtle subjects, it is so complete, so total a journey. I was very moved and very stimulated. You express with such exactness the meanings which often escape synthesis. I learned a great deal from it. It reassembled diffuse knowledge and made some of the evolutions so human and understandable. It is a major work. I wish I had read it before I [made] a list of women writers [for] women's studies. I would have mentioned yours as a means of increased awareness. I read it all through, but I intend to *study* it as soon as I finish a far too heavy schedule of lectures. Your writing is imaginative and incisive. Thank you for sending me this valuable book.

Letter to a reader:

I do realize the absence of my husband is a serious lack in the Diary, but my husband did not want to be in it and I had to respect that, because I have a right to share my life but not to force this on others more reticent or shy of sharing.

All I can say is that I had *all* the problems we have all had with marriage but that they can be worked out with good will and awareness. For the moment that is all I can say. I realize your question is natural, and it has been asked often. Someday the entire Diary will be published. I'm sorry I cannot share more at this time. But I don't consider marriage any more difficult than all our other relationships to family, children, friends. They all demand our fullest creativity. They do not happen miraculously.

Letter from Lawrence Durrell:

Nothing that happened to me in Los Angeles gave so much delight as to hear your voice again and to think that with your characteristic generosity you had decided to forgive me my shortcomings and think only of our long and affectionate association and friendship. Wonderful! Thank you, dear artist. We spoke much about you as always, Henry and I, and of course we saw once again the beautiful film which Snyder has made of you, and where you speak with such force of my favorite woman, Lou! I have always thought of you as a sort of incarnation of Lou Salomé in your knowledge of and feeling for artists. Why has not more justice been done to her name? It is a great mystery to me. Even Henry, who is very curious about her, can find nothing except one rotten and pretentious biography. . . . Perhaps you will manage to rectify this state of affairs.

On the way back a strike at Paris diverted all planes so that it is actually in Geneva that I am writing this hasty and rather scrappy letter of thanks and solidarity. I think the Artaud film will be a good one, and it is a thousand pities that you were not in it. We were working mostly in French for an all-European viewing, which made the whole projecting somehow more congenial. The level of intelligence I suppose was the key really—and consequently you should really have been up center of stage. Never mind. They seemed very happy with what they got, the French.

Tomorrow I take the train back to my gloomy old house in Sommières. When you are next in Europe, please come and stay with me if the mood for country life is on you. I don't have to tell you how much pleasure that would give.

Letter to a reader:

Your letter distressed me, you are going through such a terrible experience. There is so little one can say in the face of either death or madness, for they are the same. People do not wait for the artist to die. People are simply afraid of whoever might change their life or vision. Fear of change. Art is not only for artists. It was once therapy, like religion. America disparaged it, reduced its value to our need of it for solace and healing.

The film [*The Music Lover* by Ken Russell] was a caricature of Tchaikovsky by a man who hates women. Why believe it instead of his music? Why judge the man [for] human fallibilities? Would you judge Dostoevsky for gambling . . . ?

Letter to a French friend:

We all hate American politics as much as you do. It was a terrible disappointment to see Nixon voted in again. But there is another America, unknown to the press, to other countries, people who are against power politics, war, commercialism. They are struggling . . . against great monopolies such as the oil companies, fighting Goliath. . . . I am now involved with the new generation, their struggles; they are *absolutely* different, and I had something to do with this change. But the press ignores them. I don't know how to make them known except through the Diaries—in time.

Yes, I want very much for the Diaries to be in paperback [in France]. . . . *Nouvelle Revue Française* after receiving me warmly (I thought) never answered . . . about my short stories. *Are they interested in me sincerely?* . . . Tomorrow I am seventy—and have no time to wait wait wait.

Letter from Henry Miller:

By all means print this letter. To me it doesn't sound so terribly discouraging, particularly when I compare its tone to that of greater writers than myself, men who howled like wolves from the depths of despair! Strindberg, Nietzsche, Dostoevsky, Byron, Rimbaud, to mention just a very few. I grew up with the idea that creative people must pay a terrible price for being different from the herd. The pattern never changes. All in all I was very lucky.

And I was especially happy to see that I was human enough and father enough to want to be with my children rather than adrift in a meaningless world of "culture." When I returned to Big Sur it was the children who sustained me and who taught me more than books ever could.

I don't think I was far wrong either in predicting the end of Europe. She will go down with America, I feel, before another twenty years are up. The people who are advancing with giant strides today are the Chinese. I see them leading the world in less than twenty years. (All this doesn't mean that I've become a Communist—far from it!)

I'm writing this from bed, am down again with the flu or something like it. I also want to let you know that I am *not* going to have the hip operation—my constitution won't permit it, say the doctors. So, I'll just limp along and be thankful that the rest of me is not in too bad shape. (There's always something to be thankful for, be it another square foot of floor space in your prison cell.)

I'm glad too that you telephoned Larry. Glad for *you*. A woman of your stature can't afford to take such umbrage over such trifles. As that famous killer once said, "I gave every man a chance" (before shooting him down). He meant: to hold up his hands.

I must send you the little Chapbook ("On Turning Eighty") which Noel Young printed recently. Not so much for your delectation as to show you that we are what we are, and the Devil himself (or the analyst) can't change us. . . . Good luck in New York and bravo for ending the lecture tours in May.

Dream: I am walking along the beach, and I am looking for Varda. I keep asking people and they direct me. At one moment I am climbing stairs (a place like Eze in the South of France). I arrive before a stretch of sea—a real Mediterranean blue sea. I see a place high above, a rocky mountain, an ancient city (like Eze), ramparts and old houses, very beautiful. I am told that is where Varda lives. I think to myself: It is like Varda to live in such a beautiful place. He always talked about Paradise.

[Spring, 1973]

The astrakhan dream: I am walking with someone. We find some clothes hanging on a wall, or fence. It is a beautiful astrakhan coat, muff, bag, cape, boots—all in glossy black astrakhan. I know people will steal these beautiful objects but I don't have the courage to do so, although I am tempted. (If I were alone . . .) I express my ambivalence, regrets (with a feeling of honorability winning out). When we return, all the astrakhan items are gone and I am regretful.

Association: I only possessed one fur coat in my whole life. It was an astrakhan coat and muff bought when stocks were going up (before the crash [of 1929], illusion of wealth). I wore it for ten years. Finally it was made into a small cape, hood and muff. I associate it with a false wealth. Or has it to do with my being taxed half of my lectures—anger, knowing it goes to bomb Cambodia?

The lectures were overwhelming. Fifty-eight since September. Finally my body rebelled. The moments of pleasure, the moment when a beautiful young face stands before me, deeply moved, and we look at each other with total receptivity, connecting, and I hear the words: "You have saved my life. You have awakened me. You have liberated me. You have revealed me to myself," that moment to which I respond with love and an amazing sense of communion, became finally drowned by the pressures of the crowd, the overflowing halls, the books to be signed, the poems to be acknowledged, more and more letters to answer, requests for lectures, requests to be allowed to visit. I felt submerged and this clear, warm, intimate moment I cherish was endangered. At no moment did I not feel, or respond, but feeling and responding left my body worn out. I would retire to my hotel room, or to my dormitory room, empty.

Two meetings stand out: one with Henry Jaglom and the other with Ira Progoff.

Henry Jaglom was happy. Tomorrow night *A Safe Place* will be shown at the Cinémathèque (in Paris) with my review translated into French. In Europe he had good response. In London a beautiful critique came out which I liked. Henry said over the telephone after I wrote my review: "Coming from you, I can't tell you what it means. I read your books in college."

He came to visit a few nights ago. He is imaginative, bold, and also practical. He wants to film my five novels as they were intended, as *Cities of the Interior*. We talked. He reads and rereads and penetrates the work. What an incredible year of correspondence. He talked about his obsesssion with *recording*—from childhood on. He reproached his parents for filming his childhood but stopping when he was six. What of the missing years? Now he films his parents endlessly and tapes their talk. To him, film is the preservation, the enduring record of life. When it is filmed, he is content. He fears to forget or to lose.

He has set up his own film company; he has absolute control. He is articulate. His talk flows.

Ira Progoff is a teacher. He writes deeply on psychology, evolved a course on the "Intensive Journal," understands Rank's *Beyond Psychology*. He is wise, gentle, inspiring. I'm renewing my interest in psychology. We had two evenings of talk. His work is far-reaching. He can work in Harlem, with returned soldiers, he has a wider range than I have and this always awes me, the power to teach, impart. There are many parallels and he confirms me in my orientation. I listen to his talks on cassettes and read his books.

I was troubled by those who, after listening to me for an hour talking about life, inner and outer, affirmations, transformations, would ask about suicide (Sylvia Plath's), or death. Ira explained that whenever one affirms, it arouses contraries, the negative. I took it that my talk had failed to impart life, but he did not interpret it that way. He talked about the black man in Harlem who sulked and was silent until they discussed dreams, and then he lay on the floor and told astounding dreams. In his *Dialogue with Figures of Wisdom* Progoff decided to dialogue with Shakespeare.

His sphere of influence is wide.

Letter to a reader:

I feel the crux of your conflict is that you want to go too fast. At twenty-five I was like you—ambivalent, uncertain. Take time. It is an organic, slow

growth. You hurt yourself by looking at me *now* in late maturity and comparing me with your youth. You're hard on yourself. The neurosis is there—
shocks, wounds, losses. I turned for help at those moments. The neurosis
keeps us from growing. Can you deal with that? Can you get help? You are
rich within and full of potential, humanly and poetically.

Letter to a friend:

Don't fear for your sanity, you are living fully and richly, on all levels.
Your letter was not depressed. You have done what I did in early journals,
and still do, say yes to everything and then find living complex and naturally
at times painful. But that is the only way we can live, having only one life.
We are more aware of that and so we live on many levels at once, and then
like Sabina we may feel at times we will never be whole again. . . .

Diary Five won't be out till next Spring, 1974. Next will come Six to bring
it up to publication of Diary and full expansion. Be patient. At the end there
is this feeling of communion with the world, contact, warmth, facility for
exploring new realms. It all harmonizes and fuses after a while. . . .

I correspond with, respond to people who write me letters for the
same reason I made friendships all through my life. I care about people
and their lives and work. Every human being is valuable to me. I consider the writing of the kinds of letters I get an act of friendship. It
requires a personal response. I never receive merely flattery or self-
interested requests. True, young writers want me to read their work.
And often I have to return it unread. It is too great a burden.

I keep the Diary spasmodically, less consistently. I will write a lot
when I am traveling or on vacation, less this year because of intensive
lecturing which I am giving up.

Some of my friendships have endured, some not. It would be too
difficult to say which ones did and did not. The only person I am
ashamed to have known at all is Gore Vidal. Usually I do not regret
my mistaken concept of people. I prefer to maintain my attitude of
faith until they prove they do not have a right to it. Those who have
continued to grow with me remain permanent friends.

The women who think everything is solvable by politics and no other
means are not those I believe in. Those who are willing to make individual efforts as well, to seek to create their own freedom rather than

demand it of others, with them I work in deep harmony. The militant women who seek to impose other dogmas and prejudices I fight. The humanistic women and those intent on finding another way to change human beings, I work with. Those who reject psychology and adopt ready-made formulas and definitions of "liberation" are inventing new taboos.

We have to face the nightmare, which indicates the fears, anxieties, traumas, shocks we hold within ourselves; we have to face them because they are like abscesses of the soul and prevent growth. Facing them does not lead to death. Avoiding them, repressing them, is what causes death in life.

Dream:
Two smiling, charming black boys about fourteen and fifteen. One polishes my nails to perfection and shows affectionate gratitude. The other simply hugs me, and I hug him back. An atmosphere of playfulness and affection.

Comment: Is it the buoyant, childish, generous quality of Barry Jones? He is pixie, debonair, spontaneous.

I want to write about
> Sas Colby
> Geri Olson
> Loren Eiseley
> Henry Jaglom
> Diane Northern
> Michael Jackson
> Lance Freed
> John and Liz Pearson
> Barry Jones

The girl who gave me her favorite ring at Chicago University, quoting me from the Diary: I always gave what it hurt me to give. The girl who gave me her mother's bracelet. The paintings. The poems. The flowers. The hand-woven fabrics, a collage, a crystal, sea shells. Will I have time? Oh, time!
> Tristine Rainer
> Priscilla English
> Johanna Demetrakas

I have lived long enough to see great changes in America.
Must write about the students. They achieved their own naturalness,
like the Latins and the blacks. Johanna takes off her sandals when she
arrives. She brings me flowers from her garden in a jelly jar. She
brings me rice cakes wrapped in leaves, made by her Greek grandmother. She sits in the yoga position.
How long it took me to achieve ease in the world!

Finished Volume Five. Monday we Xeroxed it.

Renate, who has to struggle to survive economically, disperses her
energies on many fronts, tells me my portrait of her keeps her from
going to pieces. She only has to read it to reassemble herself. Particularly my comparison of her to mercury, dispersing but always returning totally to its center, its wholeness never breaking off.
A friend gives me a compliment I dislike: "You would have succeeded in business." "That is not true," I said, "the artist needs to be
organized too."

Letter from Henry Jaglom:

I have just read *Nightwood,* then reread *Collages* & feel I understand more
deeply now; and unable, at the exact moment, to fly like Doctor Mann from
Israel, I send you this sunset [from Jerusalem] with the feelings which *Collages*
has once again stirred up in me as my substitute for his brandy & chocolates,
but with no less ardour or gratitude, for being able to move me, to reach out
across two oceans & three continents and touch me so perfectly in this extraordinary land of Kaka'tuv.

Letter to William Burford:

The sixty strenuous lectures are over. I am beginning to relax and finally
write the letter I owe you. It is true I cannot sustain any correspondence, but
there is another factor I must try to make clear. After twenty years of harsh
treatment and exclusion from American literary life, I finally at the age of
seventy achieved a deep and serious acceptance. I would like to enjoy this
acceptance which helps me finish the difficult editing of Volumes Six and
Seven. I do not have much time left. I can only consider as friends those
who can sustain this effort by their love and understanding. Your letters

remind me strongly of the doubts, hurts, criticalness and negativities of which I received more than my due. You questioned the validity of diary writing itself. Forgive me if I turn away. What I accomplished I did by not listening to anyone. This is the year of my reward. If you cannot, by your very critical nature, celebrate with me, then spare me an attitude which reminds me of what I had to overcome in the past. Attacks by Vidal do not disturb me. They are too crude.

But your subtle doubts, warnings, are possibly harmful to a peace of mind I need for work.

Anything which would waste my energy I must lay aside.

Do you think you can be that kind of a friend? Or is your concept of friendship the critic's role? . . .

If this is too difficult and negative criticism is a necessity for you, then let us keep the good feeling of reconciliation which followed a shared ordeal and not venture into more difficult areas of possible discords.

My last lecture at Redwood City. It took me time to find myself again—all given, all dispensed, my attention still on the students, on their needs, work. The intense rapport with the world emptied me.

I gave Volume Five to John Ferrone, my new hardcover editor, yesterday. He was the paperback editor of the Diaries for years.

The most exciting week in American history—the freeing of Daniel Ellsberg, the unmasking of a gangster government. For the first time I celebrated emotionally. Other memories of sorrow—the death of Dr. King—were followed by repulsion for the political; but now the battle is even between good and evil, sincerity and hypocrisy; and hope is raised. Before, it was like a sewer—anything you looked at was putrid. Now at least a few clear-thinking, courageous men emerge. Every word Ellsberg says, I can believe. The oppressive power structure totters. And it was not done by violence, bloodshed or the revolutionaries. It was the principle of self-destruction. Nixon is mad and dangerous—as dangerous as Hitler. He hypnotizes the ignorant, the middle class and the rich.

Talk with Bogner:

A.N.: This whole year I had to resist the image thrust on me by the students, by the public. An idealized image, a legendary one, a heightened one.

I do not succumb—I know this is not me. It is created by people's need of heroines, of someone to believe in. Some artists come to believe they are what their lovers say, but I don't.

DR. B.: But I observe that although you do not believe this image, you try to live up to it. You try not to disappoint the students. You answer every letter. You give help. You send books to libraries for women's studies when they have no funds. You write recommendations for jobs and grants. In other words, you try to live up to this impossible ideal.

A.N.: That is true. I feel faith is a precious element; it should not be betrayed.

DR. B.: But can't you see the source of the strain, why you don't want to lecture anymore?

At Dr. Bogner's I see Lauren Frost, who is trying to adapt sections of the Diary for the stage. She is emotional and sincere, warm and intelligent. But she chose the wrong writer, Shelagh Delaney, the author of *A Taste of Honey*.

With Bogner I examined depression. My writing began to bring me business problems, which I dislike.

Anna Balakian and Nona came to see me. A good nourishing talk. Anna is immensely intelligent. To hear her talking about surrealism is inspiring. Nona has been at the *New York Times* longer than anyone. She knows literature and fights fruitless battles. Who is Breton? Who is Varèse?

I went to the Brooklyn bank vault and brought back volumes to work on Diary Six this summer.

I met the Harcourt Brace Jovanovich salesmen. They clapped when I entered. Not at all like the concept we have of salesmen, the cliché concept.

Trew visits me, the potter from Washington. She is so utterly sincere, and troubled with closeness to woman. How close? What does it mean? All the questions I asked myself about June.

Reentry is not without pain. But it had to be. I could not continue to live as a public figure, dress for it, speak in a way which moved people, answer questions, star at receptions, receive gifts, answer letters, be recognized in the street, accosted by a thunderous motorcyclist all in black leather who said: "Are you Anaïs Nin? I'm a poet."

I had to return, to write a preface for Marcel Moreau, whose poetic volcanoes intimidate me, his power with words overpowering. His last delirious manuscript lies on my desk.

Also on my desk, a folder with instructions for the commencement at Philadelphia College of Art where I will receive a doctorate. Honorary Doctor of Art. A briefcase now empty because I have answered all the letters.

Millie Johnstone arrives in a white monk's robe, her gray hair hanging loose on her back. She has spent seven weeks in a Zen monastery in San Francisco, a communal life. She carries an exquisite basket with a cup, green tea, a napkin, a bamboo mixer, a delicate spoonlike stirrer, and makes the tea ceremony for me.

Pathetic how in 1973 the Westerner can only imitate another culture, another religion, rather than turn to the healing power of psychology. Zen did not heal her. It merely persuaded her that marriage was not a "personal matter."

Lunch with Jill Krementz, whose photograph of me in my black cape was the favorite of the year. She is a sensitive and interesting young woman, with plenty of courage. When she was assigned to cover the Harlem riots in 1964, as a staff photographer for the *New York Herald Tribune*, she went. The publisher was furious that they had not sent a man on this dangerous assignment.

Afternoon with Pamela Fiori. I like her warmth, her humanity, her knowledge of many countries, having traveled so much for *Travel & Leisure*. Her talk is full of interest and color. We are both Pisces, and she is suffering a relationship similar to mine with Gonzalo. She likes *The Wilder Shores of Love*. She liked my article on Fez.

[Summer, 1973]

Bellevue Stratford Hotel, Philadelphia.

I took the Metroliner to Philadelphia. President Culler [of the Philadelphia College of Art] met me and drove me to my hotel. I went to dinner with Mr. and Mrs. Howard Wolf, trustees of the college. I met Dr. Grimm, teacher of literature, who was to introduce me the next morning. We were ten at the table.

Tomorrow the graduation ceremony and my doctorate. I wear a classical, long-sleeved orange dress. I know that public life does not appeal to me as such; I do not need it. I have known it well, the crowds, the messages, the flowers, the autographing, the praise, the love, dinners and receptions. But I am not finished yet. In June, Robert Snyder inaugurates his film *A.N. Observed* at the Vanguard Theater. In June I speak on Ingmar Bergman at Schönberg Hall, UCLA.

Will my honorary doctorate prevent some faculty members from discouraging students who want to do their thesis on my work—as Amherst did, saying I was an "eccentric writer"?

Praise is not necessary when obstacles are removed. It is only necessary during battle, during construction.

Reentry. Change of atmosphere. Sometimes the letters tire me, when they bring problems, when they pray for consolation, for encouragement, for help in getting published. Will you read my diary? Where do you think I should live after my divorce? I am going to Paris, please give me names of your friends.

The next morning, rehearsal at room 217. My hat is too small and my black gown too short. But we solve the hat problem by an exchange. Everyone is pleasant to me. It is the black woman serving coffee who is ecstatic over my orange dress. We walk ceremoniously into the packed ballroom. We sit on the stage.

Dr. Culler speaks. Dr. Grimm speaks about my work. I come forward and receive a hood or capelet, and my Certificate of Honorary Doctorate of Art. Then I speak, impromptu, inspired as always by the theme of artist as magician. Warm response. Lunch. Richard Centing is there. Sharon Spencer in a red dress and gold earrings, radiant. Georgiana Peacher and Lynne Honickman.

Lynne generously treated us to a limousine with chauffeur for return home. The car was filled. Lynne only stayed with us part of the way. We talked a lot. Sharon's novel is out, *The Space Between*. She looked so beautiful, so alive and bright.

I'm pleased at the honor, but detached from praise. I feel it is not good for me, too much praise.

From the transcript of my commencement address at the Philadelphia College of Art:

I am particularly touched to receive an honor from this college because I was always accused of favoring the artist. It was not only being one but also learning from them that convinced me that perhaps the only magician we have is the artist. And it was James Joyce who said that history was a nightmare from which we hope to awaken. I would like to tell you how my love and feeling about the magic powers of art began.

My father and mother warred constantly, but when the hour of music came, the house would grow peaceful and my mother would sing beautifully and my father would play the piano and string quartets came to the house, and as children we thought: Now the magic begins, everything is peaceful and beautiful. And I learned very early in my life that music could transform, could transfigure, could transpose a human battle into beauty.

When I was sixteen and I became a painter's model, when the other young women around me were bored and looking at their watches, I was learning about color from the painters. Later on, I learned the importance of the image, which I have always used in my writing as coming from the dream, a way of thinking which no modern life has ever been able to eradicate.

As a writer I wanted simply to take all the various expressions of art into writing, and I thought each art must nourish the other, each one can add to the other. And I would take into writing what I learned from dancing, what I learned from music, what I learned from design, what I learned from architecture. From every form of art there is something that I wanted to include in writing, and I wanted writing, poetic writing, to include them all. Because I thought always of art not only as a balm, as a consolation, but I thought of art, as I said, as a supreme act of magic which is contained in certain words that I always tell students to write on a large piece of paper and to live with. These were all the words concerned with *trans-*: transcend, transmute, transform, transpose, transfigure. All the acts of creation were to me contained in these words, and I felt that no matter what we were living through, we had to find our strength, our harmony and a synthesis by which we could live, and make a center to resist outer events and whatever experience shattered us. I always used art to put myself together again. That is why I favored the artist, because I learned from him this creating out of nothing.

I learned from Varda how to make collages out of bits of cloth; in fact, he made me cut out the lining of my coat to make a collage, and it was certainly more beautiful as a collage than just as the lining of my coat. I learned from Tinguely how to go to a junkyard and make a satire of the machine. . . . The power to create out of nothing. The feeling that on depressed days, for example, in New York, I could go to the Metropolitan Museum of Art and look at *The Sun* by Lippold. Some of you must have seen this; it takes the whole room; it is actually more radiant than our natural sun. And, just sitting there and looking at the Lippold sun, my melancholy would be dissipated. That is why I call the artist the magician, because he holds the antitoxins. And when we are shattered, or when we are in a state of despair or sorrow about what is happening outside, being able to create something out of clay, out of glass, out of bits of material, out of junkyards, out of anything, was the proof of the creativity of man. But in history, I saw only the struggle for power, the struggle for possession. In the life of the artist, I saw that he had to be a dedicated person, that he was not sure of worldly rewards, that he would have to wait, that he had the most difficult task of all, which is (as Otto Rank put it) to balance our two wishes—one, to stay close to others; the other, to create something which may alienate us from our culture. The artist is the one who has to risk the alienation, as I did for many years because I was writing something which was not in the trend of that moment. I had to wait for many years for synchronicity between the feelings of this generation and their attitudes and their values. So this waiting is difficult, and I know many writers will have to go through it, and that they have to separate themselves; they have to, at the same time, understand and reflect their culture, but they also have to see beyond it. And it's in this moment that they begin to shape the future for us, the future of architecture or the future of music. This is the difficult moment when we sometimes repudiate them or disregard them or treat them with great indifference. So I feel the artist has the will to create, and that this is a magic power which can transform and transfigure and transpose and transmit to others.

Gaston Bachelard, the French philosopher, said something very touching; he said sometimes he thinks that what we have suffered from most is silence: the silence which surrounds our acts, the silence which surrounds our relationships, the things we cannot say, that we cannot tell to others. There was a moment in America when I was afraid that people had decided never to read again, never to depend on literature, and never even to talk again. I was very troubled until I realized that what they objected to was babble and not talking together; what they objected to was a literature that didn't bring them life, but abstractions. And therefore, for the novel not to die, for writing not to die, we had to return to the sources of life, which meant biography, which meant basing all happenings on truth, but not forgetting that art would then transform this truth, transmute this truth into poetry. And poetry will teach us how to levitate. That is what the poet teaches us, to levitate.

Bachelard also said that what the artist has done is to make it possible for us to believe in the world, to love the world, and to create the world. And I really believe this because when I began the creation of the Diaries, I never knew that I was creating a world which was an antithesis to the world around me which I rejected, which was full of sorrows and full of wars and full of difficulties. I was creating the world I wanted, and in this world, once it is created, you invite others, and then you attract those who have affinities, and this becomes a universe, this becomes not a private world at all but something which transcends the personal and creates this link. Bachelard says we suffer from silence; what the Diaries did was to speak, and then you spoke to me in return . . . So the universal link can be created by each artist when he really turns to his individual creation and is not afraid of ignoring the fashion or the current dictatorship. When the artist starts out on his road, it seems a lonely one, but he dares to follow it. And this daring is so important, this sense of adventure. Even beginning a diary, you see, was already conceding that life would be more bearable if you looked at it as an adventure and a tale. I was telling myself the story of a life, and this transmutes into an adventure the things which can shatter you. It becomes then the mythical voyage which we all have to undertake, the inner voyage, the voyage in classical literature through the labyrinth. And then you begin to look at events as challenges to your courage, and I'm not saying that we all have to be heroes but that we do have to fulfill the journey and believe that there is a way out of the labyrinth. . . .

In the afternoon I was interviewed by Michiyo Ambrosius, a young Japanese woman. She was first influenced toward independence by Simone de Beauvoir; then, dissatisfied with intellectual abstractions and philosophy, she found the Diaries a materialization of a woman's development. She wants to retain her femininity. She tells me her story. Her grandmother died. She could not weep. Then one day she went into her room and wept for hours over her grandmother's wasted life. It was her grandmother's life she did not want, which frightened her.

In Japan not only parents watch you but everyone else. She saved money, won a scholarship, came to an American college, worked terribly hard, often starved herself, married an American and is now working to see him through law school. In her struggle for independence she studied filmmaking.

During lecture at Marin College a man brought his Irish harp and wanted to play for me.

Iris Rosenfeld told me she had a new name for me in the Arabic language: *Nur al-Nisa*—"Light of Womanhood."

Marcel Moreau came to New York to see me. His violent writing did not show in his body. He spent his first night at the apartment of Sharon and her husband, Srdj [Maljković]. He watched while Sharon opened two locks, and then removed an iron bar pressing against the door. This was on West 95th Street, and twice they had been robbed. Moreau was amazed at these precautions.

Bogner and I still discuss the responsibilities and obligations of my writer's life. The Diary has continued and reinforced people's expectations of my responses, my help, my inspiration. I'm deluged. I find it hard to have a day of no work, to be at leisure, walk the streets, rest, buy Indian cotton dresses, book-browse.

First impression of Marcel. Soft, dark, glowing eyes. Sweetness. He has long black hair and a small beard. He is stocky. Srdj says he looks like a mixture of Balzac and Gorky. His writing is one long violent nightmare. He belongs to the new generation though over forty, and to the American one. He is an articulate primitive. My Diaries changed his life, brought out tenderness. The concept of a loving approach to the world, the concept of love. He began to write me. He dedicated *La Pensée Mongole* to me. We know each other by way of writing, and talking is difficult. I do understand his subterranean course. We had lunch with Bill Hayter. Bill is seventy-one but alert, vivacious, observant, keen; he is thin and wiry.

We had a dinner for Marcel with Sharon and Srdj. We took him to the Balakians', to one of their warm, lively evenings. Everybody liked him. We tried to warn him about the dangers of going to Harlem or to the Bowery. But he went. In Harlem they accepted him and invited him for a drink at a bar. Did they feel that he was not afraid? In the Bowery they accepted him too well: made homosexual advances.

The warmth of the Balakian family is my greatest delight. The beauty of the children, who are musicians, at home with writers, with every race, every age. Husband so gentle and loving. Marcel flowered in their presence.

Marcel said he had a beautiful week, that he felt relaxed and free of his demons. He talks exaltingly about my work though we are opposites. *"Vous faites votre démarche par l'amour."* He is a revolutionary, a rebel. His books are nightmares occasionally illumined by poetic depths.

Shocked by Richard Centing, who carefully records gossip against me and who, when we talk about the lessening of negative criticism, says: "What of Gore Vidal?" I answered: "He is no literary critic. He is a poison-pen writer, a hatchet man for the *New York Review of Books* and *Esquire.*"

And this right after I had told Richard I had written to William Burford that I was enjoying total acceptance of my work and that if he could not rejoice with me I could not continue a correspondence full of innuendos, negative comments. This has shaken my faith in him. Yet he wrote about symbols in the Diary so understandingly and seemed so devoted and loyal.

An interviewer asked Margaret Mead: "What do you tell your grandchildren?" Her answer was: "I listen to them."

I am trying to clear my desk to begin on Volume Six, but it seems impossible. My documentary film was premiered. I hope colleges will rent it when I cannot come, for this year I will have to accept very few lectures for the sake of my energy and editing, which suffered last year. I hope it will be considered as a visit from me.

The women's movement has given a tremendous impetus to the study of women's writing. We are truly discovering woman.

———

Today I met a most remarkable woman, Margalite Ovid, small, dark, fiery, born to a tribe in Yemen. The strength is tempered with charm, the intensity of her body so eloquent that even her hands on the drum take six or eight eyes to watch. Her hands at one moment are like the flight of many birds. Her voice has as much range as her gestures. She is mythology personified. Every part of her body is dominated by expression.

I saw her first in a film by Allegra Snyder. Even on film I felt struck by a meteorite. The other night, in person, emerging from the car, she seemed like a figurine from ancient times. When she talked about her training of forty students, I felt magnetized, as if I could get up any moment and dance according to her wishes. "It is a heart to transplant," she said. She communicated her fire and eloquence. Bob Snyder was seeking to interest her in *Collages*, but I felt she was so steeped in legend and myth that she might not make the leap into *Collages*. Her aliveness is startling. Not since Martha Graham have I seen so eloquent a body and face. Also, she possesses what Martha did not have: passion, love, responsiveness. The room was set aglow with her smile and her laughter, her beautiful balance as she sat on the Esalen pillow.

At Henry Miller's:
"At peace with myself."
Writing portraits of some of his friends—seventy pages so far. His etchings, his watercolors on all the walls. Japanese book of his watercolors.
Nightmares. Loss of identity. Madness. Punishment. Henry does not seek to know. He says: "I don't care." Never saw the paradox of joyous self and anxious self so clearly. House neat and clean. He was washing dishes last night at two A.M. Went to sleep at five A.M. "Full of ideas. Too many. Acceleration. Never felt better. One gets used to the pains and aches. When they last so long you become used to them, you forget them."

Suddenly I began to feel the loss of leisure to write. I realized I would prefer to stay home, write and swim and see friends.
Friends:
Leslie Caron—always young—a purity and musicalness—charm.

Jody Hoy—a dainty, tiny figure—enormous eyes, delicate features—brilliant.

Gwen Raaberg—sea eyes, large and illuminating—writing on two surrealist writers, Henry Miller and Anaïs Nin.

Robert Snyder—positive qualities: enthusiasm, optimism, creative will—came nearest to going beyond documentary in film on me—wants to become imaginative artist.

Dream: I am dead. But *I am still there*. Invisible but present.

Caused me concern as to handling of Diaries. Problems: what to seal, what not to seal. Made a catalogue. Trying to forestall problems and confusion. Planned each portion. Need time to edit Volumes Six and Seven, and 1914 to 1931. Concern about matters after my death has been the theme of this year. A strange paradoxical concern because I never felt more alive. In the pool, suntanning, early morning in the garden—I feel whole physically.

At seven A.M. I am at my desk. Working on 1955 to continue Volume Five.

Friends visit. Devotees of my writing. They are intelligent, loving, intuitive, natural. They take off their clothes and swim in the pool.

My political friends chide me for not listening to [the Senate hearings on] Watergate. This gangster's world we have been ruled by, now being cleaned up like a festering sore, justifies my lack of faith in politics. But I realize how dramatic Watergate is and that it may affect our future. The battle of good and evil. But again, I will not *live* with such men, let them invade my home so that their ugly faces are more present than my friends' beauty, so that their low, greedy, twisted selves accompany the meals. I seek other company, other worlds, other atmospheres. I can't breathe in the gutter. I pay homage to Nader, Ellsberg, rejoice over victories of the good, as in samurai films—the hero against fifty attackers. I admire the men who dare to defy oil companies, Nixon, expose corruption; but I also hear the refrain: *Everybody does it*; why make such a fuss?

Margaret Lee Potts writes a brilliant study: "The Genesis and Evolution of the Creative Personality: A Rankian Analysis of *The Diary of Anaïs Nin, Volumes 1–5*."

With Jody Hoy, I work on a good videotape interview; we work all day. She brings champagne and homemade pâté for the crew. She wears her hair à la Henry James character, only charmingly loose, so it falls over her delicate face. These young women writing about me are extraordinary. They manage in academic terms to impose their understanding of a non-academic work. They are well trained but manage to escape conventions.

I divert all my troubled friends to Dr. Bogner. Lauren Frost, the young actress who wants to stage the Diary. Sharon, who has grown out of certain conventionalities, has lost her nervous giggle. It is like watching plants in a hothouse, properly nourished, in a proper temperature, all damages repaired. It gives me pleasure.

Bogner playfully analyzed one of the "Help me" letters I received and my answer and success in sending the writer to therapy. In answer to her letter—"I feel nothing at all. I do weep at music"—I wrote: "If you weep at music this means you can feel, but the circuits of feeling toward human beings are blocked." Bogner commented: "You deserve a doctorate for knowing how to steer people toward seeking help." She had wanted to see whether or not I encouraged dependence.

Puerto Vallarta, Mexico.

First of all the warm, caressing air. It dissolves you into a flower or foliage. It humidifies the sun-opened pores. The body emerges from its swaddling of clothes. Rebirth. Then the colors, the infinite variations of greens, deep, dark or golden. The banana tree the darkest foliage of all, wide, dense, heavy. The fringes and interlacings of palms Then the birds, vivid, loud, vigorous, talkative, whistles, cries, gossip, clarinets and flutes. Trills, tremolos, vibratos, arabesques.

Then the flavor of margaritas, ice cold, with salt on the rim of the glass.

Rented a jeep and excursions began, to Los Tres Arcos, three huge rocks with caves and tunnels, delight of snorklers from which they return with descriptions of fish which rival descriptions of fashion shows. Blue stripes and gold tails. Three fan tails of bright red on a silver-gray body, small transparent fish like Lucite. We hike up the mountain, past a little village, along the river, to find a pool. Marianne Greenwood had made a map of what we should see.

Nightmares: My mother and I are cleaning up the kitchen, a terribly messy one. We are in our slips. Drudges. My father is coming. Anxiety at what he will think of us, he with his mania for aesthetics and beauty.

But the body is healed by the Mexican life. There is a stillness in my head. I am content with warm little pleasures, because of the warm cuddling by the air, the feeling of nervelessness. Passive drinking in of color, the cafés, the shops, people; and the thrill of looking into open homes, open windows, open doors. An old lady in a rocking chair. Photographs on the walls. Palm leaves from last year's ritual at Easter. One room reminded me of Barcelona. The whitewashed house. The room painted sky blue. I have known such a room, with potted palms, lace doilies on the table. Pictures of Christ, of course, artificial flowers and bric-a-brac.

I do not understand the nightmares. Again last night I was cleaning the rim of an incredibly dirty bathtub, picking up dirty glasses. My mother was having a sewing party. I went in to consult with her. Why should my spirit be so heavy when my body is at home in Mexico?

Returning on the boat and looking at the lush tropical vegetation, my eyes filled with tears. I do not want to die. I love this earth, the earth of Mexico, the sun.

I sit now on a small beach, facing a huge rock. The snorklers swam through caves, saw bats and darkness. I am surrounded by butterflies, black with gold stripes and pearls at the tip of their wings.

I answer a letter or two a day.

This morning I saw the most beautiful fern in a wild field, feathery, lacy and of a green so light it seemed touched with gold.

I have been reading Arthur Clarke. He envisages a future where our minds are influenced by machines, programmed. People can erase others' memories. Memory banks can distort history. Some practice telepathy. But all this has happened already. TV is the machine which brainwashes us. We do erase others' memories. Our minds are constantly tampered with (distorted, lying history and lying media). We influence each other more than we are aware.

My purple postcards have given stimulus to so many. I drop ten or twenty cards in the letter box each day. I can't answer in many words, but I respond. What they write me is usually gray. It is usually negative. Respond, respond. Turn gray into red, respond, transform gray into gold.

The women washing their laundry in the river. Some have planted umbrellas. They choose a smooth rock. They rub sheets, tablecloths, shirts and underwear. They rinse and fill baskets with clean clothes. The children play at the edge of the river.

The market. Stuffed animals, snakes, iguanas, raccoons. Armadillos, coatamundis, squirrels. Orange, purple, white shawls. The dress I found has the tones of Balinese batik, all brown and gold, with designs of birds and impalas.

We followed Marianne's map. Marianne was born in Lapland. Perhaps because of this she has an obsession with the sun. She travels all the time. She is only happy when she is traveling. She carries a camera and very little or no money. She has blond hair and icy blue eyes, close together like those of a Nordic fox. She has courage, and people in the jungle of South America are so astonished at her appearance, alone, that no harm ever befalls her. Yes, a shark bumped into her and cut her forehead above the eye. Scar. A lonely beach with a first-aid sewing job done by a native. Another time, after a hot climb in the jungle, she swam in an icy cold mountain pool and caught pneumonia. Another time the Huichol Indians broke her camera but did not harm her. She adventures everywhere. She has a lean, boyish body. In Brazil she met Alain, who had sailed from France alone on his sailboat. They traveled together. They caught malaria in the New Guineas. While he was repairing his sailboat in Puerto Vallarta, lying under it, it fell on him. Friends of Marianne saved his life in Guadalajara. She described his hospital bed in a cheap *pensión* frequented by prostitutes. They covered his sheets with holy cards to invoke the saints to save his life. It was saved. He limps. He has a radiant smile and warm dark eyes. He is twenty-four or twenty-five. She is a grandmother. They are happy together. They are linked by courage and a love of adventure. The sun has tinted her skin with warm tones. The sun has adopted her. It is natural to evoke Marianne here in the tropics where she belongs.

Dream: All my friends are acting in a musical comedy. I am in the theater. I am not too interested, so I move about, hearing fragments of the songs and parts of the speeches. As I move about I become aware of a plant which needs water. I go to a restaurant table and ask to be given some water for the plant. The women refuse me coldly. I go to the back of the restaurant. They send me away. My whole concern is for this thirsty plant. I wake up.

I am still trying to reach the sun, to immerse myself in the sun, but for several days we have had thunderstorms at night. Drops of rain fell on the diary yesterday while I sat at the beach. Count them.

Snorklers describe a three-foot sea snake, a fish that is blue, purple, with three light blue electric dots which shine like lights. A fish with a gray body and a bright yellow stripe running along its body, and a magenta tail. Another was all black and white, with three fan tails. Another pure yellow, small, with two black tails. Another was exactly divided into two colors, front half gray, back jet black.

River scenes. All the women at work. As the clothes are laid out to dry on the rocks, they form an abstract pattern of red, yellow, blue, orange, white. Later the women go home with basins filled with clothes balanced on their heads. One was climbing a hill with her load. A merry scene because of the children playing around them, naked, splashing, swimming, teasing each other.

Here comes the sun.

In the sun the pelicans sit rigid on the rocks watching for fish. The black-and-red butterflies mate on the sand just barely out of the reach of the waves. The birds sing with a lust unknown to Northern birds.

In Los Angeles I became enslaved by my correspondence, such touching, moving, poetic letters. They must be answered. I felt enmeshed by my own responsiveness.

It rains every afternoon, every night. I don't go dancing because the electronic music is too loud. What a difference between the Latin orchestras of Acapulco, so soft and seductive, and this shrieking ugly rock and roll. It was too loud on the boat too, ruined the sailing, but I loved watching the dancing. The boat trip took us to a beach. From there we hiked up a mountain to a pool and a waterfall.

Warm rain. Real steamy jungle. Overloaded mango trees, gliding frigate birds. We sit in a café by the seaside and drink beer.

———————

Last night, in Los Angeles, Henry Jaglom came. He has long hair, the most intelligent, aware eyes behind eyeglasses, with super vision, one feels. A genuine, open smile. He is magnificently articulate. His descriptions of his parents and his relationships to them complete. His father "the most interesting man in the world," powerful, convinced he is always right because he has always made the right decisions. A Russian Jew, he left Germany at the right time, influenced and dominated influential people and cannot believe he can ever be wrong.

But with Henry he found the most diabolically effective way of tyranny: love. He loves his son. "I know I should let you make your own mistakes, but I love you and if I see you about to fall out of a window I must hold you back." He came to see *A Safe Place*. He was proud that he could look at it as if it were made by somebody else, not his son. "Yes, it is like you, crazy, but it has something, it has some quality at moments. . . ." A quality which made him dream that night and remember his dream for the first time in his life. Henry is almost overwhelmed by the significance of this subliminal influence we both practice, he is ready to weep. The shell has cracked, at last. He dreamed that Henry was the girl, dreamed it was Henry's life. But just as Henry expects more, fearing to have crossed the border into the irrational the father will not concede to, he adds that the dream was probably due to a pillow that kept sliding behind the bed.

His mother is beautiful and intelligent. They understand each other. When homesick for Europe after they came to America in 1940, she played *La Mer* over and over again while pregnant with Henry, and later when he chose the music for *A Safe Place*, he selected the pieces which made him weep. One of them was *La Mer*. He has been taping all his conversations with his parents for five years (to keep, conserve, preserve what may vanish). This, in a period when links to parents are so often broken, amazes his contemporaries. I saw his diary, a real date book. He makes entries in different colors, mostly designs indicating color of person or place. Calligraphy, Pop Art, one word, a name, to remind him.

In Israel he met a man who asked him if he knew my work and then offered the information that he was Dr. Mann in *Collages*. I told Henry his real name. But he introduced himself: "I am Doctor Mann."

People connect his film with my work. There are affinities. Discovered word "Numinous." We looked it up in the dictionary. It pleased Henry Jaglom. "Spiritually elevated. The strange numinous sense of presentness, like a spell. From 'numen,' the presiding divinity or spirit of a place. Creative energy regarded as a genius or demon dwelling within one."

Before Henry's visit I had a difficult week. Illness, depression. The day before I emerged from the doldrums I had a dream: I was condemned to die. I was lying on a board and I was going to be electrocuted. First I was given a sedative, which did not have any effect. The man who was going to execute me finally could not do it. He loved me. He freed me and I knew he was going to pamper me. It was after this dream that I awakened well and began spiraling upward.

Wakened at seven and began work on article for *Westways*. Since I returned I had to answer letters, take care of the "business" part of writing. With Henry Jaglom's visit I was inspired again.

Outside in the world the climate is suffocating. Everyone watches Watergate on television from seven A.M. to two P.M. They call it a morality play. At last the evil is exposed, the corruption being judged.

But I refuse to spend my day in the company of such a low breed of men. I rejoiced wildly when Ellsberg was free, but newspapers and television give me the feeling that people are nourishing themselves on garbage. I find history repellent, not worthy of attention. It is an escape from the real tasks. Ha ha, they called the artist an escapist but the real escapists are the spectators of history, avoiding the active tasks of changing themselves, because the men being tried were chosen by them when they voted for Nixon.

Nature was kind to me. First of all, sensual love can continue as long as emotional love is alive. In my case my body was never distorted. My feet are unchanged—the ankles not swollen. I have no varicose veins. I have kept my weight at 120 pounds and wear the same size dress I wore at sixteen. I hold myself erect and walk lithely, swiftly. The only signs of age which were ugly were wrinkles on the throat. I have no frown lines between the eyes. I have wrinkles around my eyes, laugh wrinkles, but no pouches. My forehead is smooth. My legs are slim, and I can wear miniskirts. The flesh under my forearm is a little loose. But my breasts are like a young girl's, the nipples pink. I have a slim, indented waistline.

When you love someone for a long time, the expression of the body, its presence, takes on emotional attributes; and lovers do not lose desire because of the signs of age. Deep love grows deeper with the loved one's flowering. The body changes but so does the spirit, and its numinous qualities increase.

I am youthful when friends come, and I talk with brightness and catch all that is being said. I am a tireless walker and I walk fast.

It is not so definable—age, desire and love. I still arouse desire and receive love letters.

At Robert Snyder's suggestion, International Community College asked Lawrence Durrell and me to take a few writing students. This "university without walls" uses the old guild system of a master teacher working with each student on a "one to one" basis. Their offices are in Westwood Village, next to UCLA, but they now have teachers all over the world.

I wrote for their catalogue:

Anaïs Nin, Los Angeles, California, will accept ten students, graduate or undergraduate, for individual, independent study in diary and fiction writing. The following expresses Anaïs Nin's philosophy of teaching writing:

"The summation of my methods of inspiring writers is contained in *The Novel of the Future*. It means studying all the ways of revivifying writing and reuniting it with the rhythm of life itself. It means discovering the ever-renewed sources of its vitality and power. It means restoring its lost influence to help us out of the desperate loneliness of silence, out of the anxieties of alienation. It means giving a voice once again to the deep sources of metaphysical and numinous qualities contained in human beings and inhibited by our cultures. I think of writing as the ultimate instrument for explorations of new forms of consciousness, as a means to ecstasy, to a wider range of experience, to a deep way of communicating with other human beings. That is why I wish to teach both diary writing, which keeps us in close contact with the personal, and fiction writing, which is the expansion of what we have learned and experienced into myth and poem. I teach writing as a way of reducing distance between human beings, opening vision into experience, deepening understanding of others, as a way to touch and reach the depths of human beings, as nourishment; as a means of linking the content of the dream to our actions so that they become harmonious and interactive. I teach the source of writing, which is ever fertile, the images of dreams, how to use them, how they can become the starting point of a saga, an adventure, a drama. By the interaction of diary writing and fiction, I show how experience can be heightened, expanded, developed. The image of the Japanese paper flower which expands in a glass of water is apt in this case. I teach writing as a way to reintegrate ourselves when experience shatters us, as a center of gravity, as an exercise in creative will, as an exercise in synthesis, as a means to create a world according to our wishes, not those of others, as a means of creating the self, of making the inner journey, of giving birth to ourselves. I teach the value of the personal relationships to all things because it creates intimacy, and intimacy creates understanding, understanding creates love and love conquers loneliness. Before becoming a perfect novelist, I teach it is important to possess empathy and identification. I advise whoever wishes to study with me to read *The Novel of the Future* in order to understand what I believe writing can become and the vital role of the writer."

My sweetest moments are spent in the pool. I swim two or three times a day throughout the year. Though it is right next to the house, the pool with its dark green color, with plants growing over its sides, with huge red sandstone boulders at the corners, becomes part of the garden. While swimming, you can look out over the edge and see the lake below. The trees give me complete privacy so I can swim *au naturel*. On the rare occasions of a writing block, often I can float it away in the pool. The side of the house facing the pool is glass, and sometimes when it is raining I leave my tiny writing cell and write in the large room like a Buddhist monk meditating in front of his reflecting pool, hypnotized by the lacework of interlocking circles formed by the raindrops. Fortunately (even though it *never* rains in the summer in Los Angeles), it rained a little one day that Robert Snyder was making his film and Baylis Glascock was able to capture this with his camera. The Garden of Eden effect is enhanced by the perfume from the forest of pittosporum trees, like a blend of lemon and jasmine.

I am beginning to appreciate Los Angeles. True, Frank Lloyd Wright called it a lot of suburbs looking for a city (he also said the United States tilts to the southwest and everything loose ended up in Southern California), and I still resent the long drives on the freeways.

278

But I now feel this is the only large cosmopolitan city where I can be warm all year, close to the sea and still create my own small paradise just five minutes from downtown.

Frances Ring, editor of *Westways,* asked me to write about Los Angeles.

I first met Nan Fuchs at a poetry reading when she read a poem of her own which I liked and described as iridescent. Years later we met at the post office where we both have a box. She was now "the Herb Lady." She stepped out of a station wagon all painted with leaves and flowers. She walked lightly, a big bag slung over her shoulder, her Michelangelo hair curled around her face. Even her slacks were covered with leaves and flowers. We talked and she described her activities. The next day I found my mailbox filled with herbs, and I will never forget the marvelous smell which greeted me when I opened it. All the smells of flowers, plants, grasses, of the forest concentrated in neat little packages.

What I did not know then, after this introduction to the sensuous herbs, is that Nan's whole intelligent and intuitive self is not merely concentrated on herb lore and their properties but on total healing, psychic and physical.

She began as a graduate English major, became interested in botany, then in drugs at the time of Timothy Leary's and Aldous Huxley's early influence, then developed from drugs to healing herbs because, as she explained, with drugs the sky appeared intensely and magnificently blue only once in a while and she wanted to see it thus continuously, out of physical well-being.

She wanted to achieve a natural energy, a naturally tuned instrument through which joys and high moments would be reached continuously without hangovers. She wanted the natural energy which feeds creativity.

The names of the herbs and teas alone have suggestive properties: Puri-Tea, Celebration Tea, Tranquili-Tea, Capsium, Fenugreek seeds, Fu-tse powder, Golden Seal root powder, Gotu-kola leaves, Guarana powder, passionflower, Gin-ja and Fong-fung, Mu Tea with added Korean ginseng. The healing properties one learns gradually. Like all

279

esoteric knowledge, it is transmitted only as you advance willingly into the knowledge, without disbelief.

Nan's persona is the light-footed, ever-smiling magician carrying armfuls of little packages to be mailed far and wide. In intimate talk she reveals a deep compassion and concern for suffering. She has learned to sustain, to transmit courage, strength, without being infected by the illness of others. This is the wisdom of the true healer, who is immune to contagion.

Her energy is articulate. She is willing to talk, to teach, to impart. Her curiosity is alert, her mind is open to all research. Her interest in herbs is in harmony with today's generation seeking the natural sources of energy to combat technological poisons. She is a symbolic figure, Nan, with her enthusiasm, her willingness to try everything on herself first. A few years ago these herbs were only known to the Chinese in quiet shops of downtown Los Angeles, where the purveyor was suspicious of the white man's questions. I was there once when a prominent doctor was asking questions on the properties of the herbs and the answer was silence.

Nan's work seems to bring in little packages all the magic properties of trees, flowers and bushes around us. It takes knowledge to separate the toxic from the healing.

The letters I pull out of my box are often confessions of distress. The herbs, which have spilled fine powder and their incense over them, are Nan's answer to these requests for help. What would happen if instead of answering the letters I mailed a neat little package with the Herb Lady's trademark and aromatic presence?

[Fall, 1973]

As soon as I am freed from obligations—the briefcase full of unanswered mail, Volume Six to edit, the phone, talks with Bob Snyder
about *Anaïs Nin Observed* (I try to get him college rentals), talks with
Tristine Rainer, with Lynne Weston, with Tracey—I can write in the
Diary.

On the plane, Saturday, September 29. Great sorrow at confronting
for the first time the limitations of my energy. The invitation [to a
performance based on my work] in Boulder and Denver was tempting
(from Lee Potts, who wrote remarkable study of my work, and Linda
Barnes—personality in her letters).

I was honest and refused a seminar in the morning, lunch, a bookshop appearance, newspaper and radio interviews, dinner with a large
group before lecture, etc. I dislike setting barriers, closing doors. But
even with precautions I was swept into a vortex. Lee met me at the
airport. Irresistible—all of them were so immensely lovable. Lee's
friend, John—never read me, but I felt such warmth and quality
of spirit. Long drive to Boulder. John loves his mountains and points
to their beauty. They chose a motel for me among the pines. I had
dinner in their home. No time to talk. We have to leave for the performance. This was planned in three weeks by Lee and Nancy Spanier.
Dance, symbolic interpretation, electronic score, narration, background
of slides—some excellent moments. The best, the dramatic reading of
the "Birth" story by a very young woman who fainted twice after re-
hearsals and wept when we met afterward. A reading of the Varda
passages, although not done with lightness or humor; acting of the
chess player by a skillful actor with a powerful presence; a reading of
the bicycle passage from *Ladders to Fire*; dancing—out of daughter
and father passage in *Winter of Artifice*. Minor flaws—the last dance,
which should have expressed lightness, ecstasy, liberation, not light
enough; the narration, with electronic echo, not clear; but as a whole
a remarkable feat of interpretation, and very moving. They are all so
young. The dance of birth was striking.

After the performance I stayed a little while to sign books, to exchange a few words, never enough time for all, and I wish to know them all. I would like to take more time; it is passing too quickly. These faces always offering the deepest feelings—the mute ones, embracing me in place of words, or the ones who do not know how to talk, asking the endless questions which, I know now, is a form of seeking exchange, a clumsy way—not feeling at ease. Then we went to the home of Professor Young, and I met many people besides the performers and left only when a small group remained. Before sleeping I read loving notes, letters given to me. They are all saying: You have given me strength, you have freed me, they are all about the life currents. They speak of my radiance and I myself wonder at the miraculous love which continues to be transmitted in spite of my physical handicaps. The food has given me pains; I'm so deeply tired. Next morning Lee comes at nine and we go to have breakfast at Nancy's house—a colorful table. Frederick Eversley, the sculptor of rainbows, has come from Venice, California, to meet me. He is a childhood friend of Nancy's. He cooks the omelet. Now it is raining, a bitter, windy, wintry rain, and I am fearful of wet feet, of paying with a cold. In the rain we drive to the bookshop. It is utterly charming, created like a personal library—plants, couches, space. A series of rooms where people can sit and browse—a communal venture—personal and sensitive.

I signed books for two and a half hours, received flowers, homemade cookies and *The Life of Lewis Carroll* by Florence Becker Lennon, a gift from a very old lady—scarred face—who dedicated it: "For Anaïs Nin, whom I have finally discovered just before closing time *avec éclat!*" A wonderful, learned book, which I read from before sleep.

From the bookshop, Linda Barnes drove me to Denver. The students had asked for a seminar but I could not do it. I had barely an hour to dress, rest, bathe before the lecture. Linda's husband, Arden, another one of those tender, lovely men, the mates of my daughters, who had horrifying stories to tell of Boulder's architectural school (I must note them; they justify Lloyd Wright's tirades) so that he dropped out before getting his license. But building just the same because he also knows how to be a contractor. (Story of assignment to draw planting around a house, and he drew such a beautiful tree the Master gave him a C because the tree overshadowed the architecture. When drawing a poster he could not afford to buy letters so he hand-drew them and also received a C for not using printed letters!) So he was astonished because later in my lecture I mentioned a book on handmade houses as a proof of man's natural inventiveness and imagination.

The *natural* courtesy, thoughtfulness and sensitivity of these Americans far surpasses the learned courtesies of Europeans.

I didn't give my best lecture. But perhaps because all they want is a confirmation of what I wrote—my presence (they gave me an ovation before I talked)—I feel that my improvised talk was better than any prepared lecture. I also follow the contours of the questions, talk around them, beyond them.

Stayed until lights were turned off. Went with a small group to Lee's house, where we talked easily.

Breakfast with Linda and Arden and their baby. Airport. Lee arrived from Boulder with the eyeglasses I left behind—photographs. Great affection between all of us.

When Linda first went to the faculty to ask for the lecture hall and collaboration, the faculty said: "Who?" All but Miss McIntosh, who filled my room with three bowls of flowers. They left Linda to worry about tickets, doors, chairs. Could not supply a tape recorder except at cost of $25. Linda was too immersed in the technicalities and I finally discovered she had supplied $500 from her savings account so I wouldn't have to wait; and next week they are going on their vacation and need the money. So I have to remedy that immediately. Once again the rigid institution versus student needs and the influences which nourish them. What is beautiful is that American students have taken things into their own hands.

The women set up their women's studies independent of the faculty. If they are not integrated with the faculty, they go on just the same. I never realized before, the *predominance* of men in all professions, nor did I realize fully the constant lowering of women's status. It is wonderful to see them struggling to get into filmmaking, into law, all professions. But I also find the radical feminists damaging, the men haters, the artificial lesbians, the vociferous, bitter, violent women who achieve nothing. At last the International Institute of Women Studies is honoring me as useful to women.

Ever since this communion with the world has happened I no longer suffer from loneliness. I come to the little writing room and close the door; my briefcase overflowing with letters fills the space with entrancing figures. Gentle men artists who send lyrical letters and presents of artwork.

Marcel Moreau's new book with my preface in French.

Nancy Jo Hoy, so beautiful and so clever, with her handsome poet-builder husband, dean of Irvine.

Barbette Blackington, whom I only heard once at St. John's College, so powerful and witty in her feminism, honoring me in Washington.

A visit to Henry Miller just recovering from very serious, near-death surgery—so frail and small.

A blind black girl sends me cassettes in which she talks to me. She tried to shoot herself. She is writing (or dictating) her story.

So much work. A calendar of dates to find my way through undated letters or diaries.

Wasted time on a girl who came saying she was writing a book on Varda and was actually totally disassociated, rambling, disintegrated by drugs. She monologued uncontrollably and I quickly escaped from her. The monologue of drug addicts is no more interesting than drunks' monologues.

My faith in psychotherapy revived by Rollo May. He knows the cure for violence. He explains it. We won't follow it, but we could have mitigated it. I long ago suspected it grew out of powerlessness and humiliation. And America is the greatest humiliator in existence. It is always cultivating the power you get from humiliating others. The lowest kind of power, the power of Moloch. Rollo May is right. But how do we train a culture not to humiliate minorities? He is illuminating on true innocence versus false innocence. He does understand our times. So I return to the only solution for humanizing the world. Why do people regress to Jesus, to the East, when a new solution was offered us? Compatible with science. (Duality of the brain. Abnormalities of the brain of the young man who shot thirteen persons from a tower.) Prison has fostered crime. The media has carried the contagion. It does not perhaps create it, but it spreads the contagion. But the solution, psychotherapy, is far away. It is a luxury. Dr. Stone charges forty dollars an hour! It has to be free clinics, care of schoolchildren early.

Nine o'clock.

I have been at work since 7:30. I have returned at last to the intimacy of the Diary—after letting the whole world walk through it. Some damage was done, but fortunately not the damage of consciousness.

I see Tristine going through the fear of being becalmed, of missing more intense forms of life, her restlessness, her hunger for high moments. The fear she will not find them again, fly. She has a home by the sea, a blue tent, a devoted lover. She takes me back to Louveciennes. My work is crystal-clear for her. Nothing is strange to her. We have strange affinities. Talk on sexual frankness. Our culture is savage toward sex and only accepts it as pornography, "dirty." It has been vulgarized beyond salvation. Reviews of Violette Leduc are all based on morals. The immorality of politicians does not incense anyone. I do not have the ultimate courage to deliver my body's life to the public. In Volume Six I skipped the return to childhood eroticism. When will we be ready to confront all the ignorant cultures who punish every rebel who brings a new vision?

Last year, the year of the sixty lectures, from September 1972 to June 1973, I had the feeling of living outside of myself, or of myself coming entirely out of myself to meet the world. It was out of myself that I gave all I knew, and the love I responded to, but at times the constant appearance before the public created a mirror image, like an echo, which was not good for me. Too many images of Anais in a red dress, a white dress, a pink dress, a purple dress appearing on stage. Even if my *feelings* were strong, the repetition deprived them of their spontaneity. I knew what they were going to say and I knew my answer.

Letter to Daisy Aldan:

I agree with you. We need to live on many levels, not writing alone, though I must confess the public life appeals less and less to me. And I love sitting at my desk and working on Volume Six. I did read Kazantzakis, but as you know I do not respond to religious preoccupations. I'm a pagan. Religion comes from within us and is expressed by our humanity. I believe more than ever that psychology is going to cure hostilities and prejudices, which prevent us from living at peace with each other. Religion, as you can see, causes war. I may be wrong, but I think war is pathological, never sacred. Read Michener's history of religions, all trying to annihilate each other. There must be another way to humanism.

John Ferrone has become a close friend. He came to Los Angeles for the Book Fair. I made dinner for him. He is an inexorable editor but *always right* and he suggests remedies. Perhaps because I was overworked I found revisions arduous, endless. I like him so much. He is gentle and keen, human and yet firm in his judgments.

Daniel Stern teased me about "I insist on being in the Diary!" We were talking about the problems of editing. How one can damage a life even when not intending to. I sent a friend the pages on him describing our bohemian Village days when drinking or lesbianism or homosexuality were fully accepted. He asked me not to publish this because he is working for the State Department and would lose his job. The same with a woman friend who is now a therapist. Another woman friend is married to a society man and has children. Wants nothing about her past life.

Marguerite Young said today: "I hope to become a capitalist by my socialist books." She is writing about the noble men of American history at the lowest moment of American history, when Nixon is about to be impeached. She is writing about the utopians, the idealists, the socialists.

Cutting down the lectures has helped me regain my energy. In New York I have time to type ten or fourteen pages for Volume Six. I see friends as well as interviewers. So much is happening I can't note it all. *The Publish-It-Yourself Handbook* [with "The Story of My Printing Press"] came out and was well received. It not only contains the history of my press but of my friends' presses—Daisy Aldan, Adele Aldridge, Alan Swallow. The weekend at Rye produced another book, *Celebration with Anaïs Nin*. Lynne Honickman published her poems with my preface.

Before I left California, I visited Henry Miller after serious surgery, fourteen hours and eight hours on separate days. He was so weak and frail. He is blind in his right eye from being too long on the operating table. He does not hear well. When he asked to have the pillows removed so he could slide into bed and rest, I felt almost as if he was going to curl up and sleep forever.

The outrages of age, the cruelties, the slow corrosions. No wonder W. H. Auden asked to die swiftly and not as an invalid. He died of a heart attack recently before age crippled him. I am glad Gonzalo died before being crippled. I hope the same will happen to me. I don't want to live as Miller has, limping, in pain, not able to travel and now for the second time undergoing major surgery. Henry once so healthy, joyous, lively. Tireless walker, hearty eater.

But let the sun shine on a beautiful autumn day, let me have a morning free of engagements when I can work on Volume Six and I am light again. Stay alive, Anaïs.

Father Monick of the hippie St. Clement's Church where I spoke, who invited the women to say mass with him, to become priestesses, to present poetry, films, jazz and theater instead of sermons, or me instead of a sermon, speaks of the way I looked on the platform as if he were speaking of a miraculous apparition, luminous.

Jean Stevo, the Belgian surrealist artist, sends me his daughter, who teaches at Yale.

A private airplane was named after me. Whose?

Every day a college asks me to lecture. I only accept one a month.

Every day a surprisingly beautiful, poetic letter. Every day a surprise, a gift. Books from the Jung Society. Invitation to talk with Ira Progoff at the New School.

John Ferrone, to please me, obtains a golden cover for Volume Five, a painting by Susan Boulet, *Daughter of the Sun*, chosen by me.

Jim Herlihy, now calling himself, as he was called originally, "Jamie," is back in Los Angeles.

Frances and I take a walk in the Village looking for an apartment for her and by chance find the ideal apartment. My reaction to it confirmed hers.

In the sun it does not bother me to be walking toward Dr. Parks's office for a weekly injection because I am bleeding slightly and afraid of a recurrence of cancer. But he says no, it is not that. I must increase the injections.

The first few days in New York I can type in the mornings, but after that the telephone rings every ten minutes.

Barbette Blackington arrived from Washington.

I call up those who will be invited to the Gotham Book Mart to see the one-hour documentary *Anaïs Nin Observed* by Robert Snyder.

Dream: All night long I was doing or trying to do mathematics. A sense of inadequacy and frustration—I could not do it. (When I took LSD I said I understood the infinite.) I also dreamed that I kept someone from entering my house. I shut the door and windows. I knew it was a man in distress who wanted to enter.

With Ira Progoff's book, *Jung, Synchronicity and Human Destiny*, I recall instances of synchronicity.

The same day I was writing the "Birth" story in Paris, I walked into a café and ran into the doctor [who is in the story]!

Only the other evening a young man who came to the film showing and works in a bookshop brought me the book I most wanted: a biography of Erik Satie.

John Ferrone imagined me the freest of all spirits. He was amazed to find me with family duties. "No one is ever free," I said, "if one has a human sense of responsibility."

I cannot solve the contradiction between Eastern religion—all evil comes from the ego, get rid of the ego—and Western psychoanalysis, which says: All evil comes from the lack of knowledge of our unconscious self, the self we do not know. They seem hopelessly contradictory and I feel that I have reached a oneness with nature and a oneness with humanity by Western methods of removing the obstacles to this unity. I feel a complete repudiation of Buddhism and Zen, a deep and natural one. It is not my way. I have achieved satori by other means.

But I cannot explain this intellectually or argue it. *Through* and *beyond* the self, I would say. But not beyond the self by elimination of it. Elimination of the self has been the destruction of India, and to a certain extent of Japan. But the *not going beyond* and remaining at the primitive stage of greedy infantile ego has been the destruction of the West. The West is selfish and grasping and power-hungry, not spiritual. But the East is a failure too; look at the life of India.

There is some confusion between ego and self-creation. For Americans all self-creation is termed "ego trip" as a disparaging judgment. That is wrong too. Then others warn us that a scientific and technological culture will destroy the individual. Television has already brainwashed millions of individuals. It carries the germ of not thinking—of passivity.

The feeling of oneness. How can one describe it?

All who come to the door I begin by *liking,* by being open to their invisible messages, by seeking links, correlations, affinities, by seeking to know them.

If later this is betrayed, as by the cold-blooded thesis of Nancy Zee, the most destructive and negative of all, I do suffer, being still vulnerable to disapproval, but I measure it against all I have achieved in giving inspiration and courage. Bogner stresses the great difference between defensiveness and self-protection. In defensiveness I would have written an angry letter defending myself but exposing my vulnerability publicly, giving her the satisfaction of having wounded me. In self-protection, I will write an objective letter for which I'm not yet ready. I have found I cannot trust my anger.

When I became angry with Benjamin Franklin, I obtained nothing but silence and a break. I should have gone about it in a cool, studied way. I should have written to Richard Centing my objection that Benjamin Franklin is a totally negative critic, that in the newsletter he constantly disparaged my friends, that the spirit of the newsletter was fraternal ("A Café in Space"), while his belongs to that of the bitchy society I am struggling against.

Nancy Zee offended me by her false premise that what I had left out of the edited Diaries was for the purpose of self-idealization. And thinks herself a genius at detection by putting together Diary and the novels as complementing each other. The keys I gave myself, giving in another form what I couldn't give in the Diary! Noblesse oblige! She thinks to destroy me by her great discovery. Never for a moment suspecting I might be protecting others or have human conflicts!

I awaken at four A.M. to write a defensive letter, but feeling on irrational ground I take it to Bogner. She reads the thesis and finds it brilliant and accurate and objective. I believe her. Some of it seemed to me to be negative. Bogner thinks I judged it with the *self destroyed by the father*. She read Nancy's letter and dissipated the old nightmare of being annihilated by criticism.

Two days on tea and toast with my recurrent "crisis."
Keenly enjoying study of Erik Satie. I would have understood him if I had heard him from the beginning. The twenties seem more brilliant and inventive than the thirties.

The late Dr. Félix Martí-Ibáñez wrote about Zen and I understand it for the first time.
Bogner talks eloquently about Nancy Zee's thesis. My vulnerability to criticism made me pick up only negative vibrations. I misinterpreted the study. She feels I should be proud of it. She herself believes an artist reveals more of himself in his art than in his biography. Self-idealization was only used in Jungian terms, says Inge, everyone's method of self-protection, and not a lie. I can be proud of this study. She wants me to read it again and become more objective.

[Winter, 1973–1974]

I walk into an Indian shop where I buy cotton or velvet Indian dresses, Tanagra style, for twenty or twenty-five dollars, but I still look sumptuously dressed. The last one from Pakistan, red and black.

At Lewis and Clark College [in Portland, Oregon] I had met a remarkable woman, Barbette Blackington. She was trying to create a center for women which would serve many functions: research on women's questions, publication of a magazine with articles from all over the world. Her project was large and ambitious. The first number of the magazine was to be dedicated to me. She prepared a newsletter; I mailed it in every letter I wrote. Barbette came to New York to see foundations. No one wanted to take it, as they would need continuous support.

Soon after, Mrs. William O. Douglas arranged a cocktail party in my honor. Nothing could be more unexpected than that a French-Spanish child of eleven starting a diary on an old Spanish ship on the way to New York should find herself at seventy standing next to Justice and Mrs. Douglas in the Supreme Court's vast conference room receiving hundreds of persons. Half came for Justice Douglas and charming and beautiful Cathy Douglas; half came to meet me, saying something lovely about the Diaries.

And I felt amused, too, at sitting at a long table before the cocktail party, at a board meeting [of the International Institute of Sexual Identity] discussing the painful subject of raising money and budgets!

Mrs. Douglas was on the board. It was my first meeting of this kind. Inevitably it centered on matters of fund raising, budget and suggestions from the members as to the function of the center. I felt out of place and rather useless, but the fervor, dynamism, the powerful personality of Barbette magnetized me.

The journal has not yet appeared, and people subscribed three years ago!

Barbette refers obsessionally to my five-minute therapy at St. John's because I hugged her and loved her speech. She loves me. She looked beautiful in a long black dress, her bosom half exposed in a plunging neckline; her healthy gray hair, clear-skinned face, exuberance and brilliancy. She introduced me as a "woman's woman."

I gave a very brief talk:

I'm here because I believe we need to coordinate and integrate our knowledge of woman. Women's liberation has lacked such a center. It conforms to my belief that the more knowledge of ourselves we reach, whether historical, statistical, or psychological, the greater our hope of controlling those irrational swings of the pendulum, violent revolutions which cause more misery than progress.

This lack of knowledge has brought prejudice, hostility and eventually war.

Let us hope the Institute [of Women Studies] will bring lucidity and guidance to women concerned with growth and creation.

And for the men who have feared an invasion, let us hope the Institute will reveal not a rival but a powerful ally.

As an example of enrichment of knowledge: Forty years after D. H. Lawrence's death, a book was finally written about Frieda Lawrence—and then was revealed one of the most interesting collaborations, a far more human and fascinating story of interaction and interdependence.

Another recent discovery are the letters of Mme. Lafayette, which showed how much she contributed to the work Lafayette had given his life to. While he fought in America, she collected money in France, sent shoes and ammunition, dealt with the American ambassadors. Lafayette called her "his other self. "

At eight I left with one of the attorneys, whose manners were so astonishingly romantic and courteous that he felt he had to explain: "My mother was French."

I can truly say I have had my full share of thanks and honors.

The taxi driver Rosenberg.

When I gave address of the Gotham he said: "That is a bookshop. I used to go there for the James Joyce meetings." So we talk. He is a schoolteacher out of a job. He is a sociologist. He is bitter. I tell him it is not a personal failure, it is the times—history. I invite him to the film showing. He comes. He tells me at the end that my talk with the students dissolved his anger.

About 200 persons came [to see *Anaïs Nin Observed*]. But their demands upon my friendship overwhelm me. The old Kalahari greeting: "I see you! I see you!" is still true.

Humorous: When I talk to John Ferrone about the harmfulness of being a "performer," of repeating public encounters, he tells me to write it in the Diary, not to lose it! I say: "You want to edit it?"

On the way to Buffalo:

I think I am withdrawing from public life because it focuses entirely on an idealized Anaïs. They have extracted from the Diaries only my faculty for giving hope, for inspiring, for changing their life, only the life-giving quality, so that what is expected of me, what is heavily unbalanced, is again the practice of healing. If Colette Neville calls me up minutes before I set out for Buffalo, it is to confide her distress. "In theater work everything is intermittent. When I am working I give all to the work and cannot write. When I'm not working I don't write! I have a violent need for recognition." If others call me it is praise for how I appear in the film. I feel the Anaïs who is mirrored is an enhanced one I mistrust. I have work to do. I need an atmosphere that is more natural and better balanced. This is like too many flowers. I need severity and I find also in others a desperation to become me. The actress said: "I want to be you."

So I must return to this unflattering mirror to my basic seriousness. Do I feel this image of A. on stage too close to that of my father on his concert stage, to his telegrams which came regularly and were read aloud by my mother: "*Succès fou!*"

Well, enough *succès fou.*

The positive beauty was the emotion of oneness with others—the miraculous communion with those who came up to me, the *sincerity* of the praise, which is more like gratitude.

At a certain point I started to carry the Diary around—to feel the need of it. Here there is no performance. An old friend disturbed me by speaking of my aura, which he traces back to the beginning of our friendship. The present A. is a denial of that one, but he only notices the original one.

On the plane [to Los Angeles] I wrote fifteen letters.

Theme for story:
Winchester Mystery House, San José: Widow inherits fortune made from guns. Haunted by ghosts. Building false stairs, false doors, false balconies to mislead and detour them. Image of maze against guilt.

Receive my first International Community College student, a sensitive, talented, mature woman.

Dr. Weston. "Bleeding *may* or *may not* indicate recurrence of cancer." Dr. Parks had said definitely: "It is not a symptom of recurrence." Depression.

Henry Jaglom's *A Safe Place* will run in Paris as *Souviens-toi*. We have long talks over the telephone.
I spoke at UCLA's program honoring Ingmar Bergman.*

Saw Johanna Demetrakas film on "Womanhouse"—Skillful, moving, perfectly done.

Careful of dates because in the fifties I became careless. Also I didn't write immediately after event, which confused chronology—at times important.

The musicians playing—beautiful waterfalls of sound. At seven A.M. I was finishing the Diary for 1958, which is full of new themes: LSD, Brussels Fair, trip to Europe, Jim's success, painful friendship with Geismars, Durrell's unexpectedly inadequate preface to *Children of the Albatross*. Rain. Post office. Always interesting mail. Work on Diary catalogue for libraries. I would like to settle the matter of the Diaries while I'm alive.
Someone sends me a fancy selection of tea, shocked that I should use Lipton in the film! Trouble getting Bob to polish and finish *Anaïs Nin Observed*. Meditating on my lecture at Esalen. The necessity to

* See "Ingmar Bergman" in *In Favor of the Sensitive Man and Other Essays*.

know our unconscious has become more vital since women are studying programming. How can you separate the true self from the persona? So many elements have to be sorted out. On the table lie the *Notebooks of Martha Graham* given to me by John, a sketchbook of Sausalito houseboats, and the *Ascent of Woman* by Elizabeth Mann Borgese.

Ruth Ross is here and should have been introduced long ago. I don't remember how we met at first. She has a lovable nature, a keen scholarship allied to a feminine gentleness and thoughtfulness. Her talent was never imposed, loud. She is a teacher of social science, has written a book. She is an adopted child, began her life during the cruel Depression, self-made, highly educated. I liked her as a person, her voice, her large green eyes, her full, generous mouth and turned-up nose. But we were at first on such different wavelengths. I lack political science, and she was not interested in psychology. But with time the disparity lessened; I became more knowledgeable about politics. She came closer to my world. We respected each other. I think we learned from each other. She was always cheerful, loyal. Then she turned to me in moments of difficulties. It was the first time that because of personality I could listen to statistics, to history, to social science at its best. I changed too. In a sense I feel she persists in her faith in political science as I persist in mine. Now her teaching has taken a feminist turn. There is our meeting ground. We exchange books, magazines, information. She works terribly hard.

When I travel she moves into the house, which she calls her summer home. I call her Piccolino's stepmother. She likes the pool.

I think of Ruth as one of the courageous women, emerging from a destructive background, educating herself.

Henry Jaglom tells me over the telephone how he handles the "business" of filmmaking. The male investors, lawyers, etc., he treats as if *he were a woman.* He asks for things to be simplified, he admits to not understanding intricacies, he *suggests* what he would like. *They* begin to feel protective. They put out their cigars when he is there. He describes the whole game, because he says if he tried to deal with them in their own terms he would hate the whole structure, quibbling, details, complexities. He goes so far as to put perfume on himself in the middle of a board meeting. It was diabolically intelligent. I could understand it. I told him I was glad he had told me this, as I wondered how he managed in the business world and whether he found it painful. "Not at all," he said.

He talked about the film *Tracks* which he wants to make. He told me the story. He will spend months on the train. I suggested a diary which did not require the turning of pages, to parallel the train journey, a Japanese sketchbook. Accordion-folded, it can be continuous, one page running into the other. He sketches in it. He is an intricate and many-sided person, which disturbs Tristine [who is working on a script for him].

Tristine taught diary writing and asked me to talk with her students. I did and we became friends. She read her essay on my work* at UCLA. She has big brown eyes, a nose with character, a vulnerable voice. I have watched her develop, from a suffering woman to an assertive one. But Henry demands total abdication because he is her age (thirty-five). She is full of anxieties and spoiled the mood of the association by her need of a concrete solid contract. In films everything is a mirage, including contracts. I trust Henry as an artist. He is gambling on Tristine, a young, unknown writer.

I asked a scientist if he could explain scientifically why our computer-like brain should retain childhood and become blurred or even totally erased in old age. *Why* do we remember our childhood and lose our grasp of the present as many old people do? Why do the later cells distintegrate? Why do we regress to childhood? An old friend, after a stroke, is senile. She behaves like a bad child, won't go to the bathroom, won't dress, runs away down the stairs, etc., and even lifts her cane to strike the nurse.

Why should the first recording be more vivid than the later one? I have been reading books about the brain, the two sides of the brain, the duality inherent in man's body.

My only conflict now is that under incredible pressures (every day a visitor wanting to come, every day ten letters or more, every day an interview or a photographer, every day a request for a preface) I had to learn to say NO. It goes against my nature and I react with depres-

* See *A Casebook on Anaïs Nin* (1974).

sion, as I react after anger. It is easier to say yes, but my health, energy and work are in the balance. I have to say no. One interviewer from Toronto pressed the wrong button [on her tape recorder] and nothing was recorded. When she asked for a second interview I said no. It is difficult. I have guilt, regrets, I feel ugly and hard! I say, Anaïs, you're changing. I fear hardness, defensiveness. I disapprove of them.

In 1958 I suddenly expressed my true feeling about *Balthazar*. Decided Durrell does not have a deep knowledge of character. It shows in this Balthazar, *soi-disant* psychiatrist. He promised relativity of truth but that lies in acceptance of subjectivity, and that means introspection, going inward, which he has not done.

The deep disappointment at finding out Durrell does not understand me or my work.

Why should he? I say in 1973. He lives in fiction. Like Henry, he invents. He does not *see*. Typical of his lack of art for relationships is the legend of my wealth, which he clings to.

I have to talk at Esalen. I do not want to talk anymore. I don't exactly know why. I'm happier working. I think I'm disillusioned that people only bring me their burdens. Occasionally I get a present which signifies thank you, but usually it is a burden.

Listen to Ira Progoff cassette on counseling. He stresses that the method of the Intensive Journal unburdens the counselor. He discards "analysis" as if analysis were a purely intellectual-medical formula, when in the hands of Bogner it is the greatest stimulator of growth. She helped me to see the thesis of Nancy Zee, and now we can exchange opinions.

My student is a skilled writer, educated, literate and trained in psychology, yet she sees the two hours we spend together on Mondays as a duel, parrying—on her side defending her armor, on mine probing—but she asked to be delivered of inhibition. She tries to convert me to Hemingway! She had fifteen years of Christian Science, and is now a Catholic convert! But the tutoring is effortless because she is sensitive. She is already writing a whole yellow pad every morning. I suggested she show me only what she wants to. She reads certain pages and we analyze them. For example her *censor* is a formidable figure, Army and Navy! Impossible to dislodge. I said: "Rules are necessary for our own protection!" How to free the writing without going too deep? An interesting challenge. "Examine your fears," I said. She wrote: of becoming sloppy, loose, unstructured, chaotic.

Lectured at Esalen in San Francisco. Lectured at the Kabuki theater, stayed at Hotel Miyako in the Japan Center. Loved even this pale echo of Japan. Eleven hundred persons [at the lecture]. Seeking this time the answer to how we deprogram ourselves and find our genuine self. Received poems, flowers, letters, kisses, tears. I would like to carry this Diary to Tahiti, but too heavy to hide!

So I start a fresh one for the journey. It is my rest from burdens, students. My dreams have been heavy, active, but vanish in the morning. I wrote a preface for Deena Metzger (an act of friendship); an article on "Eroticism in Women" for *Playgirl** (to get Frances Field's drawings published); 400 pages of Volume Six. I think when I reach Volume Seven, I will rest (dialogue with the world). Tristine is working on script for *Cities of the Interior*. Script for *Minotaur* a disaster. "I tried to modernize it, to make natural dialogue." I suffered so much from the false tones that I could hardly read it.

"The audience . . ." One doesn't write for the audience, I said. "You do your work, as I did mine—the audience came to me. I did a timeless, poetic work, not a colloquial work. [The film] *Women in Love* was faithful to Lawrence. Why can't you be faithful to me?"

I wish I had a record of the lessons with my student. I feel I am doing something life-giving. I'm afraid to spoil the spontaneity by turning on the tape. To dissipate her inhibitions—that was the challenge.

Joaquin is traveling, retired.

I have to say no to the colleges who ask me to lecture.

A woman writes me: How do you deal with aging?
Answer:
I wish we could talk about aging. I was more concerned about that at thirty and forty than now at seventy. Because I found that if you live deeply, remain emotionally alive, curious, explorative, open to

* See *In Favor of the Sensitive Man and Other Essays* (1976).

change, to new experiences, aging recedes. It is not chronological, it is psychic. I was against the depressing acceptance of chronology by Simone de Beauvoir. Bow to age, she says. I say transcend it. I'm able to write all day, to swim, to lecture, to travel. Of course, I had to learn my energy was not infinite, but only this year. I think the youthful spirit wins over the face and body. You look beautiful and interesting in your photograph. Free yourself of the false mask of aging: It is merely a moment of tiredness.

For months now I have been bleeding, like a light menstruation. It has worried me. The fear of recurrence of cancer is there. So today, I am having an examination by Dr. Trotter and Dr. Parks in the same Presbyterian Hospital [in New York], where I had radiology treatment. Same dismal rain and snow, same long, ugly taxi ride. America has a gift for creating the ugliest environment; the speedway is lined with discarded cans; the hospital is unspeakably ugly; the cafeteria a manger for animals, with cardboard trays, paper cups and the pile of discard next to where you eat.

I wait in rooms which could be a set for *No Exit*.

I remember telling students how I dealt with a grim situation by inventing a film of happiest days during radiology—as an example of transcending experience.

Dr. Trotter and Dr. Parks not alarmed. I asked if the prognosis was bad. They said no. Dr. Parks will make a test. Nothing for the eye to see. I came back in the slush, snow, rain, not entirely reassured. What does the bleeding mean?

Test made. Yes, there is something brewing. I have to go to the hospital for four days for painful insertion of radium bullet.

Between December 21 and 31 I wrote another small red Diary on Tahiti. I couldn't carry this one around.

Tahiti was satori.

Ecstasy and oneness, with nature. I can add that to my life-giving adventures. As with Puerto Vallarta.

———————

A happy dream at last!

Expressed in a room entirely decorated by collage bits of colored clothes, young women in colorful hippie dresses, I also in colorful Indian cotton—atmosphere of color and warmth of texture. No happening.

Talk with Sharon over the telephone: She laughs like a schoolgirl —almost exaggeratedly feminine before I sent her to Bogner, playing at schoolgirl rather than brilliant scholar and teacher. Her book is dazzling. Now she tells me she finds it hard to accept her maturity.

She and I repudiate the homely role of liberated women. She dresses exquisitely. In fact she is the only woman to wear a dress I hungered for. She loaned it to me. I knew what it meant, because it was done to me so much; I knew [the borrowers] hoped to become me, as I hoped to look like Sharon the day of my doctorate at Philadelphia. Voodoo. The dress arrived from the cleaner with all the elasticized waistline loosened, so I had to give it to a dressmaker, who kept it three months, and finally it hangs in my closet, never worn by me! Was it because I was ashamed of wanting to be Sharon the beauty? She has a delicate face, big eyes, finely designed features, a delicate long neck. Her expression is seductive, lively, playful. She is slender. Her voice is light.

The whim passed. I am back into acceptance of myself, of my age, which surprises everyone. Why should it have taken so long to gain in confidence, in decisiveness, in consolidation?

In fun, if I wished to look like Sharon, June 1973, I also wished to be Marianne Greenwood, the bravest woman I know. She is as brave physically as I am psychically. Bill Lewis is writing about her. I wonder if he will capture her narrow face, her iceberg eyes set close together, fox and wolf. She is a fine photographer. She wanted us to go together to Cambodia.

Pamela Fiori. Immediate sympathy. She likes the Diaries. She is a Piscean, and twice we appeared wearing the same dress, hers the short version, mine the long; we laughed.

Henry Jaglom is nowhere. Tristine can't work without his response, so she is ready to quit and accept a teaching job. I sent him a beautiful Japanese diary. No answer. I put my trust in him. I will present his film *A Safe Place*, at Marin College in March. I believe in his talent.

Tristine identifies with my characters to the point of losing herself. She becomes each one as she writes. But she is apprehensive, suspicious. She *is* one of my characters. She has a lover who adores her, yet she is restless. She sees Dr. Stone, one of the best analysts, and she boasts of confusing him. Compared with Bogner they all seem inadequate. Tristine's alternatives are not fatal. If she teaches, she can still work at scripts. Her lover is willing to support her. "Your restlessness is merely anxiety, you are uncomfortable where you are and you think you will be comfortable elsewhere." A little house on the beach, a blue tent set up for her work, a horse.

She did ask once if the "phantom lover" could come true. The sensitive men are too soft. The phantom lover is sensitive but strong-willed, independent.

Strangely, as we playfully act mother and daughter, she told me she had been awakened sexually by D. H. Lawrence's *Lady Chatterley's Lover*—as I was, at the same age, on a train on my way to Switzerland.

I paid my tribute to Lawrence by defending him against the narrow-mindedness of the militant women.

Viveca Lindfors does an astounding job of impersonating various women—witty, vulgar, rebellious, obscene, comical, sad, bawdy—with an incredible range of voices and accents. A superb, rich, complex performance. She looks young, old, decrepit, radiant, inspired. It was very moving and disturbing too. One did not know who the writer was and did not care. It was a collage of women. She was so generous; after the play she made a reentry to read a section of my Diary and to make me stand up. I will never forget her passing along backstage as if behind a window, all in white, carrying a metal object which may have been an abstract lorgnette.

Her voice, her eyes, her frowns and her smooth brow, her young girl's voice and her comical French takeoff. She is earthy. Her legs are often spread apart in a masculine way. Her performance was truly complex and inexhaustible. How much more difficult it must be to live with so many selves!

New York:
John Ferrone cooked an exquisite dinner. He has the neat figure of

a young boy. The Italian bold features, full mouth. He invited Frances. That morning, Dr. Parks had advised me of a recurrence. I didn't mind the pain (which is great), I minded the effects of the radium implant. But our dinner was cheerful. Both Frances and I held a spirited conversation, a real spiritual tennis match. John gave me a Japanese diary for the hospital. He gives me wonderful books—Wasson's *Soma: Divine Mushroom of Immortality*, John Simon's book on Bergman, a book on the brain, Simenon's memoirs and Martha Graham's notebooks, the latter a precious document.

Today a mournful day, as I have to cancel my *Village Voice* television show, Johns Hopkins University, Kalamazoo University, dinner with the head of the Jungian Society, lunch with Hilda Lindley, lunch with Anna Balakian, evening with Nona Balakian, meeting a German interviewer, etc. John's calls were a relief. And I feel so much love around me, so many women loving me that I feel this will help me once more. In one day I received flowers from Sharon, from Barbette Blackington, from Beatrice, from Dolores, from an anonymous girl.

Tomorrow I can give my talk at the YMHA with Nancy Milford and a small group, because Dr. Parks could not get a hospital room. I'm in his office now.

Did I note the letter from the Institute of Arts and Letters? Second honor.

Friends wish to visit me in the hospital. I say: "No, I feel humiliated when I'm ill." I'd rather hide.

Women always refer to children and husbands as obstacles to creation.

I told about the many people I watch over although I still do my work. It is the equivalent of motherhood. I spoke of the need for continuity and for romantic intermittences.

Hospital:
I had planned all kinds of activities during the four days at the hospital: to read into the Sony cassette, to write in the Japanese diary John gave me, to read six books.

But the anaesthesia diffused and weakened me. For four days I was a more or less inanimate object.

Came home Monday.

The hateful, harsh winter outside.

The kindness of friends.

Flowers.

A doctor wrote me an anonymous letter of admiration.

I had to cancel lectures and an appearance at Town Hall.

On Friday I managed to pack, sent baggage by freight, arrived in Los Angeles, turned up my nose at a friend's wheelchair! He took over care of me, tender and attentive. This morning at 5:30 I awakened. I hate to awaken at night, in the silence and the dark, the suspended living. I feel the *passage of time*. It is only then I feel the course of time like some precipitation toward death.

I have been reading about the first farmers, emergence of man, Time-Life's only useful contribution that I know of, to the history of man.

Awakened earlier than usual. From the post office, brought a carton a yard long and a half-yard deep of correspondence.

In two days I answered all the important letters.

The house is healing, serene. Piccolino so gay. My student came and I could teach for two hours.

I make others write. By creating a climate of secrecy, my student writes a lot. She gained courage enough to read me her first impressions. Slowly we will transpose what she cannot tell in an acceptable form to herself. I'm interested in the effect of psychoanalytical treatment of writing. She can write, so what I had to cope with was the inhibiting factor, censor.

My student was afraid of my lucidity. I convinced her she had as much of that as I and that we were like two scientists working at the same problem: to free her writing. My insights had no other purpose.

Found that Isak Dinesen said exactly same thing about the power of the *tale* to deliver us from life.

Renate asks my secret.

I never accept being pinned down by a catastrophe. I think of the future. I *displace* myself. In the hospital I thought constantly of Bali, where I want to go this summer. My imagination takes me away from the eye of the cyclone.

People are amazed. I could talk at the Poetry Center the night before going to the hospital. But that is what saves me. I am not enslaved, possessed by what strikes me.

Half awake, I practice the meditation Dr. Harold Stone came to teach me yesterday. I met him in Berkeley years ago, for a few minutes, trusted him instantly. Sent him my troubled friends. Talked to his future therapists. Upbraided him for charging Tristine forty dollars for fifty minutes. But he excused it by saying he was putting all his money and energy in the Center for Healing Arts. When he heard I had a recurrence of cancer and the way I spoke of the burdens I was trapped in, he came immediately.

My method of fighting negative happenings is to shift my attention to the positive, displace my attention. He believes I must look at the cancer. I will transcribe what we talked about and subject of meditation.

First meditation:
Vision of dark spot—burned—dead.
Vision of white angel wings, or clouds.
Remembrance of wondering if illness was a punishment for being a pleasure-loving woman.
Vision of white spreading out over the black, gold light coming over whole scene, lightbox.
Impression that black spot is dead, cancer cells not active, killed by the radium.
White cells versus cancer cells a struggle between light and darkness.
Conscious:
1. Voice of responsibility; as a child of nine, wanted an orphan asylum.
2. I felt I have to give the gift of love, of life to everyone.
3. Anyone in trouble has a claim on me.
Voice of pleasure-loving Anaïs:

1. Love travel, tropics, real nature woman, want to do nothing.
2. Always overruled by sense of responsibility (giving family addresses when I travel).
3. Loved assignment to travel because it gave me permission to enjoy.

Second meditation:
The cancer is the crater I saw in Hawaii. I hated it. Black and smoky, smelling of sulfur. I wanted all the beautiful young women who love me, and all the young men who embraced me, to come. They filled the crater with water, and it was a beautiful crater lake and we all swam in it and the sulfur-smelling devil was drowned.

Third meditation:
Black is covered by snowstorm in a crystal ball I played with, enclosing a castle.
Spent a long time dressing for my Spanish dance, half rehearsing. Thought was that it was a *strong* dance. But at last minute, as I take first bold step, there is no music.
Awakened.

Fourth meditation:
All the white subjects in the world: snow, sugar, flour, cream, white lilies, clouds, white cells, white rice, white tapioca, white crystals, white smoke, white mint candy, white cotton—all beckoned by me. They light up the dark rotten spot in the peach. I take a knife and cut it out.

I am tired normally, not abnormally.
Dartmouth will give me a doctorate, June 9.
The same day, Scripps College invited me to speak at commencement.
Pleasure-loving Anaïs chose Dartmouth, and Scripps understood: "Of course you have to go and get your doctorate."
Dr. Stone admitted it would be a pity to cut off the correspondence completely.
What he taught me was that it was not enough to combat the destructive forces by moving *into* a positive area (in one hospital the

305

desire to see Yucatán sustained me; in another, the lost images of Bali). The *killer* in one's self must be met. You have to confront the evil. I have never done that. My magic was to *move*. He insists on changing the *way* of life which harms one.

Encounter with Larry [Durrell].
I had forgotten how he parries off with humor, how he talks to be amusing, not out of feeling. He has no sense of reality of others. He lives in his intellectual Buckminster Fuller domes.

Fifth meditation:
No more angel wings.
Tennis balls with knives attached attacking cancer, which looks like caviar eggs!

Sixth meditation:
A coal mine.
Long shaft for elevator.
Snow falls into the mine through the shaft.

Seventh meditation:
I am Joan of Arc in battle dress, on a horse, with a lance, attacking masses of locusts and bees. (Cancer?)

Yesterday. Talk with Dr. Stone. Duty-ridden Anaïs sits on one chair: I am rejoicing because the trip to Bali will be paid for, in exchange for an article, so I feel I am earning my way. I do not feel I am indulging myself. I'm concerned over others' need of money: a friend who asked for a loan; Bob Fitzgerald, who reminded me that in desperation to get *Anaïs Nin Observed* finally polished, he worked without pay.
I offered to pay him for final editing hours. He took me up on it because Bob Snyder is deep in debts and has not paid him. When Dr. Stone asked me to sit in a chair and be my father, I *did not let my father talk.* I merely repeated my mother's words. "He was a dandy. He always had to be dressed to the hilt. He was vain and utterly selfish."

In my mother's seat: "I am a very angry woman. People say I have a heart of gold but an uncontrollable temper. I like to fight."

Anaïs: "I abhor fighting. Even the idea of fighting the cancer borders on a revulsion against aggression."

In my meditation the crater I descend is tumultuous and about to erupt. I see no images but feel tumult, lava heaving, hot waves, fire. My anger at being used, at everyone bringing me only their distress, little joy. I can only be joyous and free in Mexico, or Tahiti, far-off places where the culture encourages joyousness. In Japan pleasure was in aesthetics, the cult of the bath, body ease, quiet, harmony.

I said: "Dr. Stone, I thought I had liquidated the parental influence."

Dr. Stone: "Your mother did a good job. As against the pursuit of pleasure and sensuality—the cult of work and duty. She reproached you for evading the duties of woman, avoiding having children and being domestic." (I refused to learn to sew or iron.)

In Europe domesticity was lightened by the inexpensive hiring of servants. In America I reduced it to a minimum, a bohemian rather than a formal life—no formal dinners, etc.

He caught me apologizing: "It was nature which decided I could not have children, not me."

Results: I let Mary Morris help me twice a week. She writes appropriate, tender notes in answer to touching letters. She returns manuscripts, books unread. I turn down lectures.

Visit to Durrells. Ghislaine is delightful. They were loaned a house on the beach. She is amusing and friendly and cooked a fine lunch. Larry was in a good mood. We all talked and laughed, told stories, compared memories, wondered why Henry defends and loves all the shabby characters who are not loyal to him: Hoki, Robitaille, others. After many years he became angry at the Japanese.

Larry and I had an amusing exchange, understandable only to writers. I was describing adventures in Cambodia to disprove his statement that films give us everything. At the end he said: "You wrote about it, I hope." We laughed at our unconcern for the cuts made in our articles for travel magazines. "I can always use them in a travel book," said Larry. "I can always use it in the Diary," I said. Nothing wasted. Like seamstresses saving bits of textiles.

His story of how he read my Diaries does not match my record. He says a chauffeur in a uniform came carrying two tall piles of Diaries. We never had a chauffeur, and I would not let anyone carry the Diaries just like that in his arm. And I wouldn't give my sacred Diaries to any chauffeur, least of all a bank one! The originals were in the bank vault, but I kept typed copies in a metal box at home which he described as my black children.

He clings to his tenacious fantasy about my wealth. My memory is that on Quai de Passy I opened the Morisco wedding chest and let him read the "black children." The Diary will settle the point for me, not for him. These affirmations were at the root of early quarrels; he told the same story when I visited him in the South of France.

But he loves Lou Andreas-Salomé and hates as violently as I do, Rudolph Binion, Frau Lou's prejudiced biographer. Wants to torpedo him. He can do that for the newsletter. Ghislaine caricatured Larry's science students at Cal Tech. We talked about the problem of protecting Henry from unscrupulous biographers who go around saying they are "authorized." Larry was mellow, tender and humorous.

He dismisses our fear that a madman like Nixon would push the annihilating button of the atom bomb when we push him to the wall by impeachment. He said: "Oh, I'm so bored, it would be a relief." How can Larry be bored? He has just finished a novel. He has been pampered and honored. He received an advance of $50,000. He has a delightful wife. He is admired and solidly established in literature.

He said he did not begin a diary at twenty-eight because I told him not to, that it was a trick, that I only believed my life real when I began to write about it. That was true at one time, but no longer. It is not when I write it that our lunch becomes real, but when it happens. When Ghislaine opened the first bottle of champagne in the sunlight and we looked out to sea, Larry said he had never had the sea *and* comfort.

Our evening with Henry was warm and lively. Henry has lost the sight of one eye during surgery. His legs are weak, so he uses a walking chair. He is in his blue pajamas and kimono. He tells the story of Caresse Crosby's house in the South, of Dali and his wife, of Caresse's alcoholic husband arriving in the middle of the night to throw everyone out. All our stories [of the same event] differ. *Rashomon*. Larry incites him.

When Larry uses the word "boredom," I'm startled. Is the veil of neurosis cutting off his enjoyments? I am never bored. I don't know the feeling. Everything interests me. And there is so much yet to see, love, experience. He has everything and it came to him ten years earlier than for me. Today, at seventy-one, I'm invited to the National Institute of Arts and Letters.

While Henry and Larry incensed each other, the women discovered me.

Larry talked about a discussion with Joaquin in the thirties on wanting to achieve polyphony. Joaquin said it could not be achieved in writing: "Don't try to be a Mozart." But Larry did try and describes it in an interview as "palimpsest." Is he aware that I have done it? He has gone into intellectual abstractions (*Tunc*). He is sterile. With time could I have reconnected him? His defenses, humor and impersonality are slippery.

Dr. Stone stirred up my angers. They awakened me at 5:30. He believed there must be a lot of hidden anger at the way people use me. Anger at demands: Read my poetry, read my novel, read my essay, give us a comment on this book. Thus while working on 1959 [in the Diary], I came upon such a masochistic episode I was shocked. I had a terrible cold. Tana [de Gamez] called up and said: "I must come over. I have just divorced my husband and I'm leaving for Portugal." I protested *feebly*. She came. She talked to me for two hours. I finally went to bed. I awakened at four with earthquaky chills and 104-degree fever. I could not get a doctor, only an answering service. Dr. Jacobson came at dawn and said I had pneumonia. When I got to the hospital I was told it was double pneumonia. The cold started with my giving a friend my heavy winter coat. Suicidal? She was a minor friend, a disturbed young woman who wanted to write, and we exchanged writing lessons for her typing the Diaries. Under the influence of LSD she wanted a trip to New York. Everyone was appalled at my sponsoring her. She lost her nerve and became a frightened child. Wearing my ruby-red fake fur coat seemed to give her strength. And she kept it.

I work on Volume Six from eight to ten. Mary Morris comes and we work at correspondence for three hours. Monday at ten my student comes. Other days Barbara Kraft studies writing with me.

Why did Varèse, who mocked psychology and all references to the unconscious, turn for his last work to *House of Incest*? Why did Larry at twenty-eight believe me when I advised him against writing a diary? He thought it was a profound remark. Life only became real when I wrote about it. Today that sounds like nonsense. The present is real. That is why I write less in the Diary. I talk to friends, I write letters, I confide to young women.

Henry Jaglom: "Why no one has been able to write a script is because they refused to see that it was all there, the work was all done, every word was perfect, every scene. They insisted on changing the book. Tristine did that too, changed dialogue, added scenes. It should be done like a collage: just cut up the book and select scenes. A link or two may be needed. The point is that all the women, different as they are, are ultimately *one*. Perhaps each one should be in a different city—London, Paris, New York—to show the universal woman. Nothing should be changed or added. It is nonsense to make it contemporary. It is timeless. At times the interior writing may be difficult to make cinematic, but that's my problem, not the writer's."

Anaïs: "Last night I felt almost like the sixteen-year-old girl who no longer wanted to commit suicide because she found someone who felt and saw as she did. It made me *very happy* the way you see the novels, your profoundly imaginative and daring poetic flights *around* them, and your absolute parallel vision of my intentions. I really felt strengthened. I want to do the collage you indicated. Your technical hints helped me to see how to extract from the books what could be visible." (Within the world of pure creation, last night was a *gold* night. We talked about our gold visions and sensations during LSD trip.)

The conflict over the correspondence was mainly due to the beauty of the letters and my desire to answer them. As I told Dr. Stone: "They are love letters. It hurts me not to answer them." Mary answers sensitively, tenderly. "I am a friend of Anaïs Nin, helping her because she has been ill and overworked. She read your beautiful letter and hopes to answer you later."

Tristine Rainer—slender and dark-eyed, hair fashionably over-curled. My young women friends are all incredibly beautiful and brilliant. Nancy Jo Hoy is small and delicate with big eyes and fragile features, dark hair. They are beset by difficulties. She became the wife of the dean, with a million duties and no status. She is writing on my work. Her master's thesis on Sartre is dazzling.

I can't do the meditation. I'm filled with Volume Six, what is missing, what to select. I don't like to describe Durrell's preface to *Children of the Albatross*. It was such a shock to me that he did not understand my work.

But I have now beside me hundreds of studies by women who do!

The psychologists are so right when they describe our reaction to pain or pleasure as creating tracks. The deep track made by pain renders one more attentive, more responsive to painful impressions. The same habit of joy will make one more susceptible to joy. In 1959, the pain of not being published should have been erased by two beautiful letters I received from Alyse Gregory and Elizabeth Moore.* So pain forms a rivulet of its own. Or what Bogner once described as "tuning in" on criticism and *not hearing* the praise or believing in the pleasure. But now I do. The beautiful, loving letters. The new brochure for Volume Five bears the most beautiful photograph of me dancing on the beach at Puerto Vallarta.

A strange case (so rare) of justice. Jim Herlihy sustained my writing by his articulate appreciation. Now I interested John Ferrone in his diary and it may be published. John agrees with my evaluation of it.

* See Volume Six, pp. 183, 185–186.

They met and liked each other. John said he was amazed at what Jim Herlihy so young and so long ago perceived in my work.

John was in my home for three days selecting photographs. He was from the first devoted and affectionate. Poor Hiram Haydn was patriarchal and made me very unhappy when he brought me my first beautiful review (Jean Garrigue on Volume One in the *New York Times Book Review*) and gave it to me, saying: "Why does no one write about me like that?" Sensitive to Hiram's sense of failure as a novelist, I persuaded William Claire to dedicate a number of *Voyages* to him as editor, as teacher, as publisher, and I stirred up the writers he had helped. Daniel Stern wrote an article, and so did others. But William Styron, who owed Hiram everything, did not. Hiram was immensely touched by the praise. I should be always grateful to him, for the very day the Diary was refused by another publisher, Hiram came and said simply: "I love it. I'll do it." But, like André Bay, he thought it would only appeal to my contemporaries as a piece of nostalgia. I never enjoyed our lunches. Though he was ten years younger, it was a father-and-daughter affair.

But with John, there was familiarity and ease and rapport.

At eight A.M. I am editing a description of Venice in 1959. At that time in my tiny Occidental Blvd. apartment I wanted to scream: "I am dying! My life is too narrow."

I find the same cry in one of Eve Miller's letters, which may be the key to her suicide. She wanted to live in Europe. Henry did not want to leave Big Sur. Later they separated. She married a neighbor, a sculptor. She never escaped Big Sur. "I can't breathe here," she wrote to me.

The Diary has one blessed function. When a friendship breaks, the good is erased. Only the disappointment is engraved in the memory. In the Diary, I found the friendship with Jean Fanchette intact, in its period of honeymoon.

Visited George and Ruth Barati. George is a Hungarian composer and orchestra conductor. Ruth is American. They are charming, sincere, warm. They came to my lecture at Santa Cruz and decided to use some of my text for a cantata for the Centennial. They asked me to come and listen to what George had done to date. The singer was an Italian woman, with the full-blown voice of old-fashioned opera singers (more power than subtlety), unsuited for my text. The kind I cannot bear. It was so difficult. The music was played on the piano, so I could only imagine what it would be when orchestrated. I tried to *hear* his other compositions. He is classical, not modern. I, who worship Satie!

We looked out of the windows of the Music Institute at the acacia in full bloom. Donna, the Baratis' daughter, had written a beautiful poem. Music, a delicious lunch and I unable to say: "Silence that voice which mouths words one can't understand."

I did not mind the full-throated voice of Italian men singing at the prow of the tourist gondolas in Venice. They brought tears to my eyes. In women I can only love black voices or clear voices like Dory Previn's which make every word understandable.

I could only offer encouragement. All I asked for was a more muted voice. (When the singer later sang a Ravel song, she *had* to be muted.) The struggles of musicians touch me particularly.

Meanwhile I meet a lively charming Frenchwoman, through Hilda Lindley. She is a travel consultant. In exchange for an article I can have a free trip, both my friend, who is a photographer, and I, to Bali and Nouméa. We had heard about the world-famous aquarium and the undersea life. I could hardly believe it!

I had dreamed about Bali for years. To think about Bali was my way of healing myself, but Dr. Stone insists I apply my energy *directly* against the cancer and unburden myself. Stress causes depletion. Cancer is a virus. He does not eliminate my way of healing myself but insists I have to face the *killer* in myself. Some of the killers are the loving, innocent people who want my presence, my answers to their letters. Such irony!

Norman Brown's prediction, in *Life Against Death*, applies more to men than to women: "Freud's intuition that civilization moves towards the primacy of the intellect and the atrophy of sensuality may be correct."

[Spring, 1974]

I say good-bye to Larry and Ghislaine by telephone because Ghislaine had the flu when we were to have dinner together.

A gray morning. Preparation for tomorrow's trip [to Fresno State University]. Tinting hair, nails; notes, packing, telephones.

At ten A.M. my student will come, neurotic but intelligent and responsive. She had to spend much energy and an hour of tape-recorded preaching against [the film] *The Exorcist*. More important to moralize and fight corruption than to create. I try gently to guide her into affirmation and storytelling. She is at the moment more of a Catholic militant than an artist. It is true that whatever we fight in America is gigantic, David and Goliath, but the men of sixty fired by the oil companies just before retirement believe in David's success. I admire them. Coming out and telling their story on television, getting a lawyer against Goliath.

We are now slaves of big companies, all of us. The Hitlers are replaced by men of power and wealth. I begin to see the need of socialism and listen to Herbert Marcuse. Before, I saw the tyranny of communism equal to the tyranny of money.

I flew to Fresno with a sense of obligation because last year I canceled from the airport; I was ill. I have begun to hate the strain of the lectures. But I was able to talk, and the love, the tears, the fervor of the women and some men, touch me. The man who was so eloquently admiring stressed the fact that I transcended feminism and did not allow the questions to become the usual accusations. I challenge women's courage.

Before leaving for Fresno I was angry, at my ambivalence, the desire to respond to the love I receive and the need to reduce my activities. I fell into the deepest depression.

I passed by Henry Miller's to please Jill Krementz. She wanted photographs. Henry delights at being interviewed and photographed, and I am withdrawing from it because it is uncreative. Jill took photographs of Henry, myself, then Durrell, who happened to drop by. I was in no mood for publicity frolics, but Jill has been sweet to me.

I ask Judy Chicago if she can ask Doubleday to pay me for my preface to her book. She reacts badly. "Why didn't you tell me before?" Before, there was only a question of the book's being done by a small press. All her warmth is gone because I state a rightful demand.

I have a nightmare: Two dogs steal my money. A man decides to use the choke chain on them to force them to return the money.

It is difficult for me to ask to be paid for my work. It endangers the love.

We cleared it up. Judy reacted brusquely because she felt bad, and she did not know anything about publishing. "You know how much I love you, and I was upset." And I had mentioned it too late. "You know I'll do the preface anyway. I was only trying to learn to ask for what is due me." But it may be also because it is Doubleday, and they have been consistently nasty to me. I was introduced there in the forties by Wilson, and in the last episode they refused to pay for my preface to Anna Kavan's *Ice,* a preface which was used in England. "Let's forget about it!"

My dreams are heavy. There is a heaviness *au fond.* I can't analyze it. Is it because I have to give up the lectures, because of my physical state, which is marked periodically by digestive troubles? Is it that I feel the lessening of energy? Last year when I was asked by a teacher how I dealt with my diminishing strength, I answered flippantly, "Better ask Picasso," and named my activities. But now I am defeated. The talks I give come out of spiritual energy, not my body. I went to Fresno on a two-day diet of tea and toast.

Yet I want to dwell on so many happenings. A sensitive Frenchman who lives in Louveciennes sends me photographs of 2 bis rue Monbuisson under the snow, because he said this way the deterioration would not show, the rust, the facing. It would recover its magic beauty. On the back of each photograph he copies the passage in the Diary which corresponds to the image. He writes of the Diaries being an initiation to a new form of life. He was a classicist, had never read any of the people I mentioned. He also sends me a guide to Louveciennes, in which "2 bis" is listed as a place to visit, once my home!

Friends await me in France, new friendships born of correspondence: Marcel Moreau, and Claude Louis-Combet and Cortázar. And every day a love letter. And I can still feel the tender kisses of the students in Fresno. They either kiss me or they cry.

So much to live for—the shining love of friends, Piccolino's clowning, the life-giving pool, the birds. Nan coming in her truck to take me to the post office. Always fascinating letters. Valerie Wade brings me beautiful photographs. John is working on the book of photographs.*

If the *weight* on me is physical, I must try to relieve it. If it is psychological, I must examine it. Dr. Stone, after coming spontaneously as a friend one Sunday to teach me meditations, has made me come to his office for talks. I felt they might help me to accept these new restrictions to my expansive nature, these controls over the exchanges with the world. I have to distinguish between those who love me and those who use me. I am trying to do that. But I can't control the blowup which is part of fame. I accepted an invitation to talk with Progoff at the New School because he teaches the Intensive Journal, and it was to be a small group, but now the group has increased by four times and there will be videotaping. I accepted an invitation to talk to Larry's fifteen students [at Cal Tech], and the place was filled with photographers, reporters with tape recorders, video lights, etc. The reception at Fresno was a crush, with only five minutes to give to each student.

Jim Herlihy is moving into a new home across the lake from me with a gentle, sweet, radiant hippie called Rainbow. Tomorrow I fly to Marin [College] to show *A Safe Place*.

I am helping women to live, to have courage, to feel, to believe in themselves. Evelyn Hinz is collecting the talks. I put down all the facts which give me pleasure.

Volume Five is out—golden, luminous cover.

Liz and John Pearson came yesterday. They are both so lighthearted, even though John has been fired by Berkeley after directing the most successful and imaginative programs, which made money for the university and brought distinguished people. Even though his publisher

* *A Photographic Supplement to the Diary of Anaïs Nin* (New York: Harcourt Brace Jovanovich, 1974).

will let *Kiss the Joy*, which has sold well, go out of print, because nothing satisfies their greed but best-sellers. The same with *Miss MacIntosh, My Darling*. But Liz has a job teaching music. And John's life as a photographer is assured. Liz has a body like the Venus de Milo and when she is swimming nude she looks like a smooth, firm statue. Her eyes are of a blue which often looks violet. Her cheeks are pink. The Pearsons come in their VW van, eat and sleep in it—anywhere, in parks, on the beach, or in friends' gardens.

The difficulty with me is that everyone wants to do things in groups. None of the couples I know want to be by themselves. Why?

So much to do! That always pulls me out of whatever abyss I fall into. Larry's skepticism (boredom as he calls it) shows, but mine doesn't and my students almost leap out of their chairs with excitement at what we discover together (removing the obstacles to writing).

Simone de Beauvoir and I dislike each other equally, except that her comments on the Diary were petty and personal, whereas mine on her work were about the dreariness of her writing, her antipoetic, anti-transcendent flatness.

Weekend. Wrote twenty-four letters.

What saddens me is that I have never recovered the same energy I had before January's recurrence and hospitalization. I can swim only six laps instead of ten. I have to help myself out of the bath by holding the handle. I have to make an effort to straighten up after crouching over my files. The martini I love, which breaks the tension between day and evening, gives me pain. I dread crowds, standing up for hours, talking to admirers.

Bob Snyder still has only *one* print of the film to show around.

I think of the friendships I did not make, and regret. One is Colin McFee. I met him through Peggy Glanville-Hicks. I had the impression of a pale, self-effacing man who was bitter, who had failed, who lived poor in Harlem but who, as Peggy said, sought isolation. He spent six years in Bali. His book, *A House in Bali*, is responsible for my wanting to go there. I saw the footage of his film and tapes gathering dust in a museum. He had filmed without knowledge of the right speed for sound and it was too costly for him to have a laboratory do the revision. I should have been more interested in him. He had tried to preserve Balinese music. He cooked marvelous Balinese meals. I do not know what he achieved or why he died alone and poor. I don't know how to find out. He planted a seed in me. The friends we missed. Why? Inattention? At that time I needed others to move toward me because I was not sure of myself. He perhaps expected the same thing. Checkmate. No attraction, lack of vibration. I ponder the mystery of friendships which did not happen.

A difficult evening at Marin College showing *A Safe Place*, fighting for poetic concepts against the literariness of the political interpretation (I'm sick of women being portrayed as childlike, etc.). A part of the audience responded, a part clung to moralistic and dictatorial feminism, the wrong kind. But there was only one direct attack. Two critics from the Bay Area who had panned the film came to hear what I had to say in its favor. Geri Olson was there, and she understood and loved it. It will be shown in Sonoma.

From my talk about *A Safe Place*:

In most movies, what takes place in our feelings, the imagery of our dreams around events, is rarely filmed. We know it is an external image, we know the dimensions are missing, that it is hard as a wall. We are not stirred deeply. The depths have been left untouched. Here, it is this depth which is touched, it affects one almost subconsciously; it is the dream which is captured. Those who fail to understand this film will drive themselves and others to the safe place of nonexistence.

Came home that same night at 1:30. Self-criticism is still so strong. I thought I had done badly because I allowed myself to get defensive. But when I listened to the tape, I found I did stress the real meaning of the film.

In Harold Stone's office.
The meditation against cancer stopped about two weeks ago. I rebelled against it, blocked it. It was invading my life. I didn't want to focus on it. I wanted to think about Volume Six, the portrait of

Marguerite, etc. I turned to my way of healing myself, to other places, other thoughts. When he asked me to close my eyes, most of the images (the strain which frightened me day before yesterday) became an azalea; I saw a snowstorm. He said I was turning salt into sugar. It was only when he asked me to think about a cave, to enter it, that I finally reached Paracelsus' cave in Switzerland, where he cured his patients by lowering them in a net down through a crevice into warm mineral water. It made a lasting impression on me. This, Dr. Stone accepted. The healing waters. Asked me to think of this, to meditate on it. He felt I needed help, that I was actively unburdening myself, saying no to universities, no to tiring social events, tearing up silly letters, etc. Yes. But it was all in the head. The other I would not think about. Now I am leaving, and I will see Bogner and see how she deals with the feelings I have.

Preface for a book of Margo Moore's photographs:

We corrupted a beautiful word, "image."
The primitive, the beautiful and pure definition of image was a concept of the spirit made flesh. We made images of gods and goddesses, images of beauty, images of what we wanted to be, of what we wanted to endure.
Then in our time the image was misused. We spoke of it as an artificial concoction by the media. The students at Green Bay, Wisconsin, begged me not to let the media corrupt me, make a false image of me. But this can only happen to those who do not know who they are. The true struggle is to achieve an image which conforms to the spirit of a person so he can become visible to the world. We must restore to the image the integrity and purity it has lost. That is very difficult because in every individual lies a different vision of the same object: the biographer, the autobiographer, the photographer, the filmmaker . . .

I had received several books by Ira Progoff and a warm letter from his assistant, June Gordon. I had been hearing about him from Valerie [Harms], Adele [Aldrich], Frances Steloff. He gave seminars on journal writing, taught journal writing as therapy. His books interested me. He was continuing the work of Otto Rank. He wanted to go beyond psychology. Even though his system for journal writing was the opposite of my spontaneous work, I found him stimulating.

It was fascinating to see the contrast. He had prepared a workbook for his students, separated into "dreams," "memories," "dialogue with lost friends or with anyone who had an influence over your life," "the steps not taken," "imagining the future."

He and June came to see me. June was handsome and charming and more than an assistant, a real muse, his double.

We planned a dialogue at the New School [for Social Research in New York]. The auditorium was overcrowded. I expected Ira to present an interplay of two different attitudes toward diary writing. I even asked him: "Ira, tell me what I did not do in the Diary." But he could not step out of his system. He could only try to make me fit into it. It could have been an interesting dialogue. He wanted me to give a demonstration of his method. Objectively it was a startling contrast between feminine and masculine thinking, one superorganized, the other intuitive. The audience was mostly women, and they had many questions to ask me. It ended with a dialogue between the women in the audience and me.

My appreciation of Progoff did not falter. I felt that he was doing a great deal for diary writing, making it possible for all kinds of persons. I added his experience to mine. He insisted on eliminating judgment, on avoiding literary aims. He treated the journal not as an art but as therapy.

My [International Community College] student was a mature writer who was the purest example of inhibition in life affecting inhibition in writing. She was steeped in conventional ideas. She had studied writing at UCLA, had all the degrees you can get from college, but found herself unable to write. I looked at her material. Her professor's totally negative comments would have paralyzed me. No wonder she could not write. He was constantly condemning the personal: "too personal," "too emotional," "lack of objectivity," "reorganize sequences." Her writing was good, intelligent and articulate.

We started to work. We talked for many hours; she taped everything. We talked peripherally about writers and writing. We discussed writers who had written out of a persona, who did not reveal themselves, like Hemingway, whose unconscious life was far more interesting than his artificial heroes. I also had her read Violette Leduc, Genêt, Colette and others to counterbalance her conventional writers.

She talked to her tape recorder and would bring me her thoughts to listen to and comment on. I encouraged her to be personal, to believe in her opinions, to allow herself freedom and spontaneity. Her writing improved, became natural and flexible. She was concerned with the rules of her religion.

Mainly I focused on her expressing her feelings on every subject. She wrote down her dreams. Every time she read the Diary, she would respond with her own emotional expressions. She would read a passage from my Diary on the death of my mother, and this inspired her to write on the death of her mother. I had to struggle against religious taboos, against Puritanism, against conventions. The challenge was powerful because she represented every kind of religious dogmatism, Puritanism. I hoped to teach her not to judge her writing and herself so severely.

The more we talked, the more books she read, the more we studied the Diaries, the more freedom she gained in her writing. Finally she came one day with a confession of love for a woman which had been very difficult for her to make. This woman was very ill and my student was suffering at the idea of losing her. From then on she allowed her emotions expression. Her writing became more human, warmer and more natural. We seemed to have reached a trust, a relaxation, which affected the quality of her writing. I was so happy that the search for sincerity in the writing led to sincerity in her life.

And then, dramatically, she fell and broke her leg and we were not able to meet. I received a letter in which she confessed that this liberation of her true feelings and her life came too soon. Her therapist did not agree with my method of releasing the unconscious so that the writing would flow and described our work as "unstructured." The therapist disagreed with the mixture of psychology and the teaching of writing.

My student admitted that our talks had opened a Pandora's box which she was not yet ready to explore. She asked that we put a lid back on all the ideas that had begun to flow spontaneously. As we could not meet, I felt it was best to encourage her to put her faith in the therapist, which she needed more than writing achievement. When she had first come to me, the flow of her writing was completely arrested and she was hidden in conventionalities. My way of teaching writing was so connected with psychology that she felt a conflict between my method and her therapist's. I know that deep writing can only come from in-depth exploration of the unconscious. But this was no time for daring experiments. The writing could wait.

I did not change my opinion that she was highly intelligent and courageous, but I felt that the therapist's lack of understanding of my way of teaching writing made it too difficult for her. Remembering how conventional she was, bringing me a moralist sermon more often than a story, I was amazed at the progress she had made in eight months. Two hours a week! The therapist may be right, we may have traveled too fast. I will wait and see.

[Summer, 1974]

I am sure it was Barry Jones who instigated the idea of a doctorate. He spent all his time at Dartmouth making my work known to the students.

It was a beautiful, soft summer day. The day before, we had a big dinner in a lovely restaurant by the river. I was happy to see Justice William O. Douglas again. He was about to receive a doctorate too. So was Agnes de Mille and the oldest of the jazz players, whose name I do not remember.* The dinner was gay. Afterward some of us stayed in the reception room to talk.

I found flowers in my room, a history of Dartmouth. It was the first college to invite me to lecture [in the 1940s], because of Professor Herbert West, who was a fan of Miller's and mine. The college had printed my lecture in a handsome pamphlet.

I always wake early. I went down to the cafeteria and there was Justice Douglas, alone. He invited me to join him. He told me about his efforts to save the beautiful land from the developers. The only decision he regretted was to place Japanese-Americans in concentration camps during the war. The Pentagon had given the court misleading information.

We went to dress. Then we marched slowly across the lawn and sat on an outdoor stage. The students had been allowed to dress as they wished, so it was a most colorful procession. The president read the praise he had written himself.

Then Barry and his friend drove to a sculptor's studio, a most interesting place, a ghost village, where large barracks once served to house the workmen who had mined the place and ruined the land. Now it was a series of rust-red mounds. Nothing would grow again. But a big rough-hewn barrack served well as a studio. We had lunch together, admired the agriculture and undertook the three-hour drive to the airport. Barry was returning to Oxford.

---

* Eubie Blake.—Ed.

Many years ago I read Colin McFee's *A House in Bali*. As a musician and composer, he concentrated on the music of Bali, and his descriptions were so poetic and beautiful that I could almost hear the music as I read the book. At that time I made a wish to visit Bali, a wish that was not to be consummated for twenty-seven years.

In Los Angeles I was introduced to two charming Frenchwomen. Charlotte Hyde, who knows my work, is in charge of developing tourism in Tahiti, New Caledonia and the New Hebrides. Christiane Emonin represents UTA, the French airline that flies to these islands. They offered to pay my expenses to Nouméa and Port Vila if I would write articles about them. I did not know anything about these two places near Australia, on the other side of the world, and had to read up on them. In doing so, I became very interested in Oceanic art. I loved the idea of the trip. In the course of our conversations Charlotte asked me if there was a special place I wanted to visit. I said immediately, Bali. Bali does not need publicity, but because UTA flies through Indonesia on its way back to Paris, we reached a generous compromise. UTA would pay my expenses to Bali in return for my articles on New Caledonia and the New Hebrides.

From Diary notes on Bali:

As I descended from the small plane, the first impression was a soft, caressing climate, the smell of sandalwood and the overwhelming beauty of the Balinese. With their long, glossy black hair, honey-colored skin, sinuous walk, soft contours with no bones showing, their small but perfect proportions, it was difficult not to believe that they had been selected as prize beauties for the pleasure of tourists. This beauty, a soft blend of Polynesian and Oriental, is at first unbelievable and you feel it must be an exception. But later you find it is common to almost everyone. Even the old women walked so voluptuously that men followed them. The Balinese wear sarongs, tied with colorful sashes, in vivid designs of flowers, foliage, landscapes. The women's sarongs touch the ground, the men's end at the knees.

Taxis waiting at the airport. Mine took me (contrary to my instructions) to the ugliest of all hotels, a Hilton-style concrete box. The only high-rise on the island, it was a terrible eyesore. I discovered later that after its completion, the offended Balinese made a law that no building can be higher than the palm trees. I refused to get out of my taxi and told the driver to take me to the Balinese hotel Charlotte had recommended. He said, "It is full." I said, "Take me there anyway." The gods were with me; the two charming Balinese girls at the open, garden-patio-style desk said, "We have a back room for you tonight, and tomorrow we will give you a bungalow facing the sea."

The Hotel Tandjung Sari was built on the beach at Sanur, designed by a Eurasian artist (Balinese-European) who wanted to be faithful to the Balinese atmosphere. The separate bungalows were built in native style and set in opulent gardens. The gravel paths leading to them were lighted by bamboo lanterns and along them were discreetly placed small stone temples with the traditional pagoda shape and black thatched roof. Statues of gods and goddesses appeared in niches. The room, with its split bamboo walls, mats, rafts, poles tied together with bark fiber, gave off vibrations which I can only describe as similar to those one feels in a forest, as if natural materials never lost their power to conduct life. It had a quality of refuge which so few hotel rooms have. The light was soft. The walls were covered with tapestries in beautiful, soft colors; one was like an Oriental screen, a design of everything happening at the same time—temples, marches, fighting, celebrations. When I looked for the telephone, the Balinese servant, in his red sarong and red shirt, pointed to the gong outside the heavy, antique door. I was to strike this gong for service.

The dining room was an open pavilion just off the beach. A patio led to the bar, which faced the sea; it was constructed of rough-hewn stones with numerous niches for statues of important deities. I walked to the beach and was immediately surrounded by children selling beautiful postcards. Their postcards were all identical but I could not bring myself to show favoritism, so I ended up with a collection of duplicates.

Walking to dinner, I was steeped in the smell of sandalwood and spices, magnolias and frangipani, from which they make their tiaras. I remembered Bali was once called one of the spice islands, famous for nutmeg, cloves, cinnamon, pepper; and today Balinese food is strongly flavored with a variety of crushed pungent spices, aromatic roots, leaves, onions, garlic, fermented fish paste, lemon juice, grated coconut and burning red peppers.

The candlelit dinner was served with exquisite gentleness and delicacy by barefoot women in long orange Balinese pleated skirts and blouses. They reminded me of the bas-reliefs in Cambodia. Soft-voiced, soft-footed, they handled dishes and glasses as if barely touching them, soundlessly, with the same agility these hands would later show in the dances. Musicians and dancers in Bali are ordinary people during the day—fishermen, road workers, craftsmen, field workers, servant girls or young girls from the villages. The soft night was enhanced by the softness of the music. A bamboo xylophone, called a *ting kling*, played with muffled mallets, was heard all through dinner—soft, liquid sounds like wind chimes heard from a great distance. The repetitive rhythm leads to contemplation.

The next morning I was introduced to my Balinese guide, Subudi. He had a beautiful smile, very soft, dark eyes, dark skin, curly black hair. He wore a red jacket and an orange sarong. The little red cap on his head was shaped like a paper boat. He had been to college and his English was not bad. He was very sincere and very quiet. He did not deliver all his knowledge at once, continuously and tiresomely. He never interrupted my reveries. But when I asked a question, he would answer fully. He knew his history, his religion, the habits of his people. The Balinese have a cult of moderation. One should not live either too high, on mountaintops and volcanoes, where the gods live, or too low, at the bottom of the sea, where there are black serpents. Both extremes are evil. They admire softness, quietness, rhythm. This has an extraordinary effect on one; even a breakfast could be served without breaking a reverie. And of course, the state of reverie in Bali is almost continuously fed by the beauty. You really cannot think of anything else while you absorb this extraordinary beauty.

The hotel had constructed in its gardens a charming small bamboo theater for the local dance troupes. The sides were open to the gardens and the sea so the villagers could come and watch. There was a dance that night, and immediately I was plunged into one of the most magical spectacles in the world. The air is filled with iridescent music. With serene, gentle gestures the men (young boys for the "flower petal music") strike the keys of the *"g'nder"* with little hammers and mallets; those beside the great gongs hold much bigger, thickly padded knobs. Colin McFee had described its elusive beauty:

Over a slow and chantlike bass that hummed with a serious penetration the melody moved in the middle register, fluid, free, appearing and vanishing in the incessant shimmering arabesque that ran high in the trebel as though beaten out of a thousand little anvils. Gongs of different sizes punctuated this stream of sound, divided and subdivided into sections and inner sections, giving it meter and meaning. Through all this came the rapid and ever changing beat of the drums, throbbing softly, or suddenly ringing out with sharp accents. They beat in perpetual cross-rhythm, negating the regular flow of the music, disturbing the balance, adding a tension and excitement which came to rest only with the cadence that marked the end of a section of the music.

He describes the music, but the effect is harder to describe. I can only compare it to the best and most subtle jazz, the period before rock and roll, with one distinction, however—there is no sadness in it as there is in jazz. The music is made of the same elements the Balinese favor in other arts: warm, sumptuous colors, mirrors, gold, heartbeat, blood pulsations, freedom. Music is for pleasure. It pleases both gods and men. It creates an atmosphere of languor, excitement and sensuous mysticism. The tones of the gamelan ring with a radiance, a translucence which even McFee found impossible to describe except in terms of a shower of gold, a rain of silver.

The music prepares you for the dancers, whose gestures are as far from our daily gestures as possible; rarefied, transposed. They are sumptuously dressed in tight obilike sashes which contain their body like a vase. They wear batiks from Java, gold hair ornaments, tiaras of silky white frangipani flowers, mirrors and gold leaf. Scarves, sashes, corselets of gold cloth, all shimmer as they move. When they begin their great coils of movements they seem like extensions of the music. Their hands and fingers move like dragonflies, hummingbirds, like sea anemones, like fluttering leaves. They become thistledown, lightning, India rubber or steel.

Everything from their flowery crowns to their vibrating feet is of unearthly precision, perfection. The line of their movements blossoms into a thousand intricacies of neck, eyes, hip, knee, toes, so that a single dancer seems to carry within her small body a whole orchestra of movement. The men on the stage depict the fierce, fiery, angry, warlike heroes of the past. They satirize their own arrogant stance. They increase their height by standing on their toes and swinging swords and long white scarves.

The themes are stories from Indian mythology or *A Thousand and One Nights*. The same themes recur, and some dancers wear masks. The entire village comes to watch, children of all ages, mesmerized by color and sound.

The next morning Subudi took me to my first temple. There are 10,000 temples in Bali, not counting the private ones in the gardens. The temple is the heart of the village. All celebrations take place there; the costumes, instruments and masks for the dances are sheltered there.

The people of Bali were kept in isolation for centuries, thanks to treacherous reefs and currents surrounding the island. They had time to create a high form of life in which religion, art and nature harmonized, in which self and society were one.

The sense of aesthetic beauty is present as soon as one leaves the city and drives into the villages. There are no ugly houses. Rich or poor, they are designed in the same way, a stone wall covered with ivy, lianas, bougainvillaea or moss. There is always a small bridge of either stone or bamboo to cross the stream in which they bathe themselves and the beautiful, sleek cattle. What a wonderful sight to watch a very small boy washing a huge bull, usually so fierce but now completely compliant and obedient. The gate may be elaborately carved sandstone, divided to symbolize Yin and Yang, with a center of red bricks. The house is a compound of separate buildings, one for cooking, one for sleeping, one for crafts or other labors. The poorer houses are made of bamboo, the richer ones of stone; but always with a background of luxuriant vegetation so that I saw people and houses buried deep in flowers, vines, bushes against a background of trees or mountains. Decorations were in red. Sometimes over the wall you could see the tip of a little family temple. Almost every house had its small temple of such grace and beauty, always elevating the thought toward the sky and open space.

The streets are full of children. Subudi tells me they have their tasks which they take very seriously but they have their playtimes also. And their playtime is shared with the other children of the village in such a way that the parents don't feel they have to watch them. The families take care of each other's children; it is a communal effort. The children can always go into any house and ask for food or whatever they need. They are exceptionally good and are never beaten. The parents do not let them crawl on the floor like animals because they say that's a humiliating position. They rarely stumble and seem to learn to walk in the most beautiful way. Every gesture they make is graceful. The belief is that harmony and balance of body create inner balance of the spirit, and evil spirits will never enter a balanced body.

They begin to work early, the boys as apprentices to wood sculptors, stone carvers, jewelers; helping the puppeteer, bathing the buffaloes, working hard in the rice paddies. The girls begin to carry water jugs on their heads, slowly increasing the weight. Later, as women, they will carry in baskets the rocks which the men use to mend the roads. This gives them a very strong yet graceful neck. All this is done with the natural gravity due communal responsibilities, but also with joy and pride.

The first temple we visited was dramatically built on top of a huge rock, offshore, surrounded by wild waves. It looked like a ship. They had set up a rope between the rock and the beach so that those who braved the high tide with their offerings would not be carried away by waves.

The women arrive carrying offerings on their heads. These are works of art. On a flat basket they build a pyramid of fruit, flowers, cutouts of birds, coconuts, bananas, oranges, decorations of palm leaves cut into lacy patterns, ribbons, necklaces of sea shells. Each offering is an original creation. Like figures on Greek vases, they place the offering on their head, hold it in balance with their arms curved and carry it with a languid, precise walk, never stumbling although the roads are rough.

I asked how poor families could afford such luxurious offerings. Subudi explained that the offering is brought to the temple on a special occasion and placed before the statues of the gods. The women then sit in the yoga position and meditate while the children play together. After a long prayer, they take the offerings home again and eat the fruit and rice and cakes. The gods have fed symbolically and are satisfied. Such a practical religion.

I spent the day visiting temples and attending ceremonies. You stop at every place marked by a gay, fluttering pennant; it is made of one tall, slender palm branch painted in various bright colors, which floats like a feather and bends gracefully in the breeze. Umbrellas of bright red with gold fringe, or bright blue with silver fringe, tassels and tiny mirrors, call attention to a temple ritual, a craftsman's shop or a dance.

The Balinese never fail to dress for an occasion. And their sense of color is ecstasy to a painter. The women's blouses and sarongs run the entire palette—burnt orange, parrot green, emerald, orange, lime; for the men, sepia, chocolate, coffee, shocking pink. There is always a sense of harmony of colors. They are never careless, unkempt, faded, ugly, neglected. Their sarongs are always freshly washed, beautifully tied around the waist. The blouse is made of lace or silk. Care is taken to dress according to age; older women wear more sepia and brown, younger more flamboyant sarongs with huge jungle flowers and monkeys, and a sense of gaiety. During the American occupation they began to wear towels rolled around their heads to support the baskets, which often carried very heavy objects. If the towel had a pretty color they would wear it around the waist like an obi.

When there were no festivals or special occasions, I was able to see how beautiful the temples were. Some were built of wood, others of rock, but always graceful. The entrances never led directly into the temple. There was always a wall that forced you into a labyrinth which eventually opened into the temple. This was to confuse the ghosts. The roof of one temple was ornamented with sculptured iron rods resembling the three-pronged scepter of Neptune. These were intended to catch ghosts and to divert lightning.

One temple was really a huge bat cave facing the sea. It was not a spectacle that I particularly liked. The fruit-eating bats clung in such quantities to the roof of the cave that at first one only saw a mass of fluttering black wings. But they are sacred and here are protected from native hunters who consider them a choice food. Women bring offerings just the same and then sit quietly, legs crossed, a little removed from the bats. The children have learned also to be quiet during this meditation period.

To visit another temple, I was required to wear a sarong, the scarf worn around the waist, and a little cap on my head. This temple had a large sign saying that women were not allowed during their menstrual period. This taboo applied to most temples.

Subudi took me to a temple where craftsmen were repairing damage from a storm. I was able to see the wooden framework which was the beginning of the pagoda shape. I could watch them cutting the wood, shaping the rocks and carving religious figures on the stone walls.

I visited the oldest temple in Bali. It was in a village on the far side of the island. They had enclosed the entire village with a wall and had isolated themselves for centuries. Only recently did they allow visitors.

There was one broad street lined on each side with palm-leaf houses, very neat and trim. An open pavilion served as a conference room for the elders who ruled the village. Subudi told me all Balinese villages are run communally, with everyone sharing both labor and profits. I was amazed to find there are no jails in Bali. The offender is simply asked to leave his village forever. The elders considered it sufficient punishment to be exiled from family and friends and the communal protection.

At the end of the street was a very old man sitting in the shade of a huge tree. Subudi showed me he was engraving, in Sanskrit, stories from Balinese myths on thin pieces of bamboo stem. He made very fine lines with a stylus given him by his grandfather and then rubbed black into the lines with a special ink. There were very subtle illustrations accompanying the beautiful calligraphy. The bamboo pieces were then cut about the size of a fan, tied together like Venetian blinds and closed with a ribbon. These delicate works of art sold for one dollar. This was the profession adopted by all the old men of this village when they were no longer any use in the rice fields.

They are very quiet. No one in the village talked or smiled. The feeling was one of serenity and harmony.

In this oldest village of Bali, Subudi showed me some of the first musical instruments ever used. Some of them had only one string, and there were various kinds of primitive drums.

And ancient masks. The masks were extremely important. They were used at festivals, at dances and for the symbolic enacting of mythological stories. Here they were made with great care. They used only natural paints extracted from flowers, stones, bark, shells. They use little sea shells to contain the various colors.

Everything practical, useful, necessary to daily life was given a beautiful shape or texture—baskets, pottery, rugs, mats. Even raincoats were made of palm leaves. A great deal of care was given to each object used in the household, even though they used very few.

The rice paddies are architectural feats. The terraces are designed with such precision that they come down from the mountains like the rounded stairways of giant gods, the benefic water seeping gently down from one terrace to another, creating reflective surfaces in which the clouds are mirrored. On flat lands the fields are geometric. When the tender green shoots of rice first show, they are as delicate as Japanese prints. It is easy to feel empathy with the Balinese rituals of celebration for each stage of the rice's growth.

Daytime is all work, and the work is done communally. Work on the roads. Work in the rice fields. Men care for the irrigation system, till the muddy fields and finally cut the rice and bind it into sheaves. These are hung on the ends of flexible poles carried across their shoulders. They walk in formation and in rhythm, and when the sun reflects from the red-gold rice branches, they look very much like the figures in old Japanese and Chinese prints. The women take the rice and grind it with a stone into a fine powder which they use for cooking. They make rice pancakes and wrap them around a bit of chicken or fish.

For festivals the men do the cooking. Chickens and pigs are killed. The women work on the ornamental offerings for the temple. They don their most beautiful sarongs, and while the men uncover the gamelan instruments, they unpack the dancers' costumes and the masks kept in the temples. They tress white, velvety frangipani flowers into tiaras, shells into necklaces; their favored ornaments are gold and mirrors.

Life, religion and art all converge in Bali. They have no word in their language for "artist" or "art." Everyone is an artist. Creativity is natural and widespread. It is a means of honoring the gods and serving the community. They are all artists in our sense. The fisherman may be the musician at night, the village girl working all day may be one of the sophisticated dancers. Art is craftsmanship, the trancelike state of creation is simply communion with the gods.

The gestures that they employ for work are all sinuous and graceful, with a quiet rhythm. There is never a sense of pressure. It was fascinating to me that this modulated, musical way of moving while doing any occupation, at night in the dance becomes a frozen gesture of perfection. It's almost like watching a print. It's animated but so controlled, so marvelously stylized, that it has almost no relation to the sinuosity of the daily-life gestures. This transposition of human modulations into abstract, incredibly perfect gestures is the most remarkable synthesis I have ever seen in a culture.

Dancing is not just an art form, it is an interpretation of life. The harmony of Balinese life has been achieved, it is the expression of an attitude. They don't ignore the darker forces of life; they know the world is full of dangers. But gods can be propitiated by beautiful rituals, elaborate offerings, prayers, by dancing and music. The gods are human. They enjoy beauty, music, dances, the ten thousand temples built for them. The Balinese confront evil by exteriorizing it in distorted, frightening sculptures; in threatening, contorted, angry faces which they carve in masks. On the stage the witch, the evil god, never dies. The Balinese are realists, but they are artists in their expression of rituals and ceremonies. They reach peaks of aesthetic beauty unequaled even in Japan.

Everything they do has a symbolical meaning and is always in favor of beauty and freedom. For instance the bird market sells nothing but birds. But the local custom is to buy a bird and then to set it free.

The Balinese sleep with their heads toward the east. A person who does not know where north is, they consider crazy. They have a great need of orientation. They judge their reasonableness by the way they see the sun coming up.

Wealth is immaterial for the Balinese. They hold it in contempt. For the practical side of life is intrinsically imperfect and they prefer to dwell on its spiritual meaning. Margaret Mead noticed what she called "a vacancy"; that is, the absence of anger, of strong emotions, except for laughter. They feel emotion leaves one off balance and open to invasion by the spirits. The Balinese are serene and delightful, never out of sorts. They seem superficial, but this is because they are in harmony with nature, with everything around them.

In ancient history Bali was described as "the Morning of the World." Nehru called it "the habitat of the gods."

The magically powerful shadow-play is not only the first ancestor of Balinese theater, it is also the first lesson to the child in the reality of the symbol. It signifies that our life is a shadow-play, that man himself is a shadow of god. The puppets for the shadow-play are cut from buffalo hide, painted and then stiffened with glue. The stems are made from buffalo horns, colored with the juice of plants. The puppeteer sets up his stand in the village and everyone soon knows he is there. He sits behind a screen. Hanging over him is an old smoky oil lamp, but it is bright enough to create the shadows he wants. Tiny boy apprentices sit cross-legged around him, ready to hand him the puppets he needs. His art consists not only in moving the puppets according to the story but giving each one a different voice. The quality of the voices is unreal, the intonations very similar to those in Japanese Noh plays. To see the shadows talking, fighting, flying, loving in the emollient Balinese night was stirring enough; but to steal behind the screen and watch the beauty of the puppets, their intricate costumes, embroideries, ornaments, was even more impressive; to see the children so familiar with the characters that they always knew which one came next, to see the old man sitting cross-legged like the stories of old, under the trembling lamp, swelling up for the big voices, shrinking for the women's and children's voices, was to be carried back centuries into the depths of India, the origin of Balinese mythology, religion and theater.

Cremations are joyous events because the Balinese believe that death is a freeing of the soul—free to float away, join its forefathers and merge in the ancestral soul. Musicians gather in front of the house where the body lies in state, while special craftsmen complete the bamboo tower on which it is to be carried to the cremation grounds. The height and decorative richness of the tower depends on the distinction of the dead. The tower rises high above the people (thirty to fifty feet for important persons), pagoda-shaped, covered with tinsel ornaments, mirrors, festoons of gold lace, scarves, flowers, tassels, fringes, pennants, fantastic umbrellas. It is sprinkled with holy water, and incense sticks are lighted. At the very top a white dove is tied; it will be allowed to fly away when the body is burned and the soul freed.

The crowd, in its most colorful dress, waits patiently and listens to the two gamelan orchestras, sometimes both playing different pieces at the same time. Finally the body is brought out of the house on the shoulders of friends. The women of the household place themselves in front of the glittering tower and unfold a bolt of white silk, which they hold over their heads. The body has been carried to the top of the tower along a specially designed ramp. Hundreds of men now line up on the four sides of the tower base and lift it onto their shoulders. It sways like a ship on a stormy sea. To foil the evil spirits it must be turned around several times on the way to the cremation grounds. The crowd follows quietly but without sadness. The musicians manage to play as they walk without missing a note. All the children are there, including babes in arms. We all walk along the road to the fields encircling the cremation grounds.

The red-orange bull (or cow, for women) has arrived, in which the body is to be deposited and burned to signify the last journey back into the womb, the end of a cycle. It is a mythological animal, hollowed out of a great tree trunk, with an unbelievable tail and head, partly unicorn, partly a creature out of Egyptian frescoes. More holy water is sprinkled before lighting the fire. When the fire is fully started, the bird is freed to fly.

All this happens with a natural dignity. Dignity and a deep joyousness transcend their daily life. They have parleyed with the gods, contemplated eternity, eaten the food of festivities. They have considered death as mere transmigration. They are bathed in golden sounds; their eyes have feasted on shocking pinks, aquamarine, indigo, parrot green, sun yellows and oranges and all the colors of tropical birds and flowers worn by the men and women. Every house they passed on the way is beautiful with its stone walls, its gates of lacy sculptures around a heart of red bricks. They have flown kites, and bought birds at the market for the purpose of freeing them. They have orchestrated simple human life with art and religion, painted their hard-working peasant life with all the colors which great painters restrict to a canvas. They have asserted, by a million small mirrors on one of their superb gods, the Barong, that life is reflection. They have learned to enhance, transform, elevate the life given to us.

The one who travels like a lover searching for a new passion is suddenly blessed with new eyes, new ears, new senses.

At the bar, on the edge of the beach, a man sat in an utter state of dejection. He continually looked out to sea. Occasionally he spoke to the barman in Balinese. I could feel his depression. When he left, I talked to the barman. He told me what I had half guessed. The man was a Dutchman who had once lived in Bali. When the Dutch were expelled, many of them were deeply unhappy. They loved their life in Bali. Like this man, they often came back to assuage their homesickness, dreaming over the past, the lost paradise.

Today I sat on the same barstool looking out to sea and asked myself a question I have rarely asked. Will I come back? Do I need to part from Bali, whose inner and outer beauty are one? Premonition? Anxiety? The fear of loss I have with those I love? In spite of the cancer casting a shadow on my life now, this was the first time I wondered whether I would be here again.

Then I made a wish: Let me think of death as the Balinese do, as a flight to another life, a joyous transformation, a release of our spirit so it might visit all other lives.

Epilogue

[*Anaïs Nin wished the Diary to end in Bali. She did not intend to publish any material concerning the long, painful illness which led to the release of her dove on January 14, 1977. Following are a few excerpts from the last Diary books she titled "The Book of Pain" and "The Book of Music."*]

Dream (written after seeing film of Ionesco's *Rhinoceros* on television) : By the ocean. One woman is about to deep-sea-dive for something she has lost, when I notice a huge rhinoceros emerging from the water. A small dog was swimming nearby. He began to swim backward, keeping his eye on the rhinoceros, but the rhinoceros caught up with him and swallowed him. I was still concerned about the woman who was swimming in the depths.

On Proust: The eternal dimensional mobile which can be read a thousand times for different meaning. I read him over again each year, and each time I see a new aspect, discover a new meaning. It is as if he had struck an infinite chord which never ceases to vibrate on different levels. It is the quality of infinite depth which makes each reading a new experience. His work does not stop vibrating; the soundings come from deeper and deeper realms. As one matures, one discovers a new perspective. No other writer has achieved this continuum. Is it because he explored every aspect, every mood in a state of perpetual movement, that the change is achieved each time as if each word had a thousand meanings? Proust's words have a thousand meanings.

Is it that the mobility of thought and feeling was finally cornered or captured at the moment of its evolution so that the evolution never ceases? He has never described stasis, fixity, metamorphosis into stone, petrified heart or body. The life current was never interrupted, and so whenever you catch it, you are drawn into its vortex and life offers you a new vision.

I never understood why Proust was the only author I read each year whose writing left me desolate whenever I came to the end.

I was very disturbed by Painter's biography because I knew Proust

337

would not have wished his beautiful transposition reduced once more to literal facts. Proust wanted to live and leave us the legacy of a transposed life.

Because he penetrated the unconscious of his characters, they did not age and die in our imagination; the unconscious is a stream of revelation which is never touched by time, fashions, history. Proust's universality made his writing on music applicable to any music, his writing on jealousy fit jealousy at any time. He transcended time. He never fixed a date upon anything. Very few novelists escaped the stamp of time, which allows the experience to take place only once.

Dream: Varda is not dead. I lie in a Greek marble sarcophagus. Varda paints my entire body with all the colors of his palette. When he has covered me with paint I begin to levitate about twelve inches and feel very light. I wonder if this has to do with his saying to me after his first stroke: "I am no longer afraid of death. I saw the most beautiful colors during my stroke."

Dream: I order all the servants to light all the lights of the château. There is to be a surprise!

Dream: I found my bed at the top of a great waterfall with D. H. Lawrence. We wonder whether to throw ourselves in or not. We do not jump. We look down and see Lady Chatterley swimming by in the ocean. We watch terrified while she swims from one ocean to another.

From a tape made in the hospital:

The nurse who came to take my blood sample this morning turned to me and said very seriously: "You know, there's only one consolation for illness and that's *reading*. You must read a *lot*. I've read. I've read Marcus Aurelius and Mrs. Lindbergh . . ." and she enumerated quite a lot of books. I thought that was delightful. So I laughed and answered: "Yes, and what happens when you have written the books yourself and you can't live up to them?"

My meditation last night was supposed to have been on the white light, but I meditated on the difference between my love of Japan and of Bali. I tried to put it all together, and everything about Japan seemed to accumulate into a masculine quality. The leanness, the fighting (I guess), the war spirit, in spite of the aesthetics—the tremendous firmness (I can't think of a stronger word). And then I began to dream of Bali and my love for it. Entirely different. You become a woman. It's a woman's love. It's soft. It's musical. It's passive and restful. I think of it in terms of huge fans, fanning you. It's almost life in an aesthetic and beautiful womb. But there's something about Japan that I admire as . . . strangely . . . militaristic. But it's not so much militaristic as courageous, really. *Courage.* It takes tremendous courage to follow what you believe. I can't help admiring Mishima's boldness and daring, his trying everything, culminating in hara-kiri in public for his beliefs at the height of his career. The softness of the Balinese couldn't be a greater contrast. You can't imagine a Balinese hurting himself for the sake of anything. And Bali represents every feminine quality of love, the gentleness, the soft voices, the sensuousness of the walk. That's why I love it so much. I suppose my masculine and my feminine self fuse in admiring both cultures.

But what I need now is plenty of Japanese courage. And maybe I will get it from them, from the vaccine.* Wouldn't it be tremendously dramatic if it were from Japan that I got my strength and my health again?

My friend designed a very beautiful diary book, handmade, with soft Japanese rice paper and in gold on the red leather cover, my handwritten diary signature: *"Mon Journal—Anaïs Nin."* I was determined that no illness would be recorded in this diary. So I decided to make it a diary of music. I will only write in it when the musicians come, when I hear music. And it will be a separate part of my life.

----

* During the last two years of her illness, Anaïs Nin was treated with the Maruyama cancer vaccine from Japan under a special dispensation of the U.S. Food and Drug Administration.—Ed.

The quartet is playing late Beethoven. The most continuous, unbroken, life-giving thread of my life has been love and music. Over the years there were always the deep rich tones of the viola and cello contrasting with the soaring, ethereal violins. There were always the waves of music to lift the ship away from dangerous reefs, icebergs, to keep the nerves vibrating, the being resonating, never lulled but pierced with arrows of gold. The blood transfusion of love is music. As I watch the quartet sway gently, all sorrows and tensions are transposed. Love and music make of dissonant fragments a symphonic whole. It is as if the strings strain away the dross. Sharp ends soften. Dreams float to the surface. Memories pulsate, each note is a color, each note is a voice, a new cell awakened. It stills other sounds, drowns the harsh ones, it erects spirals and new planets. When the heart acquires rough edges, music is the mute. When the heart freezes, music liquifies it. When it is lonely, secret notes will escape and find their way to the pulse, restore its universal rhythms. It is remote and gentle. It sobs for you. It cries for you. It laments, it rejoices, it explodes with vigor and life. It never allows our body to die because every wish, every fantasy, breathes and moves as if we were in the place of our first birth, the ocean. The notes fly so much farther than words. There is no other way to reach the infinite.

In music I feel most deeply the passing of things. A note strikes. It evokes an image. But with another note, this image is altered, it moves, it fades, it passes slowly, it melts into another image. Images of beauty and sorrow pass thus before me and are carried away in the forward movement of music. The note that was struck, and vanished, carried away with its sound the things that are precious. It left, with its echoes, an echo of things that are gone. Between it and the other note that is coming, there is a space that holds a loss and an emptiness. Music holds the movements of life, the chained incidents which compose it, the eternal melting of one note before another to create song. The notes must melt before one another; they must be lost after they have given their soul, for the sake of the whole. It may be a beautiful note, but it cannot strike alone forever. It must pass, as all things must pass, to make up the immense composition that is life.

————

340

Dick Stoltzman, clarinetist, and Bill Douglas, pianist-composer, came to play for me. They played Bill's compositions and improvised. The tenderest, most lyrical music. Incredible people—unspoiled. Their music undulates tenderly, the waves of feeling ebbing and flowing like gentle tides. No harshness, no dissonance, no savagery of rock and roll. The sweetness of tropical climate, and outburst of joy, playful, wistful, without diffusion.

The pool is steaming like those pools in the mountains of Japan, everything through glass, through prisms, the amethyst water acquires a different dimension, it enlarges itself, its colors; it is so beautiful.

The musicians are playing the Schubert cello quintet—the long sweetness, tender accents, the wistful, lingering plaint and bursts of joy. Joy wins out. Every note is set dancing, starting gently, ending vigorously. Then the plaint again, the repetition of the longing, the tenderness, the heartbeat and a burst of ecstasy. The lyrical tones mingle with soft shadowy secrets—feelings are suspended—then burst open, step step step toward intensity. Always a reverie, gentle and in unison, and then a tempestuous meeting of all the instruments. Peace, serenity, storm and undercurrent of intensity. The intensity wins in harmony and in moments of repose, reverie. The lullaby sets you dreaming, you float on the tenderness, but a storm awakens you. Gently now, the violins, the viola, the cellos lull you, repeating your most secret wish, lulling, caressing, swinging on a hammock of silk. Then the inner fires of the world burst and burn and spill over. All the reveries are forced to hide—one does not hear them anymore. Then the instruments seem to mourn the early reverie and seek it again. Drops of water from the trees, gold sparkle on the sea, words of passion, caressing notes, all light and sorrow.

The quartet played Debussy. It unleashed a flood of tears. I did not want to die. This music was a parting from the world. Music was always the music of exile. There existed another world I had been exiled from, the possibility that music was an expression of a better world. That is why I am moved by the Peruvian flute, the conch shell of the Tahitians, by the music of Satie and Debussy, who were the most aware of that other world. Satie's music is nothing but nostalgia.

341

My attitude toward music was always nostalgic. Emotional. I was never cold or detached or intellectual about music. I never tried to explain the feeling of exile. I accepted the weeping.

I talked with Joaquin. I said that the cry of music may have meant sorrow over exile from another world, a better world. Yes, he knew about the new world lost to us, about exile and a lost land. Yes, he knew the longing. My father felt this. Joaquin mentioned at what times he wept.

Today I asked a remarkable man, my healer, Dr. Brugh Joy. He feels the same way. Yes, music indicates another place, a better place. This was the place from which we were exiled for some great punishment which the Catholics call "sin" and other religions "evil." But what I do not understand is that some evil, sadistic, cruel people do not seem to remember having lost such a place. Perhaps to them music is an undiscovered realm. But for us it enters the body, it fills the body. Brugh explained that the tears come from remembrance of that place. And we cry because we sense at last the return home. One should think of this place joyfully. Then if it follows death, it is a beautiful place. A lovely thing to look forward to—a promised land. So I shall die in music, into music, with music.

Index

343

344

345